Explainable AI (XAI) for Sustainable Development

This book presents innovative research works to automate, innovate, design, and deploy AI for real-world applications. It discusses artificial intelligence (AI) applications in major cutting-edge technologies and details about deployment solutions for different sustainable development applications. The application of Blockchain techniques illustrates the ways of optimisation algorithms in this book. The challenges associated with AI deployment are also discussed in detail, and edge computing with machine learning solutions is explained. This book provides multi-domain applications of AI to the readers to help find innovative methods towards the business, sustainability, and customer outreach paradigms in the AI domain.

- Focuses on virtual machine placement and migration techniques for cloud data centres
- Presents the role of machine learning and meta-heuristic approaches for optimisation in cloud computing services
- Includes application of placement techniques for quality of service, performance, and reliability improvement
- Explores data centre resource management, load balancing, and orchestration using machine learning techniques
- Analyses dynamic and scalable resource scheduling with a focus on resource management

The reference work is for postgraduate students, professionals, and academic researchers in computer science and information technology.

Explainable AI (XAI) for Sustainable Development
Trends and Applications

Edited by
Lakshmi D, Ravi Shekhar Tiwari,
Rajesh Kumar Dhanaraj, and Seifedine Kadry

CRC Press
Taylor & Francis Group
Boca Raton London New York

CRC Press is an imprint of the
Taylor & Francis Group, an **informa** business

A CHAPMAN & HALL BOOK

Designed cover image: ShutterStock

First edition published 2024
by CRC Press
2385 NW Executive Center Drive, Suite 320, Boca Raton FL 33431

and by CRC Press
4 Park Square, Milton Park, Abingdon, Oxon, OX14 4RN

CRC Press is an imprint of Taylor & Francis Group, LLC

ISBN: 9781032598864 (hbk)
ISBN: 9781032600154 (pbk)
ISBN: 9781003457176 (ebk)

DOI: 10.1201/9781003457176

Typeset in Times
by codeMantra

Contents

Preface

This book is about the deployment of artificial intelligence (AI) in various domains. It covers the key features of AI deployment, AI in cutting-edge technologies, computing techniques of cognitive intelligent systems, and applications of AI in different domains. The book also provides details about deployment solutions for different applications and innovative methods for the business, sustainability, and customer outreach paradigms in the AI domain.

Artificial intelligence has rapidly permeated our lives, transforming industries, healthcare, and our interactions with technology. While AI promises innovation and efficiency, its opacity and complexity raise concerns about trust, accountability, and ethical implications. To address these challenges, Explainable AI (XAI) emerged, bridging the gap between machine learning and human understanding. XAI seeks to explain how AI systems make decisions, ensure their trustworthiness, and evaluate their societal and ethical impact.

This book provides a multifaceted realm of XAI, covering its theoretical foundations, practical applications, and ethical considerations. Through expert insights, real-world examples, and accessible explanations, we demystify XAI's complexities for a wide audience.

Along the way, we explore the black box of AI models, learn various interpretation techniques, and examine responsible AI development and deployment. XAI's influence extends from healthcare to finance, and autonomous vehicles to criminal justice, making it essential for various domains.

Our aim is to empower readers with knowledge and insights to navigate this evolving field. Whether you are a student, researcher, practitioner, or simply curious, this book provides a solid foundation for comprehending Explainable AI.

This book discusses the various applications of AI in different domains, highlighting its potential benefits and challenges. Some of the key areas covered include the following:

- **Sustainable AI:** The environmental implications, challenges, and opportunities of AI are explored, emphasising the need for AI-driven solutions to address environmental issues.
- **AIoT in Agriculture 4.0:** The role of Artificial Intelligence of Things (AIoT) in transforming agriculture is examined, showcasing its potential to enhance productivity, sustainability, and precision agriculture practices.
- **EXAI for Computational Sustainability:** The application of Explainable AI (EXAI) in developing sustainable computational models and services for smart cities is discussed.
- **AI and Emotional Intelligence in Waste Management:** The impact of AI and emotional intelligence on the performance of MSME entrepreneurs in the waste management industry is investigated.
- **AI Governance and Comprehensibility in Renewable Energy Systems:** The importance of AI governance and comprehensibility in ensuring the effectiveness of renewable energy systems is emphasised.
- **Machine Learning for Eye-Blink Mistake Detection:** The use of machine learning classifiers for accurate detection of eye-blink mistakes based on EEG (electroencephalogram) characteristics is explored.
- **Machine Learning for Polymer Material Creation:** Machine learning advancements in polymer material creation, including successful prediction of glass transition temperature, are presented.
- **AIoT for Sustainable Agriculture:** The development of a smart greenhouse management system using AIoT for sustainable agriculture is described.
- **Deep Learning for Cardiac Image Analysis:** The application of CardioSegNet, a deep learning approach, for analysing cardiac images is demonstrated.

- **AI-Based Techniques for Chiari Malformation Detection:** AI-based techniques for early detection of Chiari malformation are discussed.
- **AI-Driven Restoration for Biodiversity Conservation:** The potential of AI-driven restoration to enhance biodiversity conservation and ecosystem resilience is explored.
- **Improvised DenseNet and Faster RCNN for Agriculture 4.0:** The application of improvised DenseNet and Faster RCNN to assist Agriculture 4.0 is presented.
- **Libraries for Explainable AI (EXAI): Python:** A review of Python libraries for EXAI is provided.
- **AI and EXAI in Drug Discovery:** The trends and advancements of AI and EXAI in drug discovery are discussed.
- **AIoT for Reshaping the Farming Sector:** The role of AIoT in transforming the farming sector is examined.
- **XAI for Smart Healthcare Automation**: The power of Explainable Artificial Intelligence (EXAI) in empowering decision-making and overcoming challenges in smart healthcare automation is highlighted.

Editor Biographies

Dr. Lakshmi D is presently designated as a Senior Associate Professor in the School of Computing Science and Engineering (SCSE) and the Assistant Director at the Centre for Innovation in Teaching & Learning (CITL) at VIT Bhopal. She has 26 years of teaching experience. She has addressed innumerable guest lectures, acted as a session chair, and has been invited as a keynote speaker at several international conferences. She has conducted FDPs that cover approximately ~100,000 plus faculty members including JNTU, TEQIP, SERB, SWAYAM, DST, AICTE, MHRD, ATAL, ISTE, Madhya Pradesh Government-sponsored, and self-financed workshops across India, as well as Misamis University, Philippines, on various topics. She has 20 international conference presentations and 32 international journal papers inclusive of SCOPUS & SCI (cumulative impact factor 45). She has a total of 20 SCOPUS-indexed book chapters. A total of 24 patents are in various stages, and 18 patents have been granted at both national and international levels. She was appointed as an external examiner for several PhD candidates at reputed universities. She is also guiding research scholars. She has won two Best Paper Awards at international conferences, one at the IEEE conference and another one at EAMMIS 2021 (First European, Asian, Middle Eastern North African Conference on Management & Information Systems). She received two best teacher awards in the year 2022 on the eve of Teacher's Day. She published a book on the *Theory of Computation* in 2003, *Leading Education in the Age of Disruption* in 2021, and *Smart Cities: Disruptive Technologies Driving the Force* in 2023. She acted as a SPOC to both KAVACH and the Smart India Hackathon in the last three editions. She has created 15 hours of the high-quality online course "Python Essentials" at VITyarthi Online Learning Platform. She has 5 SCOPUS-indexed book edits with three CRC Press, Taylor and Francis; three IGI Global; and two IEEE Rivers.

Mr. Ravi Shekhar Tiwari is a Researcher, Innovator, and an Engineer. He has written more than 0.5 billion lines of code that are adding value to people's lives. He has 4+ years of industry experience working as an Artificial Intelligence Engineer, Penetration Tester, and MFDI Engineer in Multinational IT companies, as well as start-ups. He also holds a position as a reviewer and editor in reputed journals and as an author in technical magazines with Indian Patents, SCI research papers, SCOPUS research papers, and SCOPUS-indexed book chapters, and as an Editor in Book Series titled *Futuristic Trend in Artificial Intelligence* and *Futuristic Trend in IoT*. He has won awards as a Researcher and contribution to Student Development. Ravi Shekhar Tiwari's research domain includes Time Series Analysis, Protein Structure Prediction and Generation, Federated Learning, the Internet of Things, Microcontrollers, Gait Analysis, AI and Healthcare, XAI, Cloud Computing, Computer Vision, and Parallel and Distributed Computing in the cloud. Currently, he is pursuing his Master's in Technology at Mahindra University with a specialisation in Artificial Intelligence and Data Science as a Teaching Assistant. As a responsible member, he always tries to enhance and uplift society by teaching students remotely. He has been invited as a guest speaker at two international conferences. He is also a teacher and mentor without the border where he teaches students to overcome difficulties and pursue their interests as their careers. He also writes poems and short inspirational stories in periodicals.

Dr. Rajesh Kumar Dhanaraj is a Distinguished Professor at Symbiosis International (Deemed University) in Pune, India. His academic and research achievements have earned him a place among the top 2% of scientists globally, a recognition bestowed upon him by Elsevier and Stanford University. He has authored and edited over 50 books on various cutting-edge technologies and holds 21 patents. Furthermore, he has contributed over 100 articles and papers to esteemed refereed journals and international conferences, in addition to providing chapters for several influential books. He has earned the distinction of being a Senior Member of the Institute of Electrical and

Electronics Engineers (IEEE). He is also a member of the Computer Science Teacher Association (CSTA) and the International Association of Engineers (IAENG). His commitment to academic excellence extends to his role as an Associate Editor and Guest Editor for renowned journals, including Elsevier – *Computers and Electrical Engineering, Human-centric Computing and Information Sciences*; Emerald – *International Journal of Pervasive Computing and Communications*; and Hindawi – *Mobile Information Systems*. His expertise has earned him a position as an Expert Advisory Panel Member of Texas Instruments Inc., USA.

Prof. Kadry earned his bachelor's degree in 1999 from Lebanese University, MS degree in 2002 from Reims University (France) and EPFL (Lausanne), PhD in 2007 from Blaise Pascal University (France), and HDR degree in 2017 from Rouen University (France). His research currently focuses on data science, medical image recognition using AI, education using technology, and applied mathematics. He is an IET Fellow and IETE Fellow, and a member of the European Academy of Sciences and Arts. He is a Full Professor of data science at Noroff University College, Norway.

Contributors

Sharmila A.
Department of Electronics and Communication
    Engineering
Bannari Amman Institute of Technology
Erode, India

S. David Samuel Azariya
Department of Information Technology
Sona College of Technology
Salem, India

Prabadevi B.
School of Computer Science Engineering and
    Information Systems
Vellore Institute of Technology
Vellore, India

Pritika Bahad
Department of Artificial Intelligence & Data
    Science
Prestige Institute of Engineering Management &
    Research
Indore, India

Sandeep Balabantaray
School of Computer Science
    and Engineering
VIT Bhopal University
Sehore, India

Meet Bikhani
School of Computer Science and Engineering
VIT Bhopal University
Sehore, India

Anuja Bokhare
Symbiosis Institute of Computer Studies and
    Research (SICSR)
Symbiosis International (Deemed University)
    (SIU)
Pune, India

Korhan Cengiz
Department of Informatics and Management
University of Hradec Kralove
Hradec Kralove, Czech Republic

Tanisha Chandak
Department of Computer Science and
    Engineering
Vellore Institute of Technology
Vellore, India

Dipti Chauhan
Department of Artificial Intelligence & Data
    Science
Prestige Institute of Engineering Management &
    Research
Indore, India

Parimalarsundar E
Department of Electrical and Electronics
    Engineering
Mohan Babu University
Tirupati, India

Dhivya Priya E L
Department of Electronics and Communication
    Engineering
Erode Segunthur Engineering College
Erode, India

Sudha G.
Muthayammal Engineering College
Rasipuram, India

Ayaan Khadir Ghulam
Department of Computer Science
Mahindra University
Hyderabad, India

Aayushi Goenka
Department of Networking and
    Communications
SRM Institute of Science and Technology
Chennai, India

Shubh Gupta
School of Computer Science and Engineering
VIT Bhopal University
Sehore, India

Vijayashree J.
Department of Computer Science Engineering
Vellore Institute of Technology
Vellore, India

Jay Kumar Jain
Department of Mathematics, Bioinformatics
    and Computer Applications
Maulana Azad National Institute of Technology
    (MANIT)
Bhopal, India

Jayanthi J
School of Computing Science and Engineering
    (SCSE)
VIT Bhopal University
Sehore, India

Jayashree J.
Department of Computer Science Engineering
Vellore Institute of Technology
Vellore, India

Nandha Gopal J.
Department of Electrical and Electronics
    Engineering
Velammal Institute of Technology
Chennai, India

Leo John
Department of Computer Science
Saveetha School of Engineering
Chennai, India

Arun Kumar K
School of Biosciences, Bio-Engineering and
    Technology
VIT Bhopal University
Sehore, India

Saravanan K
College of Engineering Guindy
Anna University
Chennai, India

Upinder Kaur
Department of CSE
Akal University
Talwandi Sabo, India

Pradeepa M.
School of Computer Science Engineering and
    Information Systems
Vellore Institute of Technology
Vellore, India

P. S. Metkewar
School of Computer Science and Engineering
Dr Vishwanath Karad MIT World Peace
    University
Maharashtra, India

Rupal Mishra
School of Computer Science and Engineering
VIT Bhopal University
Sehore, India

R. Monisha
Department of Electronics and Communication
    Engineering
KPR Institute of Engineering and Technology
Coimbatore, India

Marirajan Murugan
Faculty of Management
SRM Institute of Science and Technology
Chennai, India

S. Muthukaruppasamy
Department of Electrical and Electronics
    Engineering
Velammal Institute of Technology
Chennai, India

Rupali Pathak
Department of Computer Science and
    Engineering
Prestige Institute of Engineering Management &
    Research
Indore, India

M.N. Prabadevi
Faculty of Management
SRM Institute of Science and Technology
Chennai, India

Pragya Ranka
Department of Computer Science and
 Engineering
Prestige Institute of Engineering Management &
 Research
Indore, India

Akshat Rastogi
School of Computer Science and Engineering
VIT Bhopal University
Sehore, India

Kumaraperumal S.
Master of Management Studies (MMS)
St. John College of Engineering &
 Management
Palghar, India

Abhinaya Saravanan
Information Technology Alumnus
Abu Dhabi University
Abu Dhabi, United Arab Emirates

Shallu Sehgal
Shoolini Institute of Life Sciences and Business
 Management
Solan, India

Neha Sharma
Department of Electronics and Communication
 Engineering
Prestige Institute of Engineering Management &
 Research
Indore, India

Nisha Soms
Department of Computer Science Engineering
KPR Institute of Engineering and Technology
Coimbatore, India

Shobhit Srivastava
Department of Networking and
 Communications
SRM Institute of Science and Technology
Chennai, India

K. S. Tamilselvan
Department of Electronics and Communication
 Engineering
KPR Institute of Engineering and Technology
Coimbatore, India

Divya Thakur
School of Computer Science and Engineering
VIT Bhopal University
Sehore, India

G. Arun Sampaul Thomas
Department of Artificial Intelligence and
 Machine Learning
J.B. Institute of Engineering and Technology
Hyderabad, India

Ravi Shekhar Tiwari
Department of Computer Science
Mahindra University
Hyderabad, India

Rajagopal V
Department of Electrical and Computer
 Engineering
Dawa University
Dire Dawa, Ethiopia

A Helen Victoria
Department of communication and Network
SRM Institute of Science and Technology
Chennai, India

1 Sustainable AI
Environmental Implications, Challenges, and Opportunities

Dipti Chauhan, Pritika Bahad, and Jay Kumar Jain

1.1 INTRODUCTION

The development and implementation of artificial intelligence (AI) technologies and systems that minimize their detrimental effects on the environment and support long-term ecological balance are referred to as sustainable AI. It recognizes the necessity of addressing the environmental effects of AI technologies, which are known to have a significant environmental impact [1]. AI systems demand a significant amount of computing power and energy, particularly those that use deep learning methods and large computational models. The development and implementation of AI have transformed many aspects of our lives, including how we interact with our surroundings. AI can be used to improve energy efficiency, reduce waste, and improve sustainable practices to analyze massive amounts of data, learn from patterns, and make real-time decisions [2]. The adverse effects of AI on the environment, however, are a cause for concern.

The carbon footprint associated with AI is one significant environmental concern. AI models frequently need high-performance computing infrastructure, which uses a lot of energy during the training and inference processes [3]. As a result of this energy consumption, greenhouse gas emissions rise and help fuel climate change. Data centers are also a significant source of emissions and energy use when powering AI systems. The electronic waste produced by AI technologies is a further issue. Due to the quick development of AI, hardware components are frequently upgraded and replaced, resulting in a significant amount of electronic waste. It is essential to properly dispose of and recycle electronic waste to avoid environmental damage and the release of hazardous materials [4]. Furthermore, rare-earth minerals, which are frequently linked to environmental and social problems, are used in the production of AI hardware. These minerals are mined in ways that might be harmful to local communities, water sources, and ecosystems. By promoting responsible and ethical sourcing of the materials used in AI hardware, sustainable AI seeks to address these problems.

The potential for sustainable AI to allay these environmental worries and contribute to a more sustainable future is what makes it so important. We can lower the computational and energy requirements of AI systems by optimizing their hardware. Techniques like model compression, hardware acceleration, and algorithm efficiency enhancements can be used to accomplish this.

Sustainable AI offers opportunities for environmental contributions in addition to lowering environmental impact. There are many ways AI can be used to monitor and protect the environment. AI-powered systems, for example, can analyze satellite imagery to detect wildlife populations, track deforestation, and optimize energy use in smart grids [5]. AI can also enhance resource management procedures, such as optimizing building energy use or enhancing waste disposal techniques.

Industry-wide initiatives are being made to create sustainability standards and guidelines in order to promote sustainable AI. These programs seek to advance responsible data practices, promote the creation and adoption of greener AI technologies, and address moral questions about how AI will affect the environment. In order to address the environmental effects of AI technologies,

DOI: 10.1201/9781003457176-1

including energy use, carbon emissions, electronic waste, and responsible material sourcing, the concept of sustainable AI has been developed [6]. By reducing these adverse effects and utilizing AI's potential for beneficial environmental contributions, sustainable AI can play a substantial role in addressing environmental concerns and working toward a more sustainable future.

The rest of the chapter is structured as follows: Section 1.2 discusses the impact of AI on SDGs, Section 1.3 explores the literature survey presented in this area, Section 1.4 discusses the addressing of environmental challenges by AI, Section 1.5 describes the environmental implications of AI technologies, Section 1.6 presents opportunities for sustainability in AI, Section 1.7 discusses the future directions and initiatives, and Section 1.8 concludes the chapter.

1.2   THE IMPACT OF AI ON SUSTAINABLE DEVELOPMENT GOALS

The adoption of AI in numerous industries has undergone a significant shift in the last 10 years, from research and development to operationalization and business value creation. Whether it's creating predictive maintenance models, face detection biometric systems, or credit risk modeling, AI is enabling the development of better solutions to many business problems. In addition to business issues, social issues are being resolved with the help of AI. The 17 sustainable development goals established by the United Nations are intended to improve society overall from a variety of angles, including eradicating poverty, building ecological balance, fostering industrial innovation, ensuring gender equality, etc. (Figure 1.1) [7]. Both independent professionals and nonprofit organizations are advancing the cause.

With AI's assistance, the United Nations' Sustainable Development Goals (SDGs) might be significantly impacted and made easier to attain [8]. AI could impact the SDGs in the following ways as depicted in Table 1.1.

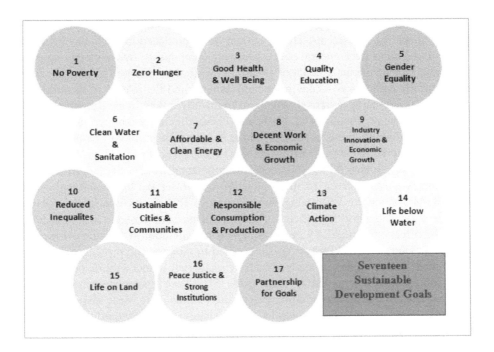

FIGURE 1.1   Seventeen Sustainable Development Goals established by the United Nations [7].

TABLE 1.1
Impact of AI SDG's

SDG	Impact of AI
Poverty eradication (SDG 1)	AI has the potential to significantly aid the fight against poverty, as stated by SDG-1. By increasing access to healthcare and education, providing financial services to disadvantaged populations, and creating job opportunities, AI can help reduce poverty significantly. AI-powered technologies can improve access to high-quality healthcare, especially in areas lacking strong healthcare infrastructure, by providing telemedicine, remote health services, and AI-based diagnostic systems. Financial inclusion is an important component of poverty reduction. Thanks to AI-powered fintech solutions, underserved populations can now access financial services like mobile banking, microloans, and electronic payments. AI has the potential to boost the economy and create more jobs. Automation and AI-powered technologies are transforming industries, creating new job roles. By reskilling and upskilling people, AI can facilitate transformation into these new industries and expand employment opportunities.
Zero hunger (SDG 2)	AI has significant potential to help address the difficulties in achieving SDG 2, which requires eliminating all forms of hunger. Using AI technologies, it is possible to improve supply chain management, ensure efficient food distribution, maximize crop yields, and reduce food waste. One important area where AI can make an impact is precision farming. By examining data from a variety of sources such as soil sensors, satellite imagery, and weather patterns, agronomists can benefit from the insights that AI algorithms can provide. Along the entire supply chain, AI can help reduce food waste. By examining data on food consumption, patterns, product expiration dates, and logistics details, artificial intelligence (AI) systems can enhance inventory management and reduce spoilage. Apart from aiding in food production and management, AI can also help in food distribution. AI algorithms can examine data on market demands, transportation networks, and infrastructure to enhance the logistics of food delivery.
Good health and well-being (SDG 3):	Achieving SDG 3 – promoting good health and well-being – is facilitated by the use of AI technology, which has the potential to significantly improve healthcare delivery systems. In numerous ways, including disease diagnosis, individualized treatment plans, outbreak prediction, and support for telemedicine and remote healthcare services, AI can be used to enhance healthcare. AI can assist in the creation of individualized treatment plans. AI can assist medical professionals by analyzing patient data, such as medical history, genetics, and responses to prior treatments, to make it easier for them to customize treatment options to meet the unique needs of each patient. AI can also support surveillance and outbreak prediction. In order to predict early signs of infectious disease epidemics, AI algorithms can monitor social media, weather information, disease monitoring systems, and other data sources. AI has the potential to improve the usage of telemedicine and remote medical care, particularly in disadvantaged areas. With the use of robotic devices, AI can support remote consultations, health monitoring, and even surgical procedures. This can be particularly useful in areas with inadequate healthcare infrastructure or in situations, like pandemics, where direct physical contact is discouraged.
Quality education (SDG 4):	In fact, AI-powered learning tools have shown great promise in advancing and supporting the Sustainable Development Goal 4 (SDG 4) goal of providing a high-quality education. These tools use AI technologies to deliver education to rural populations, offer individualized instruction, and enable adaptive testing.
Gender equality (SDG 5)	The achievement of SDG 5 and gender equality have a lot to gain from AI. It is possible to lessen gender disparities and advance equal opportunities for women and girls across a variety of industries by ensuring that AI algorithms are impartial and devoid of bias.

(Continued)

TABLE 1.1 (*Continued*)
Impact of AI SDG's

SDG	Impact of AI
Clean energy (SDG 7)	AI has the potential to promote clean and sustainable energy, which could significantly help to achieve SDG 7. We can maximize energy production and consumption by using AI, which will result in more effective resource use and a shift to clean energy sources. There may be room for improvement in the management of the energy grid, the integration and management of renewable energy sources, and raising energy efficiency.
Sustainable cities and communities (SDG 11)	Building sustainable cities and communities is essential for achieving SDG 11, which calls for the use of intelligent technologies and environmentally friendly urban planning techniques. Cities can improve energy efficiency, increase transportation effectiveness, and improve long-term sustainability by utilizing AI and other intelligent systems.
Climate action (SDG 13)	The challenges posed by climate change and the goals of SDG 13 - Climate Action can both be greatly helped by AI. Through climate monitoring, modelling, and prediction, sustainable practices, carbon emission reduction, and improved energy systems, AI can support efforts to combat climate change. AI can support both resource management and sustainable practices. It can analyze data on waste production, water use, energy consumption, and other variables to spot inefficiencies and suggest environmentally friendly practices. AI can also support carbon emission reduction. AI algorithms can find opportunities to lower carbon footprints by examining data on energy production, consumption trends, and carbon emissions.
Life below water (SDG 14)	The SDG 14 – AI can significantly support Life below Water –. It can work towards the protection and restoration of marine ecosystems, fostering healthy and prosperous life below the surface, by using AI technologies responsibly and in cooperation with stakeholders. Identifying and monitoring marine ecosystems and biodiversity are two areas where AI can be useful. AI algorithms can analyze satellite imagery, underwater video, and other data sources, with the aim of identifying and monitoring specific species, coral reefs, and other important marine habitats. Additionally, it can help identify and evaluate pollution and its effects on marine ecosystems. AI algorithms can identify and track pollution sources, evaluate the spread and impact of pollutants, and develop strategies to reduce pollution and restore affected areas by analyzing data from sensors, drones, and other sources that can help. This may aid in lowering marine pollution, safeguarding marine life, and maintaining the general well-being of marine ecosystems.
Life on land (SDG 15)	The objectives of SDG 15 – Life on Land – can be supported by AI-'s significant contributions to ecosystem conservation and management, biodiversity, and natural resource management. Deforestation, illegal logging, and illegal fishing are a few environmental challenges that AI can help identify and address. Artificial intelligence (AI) algorithms can examine satellite imagery and other remote sensing data to find areas of deforestation and monitor changes in forest cover over time. Even in remote locations, AI can analyze real-time data and patterns to spot suspicious activity and uncover illegal logging practices.
Peace, justice, and strong institutions (SDG 16)	AI can significantly advance SDG 16 – Peace, Justice, and Strong Institutions – in a number of ways. AI can help to improve criminal justice processes, legal systems, and access to justice by automating repetitive tasks, analyzing large datasets, and finding patterns. The administrative procedures in the criminal justice system can be streamlined and improved. Law enforcement organizations can use AI-powered data analysis to find patterns and spot potential threats. AI algorithms to spot trends, forecast criminal activity, and better allocate resources can analyze massive data sets. Examples of these data sets include crime records, social media posts, and surveillance footage. Automating processes like case management, document processing, and record keeping gives legal professionals more time to concentrate on important judgment calls and research. This automation can increase productivity, decrease backlogs, and guarantee that cases move forward in a timely manner.

While AI can help achieve the SDGs, it is important to remember that in order to ensure fairness, transparency, and accountability in its application, ethical considerations must be taken into account.

1.3 LITERATURE REVIEW

Sustainable AI has significant environmental implications, including carbon footprint, energy consumption, and e-waste. Challenges include ensuring fair and unbiased data collection and addressing privacy concerns. Opportunities abound in developing greener AI systems, such as leveraging renewable energy sources and implementing sustainable data centers. Various authors have done research in this domain. This section presents a detailed literature review in this area.

In Ref. [9], the challenges and potential advantages that AI can present for the sustainable energy industry are discussed by the authors, along with the state of AI in this industry at the moment. The use of AI has the capability to boost productivity, improve energy efficiency, and improve the integration of renewable energy sources. This chapter explored several AI applications, such as demand response, smart grid optimization, energy management systems, and energy forecasting. The importance of addressing ethical and legal concerns when implementing AI technologies in the sustainable energy sector is also emphasized.

In Ref. [10], the author examined the concept of sustainable AI from the perspectives of AI for sustainability and AI's own sustainability. The first point of view, titled "AI for Sustainability," looks at how AI can support environmental causes and goals for sustainable development. In the article, various applications of AI in fields like waste management, energy, agriculture, and transportation are discussed. Examples include applying AI to recycling automation, smart transportation systems, precision agriculture, and energy optimization. The ethical and environmental effects of AI technologies are examined in the second perspective, which is on the sustainability of AI. The author discusses topics like the environmental impact of AI systems, ethical AI use, and the possible social and economic effects of AI deployment. In order to ensure long-term sustainability and prevent unintended negative effects, the article emphasizes the need for ethical considerations and responsible practices in the deployment and development of AI.

In Ref. [11], the authors discussed the impact of computing on the environment and the difficulties in precisely measuring and analyzing the carbon emissions produced by computing systems. The article emphasizes how modern computing systems, such as data centers and high-performance computers, are consuming more energy and how this has a big impact on carbon emissions. It looks at several factors that affect computing's carbon footprint, including the energy sources used, the physical layout of data centers, the cooling systems, and the workloads that are used.

The authors have also discussed the challenges and limitations of precisely predicting the environmental impact of computing. The challenges of data collection, various computing system configurations and usage patterns, and the importance of considering the entire computing equipment life cycle are all topics they touch on.

In Ref. [12], the authors discussed both the function of AI in sustainable energy management and its potential to advance circular economy principles. The article examines how AI can be used to enable circular economy principles in energy management with a focus on renewable energy sources and energy-efficient technologies. Grid management, demand response, and energy consumption optimization using AI-based models and algorithms are all covered. The authors emphasized the benefits of applying the circular economy's principles to the energy sector, such as reducing waste, improving resource efficiency, and promoting the use of renewable energy sources. It emphasizes how crucial AI is for facilitating effective energy management, reducing adverse environmental effects, and improving system effectiveness as a whole.

In Ref. [13], the authors examined various sustainability-related factors and analyzed the EU's approach to AI in this paper. The paper probably goes into detail about issues like the environmental impact, ethical issues, and social repercussions of AI development and application within the EU.

This also assesses whether the EU's environmental policies are appropriate for the age of AI and whether new regulations are required. We evaluate the potential for cross-fertilization between EU and non-EU nations.

In Ref. [14], the authors explored the application of AI and system of systems theory in addressing carbon emissions. The authors proposed a theoretical framework to address the issue of carbon emissions. A carbon emission calculator using machine learning algorithms and deep learning models with the same hyperparameters but with different datasets is designed. AI has the potential to provide valuable insights and solutions for managing and reducing carbon emissions, while the system of systems theory offers a holistic approach to understanding complex environmental systems. This study focuses on applying sustainable AI from data collection to model deployment.

The assessment of the environmental effects of AI solutions is the focus of this paper [15]. In the context of the life cycle assessment (LCA) of AI solutions, it specifically aims to reveal the hidden environmental effects connected with the use of AI techniques. Life cycle assessment is a methodology that is used to evaluate how a process or product affects the environment at each phase of its life cycle. This research aims to offer insights into the environmental implications and potential sustainability challenges of AI technologies by applying LCA to AI solutions.

In Ref. [16], the authors focused on the energy and policy considerations associated with deep learning in natural language processing (NLP). It addresses the environmental impact and energy consumption of training and deploying deep learning models in NLP tasks. It also explores various policy strategies and technical approaches that can be employed to make NLP processes more energy efficient and environmentally friendly.

In Ref. [17], an AI algorithm is combined with a novel vehicle for sustainable e-waste collection to address the growing issue of electronic waste. The objective of this study is to design an effective and sustainable method for managing e-waste. The referred-to AI algorithm probably helps the e-waste collection vehicle's collection routes be as efficient as possible. The researchers want to use AI to make e-waste management more affordable, less expensive, and less costly while also reducing its negative environmental effects.

In Ref. [18], the authors emphasized how environmental robotics can help circular economies promote a sustainable future. By encouraging material reuse, recycling, and remanufacturing, circular economies seek to reduce waste and increase resource efficiency. The article explores how robotics can benefit different facets of circular economies. It investigates robotics' potential in fields like waste management, recycling, resource recovery, and sustainable manufacturing methods. Robotics technologies, such as autonomous systems and AI algorithms, are emphasized as essential components in achieving sustainability goals.

In Ref. [19], the authors discussed the use of AI in e-waste management for environmental planning. With a focus on minimizing environmental impacts, the research aims to develop AI-based solutions that can efficiently optimize the management and planning of e-waste. The article covers a range of AI methods and algorithms, including machine learning and data analytics, that can be applied to e-waste management. These AI-based methods could contribute to the collection, sorting, recycling, and disposal of e-waste by increasing productivity, lowering costs, and preserving the environment.

In Ref. [20], the authors have critically evaluated the advancements in physiochemical and biotechnological methods for long-term metal recovery from electronic waste. E-waste can be recycled and recovered for valuable metals, reducing the need for mining and its associated environmental effects. This paper discusses various techniques and technologies, including physiochemical and biotechnological approaches, for the recovery of metals from e-waste. Biotechnological approaches might make use of microbial or enzymatic processes, whereas physiochemical approaches might use techniques like mechanical separation, pyrometallurgy, and hydrometallurgy. In terms of sustainable e-waste management, the review is expected to summarize and assess the efficacy, efficiency, and environmental implications of various metal recovery techniques.

In Ref. [21], the authors discussed the management of global e-waste and its connection to creating a sustainable future and a circular economy. The authors have given a general overview of how e-waste management practices are currently being used around the world and talk about opportunities and challenges in making the transition to more sustainable solutions. The paper discusses the idea of "urban mining," which is the process of recovering valuable materials from e-waste through recycling and resource recovery procedures. The importance of applying circular economy principles to e-waste management—which includes lowering waste generation, fostering recycling and recovery, and extending the life of electronic products—is discussed.

1.4 AI TO ADDRESS ENVIRONMENTAL CHALLENGES

AI has the capability to address a variety of environmental issues, including monitoring the quality of the air and water, providing early warning of natural disasters, developing new pollution-reduction technologies, anticipating and managing the effects of climate change, reducing pollution, maximizing energy use, creating more efficient energy production systems, and finding more effective ways to recycle and reuse materials. AI can also be employed to analyze huge datasets to find patterns and insights that can help decision-makers in the field of sustainable development [22]. AI can also be used to create novel solutions to environmental issues. One example is the use of machine learning to create predictive models that can be used to foresee and prepare for potential threats. AI has the ability to speed up worldwide efforts to safeguard the environment and save resources by detecting energy emission reductions and CO_2 removal, assisting in the development of more ecologically friendly transportation networks, monitoring deforestation, and forecasting extreme weather [23]. Examples of in what way AI can be used to address the most important environmental issues are depicted in Figure 1.2.

- Clean power
- Smart transport options
- Sustainable production and consumption
- Sustainble land-use
- Smart cities and homes

Climate Change

- Habitat protection and restoration
- Sustainable trade
- Pollution Control
- Invasive species and disease control
- Realising natural capital

Biodiversity and Conservation

- Fishing sustainability
- Preventing Pollution
- Protecting Habitats
- Protecting species
- Impacts from climate change (including acidification)

Healthy Oceans

- Water Supply
- Catchment control
- Water efficiency
- Adequate sanitation
- Drought planning

Water Security

- Filtering and capture
- Monitoring and prevention
- Early warning
- Clean fuels
- Real-time integrated, adaptive urban management

Clean Air

- Prediction and forecasting
- Early warning systems
- Resilient infrastructure
- Financial instruments
- Resilience planning

Weather and Disaster Resilience

FIGURE 1.2 Action areas for environmental challenges.

1.4.1 CLIMATE CHANGE

AI has the potential to help combat climate change by identifying regions most at risk from sea level rise and severe weather, maximizing energy use, and creating more effective energy production systems [24]. AI can also be employed to analyze huge datasets to find patterns and insights that can help decision-makers in the field of sustainable development. AI can also be used to create novel approaches to combating climate change, like using machine learning to create predictive models that can foresee and prepare for potential threats in the future. AI can be used for real-time energy demand and generation optimization using machine learning, improved grid systems with greater predictability and efficiency, and use of renewable energy. Smart sensors and meters can be installed inside buildings to gather information and monitor, analyze, and optimize energy usage. Machine learning algorithms are now being used in smart transportation, such as Google Maps and Waze, to improve navigation, boost safety, and provide data on traffic flows and congestion (such as Nexar).

1.4.2 BIODIVERSITY AND CONSERVATION

AI has the potential to address biodiversity and conservation issues, such as using AI-based object detection and image recognition to monitor wildlife populations and AI-based natural language processing to analyze huge datasets of scientific literature in order to find patterns and insights that can guide conservation-related decisions [25]. AI can also be used to create novel approaches to biodiversity and conservation, such as using machine learning to create predictive models that can foresee and prepare for potential threats. AI can identify changes in land use, vegetation, forest cover, and the effects of natural disasters when combined with satellite imagery [26]. Invasive species can be tracked, recognized, and observed using the technology mentioned above. Computer vision and machine learning are also used to identify and get rid of invasive species. Anti-poaching units to help plan their patrol routes have used predictive software. Artificial intelligence is being used by Blue River Technology to identify invasive species and other changes in biodiversity.

1.4.3 HEALTHY OCEANS

Ocean health can be monitored using AI-based object detection and image recognition, and patterns can be found in natural language using AI-based natural language processing. Healthy Oceans: AI has the potential to improve the health of the oceans in a number of ways, examining sizable databases of academic writing and insights that can help decision-makers in the conservation sector [27]. Machine learning, for instance, can be used to develop predictive models that can foresee potential threats and allow for preparation. AI can also be used to develop novel methods for enhancing ocean health. AI can gather information from far-flung marine locations, assisting in the preservation of species and their natural habitats. Illegal fishing can be detected by AI. Robots with AI capabilities can monitor the temperature, pH, and pollution levels of the ocean.

1.4.4 WATER SECURITY

AI may offer opportunities to address this problem, including the use of AI-based object detection and image recognition to monitor water quality and large datasets of scientific literature to find patterns and insights that can help ensure water safety analyzing data with natural language processing powered by AI decision [28]. AI can also be used to develop cutting-edge methods for protecting water resources, like using machine learning to build predictive models that can foresee potential dangers and assist users in getting ready. Water scientists frequently use AI to forecast weather and calculate water use in a specific area in order to make well-informed policy decisions. Drought forecasting is possible using AI and satellite data, along with weather, soil, and subsurface water conditions.

1.4.5 CLEAN AIR

AI has the capability to assist with clean air-related problems, such as the use of AI-based object detection and image recognition to monitor air quality. AI can be utilized to analyze sizable datasets of scientific literature in order to find patterns and insights [29]. Machine learning is used to develop predictive models that can foresee and prepare for potential hazards. AI-enhanced air purifiers can continuously record information about the environment and air quality and modify the efficiency of their filtration. City residents can be warned about pollution levels in their neighborhoods using simulations powered by AI. There are tools that can quickly and precisely identify the sources of pollution. AI can help to lessen air pollution.

1.4.6 WEATHER FORECAST AND DISASTER RESILIENCY

AI has the ability to aid in disaster preparedness and weather forecasting. AI-based image recognition can be used to track weather patterns. Natural language processing powered by AI can be used to mine massive datasets of scientific literature for patterns and insights that can aid in weather forecasting and disaster preparedness decisions. AI can also be used to develop novel approaches to disaster readiness and weather forecasting, such as using machine learning to create predictive models that anticipate and prepare for future threats. Drones, cutting-edge sensor platforms, and other tools can be used to monitor earthquakes, floods, windstorms, sea level changes, and other natural hazards. With the aid of automated triggers and real-time information availability, this technology can assist the government and concerned agencies in taking prompt action, enabling early evacuations when necessary. A number of meteorological firms, tech firms like IBM and Palantir, and insurance firms are fusing AI with conventional physics-based modeling techniques to simulate the effects of extreme weather events on infrastructure and other systems and provide advice on disaster risk reduction strategies [30].

1.5 ENVIRONMENTAL IMPLICATIONS OF AI TECHNOLOGIES

Artificial intelligence technologies have many potential effects on the environment. Due to the high energy and computing demands of AI systems, there will be an increase in both carbon emissions and electricity consumption. A significant amount of data may be produced by AI systems, which could increase the need for data storage as well as for more physical infrastructure. The use of AI technologies can enhance environmental decision-making and resource management, but they also have the potential to worsen environmental degradation [31]. In the end, depending on how they are used and managed, AI technologies can have both favorable and unfavorable effects on the environment.

In the context of sustainable development, the environmental implications of AI technologies are significant and merit consideration. Several significant environmental effects include the following.

1.5.1 ENERGY CONSUMPTION

Deep learning algorithms used in AI technologies, in particular, demand a lot of computing power. Increased energy use results from this, especially in data centers where AI models are developed and run [32]. These data centers use a lot of energy, which strains electricity grids and adds to carbon emissions.

1.5.2 CARBON FOOTPRINT

Carbon dioxide (CO_2) emissions are produced as a result of the energy required by AI technologies, especially those that use fossil fuels [33]. AI can have a significant environmental impact, particularly when the energy-consuming training and inference processes are taken into account. Additionally, emissions from the production and disposal of hardware are influenced by high-performance computing and massive data storage.

1.5.3 Electronic Waste

The quick development and limited lifespan of AI hardware add to the problem [34]. Older versions of AI hardware become dated and are frequently discarded as it develops and gets better. Due to the release of hazardous materials, improper management and disposal of electronic waste can cause environmental pollution.

1.5.4 Rare-Earth Materials

Neodymium, dysprosium, and cobalt are just a few examples of the rare-earth minerals needed to make AI hardware [35]. Deforestation, habitat destruction, soil erosion, and water pollution are just a few of the negative environmental effects that can result from mining and extracting these minerals. Additionally, mining operations may cause labor and social problems that have an effect on the neighborhood.

1.5.5 Data Center Infrastructure

Significant amounts of energy, water, and land are needed to build and maintain data centers to support AI technologies. Data centers have an impact on the environment in terms of energy use, carbon emissions, water use, and heat production. Data center cooling systems, which are needed to stop AI hardware from overheating, increase energy use and have an adverse environmental impact.

1.5.6 Ethical Considerations

The environmental impact of AI raises ethical considerations, such as the responsible use of AI technologies, addressing biases and discrimination, and ensuring transparency and accountability in the decision-making processes [36]. Integrating ethical considerations into the development and deployment of AI systems is a challenge that requires careful attention.

1.5.7 Collaboration and Regulation

Achieving sustainability in AI requires collaboration among researchers, policymakers, industry stakeholders, and environmental organizations. Establishing regulations and standards that incentivize and enforce sustainable practices in AI development and deployment is crucial [37].

For AI systems to be developed that are environmentally sustainable, it is essential to comprehend and reduce these environmental effects. This entails reducing the amount of energy used by AI algorithms, improving the energy efficiency of hardware design, implementing best practices for data center management, and ensuring ethical sourcing and disposal of AI hardware components. Instead of making environmental issues worse, AI can be used to overcome these obstacles and advance sustainable development. A multi-faceted approach will be necessary to solve these issues. To make the switch to sustainable energy sources, the AI industry and the renewable energy sector must cooperate. Laws and regulations should also promote the adoption of sustainable practices and ethical e-waste management throughout the AI ecosystem. Ethical frameworks should be established to guide the creation and application of AI in ways that minimize their negative impacts on the environment and align with long-term objectives.

1.6   OPPORTUNITIES FOR SUSTAINABILITY IN AI

In many industries, AI presents a significant opportunity for sustainability.

One area where AI has the potential to significantly impact society is energy management. AI algorithms can analyze patterns of energy use and provide prognostic recommendations to optimize energy use. Waste and carbon emissions may be reduced as a result of this optimization.

The management of waste is another area where AI can support sustainability. AI can enhance waste collection routes, lower fuel consumption, and boost overall efficiency by analyzing data from waste collection sensors. Additionally, waste generation patterns can be identified by machine learning algorithms, which helps in the creation of strategies for waste reduction and recycling [38].

By recommending the proper fertilizer levels, diagnosing crop diseases, and maximizing irrigation schedules, AI can enhance sustainability in agriculture. These AI-driven solutions can help farmers practice more environmentally friendly farming practices by reducing the use of chemicals and conserving water.

Additionally, there are opportunities to create hardware that is energy efficient and tailored for AI, which can improve sustainability in general. The development of algorithms with lower computational resource requirements without sacrificing performance has the potential to improve the effectiveness and durability of AI systems.

Artificial intelligence can be used to great effect in environmental monitoring, conservation efforts, and the advancement of renewable energy systems [39]. We can gain useful insights into environmental data and make wise decisions to maintain and protect our ecosystems by utilizing AI technologies.

In general, AI holds enormous promise for advancing sustainability initiatives. AI can be used in a variety of industries, from waste management and agriculture to energy management and environmental monitoring, to help reduce resource consumption, boost efficiency, and contribute to a greener and more sustainable future.

1.6.1   "AI FOR A SUSTAINABLE FUTURE: ENVIRONMENTAL MONITORING, CONSERVATION, AND RENEWABLE ENERGY OPTIMIZATION"

AI has the potential to have a significant impact on environmental monitoring, conservation efforts, and renewable energy systems [40]. We can gather, analyze, and interpret massive amounts of data in real time by utilizing AI technologies, allowing for more efficient and long-term decision-making in these domains.

Environmental monitoring: AI can be used to track and analyze environmental data related to environment, air, and water quality. AI algorithms can be used to identify patterns and anomalies when applied to the combination of data from various sources like ground sensors, citizen science initiatives, and satellite images. Furthermore, this information is used to support disaster early warning systems, motivate proactive conservation efforts, and halt environmental degradation.

Conservation: AI can assist in managing and maintaining wildlife habitats, which will greatly advance conservation efforts. Using camera trap images or satellite imagery, for example, AI-powered image recognition algorithms can identify and track endangered species, detect poaching activity, and keep track of ecosystem changes [41]. The information provided can be used to plan conservation efforts, monitor wildlife populations, and put an end to the illegal wildlife trade. AI analysis of ecological and climatic models can be used to understand and predict how human activity affects ecosystems.

Renewable energy system optimization: AI can be used to improve the effectiveness and efficiency of renewable energy systems. Solar, wind, and hydroelectric power are examples of such systems. To forecast energy demand and supply, AI algorithms can use historical weather patterns, data on energy consumption, and grid infrastructure. This improves management and planning. Artificial intelligence can also be used to strategically locate renewable energy infrastructure in order to maximize energy output while minimizing environmental impact. For example, using real-time adjustments based on changing wind conditions, AI can optimize the operation of wind turbines, resulting in increased energy output and lower maintenance costs [42].

Techniques of optimization supported by AI can also make it easier to incorporate energy from renewable sources into existing power grids, balancing demand and supply and improving overall grid stability. This incorporation eliminates dependency on fossil fuels, lowers greenhouse gas emissions, and speeds up the transition to a more sustainable energy system.

Using AI to monitor the environment, conserve resources, and optimize renewable energy systems has enormous potential to advance sustainability. We can make decisions that are more informed and take more effective actions to protect the environment, preserve biodiversity, and transition to cleaner and more sustainable energy sources by leveraging AI's ability to process and analyze massive amounts of data and make real-time predictions.

Artificial intelligence has the potential to improve natural resource management and conservation, such as forest management and biodiversity conservation. For example, machine-learning algorithms can analyze satellite imagery to monitor deforestation patterns or identify areas prone to wildfires, allowing for timely interventions [43].

Artificial intelligence-powered sensors and data analysis techniques can help monitor air, water, and noise pollution. Analysis of real-time information from a variety of sources may assist in the early identification of environmental damage events, restoration actions, and improved environmental planning.

1.6.2 "Unlocking Efficiency: The Potential of Resource-Efficient Algorithms without Compromising Performance"

The potential of algorithms that use fewer computational resources without sacrificing performance is enormous when it comes to sustainability in AI. These algorithms can assist AI systems in using less energy, emitting less carbon, and harming the environment less.

We can optimize the use of computational resources and lower the energy consumption of AI models during training and inference by creating more energy-efficient algorithms [44]. This reduces the carbon footprint created by cooling and powering the required hardware, in addition to saving money.

Model compression techniques are one way to accomplish this. These methods seek to make AI models more lightweight and effective by reducing their size and complexity. Pruning, which involves removing pointless connections or weights from a model, is one technique that can drastically cut the amount of computational power needed without sacrificing performance. Further lowering the amount of computation needed, quantization techniques can be used to represent model weights and activations with fewer bits [45].

Investigating different model architectures is an additional strategy. We can achieve comparable or even better performance while using fewer computational resources by designing models with a more effective structure. In order to be effective and lower the computational cost of inference without sacrificing results, architectures like MobileNet and EfficientNet, for instance, have been specially created.

In terms of lowering computational requirements, transfer learning and meta-learning techniques also show promise. We effectively decrease the amount of training data and computation required for new tasks by drawing on knowledge from pre-trained models or prior tasks. When computing resources are scarce or expensive, this is especially helpful.

The effectiveness of AI computations can also be greatly improved by advances in hardware technology, such as specialized accelerated processing units (APUs) and dedicated AI chips [46].

These hardware accelerators are created specifically to run AI algorithms quickly while using less resources and preserving high performance.

For AI to be sustainable, algorithms with lower computational resource requirements without sacrificing performance have a lot of potential. These algorithms contribute to a greener and more effective AI ecosystem by minimizing energy use, cutting carbon emissions, and optimizing resource use. Unlocking the full potential of sustainable AI systems requires ongoing research and innovation in model compression, alternative architectures, transfer learning, and hardware acceleration.

1.7 FUTURE DIRECTIONS AND INITIATIVES

Sustainable AI initiatives in the environment will continue to advance in the future, with a focus on innovative approaches to addressing pressing environmental challenges. These initiatives will improve environmental monitoring capabilities by utilizing AI algorithms and remote sensing techniques to gain deeper insights into ecosystems and support effective conservation and management strategies. Predictive analytics powered by AI will be critical in modeling ecological changes, allowing decision-makers to respond to environmental shifts proactively and implement targeted interventions [47]. Efforts will also be made to incorporate eco-friendly practices into AI development, with the goal of optimizing energy efficiency and reducing the carbon footprint associated with AI systems. Partnership and collaboration between scientists, policymakers, and environmental professionals will boost impactful multidisciplinary initiatives that use AI for sustainable urban planning, resource management, and climate change mitigation. Public engagement and awareness will be prioritized in order to foster a shared understanding of the potential of sustainable AI in creating a more sustainable and resilient future. These initiatives can provide a deeper understanding of ecosystems and provision successful conservation and management strategies by utilizing AI algorithms and remote sensing techniques. Artificial intelligence-powered predictive analytics can upbeat decision-making and targeted interventions to address environmental changes. Eco-friendly practices must be incorporated into AI development. The carbon footprint of AI systems should be minimized through initiatives aimed at improving energy efficiency. This may entail creating energy-efficient models, relying on renewable energy sources, and implementing sustainable production and disposal methods.

1.8 CONCLUSION

In conclusion, the adoption of sustainable AI presents immense potential in addressing environmental challenges and promoting sustainable practices. The impact of AI on the Sustainable Development Goals (SDGs) is significant, as discussed in this chapter, and it contributes to the monitoring, analysis, and management of natural resources, allowing us to more effectively address climate change, deforestation, pollution, and other environmental challenges. Further, this also addresses the implications on the environment by AI technologies, which, particularly those based on deep learning algorithms, have high energy and computing demands, leading to increased carbon emissions and electricity consumption. The further discussion in this chapter highlighted various opportunities where AI can make a positive impact, including climate change modeling, natural resource management, environmental monitoring, sustainable agriculture, wildlife conservation, energy optimization, and the establishment of a circular economy. However, it is crucial to acknowledge the challenges associated with implementing sustainable AI, such as energy consumption, ethical considerations, and the need for interdisciplinary collaboration. Nevertheless, ongoing research and development initiatives, industry-wide efforts to establish sustainability standards, and public engagement initiatives provide reasons to be optimistic about the future of sustainable AI. By harnessing the power of AI innovation and incorporating environmental considerations, we can work toward creating a greener and more sustainable future for generations to come.

REFERENCES

1. D'Amore, Gabriella, et al. "Artificial intelligence in the water-energy-food model: A holistic approach towards sustainable development goals." *Sustainability* 14.2 (2022): 867.
2. Kar, Arpan Kumar, Shweta Kumari Choudhary, and Vinay Kumar Singh. "How can artificial intelligence impact sustainability: A systematic literature review." *Journal of Cleaner Production* 376 (2022): 134120.
3. De Lucia, Gianluca, Marco Lapegna, and Diego Romano. "Unlocking the potential of edge computing for hyperspectral image classification: An efficient low-energy strategy." *Future Generation Computer Systems* 147 (2023): 207–218.
4. Arain, Aubrey L., et al. "Material flow, economic and environmental life cycle performances of informal electronic waste recycling in a Thai community." *Resources, Conservation and Recycling* 180 (2022): 106129.
5. Lourenço, Justino. "The role of IoT and AI in bioeconomy." *Handbook of Research on Bioeconomy and Economic Ecosystems*. IGI Global, 2023, pp. 312–329. doi: 10.4018/978-1-6684-8879-9.ch016.
6. Naveenkumar, Rajendiran, et al. "A strategic review on sustainable approaches in municipal solid waste management and energy recovery: Role of artificial intelligence, economic stability and life cycle assessment." *Bioresource Technology* 379 (2023): 129044.
7. United Nations. "Transforming our world: The 2030 agenda for sustainable development." New York: United Nations, Department of Economic and Social Affairs (2015).
8. Mhlanga, David. "The role of artificial intelligence and machine learning amid the COVID-19 pandemic: What lessons are we learning on 4IR and the sustainable development goals." *International Journal of Environmental Research and Public Health* 19.3 (2022): 1879.
9. Ahmad, Tanveer, et al. "Artificial intelligence in sustainable energy industry: Status quo, challenges and opportunities." *Journal of Cleaner Production* 289 (2021): 125834.
10. Van Wynsberghe, Aimee. "Sustainable AI: AI for sustainability and the sustainability of AI." *AI and Ethics* 1.3 (2021): 213–218.
11. Gupta, Udit, et al. "Chasing carbon: The elusive environmental footprint of computing." *2021 IEEE International Symposium on High-Performance Computer Architecture (HPCA)*. IEEE, 2021.
12. Jose, Rajan, et al. "Artificial intelligence-driven circular economy as a key enabler for sustainable energy management." *Materials Circular Economy* 2 (2020): 1–7.
13. Perucica, Natasa, and Katarina Andjelkovic. "Is the future of AI sustainable? A case study of the European Union." *Transforming Government: People, Process and Policy* 16.3 (2022): 347–358.
14. Gaur, Loveleen, et al. "Artificial intelligence for carbon emissions using system of systems theory." *Ecological Informatics* 76 (2023): 102165.
15. Ligozat, Anne-Laure, et al. "Unraveling the hidden environmental impacts of AI solutions for environment life cycle assessment of AI solutions." *Sustainability* 14.9 (2022): 5172.
16. Strubell, Emma, Ananya Ganesh, and Andrew McCallum. "Energy and policy considerations for deep learning in NLP." *arXiv preprint arXiv:1906.02243* (2019).
17. Nowakowski, Piotr, Krzysztof Szwarc, and Urszula Boryczka. "Combining an artificial intelligence algorithm and a novel vehicle for sustainable e-waste collection." *Science of the Total Environment* 730 (2020): 138726.
18. Grau Ruiz, María Amparo, and Fiachra O'Brolchain. "Environmental robotics for a sustainable future in circular economies." *Nature Machine Intelligence* 4.1 (2022): 3–4.
19. Chen, Jie, et al. "Artificial intelligence based e-waste management for environmental planning." *Environmental Impact Assessment Review* 87 (2021): 106498.
20. Islam, Aminul, et al. "Advances in physiochemical and biotechnological approaches for sustainable metal recovery from e-waste: A critical review." *Journal of Cleaner Production* 323 (2021): 129015.
21. Murthy, Venkatesha, and Seeram Ramakrishna. "A review on global E-waste management: Urban mining towards a sustainable future and circular economy." *Sustainability* 14.2 (2022): 647.
22. Sarker, Iqbal H. "Machine learning: Algorithms, real-world applications and research directions." *SN Computer Science* 2.3 (2021): 160.
23. Vinuesa, Ricardo, Hossein Azizpour, Iolanda Leite, et al. "The role of artificial intelligence in achieving the sustainable development goals." *Nature Communications* 11 (2020): 233. doi: 10.1038/s41467-019-14108-y.
24. Chen, Lin, et al. "Artificial intelligence-based solutions for climate change: A review." *Environmental Chemistry Letters* 21 (2023): 1–33.
25. Holzinger, Andreas, et al. "AI for life: Trends in artificial intelligence for biotechnology." *New Biotechnology* 74 (2023): 16–24.

26. Muttitanon, W., and Nitin K. Tripathi. "Land use/land cover changes in the coastal zone of Ban Don Bay, Thailand using Landsat 5 TM data." *International Journal of Remote Sensing* 26.11 (2005): 2311–2323.

27. Agarwala, Nitin. "Managing marine environmental pollution using artificial intelligence." *Maritime Technology and Research* 3.2 (2021): 120–136.

28. Yang, Liping, et al. "Towards synoptic water monitoring systems: A review of AI methods for automating water body detection and water quality monitoring using remote sensing." *Sensors* 22.6 (2022): 2416.

29. Tien, Paige Wenbin, et al. "A deep learning approach towards the detection and recognition of opening of windows for effective management of building ventilation heat losses and reducing space heating demand." *Renewable Energy* 177 (2021): 603–625.

30. Aarvik, Per. "Artificial Intelligence-a promising anti-corruption tool in development settings." U4 Anti-Corruption Resource Centre (2019).

31. Savulescu, Julian, and Hannah Maslen. "Moral enhancement and artificial intelligence: Moral AI?" *Beyond Artificial Intelligence: The Disappearing Human-Machine Divide*, Springer , 2015, pp. 79–95. doi: 10.1007/978-3-319-09668-1_6.

32. Antonopoulos, Ioannis, et al. "Artificial intelligence and machine learning approaches to energy demand-side response: A systematic review." *Renewable and Sustainable Energy Reviews* 130 (2020): 109899.

33. Hoffert, Martin I., et al. "Advanced technology paths to global climate stability: Energy for a greenhouse planet." *Science* 298.5595 (2002): 981–987.

34. Bostrom, Nick. "Ethical issues in advanced artificial intelligence." Smit I.et al. *Cognitive, Emotive and Ethical Aspects of Decision Making in Humans and in Artificial Intelligence* Vol. 2, Int. Institute of Advanced Studies in Systems Research and Cybernetics 12–17 (2003): 277–284.

35. Polyakov, E. G., and A. S. Sibilev. "Recycling rare-earth-metal wastes by pyrometallurgical methods." *Metallurgist* 59.5–6 (2015): 368–373.

36. Naik, Nithesh, et al. "Legal and ethical consideration in artificial intelligence in healthcare: Who takes responsibility?" *Frontiers in Surgery* 9 (2022): 266.

37. Cihon, Peter. "Standards for AI governance: International standards to enable global coordination in AI research & development." *Future of Humanity Institute. University of Oxford* (2019): 1–41. https://arxiv.org/pdf/1802.07228.pdf

38. Nguyen, X. Cuong, et al. "Development of machine learning-based models to forecast solid waste generation in residential areas: A case study from Vietnam." *Resources, Conservation and Recycling* 167 (2021): 105381.

39. Ahmad, Tanveer, et al. "Energetics systems and artificial intelligence: Applications of industry 4.0." *Energy Reports* 8 (2022): 334–361.

40. Şerban, Andreea Claudia, and Miltiadis D. Lytras. "Artificial intelligence for smart renewable energy sector in europe-smart energy infrastructures for next generation smart cities." *IEEE Access* 8 (2020): 77364–77377.

41. Shivaprakash, Kadukothanahally Nagaraju, et al. "Potential for artificial intelligence (AI) and machine learning (ML) applications in biodiversity conservation, managing forests, and related services in India." *Sustainability* 14.12 (2022): 7154.

42. Meyers, Johan, et al. "Wind farm flow control: Prospects and challenges." *Wind Energy Science Discussions* 2022 (2022): 1–56.

43. Piao, Yong, et al. "Multi-hazard mapping of droughts and forest fires using a multi-layer hazards approach with machine learning algorithms." *Geomatics, Natural Hazards and Risk* 13.1 (2022): 2649–2673.

44. Mazumder, Arnab Neelim, et al. "A survey on the optimization of neural network accelerators for micro-ai on-device inference." *IEEE Journal on Emerging and Selected Topics in Circuits and Systems* 11.4 (2021): 532–547.

45. Park, Eunhyeok, Junwhan Ahn, and Sungjoo Yoo. "Weighted-entropy-based quantization for deep neural networks." *Proceedings of the IEEE Conference on Computer Vision and Pattern Recognition (CVPR), Honolulu, HI, USA.* 2017: 5456–5464.

46. Ignatov, Andrey, et al. "Ai benchmark: Running deep neural networks on android smartphones." *European Conference on Computer Vision,* Munich, Germany, September 8–14. 2018: 288–314.

47. Garrett, K. A., et al. "Climate change effects on pathogen emergence: Artificial intelligence to translate big data for mitigation." *Annual Review of Phytopathology* 60 (2022): 357–378.

2 Artificial Intelligence of Things (AIoT) in Agriculture 4.0

P. S. Metkewar and Anuja Bokhare

2.1 INTRODUCTION

Internet of Things (IoT) innovation has become one of the main subjects of the logical examination field in light of its likely application. This section momentarily presented the presentation of IoT innovation and horticulture IoT innovation. Farming improvement in China is traveling from customary to modernization, and gear with present-day material circumstances is earnestly required. The subsequent second section depicts the idea of man-made intelligence upheaval in worldwide farming including IoT and agribusiness of things, as well as a portion of the vital advancements of horticulture organizing applications, in particular rural sensor innovation; remote transmission innovation; RFID innovation; agrarian item quality security advancements; smart water system innovation; and accuracy cultivating and splashing methods. How artificial intelligence is utilized in horticulture? is being presented in the third section. Robotized Cultivating Frameworks were shrouded in the fourth section for ongoing headway in farming advancements. The fifth segment committed to Brilliant Cultivating utilizing IoT presents the improvement status of IoT innovation in smart horticulture and the utilization of assets in agribusiness, agro-natural checking of the climate, and agrarian creation of fine administration, application examination, and well-being of rural discernibility perspectives. With the turn of events and the progress of science and innovation, data innovation in agribusiness has become progressively significant, particularly as of late. With the improvement of new systems administration innovations, canny farming likewise shows an expansive improvement prospect. The sixth segment was centred around the following: How are artificial intelligence and IoT utilized in farming, which examines the insightful miniature water system control innovation, followed by a conversation of the three parts of IoT innovation lacking in the current down-to-earth applications, to be specific industry guidelines, data mix, and plan of action parts of the issues. Patterns in Shrewd Farming are canvassed in the seventh section that altogether centred around security and protection concerns and furthermore the part of low in latency for information handling of horticulture area. Reasonable uses of simulated intelligence in horticulture are unmistakably thought of in the eighth section by significantly zeroing in on yield and soil checking, insect and plant sickness identification, Shrewd splashing, programmed weeding, and airborne overview and imaging. Difficulties and future exploration bearings in horticulture are underlined in the ninth section and their shift to the astuteness of agribusiness.

2.2 AI REVOLUTION IN GLOBAL AGRICULTURE

Worldwide AgriSystem is India's chief agribusiness counselling bunch solely given to the farming and food areas. Key Business Regions counselling and Specialized Warning Turnkey and Task the executives Administrations Post gather the board Administrations New Produce Production network Commodity and Import.

DOI: 10.1201/9781003457176-2

Globalization is an old peculiarity. It began at the hour of colonization. In the nineteenth century when European brokers came to India, Indian flavours were sent out to various nations of the world, and ranchers of south India were urged and upgraded to develop these yields.

There are expanding pressures from environmental change, soil disintegration, and biodiversity misfortune and from customers' changing preferences for food and worries about the way things are delivered. Also, the regular world that farming deals with – plants, vermin, and infections – keeps on representing their own difficulties.

Horticulture gives the vast majority of the world's food and textures. Cotton, fleece, and cowhide are horticultural items. Agribusiness additionally gives wood to development and paper items. These items, as well as the farming strategies utilized, may change starting with one area of the planet and then onto the next.

Globalization alludes to the spread of items, innovation, and information rising above public boundaries. Benefits: Cycle to commodity and import items turned out to be simple. India is well known for its flavours, cotton, tea, and so on. Different items from different nations are accessible in our market.

What is India's horticulture issue? Disintegration of soil by heavy downpour, floods, inadequate vegetation cover, and so on diminishes ranch efficiency. Deficient water system offices and unfortunate administration of water assets have prompted an extraordinary decrease in horticultural efficiency.

The accessibility of present-day agrarian innovations, for example, food handling ventures, cultivating gear, and so on. Expanded result and efficiency. Public Pay Development. New position open doors. An ascent in exchange share Development of horticultural products.

The worldwide horticulture market developed from $12,245.63 billion in 2022 to $13,398.79 billion in 2023 at a build yearly development rate (CAGR) of 9.4%.

Multinationals give new positions and abilities. Multinationals carry unfamiliar money to nearby economies when they purchase neighbourhood items and administrations. The blending of individuals and societies from everywhere in the world empowers the sharing of thoughts and ways of life, making energetic social variety.

For what reason is globalization significant? Globalization has an impact on the manner in which countries, organizations, and individuals associate. In particular, it changes the idea of monetary action among countries, extending exchange, opening worldwide stockpile anchors, and giving admittance to normal assets and work markets.

Globalization is the word used to portray the developing relationship of the world's economies, societies, and populaces, achieved by cross-line exchange labour and products, innovation, and streams of venture, individuals, and data.

Ranchers can utilize man-made intelligence-fuelled applications to follow information on things like soil well-being, weather conditions, and plant development. This information can then be utilized to settle on additional educated conclusions about things like water system and manure use, which can prompt higher harvest yields.

Man-made reasoning is applied in different ways to work on the quality and precision of the farming business. By utilizing the force of simulated intelligence, ranchers can now come to additional educated conclusions about dispensing their assets and dealing with their yields. This prompts better generally speaking harvest quality and exactness.

The information viewpoint alludes to the method involved with getting ready datasets expected to benefit from the learning calculations. In conclusion, AI identifies the examples from the preparation information and predicts and performs errands without being physically or expressly customized.

Artificial intelligence frameworks are further developing the reap quality and exactness, which is known as accuracy agribusiness. Computer-based intelligence innovation helps with identifying the illnesses in plants, bothers, unfortunate plant nourishment, and so on. It likewise permits the ranchers to screen the well-being of the yields and the dirt.

Man-made intelligence empowers better independent direction. Additionally, artificial intelligence-fuelled machines can decide soil, yield, and well-being; give compost proposals; screen the climate; and can decide the nature of harvest. All such advantages of computer-based intelligence in agribusiness empower the ranchers to settle on better choices and do effective cultivating.

Artificial intelligence programming helps in distinguishing pest infestations and plant health issues. It also improves the fertility of the soil and recovers from the overuse of pesticides and herbicides in accordance with the specific field. Furthermore, simulated intelligence not only checks the harvests but also helps in splashing the pesticides and weedicides in the field.

The most well-known utilizations of man-made reasoning in the horticulture industry are Agrarian Robots, Prescient Examination, and Harvest and Soil Observing. PC vision and profound learning calculations are utilized to handle information caught by rambles, and additionally, programming-based innovation is used to screen crops.

The countries leading the way in information generation using computer-based intelligence in practical farming are the United States, India, Iran, and France.

In general, progressive change will be a short, sharp issue. So by that standard basically, the rise of man-made consciousness (artificial intelligence) can best be depicted as 'transformative' as opposed to 'progressive'.

2.3   HOW AI IS USED IN AGRICULTURE?

Ranchers can reduce errors and lower the risk of harvest disappointments by using simulated intelligence to provide them with the decisive and proactive research. Weather conditions determining man-made intelligence empowers ranchers to predict temperatures and foresee the number of natural products or vegetables a collection will yield.

Ranchers can gather and handle altogether more information and do it quicker with simulated intelligence than they could otherwise. Breaking down market interest, gauging costs, and deciding the ideal time for planting and gathering are key difficulties ranchers can settle with simulated intelligence.

Computerized reasoning uses PCs and machines to impersonate the critical thinking and dynamic abilities of the human psyche.

How artificial intelligence is utilized in farming in India? Man-made intelligence can assist with distinguishing field limits and waterways to enable reasonable cultivating rehearses, increase crop yields, and support India's 1.4 billion individuals and the remainder of the world. For India, horticulture is basic.

The utilization of simulated intelligence in farming was first endeavoured by McKinion and Lemmon in 1985 to make GOSSYM, a cotton crop recreation model utilizing Master Framework, to upgrade cotton creation affected by the water system, treatment, weed control development, environment, and other variables.

Simulated intelligence empowers better navigation. Additionally, computer-based intelligence-controlled machines can decide soil, yield, and well-being; give manure proposals; screen the climate; and decide the nature of harvest. All such advantages of computer-based intelligence in horticulture empower the ranchers to settle on better choices and do effective cultivating.

Computer-based intelligence empowers the mechanization of routine repetitive undertakings in regions, for example, information assortment, information passage, client-focussed business, email reactions, programming testing, receipt age, and more. Representatives are given the opportunity to focus on tasks that require human capacities.

Farming plays a significant role in the financial area of every country. Populace all over the planet is expanding step by step, as is the interest for food. The conventional techniques that are utilized by the ranchers are not adequate to satisfy the need at the ongoing stage. Subsequently, some new robotization strategies are acquainted with fulfilling these prerequisites and giving extraordinary open positions to many individuals in this area. Man-made brainpower has become perhaps the main innovation in each area, including training, banking, mechanical technology, agribusiness, and so on. In the horticulture area, it is assuming an exceptionally essential part, and it is changing the farming business. Simulated intelligence saves the farming area from various factors, for example, environmental change, populace development, business issues in this field, and food handling. The present horticulture framework has reached an alternate level because of man-made intelligence. Man-made brainpower has further developed crop creation and constant observation, gathering, handling, and advertising. Different Hi-tech PC-based frameworks are intended to decide different significant boundaries like weed discovery, yield recognition, crop quality, and more.

2.3.1 Challenges in Agriculture Using Traditional Methods

Prior to understanding the simulated intelligence effect and application in farming, we should comprehend what are the difficulties in agribusiness by utilizing conventional techniques, which are given beneath:

- In cultivating, various climatic factors like precipitation, temperature, and moistness play a significant role. Because of contamination, some of the time environment fluctuates suddenly, and consequently, it becomes challenging for ranchers to pursue legitimate choices for gathering, planting seeds, and soil getting ready.
- For a superior yield, it is vital that the dirt ought to be useful and have the necessary sustenance, like nitrogen, phosphorous, and potassium. On the off chance that these supplements are absent in a successful manner in the dirt, then, at that point, it might prompt low-quality yields. However, distinguishing the dirt quality with conventional ways is troublesome.
- In the horticulture lifecycle, it is expected that we save our yields from weeds. Else it might expand the creation cost, and it likewise assimilates supplements from the dirt. Be that as it may, by customary ways, distinguishing proof and counteraction of harvest from weeds isn't effective.

Similarly, as with the conventional techniques for agribusiness, there are so many difficulties that ranchers would confront. To tackle these difficulties, simulated intelligence is broadly utilized in this area. For horticulture, man-made brainpower has turned into a progressive innovation. It helps the ranchers to yield better harvests, control bothers, check soil, and a lot more. The following are a few critical utilization of computerized reasoning in the farming area:

Climate and Value Estimating: As we have talked about in difficulties, it is hard for the ranchers to make the ideal choice for gathering, planting seeds, and soil getting ready because of environmental change. In any case, with the assistance of computer-based intelligence weather condition anticipation, ranchers can have data on climate examination, and as needs be, they can make arrangements for the kind of yield to develop, seeds to plant, and gathering the harvest. With cost gauging, ranchers can find out the cost of harvests for the following couple of weeks, which can assist them with getting the greatest benefit.

Well-being Checking of Harvests: The idea of gathering extensively depends on the kind of soil and food of the soil. Nevertheless, with the rising speed of deforestation, the soil quality is corrupting bit by bit, and it is difficult to choose it.

To decide this issue, PC-based knowledge has thought about another application called Plantix. It was made by PEAT to perceive the needs of soil, including plant aggravations and sicknesses. With the help of this application, farmers can get an arrangement to use better excrement, which can additionally create the procure quality. In this application, reproduced knowledge's image affirmation advancement is used by which farmers can get photos of plants and get information about the quality.

Horticulture Advanced Mechanics: Advanced mechanics is by and large generally utilized in various areas, principally in assembling, to perform complex assignments. These days, different computer-based intelligence organizations are creating robots to be utilized in the agribusiness area. These simulated intelligence robots are created so that they can play out numerous assignments in cultivating.

Mimicked knowledge robots are similarly ready to truly take a gander at the idea of yields, recognize and control weeds, and gather the reap with faster speed stood out from a human.

Watchful Sprinkling: With mimicked insight sensors, weed can be distinguished really, and it moreover perceives weed-influenced districts. On finding such locales, herbicides can be unequivocally sprinkled to lessen the usage of herbicides and, moreover, save time and yield. Various reproduced knowledge associations are building robots with PC-based insight and PC vision, which can precisely sprinkle on weeds. The usage of PC-based insight sprayers can comprehensively diminish the amount of engineered materials to be used on fields, and consequently, it deals with the idea of harvests and saves cash.

Illness Finding: With reproduced knowledge gauges, farmers can get data on diseases easily. With this, they can without a doubt decide diseases to have real framework and on time. It can save the presence of plants and farmers' time. To do this, photos of plants, as a matter of some importance, are taken care of using PC vision development. This ensures that plant pictures are properly parcelled into the unfortunate and non-tainted parts. After disclosure, the unfortunate part is altered and transported off the labs for extra findings. This method also helps in the acknowledgement of vermin, the absence of enhancements, and some more.

Exactness Developing: Exactness developing strategy is about "Optimal spot, Amazing an open door, and Right things". The exactness developing strategy is a much exact and controlled way that can replace the work concentrated part of developing to perform horrid endeavours. One delineation of exactness developing is the ID of sensations of tension in plants. This can be achieved using significant standard pictures and different sensor data on plants. The data figured from sensors are then out to a computer-based intelligence model as a commitment for stress affirmation.

2.3.1.1   Computer-Based Intelligence of New Businesses in Agribusiness

The following is the rundown of well-known new companies in agribusiness:

Prospera: It is an Israeli start-up established in the year 2014. This organization makes wise answers for productive cultivating. It creates cloud-based arrangements that gather information from the fields like soil/water, flying pictures, and so on and join this information with an in-field gadget. This gadget is known as the Prospera gadget, and it makes bits of knowledge from this information. The gadget is controlled by different sensors and innovations like PC vision.

Blue Waterway Innovation: Blue-Waterway Innovation is a California-based start-up that began in the year 2011. It creates cutting-edge agribusiness hardware utilizing simulated intelligence, PC vision, and advanced mechanics innovation. This gear distinguishes individual plants utilizing PC vision, ML chooses an activity, and with advanced mechanics, the activity is performed. This assists the ranchers with saving expenses and synthetic substances in cultivating.

FarmBot: FarmBot is an open-source CNC precision developing machine and programming group, which is made to foster yields by anyone at their own place. The complete thing

"FarmBot" is available at an expense of $4,000, and it engages anyone to get done with developing going from seed estate to weed area in isolation with the help of a genuine bot and open-source programming structure. It is like manner gives a web app that can be downloaded on any mobile phone or PC structure and allows us to supervise developing from any spot at whatever point.

Fasal: The use of man-made knowledge in agribusiness is growing bit by bit in various spots across the world. Regardless, cultivation assets per farmer in the less lucky locale are less diverged from the rich district, which is beneficial for robotized checking as it requires a lesser number of contraptions with low bandwidth and size to discover the all-out cultivating data. In this field, the Indian start-up Fasal is working. It uses sensible sensors and man-made knowledge to give continuous data and encounters to farmers. With this, farmers can benefit from steady, huge information material to ordinary exercises at the residence. The association's contraptions are easy to execute for little places. They are making PC-based insight-engaged machines to make exactness developing that can be opened by every farmer.

OneSoil: OneSoil is an application that is planned to help farmers with taking a prevalent decision. This application includes a computer-based intelligence estimation and PC vision for precision developing. It screens the harvests in good ways, perceives issues in the fields, truly takes a gander at the weather patterns figure, and works out nitrogen, phosphorus, and potassium excrement rate.

2.3.1.2 Advantages of Man-Made Intelligence in Agribusiness

Benefits:

Man-made intelligence empowers better navigation.

Prescient examination is actually a shelter for the horticulture business. It helps the ranchers tackle the critical difficulties of cultivating, for example, investigating the market requests, value determining, and tracking down ideal times for planting and gathering the yield. In addition, artificial intelligence-fuelled machines can likewise decide soil, yield, and well-being, give manure suggestions, screen the climate, and decide the nature of harvest. All such advantages of computer-based intelligence in horticulture empower the ranchers to pursue better choices and do productive cultivating.

Simulated intelligence brings cost reserve funds.

Accuracy cultivating utilizing simulated intelligence-empowered gear assists the ranchers with developing more harvests with lesser assets and cost. Computer-based intelligence gives continuous bits of knowledge to ranchers that empower them to make legitimate choice at each phase of cultivating. With this right choice, there is less loss of items and synthetic substances and productive utilization of time and cash. Additionally, it likewise permits the ranchers to distinguish the specific regions that need water system, preparation, and pesticide treatment, which saves unnecessary utilization of synthetic substances on the yield. Everything summarizes and brings about diminished utilization of herbicides, better yield quality, and high benefit with less assets.

Simulated intelligence diminishes work deficiency.

There has forever been an issue of work lacking in the farming business. Simulated intelligence can address this issue with mechanization in cultivating. With simulated intelligence and mechanization, ranchers can finish work without having more individuals, and a few models are driverless farm trucks, brilliant water system, and preparing frameworks, shrewd splashing, vertical cultivating programming, and artificial intelligence-based robots for gathering. Artificial intelligence-driven machines and hardware are a lot quicker and exact contrasted with human farmhands.

2.4 AUTOMATED FARMING SYSTEMS

What is robotized cultivating? Frequently connected with "brilliant cultivating," mechanized cultivating utilizes different innovative gadgets to improve and robotize horticulture tasks and the harvest or domesticate animals creation cycle, making ranches more productive.

Robots can likewise be utilized to assist ranchers with planting. By setting the seed in the dirt, a robot can accelerate the establishing system, guaranteeing that the seeds are planted at the legitimate profundity and perfectly positioned.

Arm robotization (or shrewd cultivating) is an assortment of tech developments in customary cultivating to enhance the food creation process and work on quality. At this point, high-level cultivating innovation can be a fundamental piece of the rancher's everyday work.

The fundamental advantages of robotized farming include improvement in crop yields, diminished water use and water system costs, upgraded activity productivity, and better venture the board. Three kinds of robotization underway can be recognized: (1) fixed computerization, (2) programmable mechanization, and (3) adaptable robotization.

Robotization in assembling can assist with bringing down costs, further develop specialist security, diminish processing plant lead times, give a quicker return on initial capital investment, and permit your activity to turn out to be more aggressive, increment creation yield, thus substantially more!

A robotization framework is an incorporation of sensors, controls, and actuators intended to carry out a role with negligible or no human mediation. The field worried in this subject is called Mechatronics, which is an interdisciplinary part of designing that consolidates mechanical, electrical, and electronic frameworks.

How independent cultivating will change horticulture? The following are three different ways independent cultivating is set to surprise the horticultural business:

1. **Facilitating Cultivating Work Deficiencies with Independent Farm Haulers:**

   Independent trackers are set to reform the farming business by eliminating the human component and facilitating work supply when enlistment in the area is waning. John Deere sent off the primary financially fruitful steel furrow in 1837, and as of late, it uncovered its most memorable completely independent farm truck – the 8R – at the Buyer Hardware (CES) show in Las Vegas.

   Jahmy Hindman, CTO at John Deere, talking at CES, said that:

   > Up to this point, farming has forever been tied in with accomplishing more, with more -
   > more strength, more data sources, more sections of land - yet the new computerized time
   > is changing all of that. Somewhat recently, it has been tied in with accomplishing more
   > with less, and giving ranchers apparatuses to settle on informed choices.

   Driverless work vehicles expect to let the ranchers out of 8–12-hour long stretches of simply driving. They permit ranchers to take control through an application on their telephone or PC. The rancher can utilize the application to situate a farm truck, drive the length of a field, pivot, return, and move around deterrents.

2. **Supporting Practical Cultivating with Drones**

   Horticultural robots are assisting ranchers with expanding crop creations and screening crop development for the most extreme results. Ranchers are utilizing drone information to remove soil tests to really take a look at temperatures, dampness, and rise. Drone producer DJI offers a flying cultivating choice that offers types of assistance, for example, observing and designated pesticide splashing. The World Financial Gathering's New Vision for Agriculture (NVA) drive is assisting with guaranteeing that the farming area can reasonably feed a developing total populace. The NVA draws in with more than 650 associations and has progressed 100 worth chain drives to help a huge number of ranchers.

3. Further Developing Efficiency with Seed-Establishing Robots

Seed planting requires a significant measure of human exertion and is tedious, yet seed-planting robots are setting aside ranchers' time and cash. The independent gadgets plant seeds in the ideal position, removing the human component typically required. Cultivating gear expert Fendt is trying little independent seed-establishing robots, the size of a clothes washer.

The improvement of farming was a defining moment for mankind. People's capacity to design the climate to create sufficient food to support gigantic populace development was the primary massive change in the connection between completely present-day people and the climate. The coming of horticulture set off a more extensive scope of progressions, from developing yields, fire, and prepared food to self-driving hardware.

Farming has pushed us ahead for quite some time, yet we are presently at a defining moment. With a worldwide populace projection of 9.7 billion individuals by 2050, rural creation should increment by something like 70% from current levels to serve wholesome patterns. The strain on the horticulture business to create more nutritious items is coming down on the strength of our planet than at any time in recent memory.

New mechanical progressions in present-day cultivating, going from mechanical technology and farming robots to PC vision programming, have completely changed current horticulture. Ranchers presently approach devices that will assist them with satisfying the needs of our reality's steadily expanding populace.

2.4.1 What Is Robotized Cultivating?

Frequently connected with "brilliant cultivating," robotized cultivating utilizes different mechanical gadgets to improve and computerize horticulture tasks and the yield or domesticate animals creation cycle, making ranches more productive.

Numerous horticulture innovation organizations are presently dealing with advanced mechanics development to foster robot tasks, independent farm haulers, automated reapers, programmed watering, and cultivating robots. Albeit these innovations are somewhat new, the rural area has seen a rising number of customary horticulture organizations take on ranch robotization into their cycles.

2.4.2 What Innovations Does Computerized Cultivating Utilize?

The primary objective of horticulture innovation organizations is to execute brilliant advancements to cover commonplace undertakings. Probably, the most famous advancements executed in ranches are as follows:

Reap Computerization

Collecting products of the soil has forever been trying for farming robotization. Collecting robots should deal with the items tenderly to abstain from swelling and harm.

AgTech organizations, for example, Agrobot, which fostered the main robot to pick strawberries tenderly, and Bountiful Mechanical Technology, the world's most memorable business automated apple picker, are instances of numerous AgTech organizations attempting to change the farming business.

Independent Farm Vehicles

Makers have some control over their independent farm vehicles from a distance or pre-programme them to have total independence. Hare Work vehicle fostered an independent farm truck that lessens work costs for column ranchers, builds the productivity of all tasks, and helps increment yields.

Another organization, Bear Banner Advanced Mechanics, is creating work vehicle computerization packs to make mechanization more open for ranchers by retrofitting existing farm haulers with state-of-the-art driverless innovation and carrying out control.

Cultivating and Weeding

Advanced mechanics intended for cultivating and weeding can target explicit yield regions; in cultivating, it can diminish work and cultivate ordinary errands, though weeding mechanical technology can decrease pesticide utilization by 90% with PC vision.

Blue Waterway Innovation is an organization that utilizes PC vision and mechanical technology innovations to shower herbicides just where required, and unequivocally the sum required, empowering ranchers a better approach to control and forestall herbicide-safe weeds.

Drones

Horticultural robots can remotely screen conditions and apply manures, pesticides, and different medicines from a higher place. Symbolism and infrared examination can likewise distinguish pain points rapidly, assisting ranchers with diagnosing issues almost immediately.

American Mechanical Technology is fostering a completely independent "Robot-as-a-administration" with independent robots, base stations, and investigation stages, giving makers experiences into producers at goals, frequencies, and rates never before conceivable.

Benefits of Computerized Cultivating

Computerized cultivating resolves critical issues, for example, a rising worldwide populace, ranch work deficiencies, and changing purchaser inclinations. The advantages of robotizing conventional cultivating processes are fantastic.

Purchaser Advantage

Purchasers' inclinations are moving towards natural and practical items. With mechanized cultivating, produce arrives at buyers quicker, fresher, and more feasible. An expansion in efficiency from robotization expands the yield and pace of creation, lessening customer costs.

Work Proficiency

Work is more than half of the expense of growing a homestead, and 55% of ranchers say work deficiencies influence them. Along these lines, 31% of ranchers are moving to less arduous yields. Be that as it may, there is a huge potential for reap AI.

Routine assignments can be robotized with advanced mechanics innovation, diminishing work costs in the farming business. For instance, a solitary strawberry robot reaper can possibly pick a 25-section of land region in 3 days and supplant 30 homestead labourers.

Diminished Natural Impression

Robotized cultivating can make agribusiness more productive while additionally making cultivating maintainable. By carrying out accuracy cultivating procedures, ranchers can specifically diminish their natural impression by applying pesticides and manures, diminishing the synthetic substances in the encompassing soil and streams.

Moreover, computerized frameworks can assist ranchers with moderating energy and water, diminishing their ecological effect.

Difficulties of Mechanized Cultivating

There are still a few difficulties to survive. Significant expenses to embrace mechanical advances can be an extensive boundary to passage for ranchers, particularly in non-industrial nations; specialized issues and hardware breakdown can likewise introduce high charges to fix such specific gear. Ranchers should join their insight and involvement in these new advancements to use ranch computerization completely.

Looking forward, despite the fact that we are just at the beginning phases of computerized cultivating, obviously, computerization will assume a critical part in the horticulture business. Because of mechanical progressions, cultivating turns out to be more refined consistently, and what was state of the art only a couple of years prior will become the norm and financially savvy soon.

This training is useful for the actual ranchers as well as for the climate. Not only will robotized cultivating lead to expanded yields and decreased costs but also it can possibly make cultivating a more secure and more reasonable industry. The human component will constantly be key to dealing with a homestead; however, robotized horticulture is fundamental for human endurance.

2.5 SMART FARMING USING IOT

With the objective to follow, screen, computerize, and assess exercises, savvy agribusiness/ cultivating intends to interface the farming business to state-of-the-art innovation, like sensors, artificial intelligence (man-made brainpower), and the Web of Things (IoT).

The goal is to support crop quality and yield while requiring less human work. I will make sense of shrewd agrarian works involving the Raspberry Pi here and how it will be critical to cultivating from now on.

Controlling soil dampness, mugginess, PH level, bug identification, and different variables is straightforward with a Raspberry Pi. Barely any models are given beneath:

- Using the Raspberry Pi to control soil moisture.
- Using the Raspberry Pi to control humidity.
- Using the Raspberry Pi to control soil pH.
- Using the Raspberry Pi-based analysis to identify soil nutrients.
- Using the Raspberry Pi for smart bug detection.
- Using the Raspberry Pi for automated irrigation.
- Using the Raspberry Pi modem kit for agriculture projects.

IoT shrewd cultivating arrangement is a framework that is worked for checking the yield field with the assistance of sensors (light, stickiness, temperature, soil dampness, crop wellbeing, and so on) and mechanizing the water system framework.

IoT in an agrarian setting alludes to the utilization of sensors, cameras, and different gadgets to transform each component and activity engaged with cultivating into information.

A Brilliant Farming Framework upgrades creation rates. Utilizing the brilliant framework allows you to expand your results while limiting your feedback. For instance, utilizing your cell phone to screen soil dampness, plant well-being, and atmospheric conditions permits you to choose when to apply manures, water, and nuisance control items.

Brilliant cultivating is an administration idea zeroed in on giving the horticultural business the foundation to use cutting-edge innovation – including huge information, the cloud, and the IoT – for following, observing, computerizing, and breaking down tasks.

2.6 HOW IS AI AND IOT USED IN AGRICULTURE?

A portion of the utilization of artificial intelligence and IoT in horticulture is in the space of accuracy cultivating, rural robots and bouncing frameworks, domesticated animals observing, screen environment conditions, savvy nurseries, man-made intelligence, and IoT-based PC imaging.

Examples of AI in agriculture assist in the following ways:

- Research and development
- Faster identification of research data

- Greater efficiency and effectiveness
- Early detection of pests, diseases, and weeds
- Precision agriculture
- Analysing market demand
- Managing risks
- Weather forecasting

Agribusiness through accuracy horticulture executes IoT using robots, robots, sensors, and PC imaging coordinated with scientific apparatuses for getting bits of knowledge and observing the homesteads. The situation of actual hardware on ranches screens and records information, which is then used to get important bits of knowledge.

Horticulture AI applications in agribusiness depend on continuous information to convey outstanding additions for ranchers. Man-made intelligence and AI end up areas of strength for being driving all day, everyday security of far-off offices, improved yields, and pesticide adequacy. However, savvy AI arrangements don't end there.

What are the uses of computer-based intelligence and IoT? Computer-based intelligence in IoT crunches persistent surges of information and finds designs that are imperceptible by customary checks. Moreover, AI can gauge activity conditions and recognize boundaries that should be changed to come by ideal outcomes.

How do IoT and artificial intelligence cooperate? How could IoT and simulated intelligence uphold one another? In IoT, certifiable occasions are flagged and handled to make a suitable reaction. From a straightforward perspective then, at that point, any IoT application that utilizes programming to produce a reaction to a trigger occasion is basically a fundamental type of man-made intelligence, and simulated intelligence is then crucial for IoT.

Before the critical vehicle was made by Henry Section in 1908, all shipments were administered through carriage and horses. Affiliations are expected to fight with low security and hopeless plentifulness using these techniques.

Definitively when the vehicles started to appear in the business locales and on roads, people started including them for the vehicle of things. It achieved a lesser opportunity to move things and decreased work with task costs. Later around the fulfilment of the 20th 100 years, coordinated tasks experienced a huge change that changed the improvement cycle: structures programming. From there on out, progress has taken command of the execution and organizing of various endeavours, including work area and manual work process, while getting frail information.

Progress is constantly upsetting the methodology region and is meaningfully impacting the way how freight, bargains orders, materials, things, creation, and stock are made due. Relationship for the most part looks for a response that can give information to the techniques' requests that work correspondence and help with diminishing tremendous costs.

As speed, information and capability changed into the central picking parts; the coordinated endeavours region has taken on emerging drives, including re-enacted information, IoT, and block-chain, to fulfil the rising need and administer complex cycles.

Could we look at how to encourage custom techniques programming for arranged tasks and transportation of the board using PC-based insight and IoT. For example, composed tasks and transportation of the leaders is a field that needs examination and precision. It controls the transport of items or materials from suppliers to clients. It is the commitment of task specialists to focus on transportation, generally, the procurement and orchestrating of transportation for products and materials.

Facilitated activities and transportation of the board structure generally handle the following:

- Pickup and transport requesting
- Carrier the chiefs
- Pickup smoothing out

- Conveyance focus organization
- Travel
- Movement
- BI and declaring

Information given by IoT sensors includes the following:

- Sort of product
- Consistent region of the carrier
- Deviations from the organized course
- Pickup/movement to stockrooms
- Temperature/dampness

Completing recreated insight on the amassed data can help with anticipating the going with components:

- Surveyed transport time
- Driver lead assessment
- Nature of things, for example, brief items
- Contrasts between organized course and the authentic course

IoT-engaged trucks can aggregate the ongoing data about things:

- The temperature under which products are taken care of
- Steady region of the thing
- Clamminess receptiveness during transport
- Truck data, including speed, fuel costs

Computerized reasoning and the Web of Things are disturbing coordinated factors and transportation of the executives by making strategies and tasks more astute step by step. It is normal that defers in pickups/conveyances, and shipping limit concerns will involve the previous when computer-based intelligence and IoT come into the image.

2.7 TRENDS IN SMART AGRICULTURE

The expansion of advanced information, savvy sensors, mechanical mechanization, and different inventive methods is assisting ranchers with embracing shrewd horticulture procedure. The developing acknowledgement for cutting-edge innovations like cloud and man-made consciousness (artificial intelligence) in agribusiness is working with continuous help to ranchers.

The significant difficulties of shrewd farming incorporate nonstop checking, energy gathering, programmed water system, and infection expectation. A significant issue that emerges in cultivating is the deficiency of yields to different sicknesses.

A decision tree algorithm, a productive AI calculation, is applied to the information detected from the field to effectively foresee results. The outcomes obtained through choice tree calculation are sent through a mail caution to the ranchers, which helps in direction in regard to water supply ahead of time.

2.7.1 SECURITY AND PRIVACY CONCERNS

Despite the fact that there are a few security issues connected with savvy cultivating, like similarity, heterogeneity, obliged gadgets, handling, and insurance of gigantic information, hardly any assets have been consolidated in Horticulture 4.0 up until this point.

In the event that private associations that give IoT gadgets or administrations can get to IoT information, there is a gamble that they could involve or unveil individual data for purposes that are not in the public interest, for example, for profiling, designated promoting, or offer of the information to information representatives.

Ranchers are taking a great deal of time observing the situation with every one of their properties and yields. There is an absence of a qualified workforce ready to take basic choices. Simultaneously, the absence of convenient data and ideal, proper response can prompt tremendous misfortunes in crop yield.

What are the difficulties of savvy horticulture utilizing IoT? Challenges looked at by ranchers in taking on IoT for Farming w.r.t.

- **Lack of Framework:** Regardless of whether the ranchers embrace IoT innovation, they will not have the option to take advantage of this innovation because of the unfortunate correspondence foundation.
- **High Cost:** Hardware expected to execute IoT in farming is costly.
- **Normal Assaults Techniques Include Information Break and Fraud**: Unreliable IoT gadgets produce information and furnish digital aggressors with more than adequate space to target individual data. This might actually wind up in fraud and fake exchanges.

2.7.2 LATENCY IN DATA PROCESSING

How Low Latency Will Shape Brilliant Cultivating? As we move further into a computerized world, the utilization of the web has contacted each texture of human culture, from development to media. This has made an information blast for nearly everything, from development to media.

Society's jump into a more associated period has caused it to turn out to be incredibly information driven, as individuals hope to use the force of the web to improve. In this way, the requirement for a steady, secure, and quick web association is essential while entering the Fourth Modern Upheaval.

An illustration of this should have been visible in savvy cultivating, where ranchers are using drone innovation to gauge even the littlest of subtleties from water system levels, dampness levels to sun openness. This degree of accuracy has carried with it a store of data that should be conveyed, imparted, and broken down quickly since successful choices should be taken in view of the datasets made.

A new report by the unified countries featured that the digitization of ranches will save billions in waste and misfortunes and work on the nature of food that we devour. "The aggregate capacity of ranchers to create more food all the more effectively might be the way the world feeds the worldwide populace, which will hit nine billion by 2030," the report noted.

In equal, the development of the fifth era of portable organizations plays a critical impact in digitizing ranches around the world, particularly with the rising mushroom of vertical homesteads all over the planet.

Be that as it may, while many have proclaimed the approaching of 5G as a redeeming quality to inertness issues, it's as yet sufficiently not. Shrewd ranches will hope to support their availability to a higher level to retain the gigantic number of datasets being made by Web of Things (IoT) gadgets and sensors.

To accomplish this, powerful Appropriated Distributed Antenna Systems (DAS) are expected to give wide-scale inclusion to all gadgets siphoning out data to ranchers to settle on the ideal decision over their yields.

On-premises cell inclusion has become fundamental for associations to productively work. To prepare for this DAS Frameworks' Remote Transporter, DAS offers pre-development counselling, inclusion testing, RF configuration/designing, DAS establishment, support, remote observing, and advancement.

For those with indoor cultivating offices, indoor organization improvements can be achieved through various specialized geographies (for example, Repeaters, Conveyed Receiving Wire

Frameworks (DAS), Wi-Fi calling, and that's only the tip of the iceberg). DAS Frameworks address your cell inclusion issues by:

- Delivering mission-critical communication
- Improving business efficiencies and utilization
- Increasing user and employee satisfaction
- Future-proofing

Sending DAS Frameworks' Remote Transporter administration will empower ranch proprietors to accomplish plenty of advantages, among them:

- Places precision data analytics in the hands of farmers to make informed decisions
- Lighting fast connections with low latency for IoT devices to run at optimal levels
- Increases crop turnover rate and avoids waste
- Provides optimal resources on crop health and condition

Society is confronting a bunch of changes on the computerized side. With the quantity of IoT gadgets expected to significantly increase from 8.74 billion in 2020 to more than 25.4 billion by 2030, an accentuation on secure broadband is the principal.

2.8   PRACTICAL APPLICATIONS OF AI IN AGRICULTURE

There any many AI applications that exist in the global community but few are discussed here.

2.8.1   CROP AND SOIL MONITORING

Soil Observing with IoT utilizes innovation to enable ranchers and makers to expand yield, diminish illness, and enhance assets. IoT sensors can gauge soil temperature, NPK, volumetric water content, photosynthetic radiation, soil water potential, and soil oxygen levels. IOT innovation assists in gathering data about conditions with preferring climate, dampness, temperature, and fruitfulness of soil, and yielding web-based observing empowers for the identification of weed, level of water, bother location, creature interruption into the field, crop development, and agribusiness.

Smart detecting technology, which is used in crop observation, collects data on the state of the harvests (temperature, wetness, and well-being indicators), enabling ranchers to take appropriate measures should something go wrong. The IoT-based horticulture observation system starts by checking the water level, humidity, and humidity level. It notifies the phone user by SMS of the levels. When sensors detect that the level of water is decreasing, the water syphon naturally starts. If the temperature rises above the threshold, the fan starts.

Estimating soil quality gives an early admonition of the potential impacts different essential land use exercises might be having on long-haul soil quality. It can assist with distinguishing whether soil quality is corrupting over the long run and what factors might be added to soil debasement. Outfitted with the authentic, current, and determined climate information, ranchers can forestall the deficiency of collection and income because of weather condition stresses, as well as keep up with the ideal precipitation and soil dampness rates, hence guaranteeing improved yields.

2.8.2   INSECT AND PLANT DISEASE DETECTION

Normal strategies for the determination and identification of plant infections incorporate visual plant illness assessment by human raters, minute assessment of morphology elements to distinguish microorganisms, as well as sub-atomic, serological, and microbiological demonstrative procedures.

Visual investigations of side effects and signs, microscopy, culture media studies, and serology procedures are the most often involved strategies in analytic facilities. The proposed technique utilizes the sensor gadgets to identify the boundaries like temperature, dampness, and shade of the leaves, which are then contrasted with the dataset to check whether the gathered qualities fall into the reach determined in the dataset.

The higher exactness of the CNN model for plant illness characterization has sealed to be the best than any remaining sorts of ML and DL techniques. Reviews have demonstrated the way that CNNs can accomplish high precision rates in the scope of 99%–99.2% in ordering pictures of plant leaves impacted by illnesses and irritations.

Without legitimate distinguishing proof, infectious prevention endeavours can be an exercise in futility and cash in the event that a wrong methodology is taken. Conveying infectious prevention estimates that are not appropriate to deal with the illness-causing specialists could prompt further plant misfortunes.

The fundamental goal is to distinguish the plant sicknesses utilizing picture handling. It additionally, after recognizable proof of the illness, recommends the name of the pesticide to be utilized. It likewise distinguishes the insects and nuisances answerable for pestilence.

Diagnosis:

- **Laboratory Tests:** Many infectious diseases have similar signs and symptoms.
- **Imaging Scans:** Imaging procedures – such as X-rays, computerized tomography, and magnetic resonance imaging – can help pinpoint diagnoses and rule out other conditions that may be causing symptoms.

Biopsies:

Plant pathologists utilize various devices to sort out the thing that is making the plant undesirable, yet the three principal strategies utilized are microscopy, development, and perception on media and sub-atomic methods. Microscopy is a significant beginning apparatus in plant sickness conclusion and, as a rule, the main standard device accessible.

2.8.3 INTELLIGENT SPRAYING

The Intelligent Spray System comprises of a LiDAR laser sensor and radar ground speed sensor in mix with an implanted PC and individual heartbeat width balance spouts to examine the harvest covering and apply a relative measure of splash progressively.

Bosch brilliant showering innovation utilizes state-of-the-art advances to discretely apply herbicide on weeds without splashing unaffected areas of harvests. Maintainable specialized developments like these are basic to guaranteeing a copious worldwide food supply for people in the future.

The splash arrangement is ready by blending water with pesticide detailing in suitable amounts. This weakened blend is showered through water-powered spouts. The splashing is generally to the mark of dribble from foliage. In this technique, huge volume of splash fluid is applied.

A sprayer is a gadget used to splash a fluid, where sprayers are normally utilized for projection of water, weed executioners, crop execution materials, bug support synthetic compounds, as well as assembling and creation line fixings.

Showers and cleans are utilized to control bugs, vermin, and fungous and bacterial infections of plants; bugs, like lice and flies, on creatures; and weeds, through substance weed executioners or herbicides.

Advanced mechanics and programmed splashing innovations like variable rate sprayers, UAV sprayers, and electrostatic sprayers are developed to build the use pace of pesticides, decrease pesticide deposits, ongoing, cost-saving, high similarity of plant assurance items application. A smart specialist is a program that can decide or play out a help in light of its current circumstance, client info, and encounters. These projects can be utilized to independently assemble data on a normal, modified timetable or when provoked by the client progressively.

Kinds of sprayers: Sprayers are characterized into four classifications based on energy utilized to atomize and discharge the splash liquid:

1. Hydraulic energy sprayer.
2. Gaseous energy sprayer.
3. Centrifugal energy sprayer and,
4. Kinetic energy sprayer.

2.8.4 AUTOMATIC WEEDING

Robotized weeders eliminate weeds inside the three-to-five broad crude band left around the seed-line by standard development.

General Strategies for Weed Administration:

- Prevention: The most important factor in overall weed control is to prevent weeds from developing seed and perpetuating the weed problem....
- Cultivation
- Cover Crops
- Mowing
- Flaming
- Hand-removal
- Mulches
- Soil solarization

What are weeding control strategies? Such strategies incorporate pulling, digging, disking, furrowing, and cutting. Progress of different mechanical control strategies is subject to the existence pattern of the objective weed species. Hand pulling and digging are powerful on yearly and biennial species like kochia, musk thorn, and diffuse knapweed.

The khurpi otherwise called a hand digger is the most usually utilized hand device for weeding. The device is utilized in hunching-down position. The khurpi comprises of a sharp, straight-edged metallic edge with a tang implanted into a wooden handle.

Weeding can be characterized as the expulsion of weeds (undesirable plants) from the field. Weeding is vital on the grounds that weeds contend with principal crop plant for the various factors like water, daylight, supplements, and space and subsequently influence plant development.

2.8.5 AERIAL SURVEY AND IMAGING

Airborne photos are moment-visual records of explicit land regions. They are utilized to evaluate field conditions and distinguish harvest or soil issues that could somehow slip through the cracks at ground level. Elevated imaging is changing yield creation and land the board. By giving continuous symbolism of harvests and fields, elevated imaging permits ranchers and farming experts to illuminate agrarian practices and augment yield.

Forecast of development stage and yield: Satellite symbolism can give significant data about crop well-being and development, which can be utilized to foresee yield. This can assist ranchers with anticipating harvest and advertising, and settling on informed conclusions about crops the executives rehearse like timing for preparation.

What is the reason for aeronautical photography? Elevated photography gives a novel 10,000-foot perspective of a scene, whether that is a region, item, or subject. It grandstands the super point of convergence of the picture, like a permanent spot available to be purchased or a business' actual area, while additionally featuring the encompassing region. Airplanes are used for cultivating or for applying synthetic compounds for weed or irritation control.

The benefits of aerial application:

- It's fast and effective. Aerial applicators can spray more acres in an hour than a ground applicator in an entire day.
- It doesn't cause soil compaction.
- It evenly disperses products.
- It lowers the risk of disease transfer.

Information is caught effectively from the air, with restricted well-being and security concerns. This thus lessens arranging time and invalidates the requirement for broad well-being and security contemplations, giving a speedier circle back to the task in general. As we referenced, satellite imaging has a great many purposes. These incorporate map making and route, city arranging, climate forecast, biological observation, and military reconnaissance.

What are the upsides of satellite symbolism? Satellite symbolism covers a more extensive region that makes it ideal for bigger scope logical tasks. Conversely, elevated photography is taken at a lower height and gives more detail, so it is very helpful for business applications.

Limitations of aerial photogrammetry

- Visibility constraints such as rain, fog, or dense vegetation cover can block the camera's line of sight or limit the light required for clear photography.
- Poor weather conditions such as precipitation or wind can affect image capture and quality.

An elevated application activity is a trip by a plane to apply application material and any of the accompanying: examination of a workspace, pilot or other group part preparing or checking, and go from an arrival region to a workspace and back.

Elevated photography, or symbolism, as it is currently known, is the strategy for obtaining pictures from the air. Vertical photos are taken with the camera pointing straight down, instead of sideway photos that are taken at a point.

One of the main disadvantages is the expense. Satellite symbolism is costly, and the expense of obtaining and handling the information can be restrictive for certain analysts. Also, satellite symbolism is frequently of restricted goal, implying that it will most likely be unable to recognize limited scope changes in the climate.

2.9 CHALLENGES AND FUTURE RESEARCH DIRECTIONS IN AGRICULTURE

Environmental change is quite possibly the greatest issue confronting ranchers today. Increasing temperatures, unusual weather conditions, and outrageous climate occasions can all devastatingly affect crops. Agribusiness is at the nexus of three of the best difficulties of the 21st 100 years – supporting food and sustenance security, transformation and relief of environmental change, and practical utilization of basic assets like water, energy, and land. Following are the significant regions where difficulties are set up:

- Inadequate transport
- Lack of capital
- Agricultural marketing
- Soil erosion
- Irrigation problems
- Lack of high-quality seeds

- Lack of infrastructure in the agriculture sector
- Shortage of biocides, fertilizers, and manures

The variables affecting agribusiness are environment, soil type, water system, innovation, and populace thickness. Farming had a basic impact on the development of human civilization. Truth be told, India, in the same way as other different nations, has an agrarian economy that is generally subject to the horticultural area. Geology, soil, and environment are the vital actual elements influencing horticulture.

Different ranch sensors like independent vehicles, wearables, button cameras, advanced mechanics, control frameworks, and so on help in the assortment of information to dissect the presentation of the homestead. Elevated and ground-based drones are used for crop well-being appraisal, water system, checking, and field investigation. Therefore, future examination is expected to accomplish higher exactness and less asset usage.

2.10   CONCLUSION

Various worldwide issues, including environmental change, shortage of normal assets, socioeconomics, and food squandering, are putting strain on the general manageability of farming frameworks. For this, a summed-up technique for the entire homestead the board approach, in light of the strong cross-industry participation of partners, foundations, advancements, and applications, will be applied. Without a doubt, past the genuine contribution of trend-setting innovations, the significant test of horticulture towards feasible development dwells in the capability to establish more refined and compelling rural cycles at lower costs, give more secure and more proficient working circumstances both for the climate and partners (including ranchers, agronomist engineers, strategy producers, and so on), and lastly increase the collaborations among them, offering the capacity to settle on choices even on issues that have conventionally been outside their subject matters. In this specific situation, conventional ranch the executive approaches ought to go through central changes, empowering shrewd advancements for development as well as re-engineering the whole worth chain to safeguard maintainability in the rural area. Current progressions in correspondence advances, for example, distributed computing and the Internet of Things, will generally consolidate with other refined advancements like Computational Knowledge, Mechanical Technology, Enormous Information, and so on, prompting the fourth phase of upset in the horticultural area, known as Agribusiness 4.0. The motivation behind this study is to indicate and assess the vital advances and arrangements including omnipresent processing headways and applied developments of agrarian creation towards Horticulture 4.0, alongside their abilities, impacts, and difficulties to help maintainable homestead the executives.

BIBLIOGRAPHY

1. Chaudhary, V., Guha P., Pau, G., Dhanaraj, R. K. & Mishra, S., Automatic classification of cowpea leaves using deep convolutional neural network. *Smart Agricultural Technology, 4*, p. 100209, 2023.
2. Farooq, M., Gogoi, N. and Pisante, M., *Sustainable Agriculture and the Environment.* 2023, Elsevier, Cambridge, MA.
3. Williamson, H.F. and Leonelli, S., *Towards Responsible Plant Data Linkage: Data Challenges for Agricultural Research and Development* (p. 317). 2023, Springer Nature, Berlin.
4. Krishnan, S., Rose, J.B.R., Rajalakshmi, N. R. and Prasanth, N. eds., *Cloud IoT Systems for Smart Agricultural Engineering.* 2022, CRC Press, Boca Raton, FL.
5. Satapathy, S., Mishra, D. and Vargas, A.R., *Innovation in Agriculture with IoT and AI.* 2022, Springer, Cham.
6. Choudhury, A., Biswas, A., Singh, T.P. and Ghosh, S.K. eds., *Smart Agriculture Automation Using Advanced Technologies: Data Analytics and Machine Learning, Cloud Architecture, Automation and IoT.* 2022, Springer Nature, Singapore.

7. Chand, R., Joshi, P. and Khadka, S., *Indian Agriculture towards 2030: Pathways for Enhancing Farmers' Income, Nutritional Security and Sustainable Food and Farm Systems* (p. 311). 2022, Springer Nature, Singapore.

8. Chatterjee, J.M., Kumar, A., Rathore, P.S. and Jain, V. eds., *Internet of Things and Machine Learning in Agriculture: Technological Impacts and Challenges* (Vol. 8). 2021, Walter de Gruyter GmbH & Co KG, Berlin.

9. Pattnaik, P. K., Kumar, R. and Pal, S. eds., *Internet of Things and Analytics for Agriculture* (Vol. 2). 2020, Springer, Singapore.

10. Jogaiah, S., Singh, H.B., Fraceto, L.F. and De Lima, R. eds., *Advances in Nano-Fertilizers and Nano-Pesticides in Agriculture: A Smart Delivery System for Crop Improvement.* 2020, Woodhead Publishing, Sawston.

11. Fuglie, K., Gautam, M., Goyal, A. and Maloney, W.F., *Harvesting Prosperity: Technology and Productivity Growth in Agriculture.* 2019, World Bank Publications, Washington, DC.

12. Bernhardt, H., Bozkurt, M., Brunsch, R., Colangelo, E., Herrmann, A., Horstmann, J., Kraft, M., Marquering, J., Steckel, T., Tapken, H. and Weltzien, C., Challenges for agriculture through industry 4.0. *Agronomy, 11*(10), p. 1935, 2021.

13. Jat, D.S., Limbo, A.S. and Singh, C., Internet of things for automation in smart agriculture: A technical review. In *Research Anthology on Cross-Disciplinary Designs and Applications of Automation*, pp. 493–503, 2022. doi: 10.4018/978-1-6684-3694-3.ch025.

14. Wongchai, A., Shukla, S.K., Ahmed, M.A., Sakthi, U. and Jagdish, M., Artificial intelligence-enabled soft sensor and internet of things for sustainable agriculture using ensemble deep learning architecture. *Computers and Electrical Engineering, 102*, p. 108128, 2022.

15. Murugamani, C., Shitharth, S., Hemalatha, S., Kshirsagar, P.R., Riyazuddin, K., Naveed, Q.N., Islam, S., Mazher Ali, S.P. and Batu, A., Machine learning technique for precision agriculture applications in 5G-based internet of things. *Wireless Communications and Mobile Computing, 2022*, 2022. doi: 10.1155/2022/6534238.

16. Phasinam, K., Kassanuk, T. and Shabaz, M., Applicability of internet of things in smart farming. *Journal of Food Quality*, pp. 1–7, 2022. doi: 10.1155/2022/7692922.

3 EXAI for Computational Sustainability – Models, Services in Smart City, and Challenges

Pradeepa, M., Prabadevi, B., and Kumaraperumal, S.

3.1 INTRODUCTION TO EXAI

Artificial intelligence (AI) has flourished in all domains like medicine, finance, intelligent transportation, education, legislation, industrial automation, predictive maintenance, agriculture, energy conservation, etc. Although AI has remarkable upliftment in all the domains mentioned earlier, its widespread acceptance or adaptability has been hindered by its lack of transparency and trustworthiness. In most cases, the computer scientists and the inventors of the AI models were also unanswerable for the decisions arrived at by their models deployed. Therefore, AI models were not accepted widely. EXplainable Artificial Intelligence (EXAI) provides meaningful explanations for final decisions by breaking AI's black-box nature. EXAI provides explanations for the internal logic unanswerable by the developers and the conclusions, thereby promoting the trustworthiness of the AI models. Furthermore, all the applications developed and deployed in today's digital environment are transdisciplinary, amalgamating concepts from different technologies to provide a sustainable, automated, global solution. Therefore, EXAI would be a mandate for the sustainable adaptability of AI models and their applications.

Explainable Artificial Intelligence plays a crucial role in developing and implementing smart cities. Smart cities leverage various technologies, including the Internet of Things (IoT), AI, and big data analytics, to enhance urban services and improve residents' overall quality of life. However, as AI systems become increasingly complex, the need for transparency and understanding their decision-making processes becomes more critical, especially in applications affecting people's lives. EXAI is a fundamental component of building trustworthy and inclusive smart cities. It enhances transparency, fosters public trust, identifies biases, and promotes stakeholder collaboration. By embracing EXAI, smart cities can ensure that their AI-powered systems are accountable, fair, and reliable, leading to more sustainable and citizen-centric urban environments.

An intelligent decision support system is an artificially intelligent model that aids in deriving decisions based on inputs provided, such as relevant information, intuitions, and recommendations. This type of system is used in various fields, like finance, healthcare, customer service, etc. This artificial intelligence system processes vast quantities of data and produces predictions or recommendations using complex machine-learning models. Integrating EXAI into an intelligent decision support system enhances the system's trustworthiness and facilitates collaboration between AI and human experts, leading to more informed and accurate decision-making processes.

Adopting EXAI faces several challenges, which can hinder its widespread implementation. These challenges arise from both technical and non-technical aspects. Despite these challenges, the development and adoption of EXAI techniques continue to progress, driven by the growing recognition of the significance of explainability in AI systems and the need to address ethical, legal, and

DOI: 10.1201/9781003457176-3

regulatory concerns surrounding AI decision-making. Researchers and practitioners are working to overcome these challenges and make EXAI more accessible and effective in various applications.

Hence, the chapter analyses the utilization of EXAI for computational sustainability. Section 3.1 discusses the introduction to EXAI, Section 3.2 discusses the various existing EXAI models such as intrinsic and post-hoc methods, Section 3.3 addresses the services of EXAI in smart cities, Section 3.4 addresses the utilization of EXAI as an intelligent decision support system for computational sustainability, challenges in adoption, legal, ethical, and social issues in EXAI, and Section 3.5 concludes the EXAI for sustainable computation.

3.2 EXISTING EXAI MODELS

EXAI models are a particular category of AI models created to give suitable explanations and proper justifications for the predictions or decisions derived by the models. The primary objective of EXAI is to improve transparency, liability, and trustworthiness in AI systems, mainly in critical applications where the decision-making process plays a vital role that needs to be explained to humans.

Because of a lack of transparency in the decision-making, the conventional ML and deep learning (DL) models are considered to be "black boxes." Even though these models provide precise estimates, they don't provide clear explanations for how they arrived at those estimates. This lack of interpretability makes humans not able to completely rely on these estimates, especially in critical domains such as healthcare, autonomous vehicles, finance, and criminal justice systems.

EXAI models, on the contrary, are designed to provide interpretability. These models are more transparent, and the process of the model is designed for easier examination and understanding of how these models reach the specific outcomes. There are various approaches to achieving explainability in AI models, and some of the common techniques are categorized as intrinsic and post-hoc methods.

3.2.1 INTRINSIC METHODS

3.2.1.1 Linear Regression

These models are used in predictive analysis. The model is transparent as the relationship between the input and output variables is expected to be linear. The model predicts the dependent variable (output, y_p) based on some independent variables (x_i). The predicted output is calculated as the weighted sum of its k input feature x_i and a constant (a_0). The learned relationship between the input variables and the predicted output for this instance is given by [1],

$$y_p^{(i)} = a_0 + a_1 x_1^{(i)} + \cdots + a_k x_k^{(i)} \tag{3.1}$$

where, a_i, $i = 1, 2, 3, \ldots k$ are the learned feature coefficients/weights,

$$y_t^{(i)} = y_p + \in \tag{3.2}$$

where $\in$ is the error adjustment, the difference between the target $\left(y_t^{(i)}\right)$ and the predicted output $\left(y_p^{(i)}\right)$.

The optimal weights (a_i) can be calculated using various methods. The most prominent Least Squares method is employed to obtain the optimal weight. The weight values are calculated as

$$\hat{a} = \arg \min_{a_0, \ldots a_p} \sum_{i=1}^{n} \left(y_t^{(i)} - \left(a_0 + \sum_{j=1}^{n} a_j x_j^{(i)} \right) \right)^2 \tag{3.3}$$

The model's accuracy depends on the assumptions made on the input data, such as fixed input features, linearity, homoscedasticity, normality, independence, and absence of multicollinearity.

Interpretability of the model

The model is easily interpretable as the learned relationship is linear. Interpretations of the model can be explained based on weights of the corresponding features on changes in the output when other features are considered as fixed.

A change in one unit of the input feature x_i changes the predicted output by corresponding weight when other features are considered fixed. When there is a feature with multiple groupings, a change in the feature x_i, from the reference set to the other set, changes the predicted output by a_i when other features are considered fixed. In R-squared estimation, R^2 explains the total variance of the predicted outcome. The more value of R^2 represents better fitness of the model. Another interpretation is based on the t-statistic measure, which is obtained by the ratio of the assessed weight to the standard error. Hence, the feature with more variance in the estimated weight is less important [2].

3.2.1.2 Logistic Regression

LR model is specifically employed to solve classification problems with two classes. It predicts the dependent variable (output) based on the set of independent input features. The predicted result is a probabilistic value that lies between 0 and 1.

The logistic function squeezes the output and provides a value between 0 and 1. The function is given by [3]

$$\text{logistic}(\eta) = \frac{1}{1 + \exp(-\eta)} \tag{3.4}$$

The relation between the predicted output and the input features is defined in Equation (3.1). The relation for the ith instance is given by,

$$P\left(y_p^{(i)} = 1\right) = \frac{1}{1 + \exp\left(-\left(a_0 + a_1 x_1^{(i)} + \cdots + a_k x_k^{(i)}\right)\right)} \tag{3.5}$$

Interpretability of the model

This model is interpreted differently from linear regression since the predicted output is between 0 and 1. For interpretation, the equation is expressed in the form of log odds.

From Equation (3.5),

$$a_0 + a_1 x_1 + \cdots + a_k x_k = \log\left(\frac{P(y_p = 1)}{1 - P(y_p = 1)}\right) = \log\left(\frac{P(y_p = 1)}{P(y_p = 0)}\right) \tag{3.6}$$

Now the relationship is in the form of a linear model for log odds. To have better interpretability, the expression is rearranged as,

$$\exp(a_0 + a_1 x_1 + \cdots + a_k x_k) = \frac{P(y_p = 1)}{1 - P(y_p = 1)} = \frac{P(y_p = 1)}{P(y_p = 0)} \tag{3.7}$$

A variation in any input feature by one unit is indicated by the odds ratio multiplied by a factor of $\exp(a_j)$, which is calculated as follows,

$$\exp(a_0 + a_1 x_1 + \cdots + a_k x_k) = \text{odds}$$

then,

$$\frac{\text{odds}_{x_j+1}}{\text{odds}} = \frac{\exp\left(a_0 + a_1x_1 + \cdots + a_j\left(x_j+1\right) + \cdots + a_kx_k\right)}{\exp\left(a_0 + a_1x_1 + \cdots + a_jx_j + \cdots + a_kx_k\right)} = \exp\left(a_j\left(x_j+1\right)\right) - \exp\left(a_jx_j\right) = \exp\left(a_j\right)$$

(3.8)

When a feature is of categorical type with binary values, out of the two binary values, one is the reference. Any small change in the feature x_j with reference to the other modifies the computed odds by a factor of $\exp\left(a_j\right)$.

When an input feature has multiple categories, the interpretation can be obtained by applying the one-hot-encoding. It assigns each category to its own column. Therefore, $K-1$ columns are needed for a feature containing K categories. Later, each category is interpreted in the same way as for the binary features [2].

3.2.1.3   Generalized Linear Model (GLM) and Generalized Additive Model (GAM)

The LR model assumes that the predicted output determined based on the input features follows a Gaussian distribution. But this is evicted in many situations where the prediction outcome may be a count or a category or a period of an event occurrence. Therefore, LR is further extended to support these outcomes. Such a model is termed a GLM [4].

The mathematical representation of this model is given by,

$$g\left(E_Y\left(y \mid x\right)\right) = a_0 + a_1x_1 + \cdots + a_kx_k$$

(3.9)

where g is the link function chosen based on the outcome, E_Y is the probability distribution from the exponential family, and the right side of the expression is the weighted sum $x^T a$.

Generalized additive models replace the linear relationship with any arbitrary function. The model is mathematically represented by,

$$g\left(E_Y\left(y \mid x\right)\right) = a_0 + f_1\left(x_1\right) + \cdots + f_k\left(x_k\right)$$

(3.10)

Interpretability of the model

The estimated weight values are interpreted based on the distribution assumed and the link function chosen [2].

3.2.1.4   Decision Tree

Both LR and logistic regression predict the output based on the linear relationship between the input and the output. If there exists a non-linear relationship, the model will fail to predict the output. The tree-based model helps to solve this kind of problem. Therefore, DT can be used for solving both regression and classification problems. In this, the dataset is partitioned multiple times on the input feature using some attribute selection measures to find an attribute that best splits the dataset. There are various algorithms available to arrange the input features in the form of a tree, but they differ on the criteria used to split when to stop splitting, and the estimation of the simple model within the leaf nodes. The frequently used method is the classification and regression trees (CART) algorithm [5]. In CART, the relationship between the independent features x and the predicted output or target output y is given by,

$$\hat{y} = \hat{f}(x) = \sum_{n=1}^{N} c_n I \left\{x \in R_n\right\}$$

(3.11)

where R_n, represents the subset, where each instance of the input tuple maps to only one leaf node. I represents the identity_function, $\begin{cases} I = 1 \text{ if } \{x \in R_n\} \\ I = 0 \text{ if } \{x \notin R_n\} \end{cases}$, and c_n indicates the mean of the training tuples in the leaf node R_n.

In the case of a regression problem, the variance of y represents the spreading of y values in a node around their average value, whereas in the case of a classification problem, the Gini index of the class distribution of y represents the node impurity. The algorithm has to choose the optimal cut-off points so that the variance in the regression problem and the Gini index in the classification problem are minimal [2].

Interpretability of the model

The importance of each input feature is obtained by running through all the data splits made by the feature and by measuring the reduction in the variance or Gini index as it traverses through the tree. The overall model importance is obtained by the sum of the individual feature importance. The individual feature importance is scaled to 100, before interpreting the overall importance.

Individual predictions can be obtained by decomposing the decision path into one component per feature. Then follow up the path and clarify the prediction by contributions added at each decision node. The root node predicts the mean of the outcome, then in the next split either add or subtract a term depending on the next node in the path. The procedure is followed up at each split to find the final prediction.

For each class, the individual prediction is the sum of the mean predicted value and the sum of the contributions of the L splits on M features. This can be utilized for calculating each feature's contribution to the prediction [2].

$$\hat{y} = \bar{y} + \sum_{l=1}^{L} \text{split\_contribution}(l, x) \tag{3.12}$$

$$\hat{y} = \bar{y} + \sum_{m=1}^{ML} \text{feature\_contribution}(m, x) \tag{3.13}$$

3.2.1.5 Decision Rules

The decision rule applies the "If-Then" rule for prediction. The model predicts the output if the conditions are met. This model is highly interpretable. Sometimes, multiple rules are satisfied by the tuple instance. In such cases, a conflict resolution strategy is employed by ordering the rules as a decision list or a decision set. In the decision list, the rules are ordered based on the classes or rule quality. For instance, each rule is checked for the given predictive instance, and if more rules are fired, none of the other rules are satisfied by the tuples. If none of the rules are satisfied, a default rule is fired. In the decision set, the rules are either disjunctive, so a conflict resolution strategy is employed. The complexity of interpretation increases as several rules are involved. If none of the rules are applied, a default rule is introduced in both the decision list and the decision set.

Many algorithms are used to learn rules from the training data such as one R, sequential covering, and Bayesian Rule Lists.

Learn Rules from a Single Feature (OneR): It generates one rule for every feature and then selects one best rule based on the error rate. The rule with less error rate is nominated as the best [6].

Sequential Covering: Learns one rule at a time for each class. It aims to generate the rules in an iterative fashion adopting the greedy depth first search and beam search procedures. It starts with an empty rule and precedes by adding the conditions for each possible attribute value pair. Once a rule is learnt, it will remove the tuples covered by that rule and steps in growing the next rule [7].

Bayesian Rule Lists: This method first mines the rule antecedents and in turn combines the rules into a decision list which are learnt using Bayesian statistics [8].

3.2.1.6 Naive Bayes Classifier

As the name indicates, the naïve Bayes algorithm works on the strong assumption that the input features are conditionally independent of each other and equally contribute to predict the final target outcome. It adopts the Bayes' theorem of conditional. For each feature, it computes the probability for a class (prior probabilities and likelihood probabilities), subject to the value of the feature. With that assumption of feature independence, Maximum A posterior estimation is used to simplify the Naïve Bayes function. The probability of a class C_k given by

$$P(C_k|x) = \frac{1}{Z} P(C_k) \prod_{i=1}^{n} P(x_i|C_k) \tag{3.14}$$

where S is the scaling parameter and can be negotiated as its value will be closer to 1(sum of all probabilities) which will not affect the outcome [9]. The posterior probability is obtained by the product of all likelihood probabilities of the attributes for the classes and the prior probability of the class. The class whose posterior probability is high will be predicted as the class of the given tuple instance.

Interpretability of the model

The strong assumption of feature independence makes the Naive Bayes classifier an interpretable model. The predicted probability of a class for each input feature is based on conditional probability, so easily interpretable.

3.2.1.7 K-Nearest Neighbors (KNN)

For regression and classification problems, the K-Nearest Neighbors model is used. The model predicts the output based on the nearest data points called neighbors. For a classification problem, the KNN will assign the most common class of the test instance's nearest neighbors; whereas for regression, it predicts the outcome by assigning the average value of the nearest neighbors outcome. The major part of this algorithm is finding the value for k and the measure of distance which determines the neighborhood [10].

Interpretability of the model

The KNN model is an instance-based learning model. This model has no interpretability since the model does not have any parameters to learn. There are no global weights for explicit learning; the model has to be interpreted locally. To interpret the prediction, retrieve the k neighbors used for the prediction for each instance separately. If the instance contains many features, it is not possible to interpret. If features and the instances are reduced to the most important features and instances, then the interpretation is possible [2].

3.2.2 Post-Hoc Methods

3.2.2.1 Textual Explanation

InterpNET is a deep neural network. It is combined with classification architecture to provide textual explanations. For a simple network, the output y is given by,

$$y = \text{softmax}\left(W_1 \text{relu}\left(W_2 x + b_2\right) + b_1\right) \tag{3.15}$$

The internal activation functions are $f_1 = x$, $f_2 = \text{relu}(W_2 x + b_2)$ and $f_3 = \text{softmax}(W_1 \text{relu}(W_2 x + b_2) + b_1)$. The InterpNET uses these activation functions as input vector, $i = [f_1; f_2; f_3]$, for the language model to provide explanations. The explanations are generated based on the activation values of the deep neural network. An instance of explanations produced by the model for a bird's image is detailed as well as a valid explanation and an invalid explanation are well discriminated [11].

Various methods are available to provide textual explanations:

The most-weighted path generates an explanation based on the input-output path with an input weighing the highest in the associated neuron.

The most-weighted combination generates an explanation depending on the two inputs with the highest weight associated with the neurons of the first and second neuron layers.

Maximum frequency difference generates explanations for the input-output path with input having a maximum difference in frequency percentage [12].

Lie et al. [13] proposed a method that extracts some portions of input text as a rationale for the output predicted by neural networks in sentimental analysis. These rationales have words that are interpretable and provide predictions as to the whole input text. A "rationale generator" function with an encoder is used for generating these words which in turn acts as a binary classification model by assigning a binary label to each word, whereas the "encoder" function maps a sequence of words to a final target class.

The image classifier provides textual explanations through relevance and discriminative loss. The convolutional neural network extracts the visual features like objects and colors and provides the description for the images trained using visual features. During the training process, the loss function is reduced, so that the produced explanations are relevant to the image and the class category [14,15].

3.2.2.2 Visual Explanation

In visual explanations, using some graphical aids in the internal functions of the model is explained.

Salient Mask: One of the frequently used aids is a salient mask that effectively identifies a part of the input which may influence the model's prediction result negatively, by superimposing a mask emphasizing them [16].

Layer-wise Relevance Propagation (LRP): Bach et al. [17] proposed a layer-wise relevance propagation approach in which the non-linear classifiers are decomposed pixel-wise to provide explanations for the classification prediction problems. The LRP perceives that by decomposing the classifier into many layers of computation, the role of each pixel to the output can be identified in each and every layer to corresponding attributes to individual inputs. The impact of pixels can be visualized in terms of heat maps.

Spectral Relevance Analysis (SpRAy): To examine the behavior of the classifier model on a large dataset, the SpRAy approach is used. On the dataset of LRP explanations, the approach applies spectral clustering to discover usual and unusual decisions made by the ML model [18].

Image Perturbation: The image perturbation elucidates by way of saliency maps. This approach blurs the different portions of the image and identifies the portions of an image that affect the prediction accuracy of the model more [19].

Restricted Support Region Set Detection (RSRS): To make predictions on classification, some portion of an image is critical. This approach is used to visualize that critical portion of an image. The restricted support region set is defined as a portion of an image that is size-restricted and non-overlapping portion where removal of either of them leads to wrong classification.

This approach can be used to detect the limitation of a classifier, predict its failure mode, and determine the rules of classification and the database bias disclosure [20].

iVisClassifier: Choo et al. [21] proposed an iVisClassifier based on linear discriminant analysis (LDA). The approach reduces the dimension of input into clusters and defines the heat maps that explain the association among input clusters. The pairwise spaces among cluster centroids are identified for reduced dimension as well as the original dimension.

The Saliency Detection Method: Dabkowski and Gal [22] proposed a method that is applicable to all different classifiers. The model is trained to forecast the score of the classifier by masking salient fragments of the input image. The output map helps to find the significant portion of an image taken for classification by the model.

The Sensitivity Analysis Method: The method produces explanations based on local gradients. This gradient helps to understand how the model predicts the class based on the movement of the data points. The clarifications are given based on plotting the gradient vectors on scatter plots or heat maps. The plot shows that the part of the input needs to be updated to adjust the calculated class label by the model [23].

Individual Conditional Expectation plots (ICE): The ICE plot represents the functional association of the model output and the input feature for each instance, while other input features are considered as constant and the analysis is carried out by changing the input feature [24].

Partial Importance and Individual Conditional Importance plots (PI & ICI): The author [25] proposed plots that visualize the feature importance through the PI and ICI plots. Both plots are intended to show how the models' performance is affected by changes in a feature. The PI plot provides a global explanation by envisaging a point-wise mean of all instances of ICI curves. However, the ICI plot provides a local explanation by envisaging the variations of each instance. The significance of each feature is measured based on Shapley value which equally dispenses the model's efficiency between them based on their marginal influence.

Class Signatures: They provide a visual representation to find the relationship between the input and output using the combination of various plots and tables. The charts and tables are structured in a manner such that relationships become apparent [26].

ExplainD: The framework was proposed by Poulin et al. [27] to explain the predictions made by classifiers using additive evidence. The framework is applied to the classifiers like linear discriminants and additive models. It provides a graphical explanation of the classification method such as visualizations of predictions of the classifier decisions, visualization of the evidence for those decisions, and the competency to take risks on the consequence of variations to the data.

Manifold and MLCube Explorer: These visual analytical tools provide the explanation using comparative analysis for multiple models. Providing some set of input instances based on certain conditions will be able to find a set of input instances that make inaccurate output. Accordingly, they explain possible causes for the inaccuracies and progressively improve the model's efficiency through graphical tools such as lines, bar charts, and scatter-plots [28,29].

3.2.2.3 Global and Local Explanation

i. Global Explainability

Global explainability supports finding the features that are maximally responsible for the models' prediction. It also supports finding what portion a specific feature involves in the final prediction of the model. It explains how the model learns by presenting the changes in the particular features essential for its prediction. For various decision-making applications, global explainability identifies the data variables involved in the models' decisions. Some global explainability methods are discussed below.

a. Partial Dependence Plot (PDP):

PDP provides a global visual representation of the prediction of the model influenced by few features by keeping the other features fixed [30]. PDP provides an explanation if the objective and selected characteristics have a linear or complex association.

For a linear regression model, PDP shows a linear association of the features, and the partial dependence function (PDF) is given by,

$$\hat{f}_{xs}(x_S) = E_{xc}\left[\widehat{f}(x_s, x_C)\right] = \int \widehat{f}(x_s, x_C)\, dP(x_C) \qquad (3.16)$$

Where x_S represents the set of features in set S containing one or two features for which the PDF is plotted, and x_C represents the other set of features used by the ML model. The effect of prediction is identified for the features in set S. The total feature space contains the features in sets S and C. The partial dependence function marginalizes the model response based on the features in set C. Then, the PDF displays the association between the features in set S.

The PDF $\hat{f}_{xs}$ is calculated through finding the mean values in the training data and is given by

$$\hat{f}_{xs}(x_S) = \frac{1}{N} \sum_{i=1}^{N} \widehat{f}\left(x_S, x_C^{(i)}\right) \qquad (3.17)$$

where N is the number of instances. The PDF conveys the mean marginal effect on the prediction of model output based on the features in set S. Based on the assumption that features in set S are not correlated with the features in C, PDP is plotted. If the assumption goes wrong, it leads to incorrect results.

For classification problems, generally, the outputs are in terms of probabilities. The PDP plot displays the probability of a class for various values of features in set S. For multiclass classification problems, the plot has been drawn for each class. The PDP approach provides a global explanation by taking all inputs and delivers an explanation of each feature's affect on the predicted response [2].

b. Individual Conditional Expectation (ICE)

ICE is easier to understand than PDP. ICE can define diverse connections but can explain only one feature at a time, whereas PDP allows for two feature explanations. ICE creates a graph that depicts the average predicted outcome of some features whereas the other features are fixed. ICE plot shows one line per instance, so it explains the changes in the predicted outcome based on changes in features in each instance. PDP plots the average influence of the features, not representing the influence of individual instances [24].

c. Accumulated Local Effects (ALE) Plot

On average, the model's prediction affected by the features is explained by the accumulated local effects plot. This plot is faster and unbiased and an alternative to PDP [31].

ii. Local Explainability

Local Explainability explains the individual output of an ML model. The influence of individual instances is identified through this approach. Some of the local explainability methods are discussed below.

a. Local interpretable model-agnostic explanations (LIME)

The LIME provides explanations of each and every prediction of the ML models. LIME examines the predictions of a model when different data are presented in the model. LIME constructs a fresh training dataset comprising permuted samples and their estimates. Now the model is trained with the newly constructed dataset and the model is weighted by the closeness of the input to the inputs of concern.

The explanation is mathematically represented by,

$$e(x) = \arg \min_{g \in G} L(f, g, \pi_x) + \Omega(g) \tag{3.18}$$

To explain a model g ($g \in G$), where G is a set of interpretable models, consider the function $\Omega(g)$ that represents the measure of complexity of the explanation for the model $g \in G$, where the depth is considered for the decision tree model and the number of weights (non-zero) for the linear model. For the classification problem, $f(x)$ represents the probability of class x, and the function $\pi_x(z)$ represents the proximity measure between an instance z and x. Consider another function $L(f, g, \pi_x)$ which measures in what way unfaithful the model g is in defining the function f specified by π_x. To obtain both interpretability and local fidelity, the function L is to be minimized by keeping $\Omega(g)$ low enough [32].

b. SHapley Additive exPlanations (SHAP)

It is a game-theoretic way to provide details from the ML model's output. It explains how an estimated value is distributed equally across many inputs [33].

Shapley value is calculated as the mean marginal contribution combination of all features. SHAP provides the effect of each feature through the interpretation of certain values concerning baseline value which is computed as the mean value of all predictions. The Shapley value is used to find any prediction as additive effects of every feature value. But the computation time is high. The Shapley values can be joined together and used to make global interpretations.

Consider a linear model's prediction for a single instance given by,

$$y_p(x) = a_0 + a_1 x_1 + \cdots + a_k x_k \tag{3.19}$$

where x is the instance, x_j is a feature value, with $j = 1, 2, \ldots, k$, and a_j is the corresponding weight.

The influence of jth feature ϕ_j in the model's output prediction is given by,

$$\phi_j(\hat{f}) = a_j x_j - E(a_j x_j) = a_j x_j - a_j E(x_j), \tag{3.20}$$

where $E(a_j x_j)$ represents the average approximation for feature j. The sum of all feature's contributions for a single instance is,

$$\sum_{j=1}^{k} \phi_j(\hat{f}) = \sum_{j=1}^{k} a_j x_j - E(a_j x_j) = \left(a_0 + \sum_{j=1}^{k} a_j x_j \right) - \left(a_0 + \sum_{j=1}^{k} E(a_j x_j) \right) = \hat{f}(x) - E(\hat{f}(X)) \tag{3.21}$$

3.2.2.4 Example-Based Explanation

The method explains the behavior of the model by presenting some specific inputs from the dataset to describe the activities of ML models. The example-based explanations are useful only if the instance of the data, which is presented to the model, is easily understandable by a human.

Example-based explanations are suitable for the dataset containing images, as they can be interpreted directly. If the instances have more contexts and have structures such as images and texts, the example-based explanations are good. If the input instances are in tabular form and contain thousands of features, it is a very difficult task to present the data in a meaningful manner. The explanations are good for which the numbers of instances are less or possible to summarize instances.

These explanations are used to build an intellectual machine-learning model. The model supports understanding complex data distributions.

Some of the machine learning models provide example-based explanations such as decision tree, KNN, and neural networks. In a decision tree, the data points in the feature are split into various nodes based on similarities. The model predicts a new instance using the instances that are similar to it and provides the outcome as the average of these instances. In the KNN model, when presenting a new input, the model finds the k-nearest neighbors and provides the outcome as the mean of the outcome of k-nearest neighbors.

Some interpretation methods for example-based explanations are listed below. A counterfactual explanation finds the changes in the instances that make diverse outcomes [34]. An adversarial example predicts the inputs that are insignificant and finds the feature perturbations that make the model create an incorrect prediction [35]. The prototype method finds a set of inputs that represent a summarized view of the whole dataset to be present to the model to make predictions [36]. Influential instances are the training instances that are a more influential factor for altering the model's prediction. Identifying these instances is helpful in many ways such as debugging the model, analyzing its behavior, identifying the inputs that have problems, and identifying which inputs need to be verified for errors [2].

3.2.2.5 Explanation by Simplification

Linear models and decision tree models provide explanations using Local Interpretable Model-Agnostic Explanations (LIME). The input data have to be transformed into interpretable form so that the resulting features produced by the models are easy to understand by humans [32].

The next method is anchors used by rule-based models to provide explanations. The approach considers only the essential features and ignores the other features in prediction to provide sparse explanations [37].

The G-REX approach introduced in genetic programming initially extracts rules from the data which have been further used for explainability [38,39].

Another approach learns the rules in the form of the Conjunctive Normal Form or Disjunctive Normal Form. Then, the model provides explainability using these rules and is exploited as a predictive model [40].

This method depends on dividing the input data in similar instances by approximating the complex model into a decision tree. Whenever new instances are presented, the model is accountable to explain similar instances [41,42].

Another method is implemented with a two-step process, which is a distillation approach and a statistical test. The method examines whether the variables are sufficient to reconstruct the present model else requires any additional data to have the same performance [43].

In counterfactual explanations, the model creates instances that are close to the original instances and are easily explainable. Then, presenting these new instances to the model, and finding the changes made by the model's output with the output for original instances, provides the understanding of the model behaviors for the changes in the instances [44].

3.2.2.6 Feature Interaction

In an ML model, if the feature interacts with other features, the prediction cannot compute the sum of each feature's effect as one feature value depends on the other.

Consider an ML model whose predicted output depends on two features where each feature interacts with the other. The predicted output is based on four terms such as constant term, first feature value, second feature value, and relation among two features. The relation between two features is calculated by modifying the predicted output and the features. The relation strength measures the variation in the model's predicted output caused by features interacting with others. Friedman and Popescu measured the strength as a statistic [45]. The relation between the two features is represented by the function $F(x)$. Calculate the relation among the two feature variables x_i and x_j, defined by the function $F(x)$. The difference in the function $F(x)$ exists by modifying the value of x_i which depends on the value of x_j. For numerical feature variables,

$$E_X \left[\frac{\partial^2 F(x)}{\partial x_i \, \partial x_j} \right] > 0$$

The partial dependence function is normally used to analyze the dependence of the predictive model. If there is no interaction between x_i and x_j, the partial dependence function $F(x)$ is,

$$F_{ij}(x_i, x_j) = F_i(x_i) + F_j(x_j) \tag{3.22}$$

If x_i does not interact with any of the other variables, the function $F(x)$ is,

$$F(x) = F_i(x_i) + F_{\setminus i}(x_{\setminus i}) \tag{3.23}$$

as $F_{\setminus i}(x_{\setminus i})$ represents a function on all variables except x_i.

To examine the existence of an interaction between two feature variables x_i and x_j, the statistic is given by,

$$H_{ij}^2 = \frac{\sum_{k=1}^{N} \left[\hat{F}_{ij}(x_{ki}, x_{kj}) - \hat{F}_i(x_{ki}) - \hat{F}_j(x_{kj}) \right]^2}{\sum_{k=1}^{N} \hat{F}_{ij}^2(x_{ki}, x_{kj})} \tag{3.24}$$

Similarly, a statistic for examining whether a feature x_i has any relation with other features given by,

$$H_i^2 = \frac{\sum_{k=1}^{N} \left[F(x_k) - \hat{F}_i(x_{ki}) - \hat{F}_{\setminus i}(x_{k \setminus i}) \right]^2}{\sum_{k=1}^{N} F^2(x_k)} \tag{3.25}$$

3.2.2.7 Feature Importance/Relevance

The prediction error is calculated by presenting permuted feature values to the machine learning model. If the permutation of feature value results in a rise in prediction error, the feature is more important to determine the output of the machine learning model. If the feature is not important, the permutation of the feature value does not affect the prediction, and hence, there will not be any change in the prediction error. If the feature is unimportant, it may be ignored to reduce the complexity of the model and time consumption for prediction.

The algorithm [46] is stated as follows:

Let the trained model is f, the feature matrix is X, the target vector is y, and, the error measure is $L(y, f)$:

1. Find the original model error, $\text{error}_{\text{original}} = L(y, f(X))$
2. Every feature $i = 1, 2, \ldots k$
   a. Find feature matrix $X_{\text{permutation}}$ through permuting the feature i in the dataset X. The process removes the relationship between feature i and the target output of the model y.
   b. Find the error, $\text{error}_{\text{permutation}} = L\left(y, f\left(X_{\text{permutation}}\right)\right)$.

c. Determine permutated feature importance (*FI*),

$$FI^i = \text{error}_{\text{permutation}} / \text{error}_{\text{original}} \text{ or}$$

$$FI^i = \text{error}_{\text{permutation}} - \text{error}_{\text{original}}$$

3. Arrange the features based on *FI*.

In another approach, the linear model is constructed, and the instances presented to the model have to be described, and by calculating the Shapley value, the feature's importance is examined. Based on the feature's mean marginal contribution, the Shapley value is calculated by considering all feature combinations. SHAP provides the effect of each feature through the interpretation of certain values concerning baseline value which is calculated as the average value of all predictions [47].

Another approach, an explainable framework, provides global explanations using the Shapley method to Lorenz Zonoid. The approach finds the contribution of variables and their marginal contribution. The outcome of this framework is that it combines local attributions with predictive accuracy which is easy to interpret [48].

Cortez and Embrechts [49] proposed an extension of the present sensitivity analysis approach for the design of a global sensitivity analysis method. This approach is combined with visualization tools to simplify and communicate the prediction.

Henelius et al. [50] presented a method to identify which attributes the model uses during prediction. The approach is applied for the model having a huge dataset for which the subset of samples is used for prediction resulting in better performance.

The influence of the data points is measured by tracing back from the prediction to training data using the gradients and Hessian-vector products [51].

Another approach to finding the influence of the data point is deletion diagnostics. This method measures the effect of omitting data points that affect the quality of the model [52].

3.3 EXAI IN SMART CITY

Artificial intelligence is a critical idea concept in the deployment of AI systems, including those used in smart cities. Smart cities apply advanced techniques and data analytics for improving performance, sustainability, and overall level of life. However, deploying AI algorithms in real world without transparency and explainability gives rise to concerns about trust, bias, and privacy among humans. Hence, the role of EXAI is considered much essential.

3.3.1 EXAI in Different Services of Smart City

Explainable Artificial Intelligence (EXAI) can be applied to numerous applications of smart cities to enhance trust, transparency, reliability, and accountability in the process of AI-driven decision-making. EXAI can be exploited in various areas of smart city such as:

- **Transportation and Traffic Management**
  EXAI can provide explanations for the prediction of traffic flow and optimization approaches. People can realize the source for route recommendations and congestion administration. In self-driving vehicles, EXAI helps to take a decision by describing the facts behind it [53]. The decisions made by autonomous vehicles can also be explained by safeguarding travelers and foot-travelers who have confidence in the safety and reliability of the technology.

- **Energy Management**

    EXAI is used in building energy-efficient system in which it can forecast energy consumption and provide smart recommendations to improve efficiency. The methods and tools used by the EXAI system support trustworthiness in AI for energy systems [54]. People can easily know in what way the smart grid systems optimize energy consumption and distribution.

- **Urban Planning**

    EXAI helps to explain the features that have an impact on urban planning decisions, like infrastructure development, land-use zoning, public service allocation, etc.

- **Public Safety and Security**

    AI support can support environmental safety, supporting disaster response, monitoring and ensuring food security, and managing epidemics, where EXAI provides the explanations for the deployment of these systems and its predictions [55].

- **Waste Management**

    AI can be used to predict the water demand, monitor the water level of a specific region, forecast waste generation and classification, improve the efficiency of waste collection etc. [55]. EXAI provides explanations about waste, ensuring efficiency and reducing environmental impact. Through the proper understanding of the decision made by the EXAI models, people actively participate in the waste reduction process.

- **Healthcare Services**

    EXAI can be adopted in healthcare systems to provide clear explanations for all predictions related to health and its diagnoses and to increase trust in AI-driven healthcare services. Since the explanations are in view of human-centric orientation, medical professionals can have better understanding of AI-generated predictions and recommendations, allowing combined decision-making with the AI system [54].

- **Environmental Sustainability**

    AI together with other technologies like Internet of Things, image processing, and Big data can provide support to achieve environmental sustainability such as water resource conservation, energy conservation, renewable energy, sustainable transportation, biodiversity conservation, and ecosystem service [56]. EXAI helps to explain data-driven environmental predictions. Governments and people can work together to develop sustainable strategies based on the insights provided by EXAI models.

- **Emergency Response**

    AI can be applied to find the initial warning symptoms of natural calamities, create maps of areas affected by the disaster, and also predict the number of people affected, spotting and differentiating the structure. EXAI can clarify the basis for emergency response resource allocation, supporting better coordination during disasters.

    In all these services, the employment of EXAI models helps to rely on AI technologies that empower people, decision-making professionals, and stakeholders to apply advanced technologies in shaping the future of their smart cities.

The illustration of the various services of the EXAI in smart city is depicted in Figure 3.1.

3.4   INTELLIGENT DECISION SUPPORT SYSTEM

AI, in general, and ML, specifically, have played a vital role in enhancing the decision-making capabilities in many applications such as predicting the remaining useful life of the battery, forecasting organ transplantation risk, money laundering, and student dropout prediction [57–60]. Initially, AI struggled a lot to imitate human decision-making capability. Still, rapid advancements in AI have lent greater support to effective decision-making capabilities in various domains like biological science, economics, marketing, medical science, tourism, and marketing [61]. The intelligence of the intelligent DSS is characterized by its ability to learn from history, find meaningful

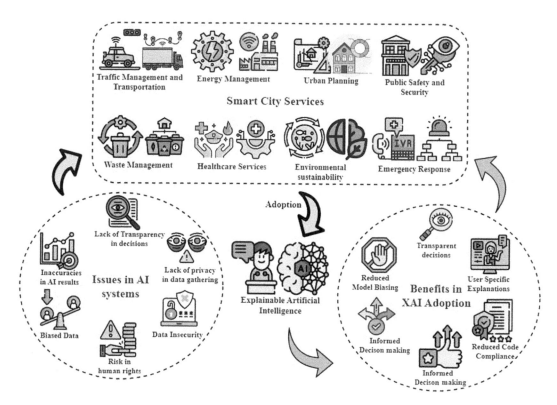

FIGURE 3.1   EXAI services in smart city.

insights from ambiguity, timely and appropriate responses, apply logical reasoning, handle perplexed situations, apply acquired knowledge to perceive the environment, and recognize the relative importance of various parameters involved in a decision [62]. Intelligent DSS is classified into three types: Intelligent DSS based on AI, Intelligent DSS based on data warehouse, and Intelligent DSS based on case reasoning [63]. Intelligent DSS based on AI, a topic of interest, is further subdivided into Intelligent DSS based on Expert Systems, which has flourished in today's computing environment, composed of a knowledge base, an inference engine, and a database. Intelligent DSS based on Expert System applies automated reasoning for solving user queries, by interpreting one or two identified human expert intelligence. The second one is Intelligent DSS based on ML, which acquires knowledge through past experiences of solving human problems by enhancing knowledge acquisition. The third one is Intelligent DSS based on Intelligent Agents, where the decisions are made through the intrinsic ability of the agents rather than prescriptive logic entrenched in the programs.

Intelligent DSS has been deployed in intelligent transportation systems for efficient traffic state prediction through the integration of Convolution Neural Networks with Grate Recurrent Unit and Grasshopper Optimization Algorithms and attained better results with overall less computational overhead [64]. An Intelligent DSS based on ML has been employed in the Freight transport sector for recommending route sequencing and inter-continental transportation of goods [65]. Efficient hyperspectral image classification has been done using deep learning-based Intelligent DSS through Manifold Batch structure and observed that it is time-consuming compared to traditional systems [66]. Intelligent DSS is implemented in numerous medical practices like cardiovascular risk prediction, epidemiological diagnostics, cervical cancer diagnosis, COVID-19 prediction, and stroke rehabilitation assessment [67–69]. Furthermore, these intelligent DSS can be offered in different interaction modes, viz., conventional AI, where patients' electronic health records will be used for predicting clinician's report, and later, further clinical decision-making is done; fully automated AI, where decisions will be taken purely by the model without human intervention and integrative AI and input is taken anonymously, and the predicted decisions are updated in patients-specific records [70]. Other applications include supply chain management, the oil industry, equipment manufacturing, parking slots management in urban areas, and IT project management. Evidently, one of the essential applications of Intelligent DSS was seen in the medical sector and has also propelled it to greater heights.

Recent advancements in AI have focused on boosting the prediction accuracy of AI models for more efficient decision-making. Although the focus is appreciable, AI models have failed to expose the explainability of the models in clarifying the decisions arrived at. This has led the decision-makers to lose trust in the models, eventually decreasing AI adoption [71]. More specifically, this has been a major issue in clinical DSS, wherever the decisions are life-threatening and determine a very sensitive issue in human life. The major ethical concerns with Intelligent DSS for the clinical sector include trustworthiness, transparency, and communication reliability among clinical agents [72]. Because Intelligent DSS directly accesses the patient's personal information, medical health diary, and diagnostic toolbox, data privacy laws should be adhered to. Furthermore, the end user and the computer scientists did not clarify how the data are interpreted for the decisions and are the data safe. Therefore, EXAI overcomes the issue concerned with AI adoption by providing detailed explanations of the decisions arrived at, thus revealing the pros and cons of the decision-making models, and also, entrusts the policymakers and decision-makers by successfully adopting AI for a more sustainable and effective decision-making process. Because the model's explainability is equally important for the managers/decision-makers to understand the parameters correctly, they can effectively communicate the analytical rationale of the decisions to their stakeholders more convincingly.

3.4.1 "Human-in-the-Loop"-Sustainable EXAI for Intelligent DSS

The "human-in-the-loop," in the perspective of EXAI, refers to creating human-centered or human-understandable explanations for the decisions arrived at. Human inputs are required to generate understandable explanations; therefore, human factors must be considered during the model development processes for computationally sustainable outcomes. Schoonderwoerd et al., have developed design patterns for generating explanations in intelligent clinical DSS for child health [73]. They analyzed the inputs from the most experienced pediatricians to determine the type of explanations that must be generated. In turn, the interactive design patterns were consequently tested with the users. The derived design pattern specifies the time the user involvement is required and how the interaction must be entertained to ensure the generality of the developed design pattern [74]. The EXAI models should be designed with design-for-fit, i.e., generating explanations specific to the application. Therefore, the EXAI model developers must have a deep understanding of the internal workings of any application and the purpose of explanation in different aspects of its use. For instance, developers of EXAI for clinical DSS must have in-depth knowledge of the decisions arrived of the clinical sector, the explanation needs of clinicians, patients, and other clinical practitioners as well as different perspectives of interactions like clinicians, clinicians to patients, or other practitioners. In weird situations, some clinicians might disagree with the medical diagnosis generated by the clinical DSS, due to some discrepancy or require additional tests for clarity. Therefore, developers must adopt a tailor-made approach for generating explanations for more sustainable and efficient DSS system development. An AI-based Intelligent DSS with EXAI augmentations was developed for solving different tasks of low-stake and high-stake circumstances [75]. To understand the low-stake and high-stake situations, the developers worked closely with the solar panel manufacturer to better understand the typical image defects and utilized the standard dataset. Consequently, human-centered design for EXAI model development needs a clear picture of the situation of use, its explainability, and transparency. Henceforth, before the development of

XAI-based Intelligent DSS, EXAI planning techniques must be devised focusing on understanding the subgoals and their related understandings [76].

3.4.2 CHALLENGES IN ADOPTION

EXAI will be a mandated solution for AI adoption to the fullest. But, there are certain challenges to adoption, and some questions remain unclear. Furthermore, bringing together the human factors in the development of DSS remains imprecise. Questions arrived from different perspectives in the adoption of EXAI-based Intelligent DSS are

3.4.2.1 Trustworthiness
  a. How the trust of EXAI-based Intelligent DSS will be assured by the different perspectives of varied participative entities in the application?
  b. How will the end-user of data-intensive applications know that their data taken for analysis is privacy-preserving and safe per Data Protection Act?
  c. For fully automated Intelligent DSS, where no human is involved, how will the end-user be assured of interpersonal communication and collaboration among the people with a stake in the system? E.g., a patient and a doctor in the clinical sector.
  d. Will these trustworthy EXAI-base Intelligent DSS define all decisions' legal and ethical principles?

3.4.2.2 Transparency
The main reason for EXAI's evolution is the opacity of the AI models, While EXAI assures transparency, certain questions remain unanswered. Further, the system must be capable of defining why and how the output has arrived.

  a. How or what degree of transparency an EXAI-based Intelligent DSS will offer, and how will it be defined?
  b. What are the different levels of transparency? From the end user's perspective, the level of understanding must be very clear, whereas, from the higher internal stakeholder's perspective, it can be generic with technical terms. How will this discrimination in the explanations be attained? [75,77].
  c. How stakeholder-specific sufficient explainability of the models be determined?
  d. What level of transparency is input-specific (data taken), output-specific (results arrived), or both provided?
  e. Assuming the level of transparency is identified and defined, how will the same be communicated to the different stakeholders (as different stakeholders have varied literacy levels on the particular application)?
  f. In the case of shared decision-making, like clinical decisions requiring patients' opinions based on budget constraints for treatments, how will this explainability be included in the processes?

3.4.2.3 Shared and Collaborative Entities in the Decision-Making Environment
In most applications, decision-making is not unimodal, it has been mutually intertwined, collaborative, and interdependent among different entities involved. The questions concerned with shared entities are as follows:

  a. What are the different types and ranges of entities participating in the decisions?
  b. How long each entity's participation or input is required to arrive at the decisions?
  c. Identify the machine-independent tasks and their acceleration for arriving at the final decisions.

    d. Are any legal issues connected with any third-party entity participation or "human in the loop" required for the final decision?

    e. What practices are enforced for "meaningful human control" in shared entity's participation alongside machines?

    f. How are the responsibilities and liabilities designated among the shared entities and machines?

These questions must be answered for the fully pledged, sustainable, and successful adoption of EXAI-based Intelligent DSS.

3.4.3 LEGAL, ETHICAL, AND SOCIAL ISSUES IN EXAI

EXAI has led to dramatic upliftment in almost all the domains specifically concerned with data sensitivity. While EXAI is explainable, providing transparent explanations of the decisions arrived at, some legal, ethical, and social issues concern EXAI explanations. As the explanations are delivered for the automated decisions to assure transparency in the modeling, it is not always possible for humans to believe or trust the explanations.

3.4.3.1 Right to Explanation

European Union's General Data Protection Act (GDPR) enforces certain basic principles that must be adopted by any data processing system dealing with personal data to ensure fairness, lawfulness, and transparency in data usage [78]. Although the EXAI has satisfied the Explicability property of GDPR on black-box models, GDPR has now framed a new "right to explanation," warranting the AI industry to adopt the ethical code of conduct while providing meaningful explanations to the decisions. It has been observed that individuals' legal status might be disturbed by the explanations provided by fully automated decisions. Algorithms can also provide a false or projected explanation by hiding the fact. Moreover, when the explanations generated have been shared among multiple parties in the loop, how data security is assured. Therefore, while generating explanations, GDPR's code of conduct must be assured, and proper descriptions of the need for explanations for every explanatory content must be produced. Furthermore, explanations must be generated according to the expertise of any stakeholder concern and based on a proper requirement statement for the need [79]. The current EXAI models are concerned with a one-size-fits-all approach [74], i.e., providing a single explanation meeting the requirements of different stakeholders. In contrast, other models are focused on inductive or deductive explanations [80]. As there is no strong separation between creating things explainable and explaining the things, Sovrano et al. have proposed an approach that leads to strong means of separation between explainability and explaining, for developing more computationally sustainable EXAI models with explanations [81]. They have proposed a model utilizing exploratory AI to provide user-centered explanations and solve the computational irreducibility problem in the decision explanations. Therefore, any EXAI models developed must adhere to the right to explanation by assuring individuals how their data are interpreted, transparent decisions, and the information used is safeguarded through proper security mechanisms.

3.4.3.2 Explanations through Multidisciplinary Domain Collaboration

The development of explanatory agents involved in generating human-centered explanations must collaborate with researchers from different domains like cognitive science, psychological, philosophical, and human-computer interactions (linguistic) to avoid the following: contractiveness in explanations, a human participant for explanations should not be influenced by biases, explanations based on statistical relationships are ineffective, and involve social disciplines [82]. In contrast, another researcher suggests that instead of involving humans in generating explanations, healthy collaboration with experts in social sciences would result in better EXAI models in the case of the healthcare domain [83]. Therefore, to abide by the requirements of different personnel in varied domains, the EXAI community should collaborate with the aforementioned expertise to promote cross-pollination, qualitative investigations, and sustainable models [84]. Similarly, the author [85] suggests that logical rules involved in framing explanations must be adopted wisely, termed an "illusion of explanatory depth" for making the human understand the explanations better.

3.4.3.3 Biases with Explanations

Bias in terms of AI means a machine or model is irrational to one form of input and another. Bias in EXAI comes in different forms like societal biases (like gender, race, and nationalism), cognitive biases (it includes different forms of knowledge interpretations and providing results accordingly like statistical biases), and algorithmic AI bias (where the model is trained on biased data). Bias results from various issues like demographic distortions, data quality, behavioral aspects, linking biases, and so on [86]. Effective EXAI explanations must contain cues assuring the human participants that heuristics are followed with cognitive biases, and appropriate logical reasoning is incorporated. EXAI models should be developed on non-bias data and generate explanations without biases.

3.4.3.4 EXAI for Heterogeneous Data Types

Currently, EXAI has been employed for text and image data only. However, different data types, such as audio, time series, spatiotemporal data, and graphs, have received much less attention. Visualization techniques can convert non-image data in images and other heterogeneous data types into an acceptable format. But, the major requirement of EXAI models for other types of data is that they may provide better explanations for understanding complex data interpretations [87]. However, this may require extra assistance from expertise in time-series data or any other complex data type. These EXAI systems for heterogeneous data types can improve the effectiveness of their application domain with more variability. This will enhance the applicability of EXAI in process industries [88].

3.5 CONCLUSION

In conclusion, Explainable Artificial Intelligence (EXAI) demonstrates its major role in addressing the challenges of trustworthiness, transparency, and accountability in the deployment of AI systems. As AI technologies become increasingly widespread across various fields, the need for EXAI becomes more evident to support humans to comprehend and authenticate AI-driven decisions and predictions.

EXAI models provide insights into the internal mechanisms of complex AI models, making their decision-making processes more interpretable to all kinds of users. By identifying the features that influence AI outputs, users can make well-versed decisions, find possible biases, and ensure the appropriate use of AI technologies.

In fields like healthcare, automobiles, finance, judicial system, insurance, manufacturing, defense, smart cities, and many others, EXAI can provide interpretation and explanation on how AI models made decisions which improve the overall system performance and user acceptance. Moreover, in critical applications, such as medical diagnosis and autonomous vehicles, EXAI can be critical for justifying AI-generated predictions and recommendations in order to ensure the safety and well-being of humans.

As EXAI continues to advance and become more united into our day-to-day lives, the development and deployment of EXAI will continue an attention for researchers. Providing the correct interpretability for the AI model output is always challenging for the researchers who are actively working on it to ensure EXAI is efficient and more effective.

In summary, EXAI plays a vital role in responsible AI development, nurturing human-machine association, and ensuring all the AI models are designed with enough transparency and accountability. Furthermore, all the applications developed and deployed in today's digital environment are transdisciplinary, amalgamating concepts from different technologies to provide a sustainable, automated, global solution. Therefore, EXAI would be a mandate for the sustainable adaptability of AI models and their applications. By making AI systems interpretable and/or explainable, AI will be deployed in all domains while upholding ethical principles and human values.

REFERENCES

1. Montgomery, D. C., Peck, E. A., Vining, G. G, *Introduction to Linear Regression Analysis*. Hoboken, NJ: John Wiley & Sons, 2021.
2. Molnar, C., *Interpretable Machine Learning*. Morrisville, NC: Lulu. Com, 2020.
3. Dreiseitl, S., Ohno-Machado, L., Logistic regression and artificial neural network classification models: A methodology review. *Journal of Biomedical Informatics*, 35(5–6), 352–359, 2002.
4. Guisan, A., Edwards Jr., T. C., Hastie, T., Generalized linear and generalized additive models in studies of species distributions: Setting the scene. *Ecological Modelling*, 157(2–3), 89–100, 2002.
5. Hastie, T., Tibshirani, R., Friedman, J. H., Friedman, J. H, *The Elements of Statistical Learning: Data Mining, Inference, and Prediction*, New York: Springer, 2, 1–758, 2009.
6. Holte, R. C, Very simple classification rules perform well on most commonly used datasets. *Machine Learning*, 11, 63–90, 1993.
7. Stange, R. L., Neto, J. J, Learning decision rules using adaptive technologies: A hybrid approach based on sequential covering. *Procedia Computer Science*, 109, 1188–1193, 2017.
8. Borgelt, C, An implementation of the FP-growth algorithm, In *Proceedings of the 1st International Workshop on Open Source Data Mining: Frequent Pattern Mining Implementations*, 1–5, New York, United States, 2005.
9. Nagahisarchoghaei, M., Nur, N., Cummins, L., Nur, N., Karimi, M. M., Nandanwar, S., Rahimi, S, An empirical survey on explainable AI technologies: Recent trends, use-cases, and categories from technical and application perspectives. *Electronics*, 12(5), 1092, 2023.
10. Wang, L, Research and implementation of machine learning classifier based on KNN. *IOP Conference Series: Materials Science and Engineering*, 677(5), 52038, 2019.
11. Barratt, S, *Interpnet: Neural introspection for interpretable deep learning.* arXiv preprint arXiv:1710.09511, 2017.
12. Garcia-Magarino, I., Muttukrishnan, R., Lloret, J., Human-centric AI for trustworthy IoT systems with explainable multilayer perceptrons. *IEEE Access*, 7, 125562–125574, 2019.
13. Lei, T., Barzilay, R., Jaakkola, T., *Rationalizing neural predictions.* arXiv preprint arXiv:1606.04155, 2016.
14. Hendricks, L. A., Akata, Z., Rohrbach, M., Donahue, J., Schiele, B., Darrell, T., Generating visual explanations. In *Computer Vision-ECCV 2016: 14th European Conference*, Amsterdam, The Netherlands, October 11–14, 2016, Proceedings, Part IV 14, Springer International Publishing, 3–19, 2016.
15. Hendricks, L. A., Hu, R., Darrell, T., Akata, Z., Grounding visual explanations. In *Proceedings of the European Conference on Computer Vision (ECCV)*, 264–279, Munich, Germany, 2018.
16. Vilone, G., Longo, L., *Explainable artificial intelligence: A systematic review.* arXiv preprint arXiv:2006.00093, 2020.
17. Bach, S., Binder, A., Montavon, G., Klauschen, F., Müller, K. R., Samek, W., On pixel-wise explanations for non-linear classifier decisions by layer-wise relevance propagation. *PLoS One*, 10(7), e0130140, 2015.
18. Lapuschkin, S., Wäldchen, S., Binder, A., Montavon, G., Samek, W., Müller, K. R., Unmasking Clever Hans predictors and assessing what machines really learn. *Nature Communications*, 10(1), 1096, 2019.
19. Fong, R. C., Vedaldi, A., Interpretable explanations of black boxes by meaningful perturbation. In *Proceedings of the IEEE International Conference on Computer Vision*, 3429–3437, Venice, Italy, 2017.
20. Liu, L., Wang, L., What has my classifier learned? Visualizing the classification rules of bag-of-feature model by support region detection. In *2012 IEEE Conference on Computer Vision and Pattern Recognition*, IEEE, 3586–3593, Providence, Rhode Island, 2012.
21. Choo, J., Lee, H., Kihm, J., Park, H., iVisClassifier: An interactive visual analytics system for classification based on supervised dimension reduction. In *2010 IEEE Symposium on Visual Analytics Science and Technology*, IEEE, 27–34, Salt Lake City, UT, USA, 2010.
22. Dabkowski, P., Gal, Y., Real-time image saliency for black-box classifiers. In *Advances in Neural Information Processing Systems*, 30, 2017.

23. Baehrens, D., Schroeter, T., Harmeling, S., Kawanabe, M., Hansen, K., Müller, K. R., How to explain individual classification decisions. *The Journal of Machine Learning Research*, 11, 1803–1831, 2010.
24. Goldstein, A., Kapelner, A., Bleich, J., Pitkin, E., Peeking inside the black box: Visualizing statistical learning with plots of individual conditional expectation. *Journal of Computational and Graphical Statistics*, 24(1), 44–65, 2015.
25. Casalicchio, G., Molnar, C., Bischl, B., Visualizing the feature importance for black box models. In *Machine Learning and Knowledge Discovery in Databases: European Conference, ECML PKDD 2018*, Dublin, Ireland, September 10–14, 2018, Proceedings, Springer International Publishing, Part I 18, 655–670, 2019.
26. Krause, J., Perer, A., Bertini, E., *Using visual analytics to interpret predictive machine learning models*, arXiv preprint arXiv:1606.05685, 2016.
27. Poulin, B., Eisner, R., Szafron, D., Lu, P., Greiner, R., Wishart, D. S., Anvik, J., Visual explanation of evidence with additive classifiers. In *Proceedings of the National Conference on Artificial Intelligence*, Menlo Park, CA; Cambridge, MA; London; AAAI Press; MIT Press; 1999, 21(2), 1822, 2006.
28. Zhang, J., Wang, Y., Molino, P., Li, L., Ebert, D. S., Manifold: A model-agnostic framework for interpretation and diagnosis of machine learning models. *IEEE Transactions on Visualization and Computer Graphics*, 25(1), 364–373, 2018.
29. Kahng, M., Fang, D., Chau, D. H., Visual exploration of machine learning results using data cube analysis. In *Proceedings of the Workshop on Human-in-the-Loop Data Analytics*, 1–6, San Francisco, CA, USA, 2016.
30. Friedman, J. H, Greedy function approximation: A gradient boosting machine. *Annals of Statistics*, 29, 1189–1232, 2001.
31. Apley, D. W., Zhu, J., Visualizing the effects of predictor variables in black box supervised learning models. *Journal of the Royal Statistical Society Series B: Statistical Methodology*, 82(4), 1059–1086, 2020.
32. Ribeiro, M. T., Singh, S., Guestrin, C., "Why should I trust you?" Explaining the predictions of any classifier. In *Proceedings of the 22nd ACM SIGKDD International Conference on Knowledge Discovery and Data Mining*, 1135–1144, San Francisco, California, 2016.
33. Shapley, L. S., A value for n-person games, In: *Classics in Game Theory*, 69, 1997. doi: 10.2307/j.ctv173f1fh.12.
34. Guidotti, R., Counterfactual explanations and how to find them: Literature review and benchmarking. *Data Mining and Knowledge Discovery*, 1–55, 2022. doi: 10.1007/s10618-022-00831-6.
35. Goodfellow, I., Papernot, N., Huang, S., Duan, Y., Abbeel, P., Clark, J., Attacking machine learning with adversarial examples, *OpenAI Blog*, 24, 2017.
36. Bien, J., Tibshirani, R., *Prototype selection for interpretable classification*, The Annals of Applied Statistics, 5(4), 2403–2424, 2011.
37. Ribeiro, M. T., Singh, S., Guestrin, C., Anchors: High-precision model-agnostic explanations, In *Proceedings of the AAAI Conference on Artificial Intelligence*, 32(1), Hilton New Orleans Riverside, New Orleans, Louisiana, USA, 2018.
38. Konig, R., Johansson, U., Niklasson, L., G-REX: A versatile framework for evolutionary data mining, In *2008 IEEE International Conference on Data Mining Workshops*, 971–974, IEEE, Pisa, Italy, 2008.
39. Johansson, U., König, R., Niklasson, L., The truth is in there-rule extraction from opaque models using genetic programming, In *FLAIRS Conference*, 1, Miami Beach, Florida, USA, 2004.
40. Su, G., Wei, D., Varshney, K. R., Malioutov, D. M., *Interpretable two-level boolean rule learning for classification*, arXiv preprint arXiv:1511.07361, 2015.
41. Krishnan, S., Wu, E., Palm: Machine learning explanations for iterative debugging, In *Proceedings of the 2nd Workshop on Human-in-the-Loop Data Analytics*, 1–6, Chicago, IL, USA, 2017.
42. Bastani, O., Kim, C., Bastani, H, *Interpretability via model extraction*, arXiv preprint arXiv:1706.09773, 2017.
43. Tan, S., Caruana, R., Hooker, G., Lou, Y., Distill-and-compare: Auditing black-box models using transparent model distillation, In *Proceedings of the 2018 AAAI/ACM Conference on AI, Ethics, and Society*, 303–310, New York, USA, 2018.
44. Wachter, S., Mittelstadt, B., Russell, C., Counterfactual explanations without opening the black box: Automated decisions and the GDPR. *Harvard Journal of Law & Technology*, 31, 841, 2017.
45. Friedman, J. H., Popescu, B. E., Predictive learning via rule ensembles. *The Annals of Applied Statistics*, 2, 916–954, 2008.

46. Fisher, A., Rudin, C., Dominici, F., All models are wrong, but many are useful: Learning a variable's importance by studying an entire class of prediction models simultaneously. *Journal of Machine Learning Research*, 20(177), 1–81, 2019.

47. Lundberg, S. M., Lee, S. I., A unified approach to interpreting model predictions, In *Advances in Neural Information Processing Systems*, 30, Long Beach, CA, USA, 2017.

48. Giudici, P., Raffinetti, E., Shapley-Lorenz eXplainable artificial intelligence. *Expert Systems with Applications*, 167, 114104, 2021.

49. Cortez, P., Embrechts, M. J., Opening black box data mining models using sensitivity analysis, In *2011 IEEE Symposium on Computational Intelligence and Data Mining (CIDM)*, IEEE, 341–348, Paris, France, 2011.

50. Henelius, A., Puolamäki, K., Ukkonen, A., *Interpreting classifiers through attribute interactions in datasets*, arXiv preprint arXiv:1707.07576, 2017.

51. Koh, P. W., Liang, P., Understanding black-box predictions via influence functions, In *International Conference on Machine Learning, PMLR*, 1885–1894, Sydney, Australia, 2017.

52. Cook, R. D., Detection of influential observation in linear regression. *Technometrics*, 42(1), 65–68, 2000.

53. Kabir, M. H., Hasan, K. F., Hasan, M. K., Ansari, K., Explainable artificial intelligence for smart city application: A secure and trusted platform, In Ahmed, M., Islam, S. R., Anwar, A., Moustafa, N., Pathan, A. S. K. (eds.) *Explainable Artificial Intelligence for Cyber Security: Next Generation Artificial Intelligence*, Cham: Springer International Publishing, 241–263, 2022.

54. Alsaigh, R., Mehmood, R., Katib, I., AI explainability and governance in smart energy systems: A review. *Frontiers in Energy Research*, 11, 1071291, 2023.

55. United Nations, *UN-Habitat, AI and Cities Risks, Applications and Governance: A playbook for local and regional governments*, 2022. https://unhabitat.org/sites/default/files/2022/10/artificial_intelligence_and_cities_risks_applications_and_governance.pdf.

56. Bibri, S. E., Alexandre, A., Sharifi, A., Krogstie, J. Environmentally sustainable smart cities and their converging AI, IoT, and big data technologies and solutions: An integrated approach to an extensive literature review. *Energy Informatics*, 6(1), 9, 2023.

57. Topuz, K., Zengul, F. D., Dag, A., Almehmi, A., Yildirim, M. B., Predicting graft survival among kidney transplant recipients: A Bayesian decision support model. *Decision Support Systems*, 106, 97–109, 2018. doi: 10.1016/j.dss.2017.12.004.

58. Kraus, M., Feuerriegel, S., Oztekin, A., Deep learning in business analytics and operations research: Models, applications and managerial implications. *European Journal of Operational Research*, 281(3), 628–641, 2020. https://doi.org/10.1016/j.ejor.2019.09.018

59. Fu, R., Huang, Y., Singh, P. V, Crowds, lending, machine, and bias. *Information Systems Research*, 32(1), 72–92, 2021. https://doi.org/10.1287/isre.2020.0990.

60. Coussement, K., Phan, M., De Caigny, A., Benoit, D. F., Raes, A., Predicting student dropout in subscription-based online learning environments: The beneficial impact of the logit leaf model. *Decision Support Systems*, 2020. https://doi.org/10.1016/j.dss.2020.113325.

61. Liu, H., Ye, Y., Lee, H. Y., High-dimensional learning under approximate sparsity with applications to nonsmooth estimation and regularized neural networks. *Operations Research*, 2022. https://doi.org/10.1287/opre.2021.2217.

62. Phillips-Wren, G., Intelligent decision support systems, In *Multicriteria Decision Aid and Artificial Intelligence: Links, Theory and Applications*, 25–44, 2013. https://doi.org/10.1002/9781118522516.ch2.

63. He, C., Li, Y., A survey of intelligent decision support system, In *2017 7th International Conference on Applied Science, Engineering and Technology (ICASET)*, Atlantis Press, 201–206, Qingdao, China, 2017.

64. Deva Hema, D., Kumar, K. A., Optimized deep neural network based intelligent decision support system for traffic state prediction. *International Journal of Intelligent Transportation Systems Research*, 21(1), 26–35, 2023.

65. Carvalho, H. D. S., An intelligent decision support system for the freight transport sector (Doctoral dissertation), 2022.

66. Sharma, M., Biswas, M., A deep learning-based intelligent decision support system for hyperspectral image classification using manifold batch structure in internet of things (IoT). *Wireless Personal Communications*, 126(3), 2119–2147, 2022.

67. Lee, M. H., Siewiorek, D. P., Smailagic, A., Bernardino, A., Bermúdez i Badia, S., Co-design and evaluation of an intelligent decision support system for stroke rehabilitation assessment, In *Proceedings of the ACM on Human-Computer Interaction, 4(CSCW2)*, 1–27, KAIST, Seoul, South Korea, 2020.

68. Bazilevych, K. O., Chumachenko, D. I., Hulianytskyi, L. F., Meniailov, I. S., Yakovlev, S. V., Intelligent decision-support system for epidemiological diagnostics. I. A concept of architecture design. *Cybernetics and Systems Analysis*, 58(3), 343–353, 2022.

69. Aggarwal, L., Goswami, P., Sachdeva, S., Multi-criterion intelligent decision support system for COVID-19. *Applied Soft Computing*, 101, 107056, 2021.

70. Yu, K.-H., Beam, A. L., Kohane, I.S., Artificial intelligence in healthcare. *Nature Biomedical Engineering*, 2(10), 719–31, 2018.

71. Shin, D, The effects of explainability and causability on perception, trust, and acceptance: Implications for explainable AI. *International Journal of Human Computer Studies*, 146, 102551, 2021. https://doi.org/10.1016/j.ijhcs.2020.102551.

72. Braun, M., Hummel, P., Beck, S., Dabrock, P., Primer on an ethics of AI-based decision support systems in the clinic. *Journal of Medical Ethics*, 47(12), e3, 2021.

73. Schoonderwoerd, T. A., Jorritsma, W., Neerincx, M. A., Van Den Bosch, K., Human-centered XAI: Developing design patterns for explanations of clinical decision support systems. *International Journal of Human-Computer Studies*, 154, 102684, 2021.

74. Arrieta, A. B., Díaz-Rodríguez, N., Del Ser, J., Bennetot, A., Tabik, S., Barbado, A., Herrera, F., Explainable Artificial Intelligence (XAI): Concepts, taxonomies, opportunities and challenges toward responsible AI. *Information Fusion*, 58, 82–115, 2020.

75. Wanner, J., Herm, L. V., Heinrich, K., Janiesch, C., Zschech, P., White, grey, black: Effects of XAI augmentation on the confidence in AI-based decision support systems, In *ICIS*, Hyderabad, India, 2020.

76. Das, D., Kim, B., Chernova, S., Subgoal-based explanations for unreliable intelligent decision support systems, In *Proceedings of the 28th International Conference on Intelligent User Interfaces*, 240–250, Sydney NSW Australia, 2023.

77. Burnett, M., Explaining AI: Fairly? Well? In *Proceedings of the 25th International Conference on Intelligent User Interfaces*, 1–2, Cagliari, Italy, 2020.

78. Regulation (EU) 2016/679 of the European Parliament and of the Council, *Regulation (eu)*, 679, 2016.

79. Hleg, A., Ethics guidelines for trustworthy AI, *European Commission*, 2019.

80. Calegari, R., Ciatto, G., Omicini, A., On the integration of symbolic and sub-symbolic techniques for XAI: A survey. *Intelligenza Artificiale*, 14(1), 7–32, 2020.

81. Sovrano, F., Vitali, F., Palmirani, M., Making things explainable vs explaining: Requirements and challenges under the GDPR, In *AI Approaches to the Complexity of Legal Systems XI-XII: AICOL International Workshops 2018 and 2020: AICOL-XI@ JURIX 2018, AICOL-XII@ JURIX 2020, XAILA@ JURIX 2020*, Revised Selected Papers XII, Springer International Publishing, 169–182, Groningen, The Netherlands (2018), Brno, Czechia (2020), 2021.

82. Miller, T., Explanation in artificial intelligence: Insights from the social sciences. *Artificial Intelligence*, 267, 1–38, 2019.

83. Hoffman, R. R., Klein, G., Explaining explanation, part 1: Theoretical foundations. *IEEE Intelligent Systems*, 32(3), 68–73, 2017.

84. Johs, A. J., Agosto, D. E., Weber, R. O., Explainable artificial intelligence and social science: Further insights for qualitative investigation. *Applied AI Letters*, 3(1), e64, 2022.

85. Schmid, U., Wrede, B., What is missing in XAI so far? An interdisciplinary perspective. *KI-Künstliche Intelligenz*, 36, 1–13, 2022.

86. Olteanu, A., Castillo, C., Diaz, F., Kıcıman, E., Social data: Biases, methodological pitfalls, and ethical boundaries. *Frontiers in Big Data*, 2, 13, 2019.

87. Saeed, W., Omlin, C., Explainable AI (XAI): A systematic meta-survey of current challenges and future opportunities. *Knowledge-Based Systems*, 263, 110273, 2023.

88. Kotriwala, A., Klöpper, B., Dix, M., Gopalakrishnan, G., Ziobro, D., Potschka, A., XAI for operations in the process industry-applications, theses, and research directions, In *AAAI Spring Symposium: Combining Machine Learning with Knowledge Engineering*, Stanford University, Palo Alto, California, USA, 2021.

4 Impact of Artificial Intelligence and Emotional Intelligence in Autonomous Operation and MSME Entrepreneurs' Performance in the Waste Management Industry

Marirajan Murugan and M.N. Prabadevi

4.1 INTRODUCTION

Environmental Protection Agency projects that 75% of the produced waste stream is recyclable. However, only 30% of recyclable materials are getting recycled. Based on 2016 statistics, global waste reached 2 billion tonnes, expected to be doubled by 2050, considering the population growth and rise in consumer culture. Researchers observed that artificial intelligence, machine learning and cloud computing could improve waste management systems rather than traditional waste management systems. MSME entrepreneurs' emotional intelligence and decision-making make entrepreneurs understand the stakeholder's requirements and provide appropriate tools and techniques.

An artificial intelligence system facilitates better decision-making from the entrepreneur's perspective [1,2]. The deployment of robotics will drive the autonomous system implementation through artificial intelligence to replace manual labour for waste collection and disposal [3]. Entrepreneurs utilise the latest technologies, such as quantum computing, artificial intelligence, machine learning and blockchain, to develop, design and scale their organisations [4]. Prediction of waste generation through machine learning approaches such as K-nearest neighbours and support vector machines positively influences solid waste generation and disposal management [5] and promotes autonomous motivation, positively influencing residents' waste separation behaviours [6]. Autonomous vehicles and their autonomous driving system for garbage collection are sufficiently efficient [7]. Artificial intelligence handles complex nonlinear problems and has become a powerful tool for exploring and managing wastewater treatment systems [8].

Based on the extensive literature review through original equipment manufacturer (OEMs) concept studies, case studies of autonomous operation and MSME entrepreneurs' performance in the waste management industry available globally, this chapter focuses on projecting the current scenario of autonomous operation in the waste management industry and further research requirements to comply complete cycle requirements and fill the gaps.

Furthermore, a well-structured questionnaire and interviews were derived to collect the responses from 23 respondents from MSME entrepreneurs. Researchers used convenient sampling to collect the data from respondents. The statistical tool used in this study is JAMOVI, and data are analysed through descriptive statistics, reliability analysis and correlation, and multiple regressions. Researchers analyse and observe that artificial intelligence and emotional intelligence in autonomous operation and MSME entrepreneur's performance have positive influences and understand

DOI: 10.1201/9781003457176-4

efficient and practical approaches for the waste management industry. Researchers recommend that government and MSME entrepreneurs update their policies to implement autonomous operations in the waste management industry.

4.2 DEFINITION, LITERATURE REVIEW AND METHODOLOGY

4.2.1 WASTE MANAGEMENT INDUSTRY

Industry produces more waste than agricultural waste, construction and demolition, hazardous, medical and electronic waste. The industry needs artificial intelligence, machine learning and cloud computing for technological improvement in their business environment to reduce waste. Solid waste generation has an impact on human health conditions and gives impact to the environment. Artificial intelligence technologies improve industry performance in waste management planning, sorting and bin level monitoring, collection, vehicle routing, waste treatment and disposal [9]. The waste manufacturing industry uses artificial intelligence to improve quality and efficiency and reduce waste. Figure 4.1 shows a global snapshot of the solid waste management system, indicating major solid waste management disposal from industrial waste.

4.2.2 ARTIFICIAL INTELLIGENCE AND EMOTIONAL INTELLIGENCE IN AUTONOMOUS OPERATIONS IN THE WASTE MANAGEMENT INDUSTRY

Researchers observed that according to Accenture, Accenture and Amazon Web Services, Inc. (AWS) Work to Help Companies Advance Journey to Water Neutrality Through First-of-its-Kind Open Platform [10], Accenture developed cloud-based water management solutions to attain the following.

- Final yield analyses
- Have the information in a centralised platform
- Cost optimisation to support decision-making
- Integrated water management
- Recycle water within the industry
- Mitigate water resource challenges

According to Advantech, they have an open platform communications unified architecture (OPC UA) solution for the wastewater treatment monitoring system [11]. Open platform communications unified architecture helps data security from the entire field to cloud-based computing to meet the following:

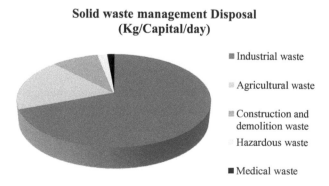

Solid waste management Disposal (Kg/Capital/day)

- Industrial waste
- Agricultural waste
- Construction and demolition waste
- Hazardous waste
- Medical waste

FIGURE 4.1 Global solid waste disposal (Archetypal).

- Engineering cost reduction
- Continuously monitoring and maintaining the IIoT network
- Control environmental challenges
- Reliable security
- Reduction of the deployment and maintenance

According to AECOM, AECOM has a more efficient future for the most precious substances. Keep it flowing, safe, viable, and sustainable: The water industry, responsible for the one thing that supports all life, bears the heaviest digital business transformation burden of all [12]. AECOM provides data-driven solutions and attains the following:

- Risk and cost management with proper balance
- Strategic and environmental expenses
- Improvements
- Upgradation
- Performance improvement
- Reduction of unplanned shutdown
- Recommendations for improvement of the quality
- Efficient and effective delivery

According to ADNOC, ADNOC and Group 42 (G42) support ADNOC's continued drive to leverage artificial intelligence to optimise performance and grow the UAE's innovation ecosystem [13]. This joint venture company provides the following solutions in the oil and gas industry.

- Optimise processes
- Improve planning
- Increase profitability
- Industrial growth
- Applications for the oil and gas industry
- Drilling performance
- Reservoir modelling
- Corrosion detection
- Product quality

According to Aqua Tech, the UK Water Utility Operating Network section with artificial intelligence, digital solutions and their impact on human workforces provides an automated part of its drinking water network with the following [14]:

- Remote control capabilities
- The high degree of instrumentation
- Real-time pump schedules
- Minimise manual overhead

According to ATOS, Scottish Water transforms wastewater network management. IoT sensors and real-time data enhance customer experience and protect the environment [15]. The outcome of its upgrade of the wastewater network is the following:

- Early warnings
- Reduced pollution incidents
- Eco-friendly environmental mandates
- Increased compliance

According to Autodesk, intelligence control of wastewater using artificial intelligence [16] makes machines and devices more intelligent and attains the following:

- Increase the efficiency of water and wastewater treatment processes
- Drive efficiency
- Reliability across the systems
- Optimising the operation

According to AVEVA, it covers artificial intelligence and the digital twin, optimises with artificial intelligence software that uses artificial intelligence technology and human insight [17], and enables self-optimisation through autonomous and semi-autonomous processes to attain the following:

- Boost profitability
- Improve plant performance
- Maximise machine learning
- Predict future ones
- Minimise the risk of failure of critical assets

According to Circle H$_2$O, delivering actionable insights and artificial intelligence-enabled insights serves as a guide to efficiently and cost-effectively operate the plant [18]. They help to identify critical points in the treatment processes and attain the following:

- Advanced analytic solutions
- Data collection system
- Cloud-based delivery platform
- Reducing operational expenses
- Avoiding plant downtimes

According to Danfoss (2023), Danfoss drives in the water and wastewater industry based on intelligence embedded in the AQUA Drive [19]. The following feature takes care of continuous running without any issues:

- Digital cascade control hot swap technology
- Backup master functionality
- Reduction in investment
- Integration condition-based monitoring
- Reduced installation time
- Cloud-free artificial intelligence embedded in the drive
- Predictive maintenance

According to Envirosuite Water Operations, EVS Water Plant Optimizer is an innovative cloud-based solution [20] – the following comprehensive solutions for designing and improving wastewater infrastructure:

- Reduce dosing costs
- Efficient plant design
- Evade environmental incidents
- Operational improvements in real-time
- Forecast plant performance

According to GE Digital, Water and Wastewater: Challenges for water utilities continue to mount while pressures to provide clean, uninterrupted water flows never abate. Digitalisation helps optimise the operations [21]. The following challenge takes care of GE Digital for the Water and Wastewater:

- Operating costs
- Drive greater efficiency
- Optimisation
- Predictive assets failure

According to Grundfos, Grundfos has solutions: Avoid unplanned operational downtime with artificial intelligence and cloud technology [22]. Using artificial intelligence, the plant can eliminate unplanned downtime with the following:

- Cloud-based intelligence
- Predictive maintenance planning
- Condition monitoring
- Adding intelligence to water reuse systems

According to KDX, intelligence water management solutions are cloud-based software that delivers real-time insights for safe and effective operations, decision-making and planning [23]. The following intelligent solution takes care of wastewater plant operations:

- Cloud-based software
- Cutting-edge technology (machine learning)
- High-performance modelling
- Automate and shape data into value

According to Rockwell Automation, Rockwell Automation delivers artificial intelligence for industry-leading wastewater trials by Severn Trent and partners [24]. Rockwell Automation provides the following solutions to automate and monitor entire waste catchments:

- Forecast maintenance
- Predict weather conditions
- Control waste flow
- Better management in storm conditions
- Automatically optimise the storage
- Forward-thinking in storm conditions

According to Schneider Electric, artificial intelligence optimises operations, helps to achieve energy transparency and consumes less energy [25]. Schneider Electric provides efficient ways to ensure wastewater industry solutions attain the following:

- Make smarter, faster and more sustainable decisions
- Cost efficiency
- Ideation in delivery
- Address business challenges
- Manage energy savings
- Manage sustainability footprint
- Cloud-based solution
- Dynamically control on-site energy resources

- Reduce CO_2 emissions
- Enable real-time analytics
- Improve the quality of service

According to Siemens, artificial intelligence and the Internet of Things reduce wastewater network blockages and pollution [26]. It helps to safeguard the high value of natural water systems with the following:

- Employ technologies with high-value
- Co-creation for people health
- Identify problems with the network quickly
- Cloud-based data analytics
- Protecting the environment

According to Suez, using artificial intelligence to improve Energy-from-Waste plant performance achieves the following [27]:

- Reduce the risk of unplanned shutdowns.
- More accurate monitoring
- Unique artificial intelligence solutions
- Detect many non-conformity items

According to Veolia, digital innovation is at the heart of the water flocculation process. Artificial intelligence is used to reach the right balance between cost and compliance [28]. Veolia focuses on sustainable solutions to attain the following:

- Lowest possible energy consumption
- Minimise the site's carbon footprint
- Maximise the reuse possibility
- Improving water treatment facility performance in real-time
- Risk mitigation
- OPEX (Operational Expenditure) optimisation
- Recycling polluted industrial water with innovative technology with a high separation level

According to Wabag, digitisation and artificial intelligence ensure operational excellence [29]. Digitalisation and digital interventions involve CAPEX (Capital expenditure) and OPEX (Operational expenditure) reduction in plant operations to attain the following:

- Lesser machinery breakdown
- Optimum energy usage
- Reduced chemical consumption
- Fewer water losses
- Less contamination of water bodies
- Earliest possible warning

According to Wipro, Smart utility is built on the right technology: A predictive system and insights tool built explicitly for wastewater supply, distribution and management [30]. Wipro utilises several technologies to forge a path into real-time insights to achieve the following:

- Efficient sludge disposal
- Control of adequate wastewater network

- Optimal management of wastewater networks
- Reducing chemical usage and treatment costs
- Maintaining toxic chemicals-free effluent water
- Maintaining operational efficiency of the water treatment plant
- Avoidance of air pollution
- Maintaining service quality
- Ensuring continuity of supply
- Ensuring proper water quality

Yokogawa [31] ensures cutting-edge artificial solutions to have a decisive market advantage and to achieve the following:

- Reliable real-time and automated data
- Predict future situations
- Improve data models
- Optimising operational efficiency
- Reducing costs and waste
- Optimise resource management
- Optimising infrastructure

According to Yorkshire Water, UK's most extensive intelligent water network pilot could revolutionise service in Yorkshire [32]. Yorkshire Water delivers innovative solutions to overcome challenges to achieve the following:

- Innovative solutions to reduce leakage
- Provide the highest quality water
- Reduce the impact of sewer flooding
- Operational decision-making

4.2.3 Research Methodology

Researchers used literature review as a method of study and compared it through descriptive.

Research study: Researchers compiled multiple case studies and empirical papers to study and examine the impact of artificial intelligence and emotional intelligence in autonomous operation and MSME entrepreneurs' performance in the waste management industry.

- Researchers studied literature from original equipment manufacturers' case studies and concentrated mainly on waste management industries worldwide.
- Furthermore, a well-structured questionnaire and interview were derived to collect the responses from 23 respondents from MSME entrepreneurs.
- Researchers used convenient sampling to collect the data from respondents.
- The statistical tool used in this study is JAMOVI and analysed the data through descriptive statistics, reliability analysis and correlation, and multiple regressions. This chapter's primary goal is to classify autonomous operations using artificial intelligence, emotional intelligence and cloud computing and MSME entrepreneurs' performance in the waste management industry. Figure 4.2 represents the proposed model for the impact of artificial intelligence and emotional intelligence in autonomous operation through digital twin technology using artificial intelligence, machine learning and cloud computing and MSME entrepreneurs' performance in the waste management industry.

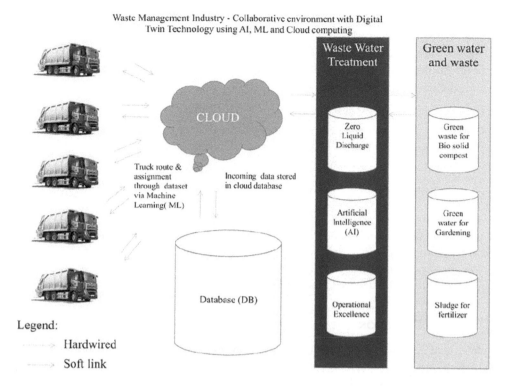

FIGURE 4.2 Model for waste management industry – collaborative environment with digital. Twin technology uses artificial intelligence, machine learning, and cloud computing for waste treatment and disposal.

4.2.4 MSME Entrepreneur's Emotional Intelligence and Their Performance

The waste management industry and statutory bodies bring an effective and efficient system for waste management. MSME entrepreneur brings new technologies to fill the gaps in the point of origin and provide the actions required to realise zero liquid discharge (ZLD) and zero waste landfills from the viewpoint of ecological, health and societal [2]. Entrepreneur's performance is achieved based on understanding existing behavioural approaches through emotions and emotional intelligence on liquid waste and solid waste disposal and mitigating with available technologies through recycling behaviour techniques.

4.3 DISCUSSION

4.3.1 Literature Review Discussion

Researchers studied through literature review and analysed the data through JOMOVI, and researchers discussed it here in two parts. The first part is the result of the literature review study highlighting that artificial intelligence and emotional intelligence in autonomous operation in the waste management industry are raising and improving the technologies based on MSME entrepreneurs' performance. The researchers outline the segregation of the digital transformation level of integration DM (Digital model), DS (Digital Shadow) and DT (Digital Twin) [33] based on categorical literature results from Original Equipment Manufacturers (OEMs) and the novelty of the findings from the study is given in Table 4.1.

Researchers outline the results from original equipment manufacturers, contractors and operating companies that artificial intelligence and emotional intelligence in autonomous operation in business transformation transformed in each phase of the cycle in the waste management industry.

TABLE 4.1

Shows Categorical Literature Review of Digital Transformation From Manual, Semi-Automation, and Digital Twin (Artificial Intelligence, Machine Learning, Cloud Computing)

Type	Digital Model	Digital Shadow	Digital Twin
Concept	—	2	—
Review	—	6	6
Study	—	1	1
Case Study	—	4	3

The waste management industry cycle starts with a waste management plant, waste segregation and bin level monitoring, waste collection, vehicle routing, and waste treatment and disposal. It provides a green revolution through the entrepreneur's emotional intelligence with zero liquid discharge and minimum solid disposal (Table 4.2).

4.3.2 Analysis Discussion

Researchers analysed the data through JAMOVI, and variables used for this analysis are waste management plan (WMP), waste segregation and bin level monitoring (WSB), waste collection (WC), vehicle routing (VR), and waste treatment and disposal (WTD).

Researchers received 23 respondents from original equipment manufacturers, consultants, contractors and operating companies through questionnaires and interviews.

Researchers have evaluated all 23 variables through Cronbach's alpha reliability test to see if multiple-choice questions through Likert scale surveys are dependable. The obtained value is 0.831 (refer to Table 4.3), which is more than 0.7, which implies that the scale's internal consistency is good and valid. Hence, the items in the Likert scale are reliable for entrepreneurs to respond to the analysis.

Among 23 entrepreneurs' responses, researchers have observed 21 (91.3%) entrepreneurs' responses from males and 2(8.7%) entrepreneurs' responses from females (refer to the Table 4.4).

Digital transformation technologies for autonomous operation providers, majorly from the USA, France, India, the UK, Denmark, and a few other countries waste management industry and autonomous operation system providers, were reviewed and analysed country-wise. Based on the latest digital twin technologies, original equipment manufacturers developed and updated their systems for fit for autonomous operation. Consultants and contractors utilised OEM technologies to achieve a green revolution for operating companies. Based on the study, country-wise autonomous system providers are given in the table, and a graphical representation is provided in Table 4.5 and Figure 4.3.

Among 23 entrepreneurs' responses from the USA, France, India and across the world, researchers have observed that 26.1% of MSME entrepreneurs from the USA, 17.4% of entrepreneurs from France, 8.7% from India and a balance from across the world participated in this study (refer to Table 4.5 and Figure 4.3).

The correlation coefficient between waste treatment and disposal and waste segregation and bin monitoring is 0.901, which indicates ($0.901^2 = 0.81$) 81.0% positive relationships between WTD and WSB, and it is significant at a 1% level (Table 4.6).

The correlation coefficient between waste treatment and disposal and waste collection is 0.825, which indicates ($0.825^2 = 0.68$) 68.0% positive relationships between WTD and WC, which is significant at a 1% level (Table 4.6).

TABLE 4.2

Shows a Categorical Literature Review of Digital Transformation, Technology, and Entrepreneur's Emotional Intelligence and Provides Minimum Solid Disposal and Zero Liquid Discharge in the Waste Management Industry

Reference Firm	Country	Type	Level of Integration	Focused Area	Technology	MSME Entrepreneur's Emotional Intelligence
Accenture [10]	Ireland	Review	DT	WMP, WSB, VR, WTD	AI, ML Cloud capabilities, Web services	CM, PE
Advantech [11]	Taiwan	Case Study	DS	WMP, WSB, VR, WTD	Automated monitoring system, Open platform communication unified architecture (OPC UA)	CM, EM, PE
AECOM [12]	USA	Review	DS	WMP, WSB, WSB VR, WTD	AI, ML, IoT	EN, CM, PE
ADNOC [13]	UAE	Concept	DS	WMP, WSB, WSB VR, WTD	AI modelling and supercomputing	EN, PE
Aqua Tech [14]	USA	Case Study	DS	WMP, WSB, VR, WTD	AI, ML	EM, TR
Atos [15]	France	Review	DT	WMP, WSB, VR, WTD	IoT platform, data analytics and visualisations.	EN, EM, TR
Autodesk [16]	USA	Case Study	DT	WMP, WSB, VR, WTD	AI, ML and Cloud	EM, TR, PE
AVEVA [17]	UK	Case Study	DT	WMP, WSB, VR, WTD	AI, ML and cloud computing	EN, CM, PE, EM
Circle H₂O [18]	USA	Review	DS	WMP, WSB, WSB VR, WTD	AI, ML	PE, EM
Danfoss [19]	Denmark	Review	DS	WMP, WSB, WSB VR, WTD	AI	EM, PE
Envirosuite Water Operations [20]	Australia	Review	DS	WMP, WSB, WSB VR, WTD	AI Modelling technology and Cloud	CM, EM, PE
GE Digital [21]	USA	Review	DT	WMP, WSB, WSB VR, WTD	AI, ML and cloud computing	PE, TR, EM
Grundfos [22]	Denmark	Review	DS	WMP, WSB, WSB VR, WTD	Artificial Intelligence (AI) and Cloud technology	EM, PE
KDX [23]	Singapore	Review	DS	WMP, WSB, WSB VR, WTD	AI, cloud-based software	EN, EM, CO

(Continued)

TABLE 4.2 (*Continued*)

Shows a Categorical Literature Review of Digital Transformation, Technology, and Entrepreneur's Emotional Intelligence and Provides Minimum Solid Disposal and Zero Liquid Discharge in the Waste Management Industry

Reference Firm	Country	Type	Level of Integration	Focused Area	Technology	MSME Entrepreneur's Emotional Intelligence
Rockwell Automation [24]	USA	Review	DT	WMP, WSB, VR, WTD	AI, Cyber security, cloud computing	MO, EM, PE
Schneider Electric [25]	France	Review	DT	WMP, WSB, VR, WTD	AI, ML and deep learning	EN, MO, EM
Siemens [26]	Germany	Review	DT	WMP, WSB, VR, WTD	AI, IoT	EM, TR, PE
Suez [27]	France	Case Study	DS	WMP, WSB, WSB VR, WTD	AI	EM, TR, EN, CO
Veolia [28]	France	Case Study	DS	WMP, WSB, WSB VR, WTD	AI, cyber security, cloud computing	EM, TR, EN, CO
Wabag [29]	India	Concept	DS	WMP, WSB, WSB VR, WTD	AI, network, cloud computing	EM, EN, CO
Wipro [30]	India	Study	DT	WMP, WSB, VR, WTD	AI, ML	EM, TR, EN
Yokogawa [31]	Japan	Case Study	DT	WMP, WSB, VR, WTD	AI, cyber security, cloud computing	EM, TR
Yorkshire Water [32]	UK	Study	DS	WMP, WSB, VR, WTD	AI, cloud and data analytics	EM, TR

A. Level of Integration:

DM, Digital Model; DS, Digital Shadow; DT, Digital Twin.

B. Technology:

AI, Artificial Intelligence; ML, Machine Learning; IoT, Internet of Things.

C. Emotional Intelligence:

EM, Empathy; TR, Trust; EN-Enthusiasm (Passion to work)-Self-motivation; CO, Cognitive (Process of understanding)-Self-awareness; CM, Compromise; PE, Positive emotions.

TABLE 4.3

Reliability Scalability Test

Scale Reliability Statistics

	Cronbach's α
Waste treatment and disposal	0.831

TABLE 4.4

Among 23 Entrepreneurs' Responses, 21 (91.3%) Entrepreneurs Responded Male and 2(8.7%) Entrepreneurs Responded Female

Frequencies of Gender

Gender	Counts	% of Total	Cumulative %
Male	21	91.3	91.3
Female	2	8.7	100.0

TABLE 4.5

Country-Wise Entrepreneurs Response

Frequencies of Country

Country	Counts	% of Total	Cumulative %
India	2	8.7	8.7
UAE	1	4.3	13.0
USA	6	26.1	39.1
UK	2	8.7	47.8
France	4	17.4	65.2
Germany	1	4.3	69.6
Japan	1	4.3	73.9
Singapore	1	4.3	78.3
Ireland	1	4.3	82.6
Taiwan	1	4.3	87.0
Denmark	2	8.7	95.7
Australia	1	4.3	100.0

Independent Variable: Waste Management Plan, Waste Collection, Waste Segregation Bin Monitoring and Vehicle Routing

Dependent Variable: Waste Treatment and Disposal

Multiple R value $= 0.912$

R^2 value $= 0.832$

We have achieved multiple correlation coefficients (R) with 0.912, which is quite a solid and positive relationship between actual and predicted values. Hence, entrepreneurs' performance is quite solid and optimistic based on the impact of emotional intelligence and artificial intelligence in autonomous operations.

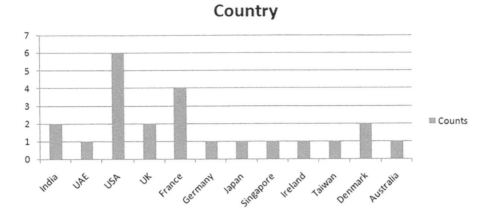

FIGURE 4.3   Country-wise entrepreneur's response.

TABLE 4.6
Correlation Matrix

		Waste Management Plan	Waste Collection	Waste Sorting and Bin Monitoring	Vehicle Routing	Waste Treatment and Disposal
Waste Management Plan	Pearson's r	—				
	df	—				
	p-value	—				
Waste Collection	Pearson's r	0.028	—			
	df	21	—			
	p-value	0.900	—			
Waste Sorting and Bin Monitoring	Pearson's r	0.062	0.916	—		
	df	21	21	—		
	p-value	0.778	<0.001	—		
Vehicle Routing	Pearson's r	0.062	0.916	1.000	—	
	df	21	21	21	—	
	p-value	0.778	<0.001	<0.001	—	
Waste Treatment and Disposal	Pearson's r	0.087	0.825	0.901	0.901	—
	df	21	21	21	21	—
	p-value	0.693	<0.001	<0.001	<0.001	—

TABLE 4.7
Model Fit Measures

Model	R	R^2
Waste Treatment and Disposal	0.912	0.832

We discovered significant regression values and found that the model fits exceptionally well. The Coefficient of Determination R^2 value is 0.832, i.e., the calculated SRP reveals 83.2% of the variation in business sustainability (Table 4.7).

4.4 OUTLOOK AND CONCLUSIONS

Researchers analysed the current scenario of the waste management industry through a literature review, surveys, and questionnaires. The extensive literature review from the original equipment manufacturers, contractors, consultants and operating companies shows that artificial intelligence and emotional intelligence in autonomous operations are either still in the conceptual stage for most of the OEMs or have an incomplete product range for the compliance of cycle requirements in a collaborative environment without manual interventions.

Researchers analysed the data through JAMOVI, and correlation results show positive relationships between waste treatment and disposal, waste management plan that needs to be improved, and autonomous operation in waste collection and vehicle routing need to be improved. Reliability analysis shows that the value is good. Multiple regression results show that the entrepreneurs' performance is quite solid and optimistic based on the impact of artificial intelligence and emotional intelligence in autonomous operation and needs to be attained without manual interventions.

This chapter proposed a model to review and to fulfil the client requirements in the waste management industry for the implementation of autonomous operation. The complete cycle was not envisaged and analysed before. Autonomous operations can be developed, updated, upgraded and implemented using the latest digital twin technologies to meet client requirements. Entrepreneurs' emotional intelligence enables them to promote digital twin technologies and achieve good business performance in the waste management industry.

4.5 RECOMMENDATIONS, LIMITATIONS AND FUTURE RESEARCH

Autonomous operations must be developed, updated, implemented and fulfilled with the latest technologies to meet the cycle in a collaborative environment to achieve business targets and entrepreneur's performance. Entrepreneurs must focus on the gaps in autonomous operation to fulfil the client requirements to comply in a collaborative environment.

Government and MSMEs must update their policies and support entrepreneurs for their autonomous operations to meet global standards and fill the gaps in existing autonomous operations.

REFERENCES

1. Amoako, G., Omari, P., Kumi, D. K., Agbemabiase, G. C., and Asamoah, G. (2021). Conceptual framework-artificial intelligence and better entrepreneurial decision-making: The influence of customer preference, industry benchmark, and employee involvement in an emerging market. *Journal of Risk and Financial Management*, 14(12), 604. doi: 10.3390/jrfm14120604.
2. Raghu, S. J. and Rodrigues, L. L. R. (2020). Behavioural aspects of solid waste management: A systematic review. *Journal of the Air & Waste Management Association*, 70(12), 1268–1302. doi: 10.1080/10962247.2020.1823524.
3. Shreyas Madhav, A. V., Rajaraman, R., Harini, S., and Kiliroor, C. C. (2021). Application of artificial intelligence to enhance the collection of E-waste: A potential solution for household WEEE collection and segregation in India. *Waste Management & Research*, 40(7), 1047–1053. doi: 10.1177/0734242X211052846.
4. Chalmers, D., MacKenzie, N. G., and Carter, S. (2021). Artificial intelligence and entrepreneurship: Implications for venture creation in the fourth industrial revolution. *Entrepreneurship Theory and Practice*, 45(5), 1028–1053. doi: 10.1177/1042258720934581.
5. Namoun, A., Tufail, A., Khan, M. Y., Alrehaili, A., Syed, T. A., and BenRhouma, O. (2022). Solid waste generation and disposal using machine learning approaches: A survey of solutions and challenges. *Sustainability*, 14(20), 13578. doi: 10.3390/su142013578.
6. Nguyen, T., and Watanabe, T. (2020). Autonomous motivation for the successful implementation of waste management policy: An examination using an adapted institutional analysis and development framework in Thua Thien Hue, Vietnam. *Sustainability*, 12(7), 2724. doi: 10.3390/su12072724.
7. Pyo, J.-W., Bae, S.-H., Joo, S.-H., Lee, M.-K., Ghosh, A., and Kuc, T.-Y. (2022). Development of an autonomous driving vehicle for garbage collection in residential areas. *Sensors*, 22, 9094. doi: 10.3390/s22239094.

8. Zhang, S., Jin, Y., Chen, W., Wang, J., Wang, Y., and Ren, H. (2023). Artificial intelligence in wastewater treatment: A data-driven analysis of status and trends. *Chemosphere*, 336, 139163. doi: 10.1016/j.chemosphere.2023.139163.

9. Andeobu, L., Wibowo, S., and Grandhi, S. (2022). Artificial intelligence applications for sustainable solid waste management practices in Australia: A systematic review. *Science of the Total Environment*, 834, 155389. doi: 10.1016/j.scitotenv.2022.155389.

10. Accenture (2022). Accenture and Amazon Web Services, Inc. (AWS) Work to help companies advance journey to water neutrality through first-of-its-kind open platform.

11. Advantech (2021). An open platform communications unified architecture solution for wastewater treatment monitoring systems.

12. AECOM (2023). A more efficient future for the most precious of substances. Keep it flowing, safe, viable, and sustainable: The water industry, with its responsibility for the one thing that supports all life, bears the heaviest digital business transformation burden of all.

13. ADNOC (2023). ADNOC and Group 42 (G42) support ADNOC's continued drive to leverage AI to optimise performance and grow the UAE's innovation ecosystem.

14. Aqua Tech (2018). UK Water utility operating network section with Artificial Intelligence. Digital solutions and their impact on human workforces.

15. Atos (2023). Scottish Water transforms wastewater network management. IoT sensors and real-time data enhance customer experience and protect the environment.

16. Autodesk (2023). Intelligence control of wastewater using AI. Dynamic, real-time data analysis provides actionable insights for immediate response to process changes.

17. AVEVA (2023). Beyond artificial intelligence: AI and the digital twin. Optimise with AI software that puts AI technology and human insight to work.

18. Circle H$_2$O (2023). Delivering actionable insights artificial intelligence-enabled insights to serve as a guide to efficiently and cost-effectively operate the plant.

19. Danfoss (2023). Danfoss drives in the water and wastewater industry. Intelligence embedded in the AQUA drive automatically defines baseline parameters for wastewater applications at all speeds and real-life operating cycles.

20. Envirosuite Water Operations (2023). EVS water plant optimizer is an innovative cloud-based solution that combines artificial intelligence and modelling technology to predict and avoid water quality incidents while identifying process improvements and cost savings for the facility.

21. GE Digital (2023). Water and wastewater: Challenges for water utilities continue to mount while pressure to provide clean, uninterrupted Water flows never abate. Digitalisation helps optimise operations.

22. Grundfos (2023). Avoid unplanned operational downtime with AI and Cloud technology.

23. KDX 2023). Intelligence water management solutions: Cloud-based software combines with leading data analytics tools to deliver real-time insights for safe and effective operations.

24. Rockwell Automation (2023). Rockwell Automation delivers AI for industry-leading wastewater trials by Severn Trent and partners.

25. Schneider Electric (2023). AI optimises operations, helping to achieve energy transparency and to consume less energy.

26. Siemens (2021). Artificial intelligence and the internet of things reduce wastewater network blockages and pollution.

27. Suez (2023). Using artificial intelligence to improve Energy-from-Waste plant performance.

28. Veolia (2020). Digital innovation at the heart of the water flocculation process. Artificial intelligence is now being used to reach the right balance between cost and compliance

29. Wabag (2023). Digitisation and artificial intelligence ensure operational excellence.

30. Wipro (2023). The intelligent utility is built on the right technology. A predictive system and insights tool built explicitly for water utilities will allow utilities to stay one turn ahead of issues at each clean and Wastewater supply, distribution and management stage.

31. Yokogawa (2023). Artificial intelligence - making technology intelligent.

32. Yorkshire Water (2020). UK's most extensive intelligent water network pilot could revolutionise service in Yorkshire.

33. Kritzinger, W., Karner, M., Traar, G., Henjes, J., and Sihn, W. (2018). Digital Twin in manufacturing: A categorical literature review and classification. *IFAC-PapersOnLine*, 51(11), 1016–1022. doi: 10.1016/j.ifacol.2018.08.474.

5 Artificial Intelligence Governance and Comprehensibility in Renewable Energy Systems

Nandha Gopal J., S. Muthukaruppasamy, Rajagopal V., G. Arun Sampaul Thomas, and Parimalarsundar E.

5.1 INTRODUCTION

Energy has played a pivotal role in shaping global geopolitics and revolutionizing our way of life throughout the past century [1,2]. Numerous historical and ongoing conflicts across the world have been driven by the pursuit of power resources like oil, natural gas, and battery minerals. The availability of energy has been instrumental in facilitating technological advancements and the proliferation of computing power, leading to the emergence of intelligent societies. However, traditional electrical power grids have been plagued by issues of operational unreliability, instability, inflexibility, and inefficiency. The complex nature of these grids, spanning large regional and national networks, has posed significant challenges in monitoring and maintaining the electrical systems and extensive distribution lines. Consequently, the shortcomings in power grid management have resulted in severe electrical system failures, the loss of human lives, and substantial economic damages.

The energy industry is going through a significant conversion through the adoption of smart grids and other emerging technologies, promoting the utilization of renewable energy sources, decentralization, and decarbonization. In this discussion, a smart energy system is employed to encompass advancements such as electrical power systems and smart grids and include associated business advancements. These innovations offer various favourable prospects, including the widespread accessibility of renewable energy sources like solar, wind, hydro, and others, for both commercial and residential use. The establishment of microgrids [2], micro grids [3], community grids [4,5], and super grids [6] has paved the way for energy self-sufficiency and facilitated energy trading among individuals, companies, and nations, among many other potential benefits.

Smart energy systems generate vast amounts of data, presenting a complex landscape. AI holds immense potential for driving innovation, optimizing processes, enhancing productivity, and delivering various benefits across sectors, including smart societies [7], healthcare [8], education, and transportation [9]. The energy sector is no exception [10]. Using AI, smart energy systems handle the immense and intricate data involved and enable intelligent and prompt decision-making. However, AI algorithms are often considered black boxes [11] and require interpretability and explainability [12] to justify decisions made by AI to different stakeholders, including regulatory and legal entities. It is critical to remember that AI algorithms are prone to imperfections and inaccuracies. These algorithms are created by human programmers and designers using incomplete data, thereby making them susceptible to inheriting biases and prejudices present within the data.

The unregulated advancement of AI has primarily focused on maximizing efficiency, economic objectives, and other goals, often neglecting human principles and objectives. According to the

National Institute of Standards and Technology (NIST), Explainable AI (XAI) systems adhere to four principles [13]:

1. **Explanation:** The system supports the outputs and/or processes with supporting data or logic.
2. **Meaningful:** The system offers clear explanations that the intended users can easily understand.
3. **Explanation Reliability:** The justifications for producing the results and/or the system's underlying operations are appropriately reflected in the explanations.
4. **Knowledge Limitations:** The system only works as intended and with a high enough level of trust in the results.

To ensure trust in AI systems, several essential characteristics, including explainability, interpretability, accuracy, privacy, reliability, robustness, safety, security, transparency, fairness, and accountability need to be considered [14]. Additionally, responsibility can be regarded as another significant aspect of establishing trust in AI systems [15].

The limited explainability and governance of AI have had a detrimental impact on stakeholders' trust in AI systems, leading to a slow adoption of AI within the energy sector. Furthermore, the energy systems' design and operational landscape have become increasingly complex, involving numerous parameters and stakeholders. The resulting risks have given the importance of social, political, national, and environmental elements associated with these energy-related issues.

This study provides a thorough analysis of AI governance and explainability in the context of smart energy systems. We used a focused query to collect 3,500 pertinent papers from the Scopus database for this review. We also found additional characteristics associated with smart energy systems with AI governance and put them in groups of four main macro-parameters: technology, design and development, operations, AI behaviour, and governance. This study provides insights into the field of research and highlights temporal progressions in this topic through a thorough examination of more than 150 papers.

The methodology employed for parameter discovery or theme identification in this study is founded on "deep journalism," a data-driven approach that utilizes deep learning and, using the aid of big data analytics, automatically finds and analyses diverse and comprehensive information from multiple perspectives. This approach aims to enhance decision-making processes and facilitate the development of effective governance tools. The concept of deep journalism has been previously introduced and applied to various sectors [16].

This contribution shows how AI explainability research in the energy systems domain is mostly focused on a small set of AI attributes like fairness, interpretability, explainability, and trustworthiness, as well as specific energy system issues like analysis of stability and dependability, energy forecasting, and the flexibility of the power system. By delving into AI regulation in the energy industry, this study contributes to existing knowledge and is expected to provide valuable insights for governments, industries, scholars, energy consumers, and other participants. It will make it easier to comprehend how AI is currently used in the energy sector, allowing for better energy system design, operation, and risk management.

Figure 5.1 illustrates the functionality of an Explainable AI model specifically designed for renewable energy systems. Explainable AI encompasses a range of tools and frameworks that are instrumental in facilitating the comprehension and interpretation of machine learning predictions.

Artificial intelligence (AI) is increasingly being used in applications involving renewable energy sources (incorporating energy sources from the wind, ocean, solar, geothermal, hydro, hydrogen, and bioenergy) as a result of its quick calculation, usability, and excellent recent outcomes. The eXplainable Artificial Intelligence (XAI) approach aids in the development of procedures, practices, and tactics that offer justifications for the suggestions, forecasts, and judgements of sophisticated machine learning (ML) systems. The "black box" of these models, or the background of

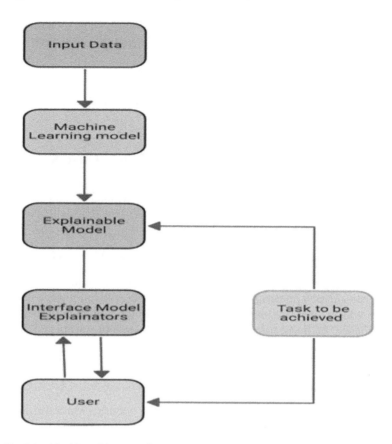

FIGURE 5.1 Explainable AI architecture for renewable energy systems.

these techniques, is what makes XAI stand as a means of figuring out how AI works systems make judgements. XAI is a leader in renewable energy (RE) solutions a fresh strategy and answers for boosting confidence in the judgements produced by machine learning (ML) algorithms, delivering more effective, assured, and affordable systems with explainability and coming up with clever answers to issues.

Since the massive quantity of data that energy firms must manage, keep, safeguard, or obtain values from in order to provide better service, quality, and product, there are several issues current issues with energy production, transmission, and distribution, such as the price, safety, security, efficiency, and uneven carbon footprint, etc. AI is being used to improve security, regulate demand, control system or stability, increase energy efficiency, decrease energy consumption and costs, and identify natural gas leaks. Due to the popularity of ML and deep learning (DL) algorithms in the recent past, this has led to an improvement in the application of AI techniques.

According to a research by Precedence Reserve, the ecosystem of smart grids is expected to be valued around $17 trillion by 2030, and they further enhance or support energy system applications. The demand for power in settlements is anticipated to rise, and one of the components allowing the global AI is the RE market industry to be equally greater, and is anticipated to be worth roughly $80 billion in 2030. AI will become more efficient in the global RE industry as the demand for smart energy grids increases. This increase has been facilitated by ML and deep learning (DL) algorithms.

The digitalization of energy [3] is another area where AI is required in the RE sector. Power generation, transmission, and distribution have all improved in efficiency and sustainability as a result of the development of smart technologies. At this point, big data and AI are critical because these technologies are necessary for making intelligent decisions when maximizing all services based on data analytics. "Smart grids" powered by data or AI can contribute to by increasing the use of renewable energy sources like wind and solar electricity, and supply management.

5.2 BACKGROUNDS

The approach and software tool design used for the automated parameter discovery procedure are briefly summarized in this section.

5.2.1 ENHANCING TRANSPARENCY IN ENERGY AND POWER SYSTEMS USING RANDOM FORESTS

Among machine learning models, Random Forests is used in groups based on decision trees. It offers the advantage of an inherent decision system, allowing it to handle diverse data constraints without the need for dimensionality reduction.

5.2.2 BOOSTING TRANSPARENCY IN ENERGY AND POWER SYSTEMS USING XGBOOST

Extreme Gradient Boosting (XGBoost) is a powerful supervised learning algorithm that utilizes ensemble trees. It has gained popularity in various fields for classification projects [20]. Notably, XGBoost has been widely employed in winning submissions for Kaggle competitions. Due to its exceptional performance, XGBoost has created numerous research prospects and opportunities for further exploration.

5.2.3 ENHANCING TRANSPARENCY IN ENERGY AND POWER SYSTEMS WITH LIGHTGBM

LGBM (Light GBM) employs continuous feature histogram binning, which further enhances its speed compared to traditional gradient boosting algorithms. The process of binning numeric values reduces the number of split points required in decision trees, eliminating the need for computationally intensive sorting methods. Unlike other algorithms, LGBM builds trees level by level, leaf by leaf. It gives the leaf containing the largest delta loss growth priority, allowing leaf-wise computations to reduce more loss compared to level-wise calculations. This approach contributes to the overall efficiency and effectiveness of the LGBM algorithm.

5.2.4 INTERPRETING MACHINE LEARNING MODELS IN ENERGY AND POWER SYSTEMS USING SHAP

SHAP (SHapley Additive exPlanations) is a visualization tool designed to enhance the interpretability of AI/ML models by providing more comprehensible insights. It enables users to understand the contributions of each variable to a model's predictions. SHAP integrates various techniques, including lime, SHAPley sample values, Deep Lift, Quantitative Input Influence (QII), among others. One crucial aspect of the SHAP tool is the utilization of SHAPley values, which enables it to establish a connection between optimal credit allocation and local explanations. The accompanying figure illustrates the pipeline of the post-hoc explainable tool SHAP (Figure 5.2).

5.2.5 ENHANCING TRANSPARENCY IN RENEWABLE ENERGY TRANSFORMATION USING EXPLAINABLE AI

Figure 5.3 serves as an example demonstrating the programme of Explainable AI techniques in the context of transforming renewable energy. XAI encompasses a range of strategies and guiding principles that Machine Learning (ML) models to be clarified and comprehended. By leveraging XAI, ML techniques can be effectively utilized for controlling and managing energy resources derived

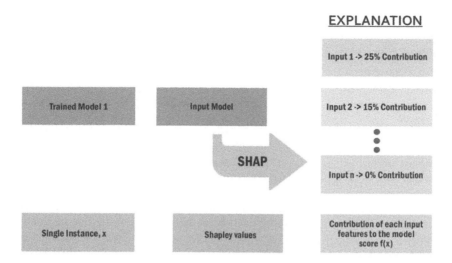

FIGURE 5.2 SHAP-based model interpretation for renewable energy systems.

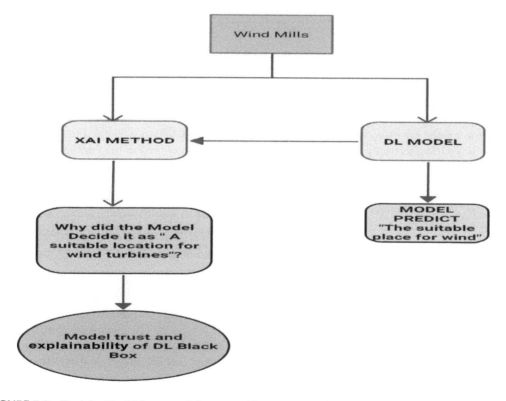

FIGURE 5.3 Explainable AI framework for renewable energy transformation.

from renewable energy applications. In many cases, Deep Learning (DL) and ML models are considered as "black boxes" due to their opaque internal workings. XAI aims to address this limitation by providing transparency to domain experts, enabling them to better understand and evaluate the outcomes of XAI techniques. However, there is a need to further enhance the explainability of DL and ML models. The assessment, evaluation, and explanation of XAI techniques often require the involvement of domain experts and must be tailored to the specific problem at hand.

TABLE 5.1

Classifications of XAI and AI Research in Renewable Energy (RE) Systems

S. No	Objective	Theme	Model
1	AI support for predictive analysis maintenance in RE systems	Developed a deep learning model using an endoscopic picture dataset with labels	Convolutional Neural Network
2	AI hybrid approach for RE	Improved energy management in a smart grid using hybrid AI for optimal management of RECs	Model Predictive Control (MPC) Algorithm
3	Geothermal AI for geothermal exploration	Utilizing Remote Sensing (RS), ML, and AI to address challenges in geothermal exploration	Machine Learning (ML)
4	XAI-driven strategy to achieve net-zero carbon	Remote sensing was used to get data on offshore wind speed for offshore wind generation	Variational Autoencoder (VAE) and t-SNE
5	Explainable Fault Detection Systems	eXplainable Fault Detection Systems (XFDS) were created to identify potential flaws in solar panel systems	Model for three diodes based on irradiance (IB3DM)
6	Electrical Load Forecasting with XAI Tool	Developed a data-driven strategy by bringing together seasoned power market and system professionals	LSTM and SHAP are two types of short-term memory

Explainable AI (XAI) has found applications in the realm of solar and wind power systems, contributing to the enhancement of energy management and efficiency. This area of research has been rapidly expanding, focusing on the transparent visualization of XAI alternative energy system solutions. Table 5.1 provides a grouped compilation of various studies that have explored AI and XAI methodologies within this area.

Using a search consisting of precise keywords, the Scopus database is queried to find the data for this study. Grid, electricity, energy, power system, artificial intelligence, machine learning, deep learning, interpretability, accountability, ethics, trustworthiness, and justice are some of the keywords utilized in the search.

The Key Dimensions/Aspects of AI and XAI Research in Renewable Energy Systems are as follows.

5.2.6 Ethical and Regulatory Considerations in the Implementation and Governance of Artificial Intelligence

This dimension focuses on the administration and control of AI in the energy sector, including the identification of specifications for creating morally upright and reliable programmes [17]. An in-depth explanation of data privacy policies, rules, and issues is also included. This parameter covers a variety of aspects of AI governance and behaviour, including AI accountability and responsibility within shrewd grids [18]. In the context of power-related general-purpose technology, it also examines AI governance and laws [19]. The use of automatic decision-making for gaining entry to basic privileges like telephones and electricity is also examined with the goal of ensuring a transparent and responsible grid management system [20]. Furthermore, the parameter encompasses analysing the ethical ramifications of AI power systems.

5.2.7 Interpretable AI Models for Power Grid Applications

The power grid is becoming more susceptible as a result of the expanding integration of renewable energy sources, the market liberalization for electricity, and the existence of transmission using direct current technologies. The application of advanced AI approaches to stability analysis and control-related issues has shown promise. Transparency issues with black-box models have hampered the practical use of these techniques [21]. Enhancing the grid security assessment model comprehensibility has been the subject of recent research. In this study [22], decision trees are utilized to classify stable or unstable system operating circumstances, with the depth of the tree representing interpretability. A modified optimum classification tree is used to achieve model correctness, and interpretability is traded off. Another work [23] adopts a model-agnostic approach utilizing a Grid Security Condition Classification Gated Recurrent Unit (GRU). In order to enable preventive control actions, a model of comprehensible decision tree is used as a substitute for an explanation-based model. Conception and knowledge extraction approaches are employed in [24], where XG Boost is used to model transient stability status. Evaluation metrics such as rate of false alarms and missing alarms are employed to assess the performance. Evaluation of transient stability is addressed in [25], where a deep belief network is used to model transient stability and a local linear interpreter model is employed for explanation. This work discusses both fidelity and interpretability, ensuring that the model maintains fidelity to particular fault scenarios at the local level. Lastly, in [26], Shapley values along with heat maps are employed as a description of the machine learning model employed to evaluate transient stability.

5.2.8 AI Models with Transparency for the Energy Sector

Machine learning representation plays a crucial role in various applications within the energy sector, influencing operational choices made during planning. Therefore, it is crucial to have explicable XAI models that can inspire end users with trust and confidence [27]. There has been a rising trend in recent years that focuses on employing XAI techniques in renewable energy forecasting. For instance, an XGBoost model is utilized to predict photovoltaic to illustrate this XG Boost model, the author uses the ELI5 Python module, which offers feature importance for ML models. According to ELI5, the authors exclude unnecessary information by using the supplied dataset. However, reducing the size of the source data set results in a decrease in model accuracy. This concept is further expanded upon in [28], where three XAI techniques LIME, SHAP, and ELI5 are employed to analyse the feature importance of a random forest regression model's forecasts for PV power. These techniques offer a more comprehensive understanding of feature importance from different perspectives [29].

Several studies have concentrated on using explainable AI (XAI) methods to ML models for predicting solar irradiation. In this study [30], the authors employ a neural network that is directly explicable to transfer the input to the output through a non-linear model, providing explainability, and a fundamental model of solar radiation predictions. A knowledge-based strategy is used in another study to understand FRLC or fuzzy rule learning by clustering, which is suggested to forecast solar irradiation [31]. In order to interpret the FRLC model predictions, membership function graphs for various attributes are implemented, and linguistic techniques are used [32]. A solar irradiance forecasting model is also explained using feature dependency analysis, SHAP, and permutation feature importance. These XAI techniques contribute to understand the factors influencing solar irradiance predictions.

5.2.9 Interpretable Building Energy Management Using AI Models

The comprehensibility of AI algorithms used to forecast building energy usage, especially those connected to energy efficiency is the main topic of this subject [33]. In this study, SHAP is used to fill the gaps left by black box models in a lengthy forecasting model for predicting the amount of energy used for cooling the building. An explanation of the Q Lattice method, a machine learning model to predict the energy performance of buildings is provided that presents an explainable model for long-term prediction of researching annual building energy performance [34]. In a different study, building energy modelling and energy use are covered, and the visualization is used to explain the model strategy. To explain choices relating to particular areas of the explanation space, localized decision trees are used as surrogate models. In addition, XAI methods have been used in models for short-term forecasting of building energy efficiency based on the performance coefficient, which is connected to the cooling load of the building. In this study, multiple machine learning models are implemented with XAI methodologies, and k-means clustering is employed to predict the high/low status of COP. It should be highlighted that even while certain models have excellent accuracy, they might not perform well in terms of metrics for trust. Similar to this, SHAP values are used in research on DL models to interpret the results of models that forecast the performance of irregular dew point coolers.

5.3 PROPOSED WORK

The Advancements in Technology and Developments are as follows.

5.3.1 Enabling Smart Connectivity and Edge Computing: Integration of IoT and the Edge

In order to efficiently monitor and manage energy systems, this parameter relies on the use of edge computing and the Internet of Things (IoT). It encompasses various aspects related to "IoT and Edge," such as identifying power use attacks to enhance the reliability of vehicular edge devices and ensure the trustworthiness of AI chips. It also involves the use of self-powered learning sensor systems to enable eco-friendly energy sources and promote virtuous power use. Additionally, it emphasizes the improvement of data transfer for portable sensors to enhance the reliability and energy efficiency of the Internet of Things network. Other dimensions encompassed within this parameter include achieving energy efficiency through trustworthy intelligent IoT environments, monitoring Wireless Sensor Networks (WSNs) using cloud computing, leveraging energy systems uses of cloud and edge computing, integrating edge-cloud computing for IoT energy systems and energy monitoring, and integrating IoT devices into the power network.

5.3.2 Decentralized and Trustworthy Data Management: Block Chain Technology

This parameter focuses on the utilization of monitoring and analysis using edge computing and the Internet of Things governing energy systems efficiently. It encompasses various aspects related to "IoT and Edge," such as identifying power use attacks to enhance the reliability of vehicular edge devices and ensure the trustworthiness of AI chips. It also involves the use of self-powered learning sensor systems to enable support for the use of morally sound stable power systems and sustainable energy. Additionally, it places a focus on enhancing mobile sensor data sharing to raise the IoT network's energy efficiency and dependability. Other aspects covered by this parameter include achieving energy efficiency through reliable intelligent IoT environments, leveraging edge-cloud computing, edge computing for IoT energy systems, and cloud and edge computing for energy monitoring in applications for energy systems are all examples of how these technologies are being used.

5.3.3 Smart Sensing and Networked Systems

This parameter focuses on the adoption of reliable methods to extend the life, effectiveness, and energy efficiency of sensor networks and Wireless Sensor Networks in shrewd grids. It includes different sizes of "Sensor Networks," the offloading of tasks at the edge of smart grids to make them more trustworthy, and improving the use of protocol of Secure Energy-Aware Meta-Heuristic Routing to make IoT-WSN work better. Additionally, it uses dependable Deep Learning techniques to identify black-hole assaults on wireless sensors and increase energy effectiveness. Furthermore, it highlights the use of DL approaches to enhance in order to maximize energy efficiency, Cognitive Radio Sensor Networks use temperature-aware, trustworthy routing and energy usage equity between the cluster members.

The Efficient Operations and Managements are as follows.

5.3.4 MANAGEMENT AND OPTIMIZATION OF ENERGY MARKETS

The identification and management of power demand levels in energy markets are the main objectives of this parameter. It includes several aspects of "Energy Markets and Management," such as the application of the Intelligent Machine Learning approach for decentralized optimal power flow management. With a focus on the dependability, interpretability, and security of power distribution systems, it also entails the construction of a clear Deep Reinforcement Learning strategy for the extension of transmission networks in wind energy systems. It also emphasizes the best for connected energy systems in co-trading market, multi-agent energy management, with the goal of fostering ethical trade and protecting individual privacy. The management of energy pipeline infrastructure, as well as the use of IML and cooperative game theory, analyse market regression and are also included in the parameter, specifically in the context of energy forecasting.

5.3.5 AN ACCURATE FORECAST OF ENERGY DEMAND

This parameter is concerned with methods for analysing data to forecast energy usage and related service costs. It includes several aspects of "Energy Demand Forecasting," such as the use of Explainable AI techniques to evaluate power system stability. One illustration is the employment of a recurrent neural network as an interpretable way to forecast stochastic load in power networks and estimate short-term electric demand. In order to increase the precision of energy consumption forecasting on a short-term basis using Intelligent Machine Learning models, the parameter also includes the use of temporary energy demand forecasting employing a two-stage interpretable model in power management. The creation of multi-step interpretable probabilistic models, short-term energy demand forecasting, load forecasting, and the use of various machine learning models all contribute to the forecasting of energy.

5.3.6 ENHANCING PHOTOVOLTAIC SYSTEMS

Solar energy predictions are the main emphasis of this parameter and its role in improving the management of power generation, as well as proposing techniques that are reliable and clear. It covers a wide span of dimensions connected to "Solar Energy Systems," including how well solar energy forecasts can be interpreted. This involves developing models that provide insights into the temporal dynamics of photovoltaic (PV) power generation, ensuring interpretability and trustworthiness in the worldwide solar radiation forecast, and estimating energy output and carbon dioxide (CO_2) emissions. Furthermore, the parameter explores the utilization of hybrid approaches that combine Internet of Things technologies with machine learning methods for solar radiation prediction and the forecast of solar irradiance. These efforts aim to enhance the accuracy and reliability of solar energy systems and improve power generation through solar energy sources.

5.3.7 ENSURING GRID STABILITY AND DEPENDABILITY

In order to assure supply security and system integrity, this parameter concentrates on expanding transparency in decision-making processes while also using trustworthy evaluation models to improve energy system operations. It includes aspects of "Grid Reliability and Stability Management," such as the examination of risks connected to managing an official electrical grid to assist sensible management and also decision-making procedures. Making use of machine learning techniques is also being investigated as a way to enhance the effectiveness of nuclear power facilities. The parameter also covers the significance of using interpretable solutions in the management of grid stability and reliability. This entails creating data integration models to predict a power system's frequency response, which enhances the results' interpretability and decision-making procedures. The potential for power system applications of AI is also examined, with a focus on fostering stability and interpretability. Additional areas involve making smart grids more reliable by analysing voltage stability to prevent power outages. It includes evaluating the performance of machine learning algorithms for identifying faults in power lines and assessing the accuracy and clarity of ML techniques for electricity system evaluation. Overall, the objective is to increase the reliability, stability, and transparency of energy systems for efficient and secure operations. The operational Workflow of AI and Renewable Energy Systems is shown in Figure 5.4.

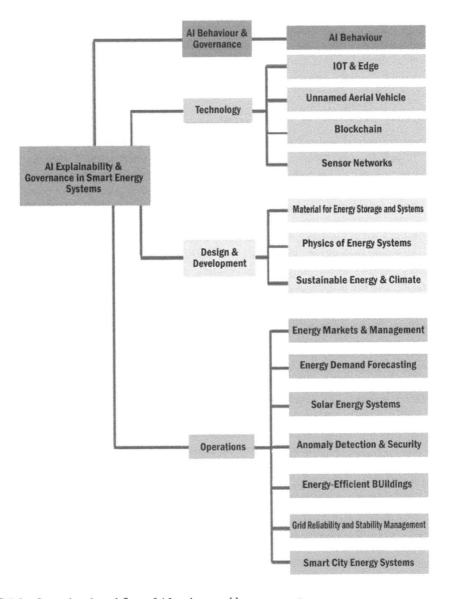

FIGURE 5.4 Operational workflow of AI and renewable energy systems.

5.3.8 Enhancing Energy-Smart Cities

The goal of this parameter is to improve the governance of smart city systems and applications in the area of energy by utilizing AI and IoT technologies. It includes elements linked to "Smart City Energy Systems," such as using cutting-edge AI and blockchain for traffic congestion relief and managing vehicle surveillance through secure and reliable vehicle communications. In the context of smart city governance, AI technologies are being used to enable smart energy trading, increasing the benefits of innovation and quantifiable adequacy of electric cars, smart buildings, and smart grids. The parameter also looks at how AI and Analytics might be included in the smart grid improvements to improve energy management, looking at the most recent approaches in this field. The implementation of AI-based fairness approaches in localizing transit is also covered. Sustainable criteria are used to guarantee inclusive and equitable governance of smart cities. The deployment of DL techniques in smart city environments for various purposes such as power forecasting is also discussed, highlighting the potential of AI to optimize energy management and efficiency. Data-driven insights can contribute to intelligent urban systems, smart city applications for IoT, and transportation. The parameter also highlights the use of cloud analytics that can be understood by AI for effective energy monitoring and management when smart energy meters are installed in smart homes. The overall goal is to enhance the governance, sustainability, the effectiveness of smart city energy systems and applications by utilizing AI and IoT technology.

5.4 DISCUSSIONS

5.4.1 Exploring XAI Opportunities in Power System Applications for Energy

This section contains the potential opportunities of eXplainable Artificial Intelligence regarding energy and power systems. Machine learning applications are currently identified, but they have not yet included XAI. By introducing transparency and interpretability into these applications, their decision-making processes can be better understood and validated. Table 5.2 provides an

TABLE 5.2

Advantages of XAI for Power Systems and Energy Applications

S. No	Approach	Gap Due to Unexplainability	Gain from XAI
1	Management of energy storage	Control laws could be challenging for power professionals to understand	Offer explanations for the control laws that have been learnt
2	Frequency/voltage control	Control laws could be perceived as lacking reliability.	Provide a rationale for control decisions during critical scenarios
3	Energy scheduling	Insufficient clarity is in explaining the reasoning behind scheduling decisions	Present reasons to support your chosen scheduling decisions
4	Non-intrusive load monitoring	Consumers lack trust in machine learning algorithms that lack transparency	Enhancing user confidence by offering explanations for the decisions made
5	Input-output management	Users are worried about employing non-transparent algorithms for crucial tasks	Offer users comprehension and reassurance
6	Detection of line faults	Insufficient understanding of critical measurements	Present essential metrics to enhance system planning
7	Surveillance of cyberspace	Unreasonable choices in critical applications	Elaborate on the factors behind identified anomalies in cybersecurity measurements

overview of the suggested study directions in this area. These directions highlight potential XAI applications in power systems and energy research. It is important to note that these suggestions serve as examples to demonstrate the diverse possibilities for integrating XAI into the field, and they are not an exhaustive list. By embracing XAI, energy and power systems can benefit from improved transparency, accountability, and trust in decision-making processes. XAI techniques can help uncover hidden patterns, biases, and uncertainties in ML models, leading to more robust and reliable solutions. The applications of XAI in this domain have the potential to enhance energy management, grid operations, demand forecasting, renewable energy integration, and other critical aspects of the energy sector. Table 5.2 provides a concise overview of the suggested research directions, emphasizing the broad scope of opportunities for incorporating XAI into utility and energy research.

5.4.2 BEST PRACTICES FOR ENERGY MANAGEMENT AND CONTROL

- As electric grids become more decentralized and less regulated, it's no longer practical to study power systems as if one entity knows and controls everything. Additionally, the complex load statistics and renewable energy source behaviour pose challenges for traditional control methods, reducing their effectiveness.
- To address these issues, researchers have turned to ML techniques for energy management problems. However, one major drawback of ML models is their lack of interpretability. This lack of transparency makes power system engineers hesitant to fully rely on ML-based control methods.
- To overcome this challenge and enhance the reliability of ML models, the application of eXplainable Artificial Intelligence (XAI) becomes crucial. By incorporating XAI techniques, the inner workings and decision-making processes of ML models can be made transparent and interpretable, providing insights into the reasons behind their predictions or actions.
- In the context of energy management, several familiar applications could greatly the addition of the XAI-provided explanations will be beneficial. These applications might include load forecasting, demand response, energy scheduling, renewable energy integration, and fault detection, among others.
- By integrating XAI, power system engineers and operators can gain a better understanding of the ML models' behaviour, identify potential biases or uncertainties, and build trust in their decision-making capabilities.
- The addition of XAI to ML-based energy management applications opens up various future research avenues. These options could include creating new XAI methods designed for power systems, trying out mixed models that use both ML and human knowledge, looking at the trade-offs between understanding and accuracy, and finding ways to test and compare XAI models in the energy field.
- By using XAI in energy management, we can overcome the drawbacks of black-box ML models and open up a path for dependable, clear, and reliable control solutions in today's power systems.

Energy storage control plays a crucial role in managing the incorporation of sporadic renewable energy sources into contemporary electricity networks. As the reliance on renewable energy increases, there is a need for effective control algorithms to optimize the operation of energy storage units. Reinforcement Learning has proven to be a promising approach for energy storage control owing to its capacity for learning optimal policies through interactions with the environment. However, the trustworthiness and reliability of storage systems are paramount. Power engineers require confidence in the control algorithms they employ, and the lack of interpretability in RL models may raise concerns. The decisions made by RL agents are often based on complex interactions and may not have easily understandable justifications. This opacity can hinder the acceptance and adoption of RL techniques in practical power system applications.

To address this challenge, a potential future research direction is to explore the use of Explainable Reinforcement Learning (XRL) for power engineers' understanding and verification of controllers. XRL combines the benefits of RL with interpretability, enabling power engineers to gain insights into the decision-making process of the learned policies. By incorporating XAI techniques into RL, the inner workings of the control algorithm can be made transparent, providing the rationales behind the judgements taken by the RL agent. By developing XRL approaches for energy storage control, power engineers can have a clear understanding of how the RL agent operates and verify its decisions against their domain knowledge. This not only enhances the trustworthiness of the control algorithm but also allows for more effective collaboration between human operators and autonomous RL agents.

Future research in this area might include making XRL algorithms that are specifically designed for controlling energy storage, looking into ways to get useful explanations out of RL models, looking into trade-offs between RL performance and interpretability, and testing the performance and reliability of XRL controllers in real-world energy storage systems. By integrating XAI into RL-based energy storage control, this study can bridge the gap between the powerful learning capabilities of RL and the need for trust, transparency, and understanding in real-world power system applications.

5.4.3 Applications for Energy Consumers Powered by AI

Modern smart grid technology developments have led to the widespread adoption of smart meters by consumers. Consequently, researchers have explored machine learning techniques being used in energy consumer applications that leverage the data collected from these smart meters, aiming to encourage energy-saving practices, flaw-finding improvements, demand projection improvements, and energy incentives, among other benefits. An example is the disaggregation of loads, also known as Non-Intrusive Load Monitoring (NILM). This includes figuring out how much electricity different devices use by analysing data from smart meters. In recent years, deep learning (DL) techniques have been successfully implemented for NILM. Another application is input-output side management, where ML, particularly robust learning, has shown effectiveness in specific tasks like electric vehicle charging optimization.

However, a significant challenge in the practical implementation of these ML-based applications is the lack of user trust and understanding. Consumers may be hesitant to rely on ML models whose decision-making processes they cannot comprehend. This lack of trust can hinder the real-world adoption of these applications. A customer might be reluctant to utilize an ML model, for electric vehicle charging if they fear that it may not fully charge the vehicle when needed. Explainable Artificial Intelligence has developed a solution to this problem, techniques can play a crucial role in improving user trust and understanding. By providing transparent and interpretable explanations, XAI can bridge the gap between ML models and end-users, enhancing the usefulness and acceptance of these applications. In the context of NILM and DSM, XAI techniques can help consumers better understand how the ML models estimate power consumption and optimize energy usage, respectively. This understanding can increase consumer confidence and encourage their active participation in energy-saving practices.

It is worth noting that while XAI techniques can improve consumer trust, some works primarily focus on making classifiers that can be understood by AI experts as well as just end users. Nevertheless, by incorporating XAI principles, these ML-based applications can provide trustworthy and straightforward feedback, increasing user understanding and confidence in their operation. Overall, the utilization of ML techniques in consumer energy applications can bring numerous benefits, but the lack of transparency and user trust poses practical limitations. XAI techniques offer a promising avenue to overcome these limitations, ensuring that consumers can comprehend and trust the decisions made by ML models, thereby maximizing the potential impact of smart grid technologies on energy consumption and efficiency.

5.4.4 ENHANCED POWER SYSTEM MONITORING THROUGH AI

Another important application that relies on ML is power system monitoring, which encompasses tasks such as finding faults, identifying power network imbalances, and identifying cyber-security intrusions. As power networks become increasingly complex, these tasks pose significant challenges, which ML methods excel at solving due to their ability to handle complex pattern recognition problems. However, the black-box nature of ML models impedes their practical use in critical applications, raising concerns about trust and hindering their adoption.

One specific application in power system monitoring is line fault detection, where ML models utilize input attributes and bus measurements. While ML has shown promising results in fault detection, the lack of interpretability hampers its acceptance. Power engineers may be reluctant to rely on models that make judgements based on incomplete or unrelated facts. XAI techniques can provide a solution to this problem by providing insights into the reasoning behind the model's predictions. For instance, XAI can be employed to identify which measurements were considered significant in locating the error. Furthermore, system planners can benefit from using global XAI approaches to place measuring equipment on buses where the model predicts it will have the most impact, improving fault detection accuracy.

Cyber security surveillance, where Machine Learning techniques are used to identify digital attacks like bogus intrusions and data injections, is another crucial use of power system monitoring. However, these models often lack the ability to explain why certain measurements are flagged as cyberattacks. This lack of interpretability hinders operators' understanding of the detected attacks, making resolution and mitigation challenging. Given the severe consequences of misclassification in cyber security, a high level of understanding of these models is crucial. XAI techniques can enhance trust and transparency by providing explanations for why an event is classified as a cyberattack, empowering power system experts to make informed decisions in response to detected threats.

By integrating XAI techniques into power system monitoring applications, the limitations of black-box ML models can be overcome. XAI provides the means to understand and trust the decisions made by these models, facilitating fault detection, imbalance identification, and cyber-security monitoring. Power engineers and operators can gain insights into the information considered by the models and the reasoning behind their predictions, enabling them to take appropriate actions and make sure the electricity system is secure and reliable.

In summary, power system monitoring applications, including fault detection, imbalance identification, and cyber-security monitoring, can greatly benefit from the use of ML methods. However, the black-box nature of these models hinders their practical deployment due to trust and interpretability concerns. By incorporating XAI techniques, the transparency and trustworthiness of ML models can be enhanced, enabling power system engineers to understand the decisions made by these models and make informed decisions in critical applications.

5.5 CONCLUSION

Modern machine learning models have performed remarkably well in applications related to energy and power systems. However, the lack of understanding and transparency in these models can undermine trust among power experts and users. Explainable Artificial Intelligence has developed a solution to this problem that aims to enhance the explainability and trustworthiness of ML models. XAI approaches have seen an increase in popularity in recent years when applied in the areas of power and energy, as revealed by a thorough examination of many sources. This study concludes with selected applications in the areas of power and energy identified through comprehensive content analysis. The analysis uncovers notable trends in current research and provides insights into the conditions under which different XAI techniques are employed. Among the various XAI techniques, SHAP and LIME emerge as the most frequently employed methods. This contribution showcases numerous examples and opportunities for utilizing XAI in the fields of energy and power. XAI approaches provide a lot of potential for explaining the choices made by ML algorithms, which are popular in the domain of energy and power systems, despite the difficulties noted above. By leveraging XAI, a greater level of understanding and trust can be achieved, which paves the way for broader adoption and application of ML models in energy and power systems.

REFERENCES

1. Vakulchuk, R., Overland, I., and Scholten, D. Renewable energy and geopolitics: A review. *Renew. Sustain. Energy Rev.* 122, 109547, 2020. doi: 10.1016/J.RSER.2019.109547.
2. Blondeel, M., Bradshaw, M. J., Bridge, G., and Kuzemko, C. The geopolitics of energy system transformation: A review. *Geogr. Compass* 15(7), e12580, 2021. doi: 10.1111/GEC3.12580.
3. Hussain, A., Bui, V. H., and Kim, H. M. Microgrids as a resilience resource and strategies used by microgrids for enhancing resilience. *Appl. Energy* 240, 56–72, 2019. doi: 10.1016/J.APENERGY.2019.02.055.
4. Gill-Wiehl, A., Miles, S., Wu, J., and Kammen, D. Beyond customer acquisition: A comprehensive review of community participation in mini grid projects. *Renew. Sustain. Energy Rev.* 153, 111778, 2022. doi: 10.1016/J.RSER.2021.111778.
5. Ceglia, F., Esposito, P., Marrasso, E., and Sasso, M. From smart energy community to smart energy municipalities: Literature review, agendas and pathways. *J. Clean. Prod.* 254, 120118, 2020. doi: 10.1016/J.JCLEPRO.2020.120118.
6. Nandha Gopal, J., and Muthuselvan, N.B., Current mode fractional order PID control of wind-based quadratic boost converter inverter system with enhanced time response. *Circuit World* 47(4), 368–381, 2020.
7. Zarazua de Rubens, G., and Noel, L. The non-technical barriers to large scale electricity networks: Analysing the case for the US and EU supergrids. *Energy Policy* 135, 111018, 2019. doi: 10.1016/J.ENPOL.2019.111018.
8. Janbi, N., Mehmood, R., Katib, I., Albeshri, A., Corchado, J. M., and Yigitcanlar, T. Imtidad: A reference architecture and a case study on developing distributed AI services for skin disease diagnosis over cloud, fog and edge. *Sensors* 22(5), 1854, 2022. doi: 10.3390/S22051854.
9. Alahmari, N., Alswedani, S., Alzahrani, A., Katib, I., Albeshri, A., and Mehmood, R. Musawah: A data-driven AI approach and tool to Co-create healthcare services with a case study on cancer disease in Saudi Arabia. *Sustainability* 14(6), 3313, 2022. doi: 10.3390/SU14063313.
10. Nandha Gopal, J., Balasubramanian, M., and Subburaj, M. Model predictive controller-based quadratic boost converter for WECS applications. *Int. Trans. Electr. Energy Syst.* 31(12), e13133, 2021.
11. Alkhayat, G., Hasan, S. H., and Mehmood, R.S., Energy: A novel deep learning based auto-selective approach and tool for solar energy forecasting. *Energies* 15(18), 6659, 2022. doi: 10.3390/EN15186659.
12. Lundberg, S. M., Erion, G., Chen, H., De Grave, A., Prutkin, J. M., Nair, B., et al., From local explanations to global understanding with explainable AI for trees. *Nat. Mach. Intell.* 2(1), 56–67, 2020. doi: 10.1038/s42256-019-0138-9.
13. Muthukaruppasamy, S., and Abudhahir, A., Indirect output voltage control in negative output elementary super lift luo converter using PIC plus FLC in discontinuous conduction mode. *Circuits Syst.* 7(11), 3685–3704, 2016.
14. Yigitcanlar, T., Corchado, J. M., Mehmood, R., Li, R. Y. M., Mossberger, K., and Desouza, K., Responsible urban innovation with local government artificial intelligence (AI): A conceptual framework and research agenda. *J. Open Innov. Technol. Mark. Complex.* 7(1), 71, 2021. doi: 10.3390/joitmc7010071.
15. Ahmad, I., Alqurashi, F., Abozinadah, E., and Mehmood, R., Deep journalism and DeepJournal V1.0: A data-driven deep learning approach to discover parameters for transportation. *Sustain. Switz.* 14(9), 5711, 2022. doi: 10.3390/SU14095711.
16. Muthukaruppasamy, S., Abudhahir, A., GnanaSaravanan, A., Gnanavadivel, J. and Duraipandy, P., Design and implementation of PIC/FLC plus SMC for positive output elementary super lift Luo converter working in discontinuous conduction mode. *J. Electr. Eng. Technol.* 13(5), 1886–1900, 2018.
17. Alqahtani, E., Janbi, N., Sharaf, S., and Mehmood, R., Smart homes and families to enable sustainable societies: A data-driven approach for multi-perspective parameter discovery using BERT modelling. *Sustainability* 14, 13534, 2022. doi: 10.20944/ Preprints 202208.0233.V1.

18. Ahmad, I., Alqurashi, F., Abozinadah, E., and Mehmood, R., Deep journalism and Deep Journal V1.0: A data-driven deep learning approach to discover parameters for transportation. *Sustain. Switz.* 14(9), 5711, 2022. doi:10.3390/SU14095711.

19. Volkova Anna Patil, A. D., Javadi, S. A., and Meer, H. D., Accountability challenges of AI in smart grid services. In *e-Energy 2022- Proceedings of the 2022 13th ACM International Conference on Future Energy Systems*, pp. 597–601, 2022. doi: 10.1145/3538637.3539636.

20. Nitzberg, M., and Zysman, J. Algorithms, data, and platforms: The diverse challenges of governing AI. *J. Eur. Public Policy* 2022, 26, 2022. doi: 10.1080/13501763.2022.2096668.

21. Przhedetsky, L., Designing effective and accessible consumer protections again stun fair treatment in markets where automated decision making is used to determine access to essential services: A case study in Australia's housing market. In *AIES 2021-Proceedings of the 2021 AAAI/ACM Conference on AI, Ethics, and Society*, New York, NY, United States, 30 July 2021, pp. 279–280, 2021. doi: 10.1145/3461702.3462468.

22. Zhang, K., Zhang, J., Xu, P.-D., Gao, T., and Gao, D.W., Explainable AI in deep reinforcement learning models for power system emergency control. *IEEE Trans. Comput. Soc. Syst.* 2021, 1–9, 2021. doi: 10.1109/TCSS.2021.3096824.

23. Santos, O.L., Dotta, D., Wang, M., Chow, J.H., and Decker, I.C., Performance analysis of a DNN classifier for power system events using an interpretability method. *Int. J. Electr. Power Energy Syst.* 136, 107594, 2021. doi: 10.1016/j.ijepes.2021.107594.

24. Machlev, R., Perl, M., Belikov, J., Levy, K., and Levron, Y., Measuring explainability and trustworthiness of power quality disturbances classifiers using XAI - Explainable artificial intelligence. *IEEE Trans. Ind. Inf.* 2021, 1, 2021. doi: 10.1109/tii.2021.3126111.

25. Zhang, D., Li, C., Shahidehpour, M., Wu, Q., Zhou, B., Zhang, C., et al. A bi-level machine learning method for fault diagnosis of oil-immersed transformers with feature explainability. *Int. J. Electr. Power Energy Syst.* 134, 107356, 2022.

26. Sairam, S., Seshadhri, S., Marafioti, G., Srinivasan, S., Mathisen, G., and Bekiroglu, K. Edgebased explainable fault detection systems for photovoltaic panels on edge nodes. *Renew. Energy* 2021, 2021. doi: 10.1016/j.renene.2021.10.063.

27. Donti, P.L., and Kolter, J.Z. Machine learning for sustainable energy systems. *Ann. Rev. Environ. Resour.* 46(1), 719–47, 2021.

28. Henriksen, E., Halden, U., Kuzlu, M., and Cali, U., Electrical load forecasting utilizing an explainable artificial intelligence (XAI) tool on norwegian residential buildings. In *2022 International Conference on Smart Energy Systems and Technologies (SEST)*, 5–7 Sept. 2022, pp. 1–6, 2022. doi: 10.1109/SEST53650.2022.9898500.

29. Dellosa, J. T. and Palconit, E. C., Artificial intelligence (AI) in renewable energy systems: A condensed review of its applications and techniques. In *2021 IEEE International Conference on Environment and Electrical Engineering and 2021 IEEE Industrial and Commercial Power Systems Europe (EEEIC/I&CPS Europe)*, Europe, pp. 1–6, 2021.

30. Samek, W. M., Vedaldi, G., Hansen, A., and Müller, K.R. (eds.) *Descriptive AI: Explanation of In-depth Research, Explanation, and Visualization* (vol. 11700). Springer Nature, Berlin, 2019.

31. Knapic, S., Malhi, A., Saluja, R., and Främling, K., Descriptive AI for web decision-making in the field of medicine. *Mach. Learn. Extr. Inf.* 3(3), 740770, 2021. doi: 10.3390/make3030037.

32. Shin, W., Han, J., and Rhee, W., AI-assistance for predictive maintenance of renewable energy systems. *Energy* 221, 119775, 2021.

33. Conte, F., D'Antoni, F., Natrella, G., and Merone, M., A new hybrid AI optimal management method for renewable energy communities. *Energy AI* 10, 100197, 2022.

34. Nandha Gopal, J. and Muthuselvan, N. B., Educational tool for analysis of PI and fractional order PI controlled quadratic boost boost converter system using MATLAB/Simulink. *Int. J. Electr. Eng. Educ.*, 2021. doi: 10.1177/00207209211013435.

6 Exploring EEG Characteristics and Machine Learning Classifiers for Accurate Detection of Eye-Blink Mistakes

Shubh Gupta, Divya Thakur, Akshat Rastogi, Rupal Mishra, Sandeep Balabantaray, and Meet Bikhani

6.1 INTRODUCTION

The purpose of this study is to forecast eye movements using electroencephalography (EEG) data. While volunteers carry out a visual fixation test, eye movements and EEG data are concurrently captured. Then, while EEG signals are being processed to provide spectral features, eye movement data is being examined to extract other features like saccade amplitude, fixation time, and blink rate. Based on the collected features, a model to predict saccade amplitude [1] and fixation time is created using support vector regression. The model successfully predicted saccade amplitude and fixation length, according to the results, proving that eye movements can be predicted using EEG data. These discoveries may be used to create neuroprosthetics [2] and other helpful technologies for those who suffer from motor disabilities. Important new perspectives on the cognitive processes underlying visual perception, attention, and decision-making are provided by EEG and eye movement data. These data are acquired by simultaneously recording EEG signals and eye movements from people performing cognitive or visual tasks. The timing and nature of brain activity associated with eye movements and visual processing are very detailed in the generated dataset.

We provide a dataset of eye movement and EEG recordings taken during participant participation in a visual search task for this investigation. In addition to it, X EEG electrodes [3] are used to measure the electrical activity of the brain., the dataset contains information from X participants about the timing and direction of eye movements. Because noise and errors have been pre-processed out of the dataset, it is perfect for a number of analyses, including research into the neural correlates of attention and visual processing. This dataset is a valuable resource for scholars trying to comprehend the neural underpinnings of eye movements and visual perception, and it may improve our understanding of the cognitive processes that underlie human behaviour.

The study discussed here focuses on the use of EEG data to predict eye movements, particularly saccade amplitude and fixation time, during a visual fixation test. The experiment involved capturing eye movements and EEG data concurrently from volunteers performing the test. The EEG signals were processed to extract spectral features, while eye movement data was analysed to extract saccade amplitude, fixation time, and blink rate features.

Based on these features, a support vector regression model was created to predict saccade amplitude and fixation time. The results showed that the model successfully predicted these variables, suggesting that EEG data can be used to predict eye movements.

DOI: 10.1201/9781003457176-6

The development of neuroprosthetics and other technologies that could aid people with motor disabilities in controlling their eye movements is likely to result from this study, which has important consequences for those people. Moreover, EEG and eye movement data can provide new insights into the cognitive processes that underlie visual perception, attention, and decision-making. To facilitate further research in this area, the study's authors provide a dataset of eye movement and EEG recordings obtained from participants performing a visual search task. This dataset includes information on the timing and direction of eye movements, as well as electrical brain activity measured by X EEG electrodes.

The dataset has been pre-processed to remove noise and errors, making it ideal for analysing the neural correlates [4] of attention and visual processing. This dataset can be used by researchers to learn more about the cognitive processes involved in eye movements and visual perception, which could have broader implications for our understanding of human behaviour.

The study highlights the potential of EEG data to predict eye movements, which could lead to the development of technologies to assist individuals with motor disabilities [5]. The dataset provided by the authors is a valuable resource for further research into the neural underpinnings of eye movements and visual perception.

6.2 PROBLEM DESCRIPTION

Examining the connection between eye movements and brain activity is the issue that is being addressed by the eye movement and EEG data. For navigating the visual environment and focusing attention on important information, eye movements are crucial. EEG signals also offer a non-invasive way to assess the brain activity related to attention and visual perception.

With the use of this dataset, researchers hope to answer a number of concerns about the cognitive mechanisms that underlie eye movements and neural activity. For instance, researchers may be interested in learning how attention is distributed during various visual activities or how visual cues affect eye movements. They may also investigate how neuronal representations of eye movements in different brain regions relate to cognitive activities such as working memory and decision-making. Researchers can learn more about the complex links that exist between eye movements and brain activity by investigating these questions.

Moreover, this research has important implications for the development of neuroprosthetics and other technologies to assist individuals with motor disabilities. For example, individuals with conditions like cerebral palsy or spinal cord injuries may have limited control over their eye movements. By understanding the neural mechanisms that control eye movements, researchers can develop new technologies to help these individuals better navigate their environment and communicate with others.

Furthermore, the use of EEG data to predict eye movements could also have implications for other areas of research, such as the interaction of human and computer and virtual reality. For example, by using EEG data to predict where a user is looking in a virtual environment, researchers can develop more intuitive and immersive virtual reality experiences.

Overall, the work under consideration here represents an important advancement in our understanding of the relationship between eye movements and brain activity. The authors' dataset is a great resource for future research into these complicated cognitive functions, with important implications for sectors ranging from health to technology.

6.3 LITERATURE

In order to enhance the detection of eye blink errors in EEG signals, the author [6] conducted research to examine 12 EEG features and 5 machine learning classifiers. The most useful factor for classification was determined to be the scale topography, while mean and skewness were less useful. Artificial neural networks (ANN) outperformed the other classifiers. The best method for identifying eye blink mistakes was found to be scalp topography in conjunction with ANN. Further research on feature and classifier selection for the identification of eye blink mistakes in EEG signals will benefit greatly from the study's useful information.

In [7], the author addresses how the enhanced categorization model might be used to create new instruments for diagnosing and treating depression as well as to deepen our understanding of the neurological underpinnings of the illness. Overall, the study offers a novel method for diagnosing depression that combines eye tracking and EEG data.

In [8], the author adheres to the restrictions of this study, while reading panoramic radiographs during the mixed dentition phase, it is advised to read each region in a clockwise rotation order. Due to task complexity and inferior learning outcomes, students who moved their eyes frequently showed reduced interest. During test image viewing, in order to improve instructional assistance on diagnostic imaging in paediatric dentistry, recommendations were made based on the classification of eye movement patterns.

In [9], the author presents EMPP, a useful technique for evaluating the VF in kids with IL. The empirical plots of EMPP could add to the GVF perimeter by detecting and characterizing the centre 30-degree VF in greater detail. A rigorous evaluation of its diagnostic performance in comparison to structural issues discovered using imaging techniques may be helpful in the future.

The author of [10] offers EyeBox, a tool for processing and displaying data from head-mounted Pupil Core eye trackers. The analysis of data could be completed much faster with EyeBox. We discovered EyeBox accomplished great accuracy by contrasting the findings with the manual processing. Next, we performed a user experience test to assess EyeBox's user interface. According to the findings, EyeBox has a decent response time and interaction fluency. Several participants, however, intended to optimize and simplify the user interface. We will eventually accomplish automatic recognition of a certain area, do away with the manual part, and enhance the user interface. Only data from Pupil Core is processed by the present version. We intend to update EyeBox so that it can handle the data collected by various eye trackers.

In [11], the author provides preliminary findings and suggestions for future research on an emerging subject. The only trials that met the criteria for inclusion in our systematic review were four out of the eight trials that produced data for our meta-analyses. According to the synthesized data presented here, the disruption of the SWS did not significantly influence post-prandial glucose or insulin levels, but it did dramatically enhance insulin resistance. No trials were found to have a high risk of bias in any particular domain. Future research should focus on developing sleep stage disruption (to understand the mechanisms involved) and sleep stage augmentation (to investigate potential therapies) approaches.

Reference [12] describes a classifier using eye movement data, the author developed a method to identify dyslexic readers. Furthermore, we chose an arbitrary threshold for reading fluency score to designate dyslexia in this article, which makes the categorization process intrinsically challenging. Instead, then employing the simple average values of fixation and saccade measures, our feature extraction uses gaze patterns inside AOIs and histograms to supplement the transition matrices that are often utilized. With the most important eye movement variables selected via RF, an SVM classifier was able to attain a recall score of 84.8% and an accuracy of 89.7%. The outcome is encouraging, and a more in-depth examination of the feature's importance offers knowledge that may be applied to direct future research towards efficient and accurate dyslexia screening systems.

In Reference. [13], the report outlines a proposal to create a novel eye movement-based dementia evaluation system. Six healthy volunteers were used to gather eye movement data for a basic recreational Tangram game. Once the COVID-19 issue has been rectified, the authors intend to look at the differences in eye movement between dementia sufferers and healthy individuals. The created system may assess cognitive functions without putting the patient under stress or additional burden. It is not a diagnosis system. In order to address the decreased opportunities for dementia patients to engage with people as a result of COVID-19, Additionally, scientists want to improve the system so that it may be used online to study cognitive performance and dementia progression.

6.4 METHODOLOGY

6.4.1 DATA PREPROCESSING

To assure the quality and accuracy of the data, there are various procedures involved in the capture and pre-processing of eye movement and EEG data. These actions can be broadly categorized as follows:

6.4.1.1 Rescaling Data

A data preprocessing technique called rescaling involves converting a dataset's feature values to a common scale, often between 0 and 1 or −1 and 1. This method prevents the issue of some features predominating others, which can result in biased outcomes in machine learning models. In rescaling, the feature values are converted to have the same range and to have modified values that are proportional to the original values. Min-Max scaling and standardization are the rescaling methods that are most frequently utilized. When the data range is known and fixed, min-max scaling is employed; however, standardization is employed when the data range is unknown or not fixed.

6.4.1.2 Mean Removal

A data preprocessing method called mean removal removes the mean value of each characteristic to centre the data. This technique is used to eliminate the effect of different mean values across features and allows for the comparison of features with different scales. In mean removal, the mean value of each feature is subtracted from each data point. This results in a new dataset with a zero mean for each feature, which is useful for many machine learning algorithms.

Mean removal is particularly important when dealing with datasets with a large number of features or when working with high-dimensional data. This technique can help reduce the computational complexity [14] of machine learning models and improve their performance. However, it is important to note that mean removal should be used in conjunction with other preprocessing techniques, such as rescaling or normalization, to obtain the best results.

6.4.1.3 Standardizing Data

The feature values of a dataset are modified using a data preparation method called standardization to have a mean of 0 and a standard deviation of 1. Rescaling the data to a standard range with this method makes it simpler to analyse the data and enhances the effectiveness of machine learning models.

Each feature value is divided by its standard deviation after being initially subtracted from its mean in order to standardize the data. As a result, a new dataset is created with each feature having a mean of 0 and standard deviation of 1, making it simpler to compare characteristics with various scales. When working with datasets with different scales and units, standardizing data are especially helpful because it eliminates the scale impact and allows machine learning algorithms to make better use of the data.

6.4.1.4 One Hot Encoding

A data preparation method called one hot encoding uses a collection of binary variables—one for each potential category—to represent categorical variables. According to this method, each distinct category is given a separate binary variable, whose value is set to 1 if the category is present and 0 otherwise. The dataset that results has a set of binary variables for each category, making categorical data comparison and analysis simple. When working with categorical variables like colour or gender that lack an inherent ordering, one hot encoding is especially helpful. It enables categorical data to be used as input for machine learning algorithms, enhancing their efficiency and precision (Figure 6.1).

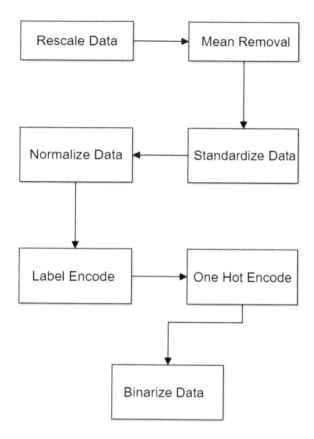

FIGURE 6.1   Figure SEQ figure * ARABIC 1 – data preprocessing.

6.4.1.5   Normalizing Data

Scaling numerical data to a common range is done using the data preprocessing technique known as normalization. The efficiency of machine learning algorithms that use distance-based measures or gradient-based optimization methods [15] can be enhanced by using this technique, which is used to make sure that the numerical values of various features in a dataset have a similar scale.

The values of each feature in the dataset are scaled to a range between 0 and 1, or between −1 and 1, as part of the normalization process. This is done by dividing by the feature's range or standard deviation and then subtracting the feature's mean. This procedure makes sure that each feature has a comparable scale, which can facilitate data comparison, analysis and data normalization.

Data preparation method called label encoding is used to transform category data into numerical values. This method gives each category in a categorical feature a numerical label or code so that machine learning algorithms can use the data as input.

6.4.1.6   Label Encoding

Each category in the categorical feature is given a distinct numerical label during label encoding, starting from 0 or 1 depending on the implementation. For instance, in a dataset with the categorical feature "colour" and the categories "red," "blue," and "green," "red" may be given a label of 0, "blue," or "1," and "green," or "2," could be given. A new numerical feature is produced as a result of this procedure, which can be used as data for machine learning algorithms.

6.4.1.7 Binarizing Data

A data preprocessing method called "binarization" is used to translate numerical data into binary values. Setting a threshold value and changing any numbers over it to 1 and any numbers below it to 0 are the steps in this strategy. When working with numerical data that has distinct thresholds, such as the results of medical tests or the pixel intensities of images, binarizing the data is a valuable technique. Setting the threshold too high or too low could lead to data loss or inaccurate results, therefore it's crucial to select a threshold number that makes sense for the particular situation and dataset.

6.4.2 ADABOOST CLASSIFIER

A strong classifier is created using an ensemble method that aggregates weak classifiers. Several weighted versions of the training data are sequentially subjected to a base learning algorithm, and the weights of samples that were improperly classified are adjusted.

A common technique in machine learning is ensemble learning, which combines several weak classifiers to produce a stronger classifier. A prominent strategy in machine learning called ensemble learning combines a number of weak classifiers to produce a stronger classifier known as a strong classifier. The theory behind ensemble learning is that by combining the results of various models, the end result will be more reliable and accurate than any one model alone.

AdaBoost (Adaptive Boosting), which successively applies a basic learning algorithm to several weighted versions of the training data, is one of the most popular ensemble methods. The weights of the samples that the preceding weak classifier incorrectly categorized are increased with each iteration, ensuring that the next weak classifiers pay more attention to these difficult cases. All predictions from weak classifiers are combined, and each prediction is given a weight based on its performance, to produce the final strong classifier.

Ensemble methods are highly effective in improving the performance of machine learning models, especially in cases where individual models might not perform well on their own. By combining multiple models, ensemble methods can reduce the variance of the final result, improve the generalization ability of the model, and make the model more robust to noise and outliers in the data.

You can express the AdaBoost Classifier as follows:

Initialize weights (w_i) for each sample

$$w_i = \frac{1}{N} \tag{6.1}$$

$$e_t = \sum_{i=1}^{n} w_i, t \tag{6.2}$$

$$\alpha_t = \frac{1}{2} \ln \ln \left(\frac{1 - e_t}{e_t} \right) \tag{6.3}$$

$$w_i = w_{i,t} * e^{-y_i \alpha_t h_t(x_i)} \tag{6.4}$$

$$F_t(x) = F_{t-1}(\langle i \rangle x \langle /i \rangle) + \langle i \rangle \alpha \langle /i \rangle_{\langle i \rangle t \langle /i \rangle} h_t(x) \tag{6.5}$$

where:

- N is the total number of samples
- h_t is the weak learner classifier

6.4.3 Decision Tree Classifier

In decision tree classification [16], the algorithm recursively splits the data based on the features that best separate the classes in the data. This separation is typically measured by information gain or entropy, which is a measure of the disorder or randomness in the data. The goal of decision tree classification is to build a tree that can accurately predict the class of new instances by learning from the patterns in the training data.

Information gain is calculated by comparing the entropy of the parent node with the weighted average of the child node entropies after a split is made. The entropy of a node measures the impurity of the data in that node. A node is considered pure if all the data in the node belongs to the same class, while a node is considered impure if it contains data from multiple classes. The goal of the algorithm is to find splits that result in the largest possible information gain, which maximizes the purity of the resulting nodes.

Entropy is a measure of the disorder or randomness in the data, which is calculated as the negative sum of the probability of each class times the log base 2 of that probability. The entropy is high if the data is evenly distributed among the classes, and low if the data is highly skewed towards one or a few classes. The goal of the algorithm is to find splits that minimize the entropy, which maximizes the purity of the resulting nodes. You may express the Decision Tree Classifier formula as follows:

$$E = -\sum_{i=1}^{K} p_i * p_i \tag{6.6}$$

$$IG = E - H \tag{6.7}$$

where:

- H is the conditional entropy of the dataset with a specific attribute.
- P_i is the proportion of samples that belong to class i.

6.4.4 Extra Tree Classifier

The Extra Trees Classifier (short for Extremely Randomized Trees) [17] is a variation of the traditional decision tree algorithm. In addition to randomly selecting a subset of features and a subset of training data for each tree, the Extra Trees algorithm also chooses splitting points randomly for each feature. This extra level of randomization helps to further decorrelate the individual trees and increase the diversity of the ensemble.

Unlike traditional decision trees and Random Forests, which consider a small set of possible splitting points for each feature, the Extra Trees algorithm generates a large number of random splitting points for each feature and chooses the best one among them. This allows the Extra Trees algorithm to consider a wider range of possible split points and potentially discover more complex and informative splits in the data.

The Extra Trees technique introduces randomization and decorrelation, which makes it a potent and adaptable machine learning algorithm that can be used for a range of tasks including classification, regression, and feature selection. To attain ideal performance, the method may need additional processing power and tweaking due to its increased complexity and unpredictability.

Extra Tree Classifier's mathematical formula is as follows:

$$E(S) = -\sum_{i=1}^{c} p_i * p_i \tag{6.8}$$

$$\text{Gain}(S, A) = E(S) - \sum_{v \in \text{Values}(A)} \frac{|S_v|}{|S|} E(S_v) \qquad (6.9)$$

where:

- c is the number of unique class labels.
- P_i the proportion of rows with output label is i.

6.4.5 GRADIENT BOOSTING CLASSIFIER

A strong learner is created by merging numerous weak learners, often decision trees, in the case of the effective and frequently used ensemble learning process known as gradient boosting. In order to minimize a loss function that evaluates the discrepancy between anticipated and actual values, the approach includes fitting a number of weak decision trees to the residuals of the previous tree successively.

The first step in Gradient Boosting is to train an initial weak model, typically a decision tree, on the original data. The subsequent trees are then trained on the residuals, which are the differences between the predicted values of the previous trees and the actual values. The algorithm uses gradient descent to minimize the loss function, which involves taking the negative gradient of the loss with respect to the predicted values. This negative gradient is then used as the target for the subsequent tree.

To prevent overfitting the training data, the new tree is fitted to the residuals rather than the original data. Each tree is fitted to the loss function's negative gradient, which indicates that it is attempting to remedy the mistakes made by the tree that came before it. By combining all of the trees' projections, the ultimate forecast is achieved.

Many machine learning applications, such as regression, classification, and ranking, benefit greatly from gradient boosting. It is widely used in industry and has been applied to a wide range of applications, such as fraud detection, recommendation systems, and image classification. However, it can be computationally expensive and requires careful tuning of the hyperparameters to achieve optimal performance. Gradient Boosting Classifier's mathematical formula is as follows:

$$L(f) = \sum_{i=1}^{N} L(y_i, f(x_i)) \qquad (6.10)$$

$$f_k = \left(\text{argmin} \left[\sum_{i=1}^{N} L(y_i, f_{m-1}(x_i) + h_m(x_i)) \right] \right)(x) \qquad (6.11)$$

$$f_m = f_{m-1}(x) + f_k \qquad (6.12)$$

$$f_m = f_{m-1} - \rho_m q_m \qquad (6.13)$$

where:

- N is the number of samples.
- m is the number of extra trees.
- ρ_m is constant.
- q_m is the gradient of the loss function $L(f)$.

6.4.6 Random Forest

With regard to classification and regression applications, Random Forest is a potent machine learning method that is frequently employed. It uses ensemble learning to blend different decision trees to predict the future. A randomly selected portion of the training data and characteristics are used to construct each decision tree. By combining all of the different trees' predictions, the ultimate forecast is generated.

One of the main advantages of Random Forest is that it can handle a large number of input variables without overfitting the model. The algorithm can also handle missing values and maintain accuracy even when some of the input variables are irrelevant. Random Forest can be used for both classification and regression tasks, making it a versatile algorithm that can be applied to a wide range of problems.

There are a number of hyperparameters in the Random Forest method that may be altered to enhance the performance of the model. For example, the number of trees, the number of features to consider at each split, and the maximum depth of each tree can all be adjusted to optimize the model. Hyperparameter tuning can be done using techniques like grid search or random search.

One of the key advantages of Random Forest is its ability to provide insight into the importance of each input variable. This is done by calculating the information gain. These measures indicate how much the model's accuracy would suffer if a particular variable were removed from the model. This information can be used to identify the most important variables in a dataset and to improve the model's performance by focusing on those variables.

The formulas used are:

$$E = - \sum_{i=1}^{K} p_i * p_i \tag{6.14}$$

$$IG = E - H \tag{6.15}$$

where:

- H is the conditional entropy of the dataset with a specific attribute.
- P_i is the proportion of samples that belong to class i.
- IG is the information gain.

6.5 RESULT

6.5.1 Simulation Environment

Python was used on VS Code to run the code on a Jupyter notebook extension. A computer with an Intel 2.30 GHz Ryzen-7 CPU and 16.0 GB of Memory was used for the experiment. The average results are shown graphically and in a table.

6.5.2 Performance Indicator

The indicators chosen to assess how well the suggested methodology performed are given.

6.5.2.1 F1-Score Performance

The F1-score, sometimes called the F1-score, is a gauge of how accurately a model performs on a given data set. Analysing the classification issue is beneficial. Moreover, information retrieval systems like machine learning models are evaluated using it. In essence, it is a technique for integrating machine learning models' precision with recall. The mathematical definition of the model is the harmonic mean of recall and accuracy. The F1 score can be manually changed to favour precision over recall or the opposite. You must correctly comprehend and recollect information in order to receive an F1 score. Let P be the precision and R be recall, then f1-score will be as in the equation.

The bar graph in Figure 6.2 represents the F1-scores of five classifiers: Ada Boost Classifier, Decision Tree, Extra Tree Classifier, Gradient Boosting Classifier, and Random Forest Classifier. The Extra Tree Classifier comes in second with a score of 0.95, just behind the Random Forest Classifier, which has the highest F1-score of 0.96. The Decision Tree has a score of 0.83, while the Gradient Boosting Classifier and Ada Boost Classifier have scores of 0.82 and 0.75, respectively. The graph's y-axis shows the F1-score, while the x-axis displays the classifier names. The graph provides a visual representation of different classifiers' performance and facilitates easy comparison between them. The high F1-scores of the Random Forest Classifier and the Extra Tree Classifier suggest that they have a balance between precision and recall, making them suitable for applications that require identifying positive and negative instances with equal importance, such as sentiment analysis in text classification. Evaluating multiple performance metrics, including F1-score, is critical when comparing classifiers' performance to make informed decisions about selecting the best algorithm for a specific application.

6.5.2.2 Precision Performance

Precision is a measure of the accuracy of a classifier or model in correctly identifying positive samples. The ratio of true positives—the number of samples that are correctly identified as positive—to the total of true positives and false positives—the number of samples that are wrongly classed as positive—is what is meant by the term. In other words, precision is the percentage of samples that were properly classified as positive out of all samples that the classifier anticipated to be positive. It represents the classifier's ability to avoid false positives, i.e., samples that the model classifies as positive even if they are actually negative.

Precision is a crucial performance metric in many applications, particularly in situations where false positives can have severe consequences, such as medical diagnosis or fraud detection. A high precision score indicates that the model is accurate in identifying positive samples, and the results can be trusted with high confidence. However, a high precision score does not necessarily mean that the model is performing well overall. It is possible to achieve a high precision score by simply predicting very few positive samples, which would result in a low recall (i.e., the percentage of genuine positive samples that were identified properly). Therefore, precision should always be evaluated in conjunction with other performance metrics, such as recall, F1 score, and accuracy, to obtain a more comprehensive assessment of the model's performance.

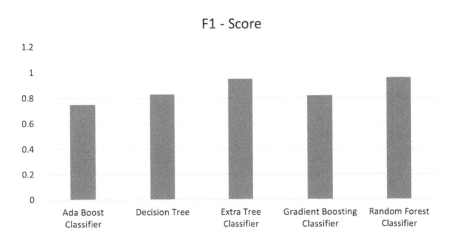

FIGURE 6.2 F1-Score.

The bar graph in Figure 6.3 represents the precision scores of Five classifiers: AdaBoost Classifier, Extra Tree Classifier, Gradient Boosting Classifier, Decision Tree, and Random Forest Classifier. The graph shows that the Random Forest Classifier has the highest precision score of 0.96, proceeded by the Extra Tree Classifier with a score of 0.95. The AdaBoost Classifier has the lowest score of 0.75. The graph's y-axis shows the precision score, while the x-axis displays the classifier names. The graph provides a visual representation of different classifiers' performance and facilitates easy comparison between them. The high precision score of the Random Forest Classifier suggests that it has a low false positive rate, making it suitable for applications that require avoiding false positives, such as medical diagnosis or fraud detection. Evaluating multiple performance metrics, including precision, is critical when comparing classifiers' performance to make informed decisions about selecting the best algorithm for a specific application.

6.5.2.3 Recall Performance

Recall is a performance metric that measures the proportion of actual positive instances that a classifier correctly identifies as positive, out of all positive instances in the dataset. It is also known as sensitivity or true positive rate. In other words, recall indicates the classifier's ability to identify all positive instances, regardless of whether they were classified as positive or negative.

Recall is an important metric in many applications, especially those where the cost of false negatives is higher than false positives. For example, in a medical diagnosis, a false negative result could result in a missed diagnosis or delayed treatment, which could have serious consequences for the patient's health. In this case, a high recall score is desired to ensure that all positive instances are correctly identified, even if it means classifying some negative instances as positive.

On the other hand, in applications where the cost of false positives is higher than false negatives, precision is a more important metric than recall. For example, in fraud detection, a false positive result could result in freezing legitimate accounts or transactions, which could damage the customer's trust in the financial institution. In this case, a high precision score is desired to ensure that the classifier is accurate in identifying positive instances, even if it means missing some positive instances. To achieve a high recall score, a classifier needs to have a low false negative rate. This means that the classifier should be able to correctly identify most of the positive instances in the dataset.

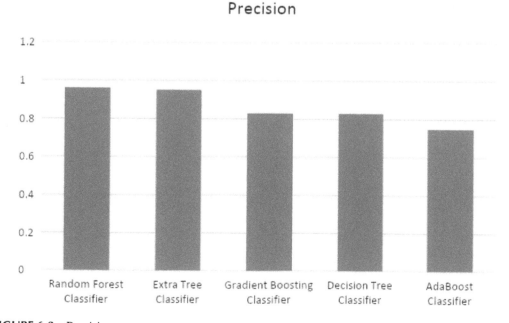

FIGURE 6.3 Precision.

However, this can be challenging in cases where the positive instances are rare or difficult to distinguish from the negative instances. In such cases, the classifier may need to be trained on a larger dataset or with more informative features to improve its recall performance.

Overall, recall is an important metric to consider when evaluating the performance of a classifier, especially in applications where false negatives have a higher cost. However, it should be evaluated in conjunction with other performance metrics, such as precision, F1 score, and accuracy, to obtain a comprehensive assessment of the model's performance.

The bar graph in Figure 6.4 displays the recall scores of five classifiers: AdaBoost Classifier, Decision Tree (DT Classifier), Extra Tree Classifier (ET Classifier), Gradient Boosting Classifier (GB classifier), and Random Forest Classifier (RF Classifier). The y-axis represents the recall scores, ranging from 0 to 1, while the x-axis represents the classifier names. The graph shows that the Random Forest Classifier, with a recall score of 0.96, has the highest score, closely followed by the Extra Tree Classifier, with a recall score of 0.95, and the Decision Tree, with a recall score of 0.83. The Gradient Boosting Classifier and AdaBoost Classifier have recall scores of 0.82 and 0.75, respectively. The graph provides a clear visual representation of the recall scores of different classifiers, allowing easy comparison of their performance. The high recall score of the Random Forest Classifier indicates that it has a low false negative rate, making it a suitable choice in applications where avoiding false negatives is crucial, such as medical diagnosis or spam detection. By considering multiple performance metrics, such as recall, in addition to precision and accuracy, we can obtain a more comprehensive assessment of the classifier's performance, enabling us to make more informed decisions about the best algorithm to use in a given scenario.

6.5.2.4 Accuracy

Accuracy is a widely used performance metric for evaluating the overall correctness of a classifier's predictions by comparing the number of correct predictions to the total number of predictions. It is an important measure when the data is symmetrical, and there are roughly equal numbers of false positives and false negatives. However, accuracy can be misleading when the data is imbalanced, and there are significantly more instances of one class than the other. In such cases, the classifier may achieve a high accuracy score by simply predicting the majority class for all instances, even if it performs poorly on the minority class. Therefore, it is crucial to evaluate other performance metrics,

FIGURE 6.4 Recall.

such as precision, recall, and F1 score, in addition to accuracy to obtain a more comprehensive assessment of the classifier's performance.

Accuracy provides a simple and intuitive way to evaluate the overall performance of a classifier, but it may not be sufficient in real-world applications where the cost of misclassification is uneven or where the data is imbalanced. In such cases, metrics that are specific to the problem domain, such as cost-sensitive accuracy or weighted accuracy, may be more appropriate. Moreover, accuracy is essential in scenarios where there are roughly equal numbers of false positives and false negatives. In such cases, the classifier is expected to make similar numbers of errors in both positive and negative classes, and accuracy provides a reliable measure of the overall performance.

To sum up, while accuracy is a crucial performance metric, it should always be used in conjunction with other metrics, especially in situations where the data are imbalanced or the cost of misclassification is uneven. The use of appropriate performance metrics can help in obtaining a more comprehensive and meaningful evaluation of the classifier's performance, leading to better decision-making in practical applications.

The bar graph in Figure 6.5 represents the accuracy scores of five different classifiers: AdaBoost Classifier, Decision Tree, Extra Tree Classifier, Gradient Boosting Classifier, and Random Forest Classifier. The Random Forest Classifier has the highest accuracy score of 0.96, followed by the Extra Tree Classifier with a score of 0.95, the Decision Tree with a score of 0.83, and the Gradient Boosting Classifier with a score of 0.82. The AdaBoost Classifier has the lowest accuracy score of 0.75. The y-axis displays the accuracy score, ranging from 0 to 1, while the x-axis shows the classifier names. The graph provides a clear visual representation of the classifiers' accuracy performance, enabling easy comparison between them. An accurate classifier is crucial in many machine learning applications to obtain reliable results, such as image recognition and natural language processing. The high accuracy scores of the Random Forest Classifier and the Extra Tree Classifier highlight their suitability for such applications, while the low accuracy score of AdaBoost Classifier indicates its unsuitability.

6.5.2.5 ROC Curve

The performance of binary classification algorithms is frequently assessed using the Receiver Operating Characteristic (ROC) curve. The ROC curve is a plot of the true positive rate (TPR) against the false positive rate (FPR) for various classification thresholds. A classification threshold

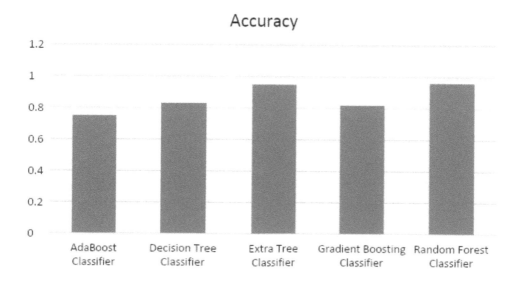

FIGURE 6.5 Accuracy.

is a value that separates the positive class from the negative class. By varying the threshold, we can generate different points on the ROC curve, each corresponding to a different trade-off between the TPR and FPR.

The ROC curve provides a visual representation of a classifier's performance that allows us to compare the performance of different algorithms. A perfect classifier would have an ROC curve that passes through the point (0,1) (i.e., TPR = 1, FPR = 0), while a random classifier would have an ROC curve that is a straight line passing through the origin with a slope of 1.

The AUC provides a single number that summarizes the classifier's performance across all possible classification thresholds, varying from 0.5 for an unreliable classifier to 1 for an ideal classifier. ROC curves and AUC have been widely used in the literature to evaluate the performance of various classification algorithms in different domains, including medicine, finance, and machine learning [18]. For example, a study by DeLong et al. (1988) used ROC curves and AUC to compare the performance of different diagnostic tests for coronary artery disease. Another study by Fawcett (2006) used ROC curves and AUC to evaluate the performance of several machine learning algorithms on different datasets.

6.6 DESCRIPTION OF OBTAINED RESULT

The Random Forest Classifier and Extra Tree Classifier models outperformed the other models in terms of accuracy, precision, F1-score, and recall, according to the data shown in Tables 6.1 and 6.2. The accuracy, precision, F1-score, and recall of the Random Forest Classifier were all 96.05%, whereas those of the Extra Tree Classifier were 94.73%, 95%, and 96%, respectively.

The Decision Tree Classifier achieved an accuracy of 82.51% and a precision, F1-score, and recall of 0.83, while the other models also produced good results. The accuracy, precision, F1-score, and recall of the AdaBoost Classifier and Gradient Boosting Classifier models were close, at roughly 75% and 0.75–0.82, respectively.

The given data represent the precision scores for different classification algorithms, namely, Ada Boost Classifier, Decision Tree (DT Classifier), Extra Tree Classifier (ET Classifier), Random Forest

TABLE 6.1
Accuracy of ML Models

Machine Learning Models	Accuracy Achieved
Ada boost classifier	74.80
Decision tree classifier	82.51
Extra tree classifier	94.73
Random forest classifier	96.05
Gradient boosting classifier	81.74

TABLE 6.2
Performance Comparison of Various Classification Models

Machine Learning Models	Precision	F1-score	Recall
Ada boost classifier	0.75	0.75	0.75
Decision tree classifier	0.83	0.83	0.83
Extra tree classifier	0.95	0.95	0.95
Gradient boosting classifier	0.82	0.82	0.82
Random forest classifier	0.96	0.96	0.96

Classifier (RF Classifier), and Gradient Boosting Classifier. The precision score measures the proportion of correctly identified positive instances out of all positive instances predicted by the model. From the bar graph, we can see that the Random Forest Classifier algorithm has the highest precision score of 0.96, indicating that it correctly identifies a high proportion of positive instances. This is followed by the Decision Tree algorithm with a precision score of 0.83. On the other hand, the Ada Boost Classifier and Gradient Boosting Classifier algorithms have lower precision scores of 0.75 and 0.82, respectively.

The ROC curve of the Ada Boost Classifier in Figure 6.6 represents the performance of the model in distinguishing between positive and negative classes. The true positive rate (TPR) and false positive rate (FPR) at various categorization levels are shown graphically by the curve. The model has a strong capacity to discriminate between positive and negative examples since the area under the curve (AUC) for all classes is 0.82. The AUC value of 0.82 is the same for both the macro- and micro-average ROC curves, indicating that the model performs consistently across all classes. The ROC curve for each individual class also shows that the model's ability to distinguish between positive and negative instances is high for both class 0 and class 1.

The ROC curve of the Decision Tree Classifier in Figure 6.7 represents the performance of the model in distinguishing between positive and negative classes. The curve shows the ratio of true positive rates (TPR) to false positive rates (FPR) at various categorization levels. The model has a strong capacity to discriminate between positive and negative examples since the area under the curve (AUC) for all classes is 0.83. The AUC value of 0.83 is the same for both the micro-average ROC curve and the macro-average ROC curve, indicating that the model performs consistently across all classes. The ROC curve for each individual class also shows that the model's ability to distinguish between positive and negative instances is high for both class 0 and class 1.

The ROC curve of the Extra Tree Classifier in Figure 6.8 represents the performance of the model in distinguishing between positive and negative classes. The true positive rate (TPR) and false positive rate (FPR) at various categorization levels are shown graphically by the curve. The area under

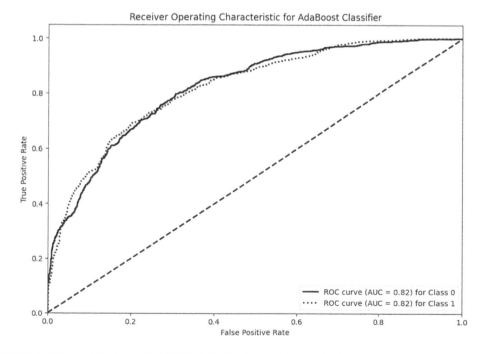

FIGURE 6.6 Figure SEQ figure * ARABIC 6 – ROC of AdaBoost classifier.

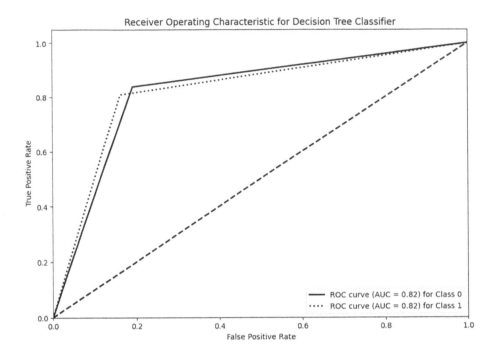

FIGURE 6.7   SEQ figure * ARABIC 7 – ROC of decision tree classifier.

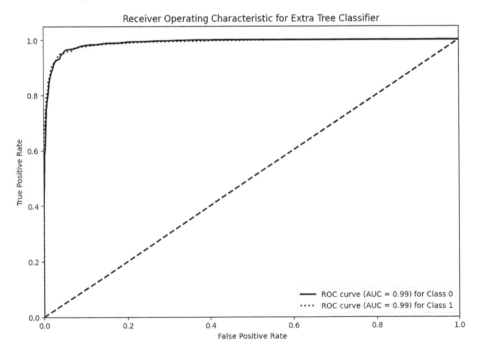

FIGURE 6.8   ROC curve of extra tree classifier.

the curve (AUC) for all classes is 0.90, indicating that the model has a high ability to distinguish between positive and negative instances. The micro-average ROC curve and macro-average ROC curve have the same AUC value of 0.90, suggesting that the model's performance is consistent across all classes. The ROC curve for each individual class also shows that the model's ability to distinguish between positive and negative instances is high for both class 0 and class 1.

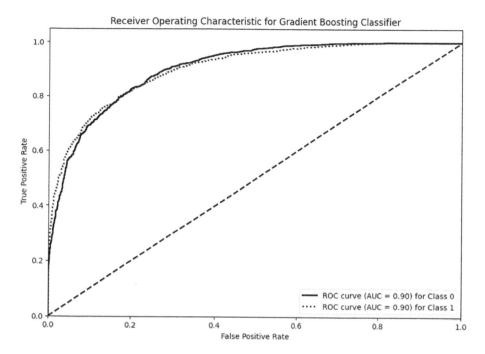

FIGURE 6.9 ROC curve of gradient boosting classifier.

The false positive rate (FPR) and true positive rate (TPR) values for various thresholds used to forecast positive and negative occurrences are displayed on the ROC curve for the Gradient Boosting Classifier model in Figure 6.9 The area under the curve (AUC) values for the macro- and micro-average ROC curves are both 0.79, demonstrating the model's strong ability to differentiate between positive and negative examples across all classes. The individual ROC curves for each class (class 0 and class 1) also have an AUC value of 0.79, demonstrating the model's high performance for each class. Therefore, the data defines the excellent performance of the Gradient Boosting Classifier model in identifying positive and negative instances with high accuracy.

The ability of a Random Forest Classifier model to discriminate between positive and negative classes is shown by the ROC curve in Figure 6.10. The true positive rate (TPR), which is the ratio of positive instances that are correctly classified as positive, is represented by the vertical axis of the ROC curve, while the false positive rate (FPR), which is the ratio of negative instances that are incorrectly classified as positive, is represented by the horizontal axis of the ROC curve.

The Random Forest Classifier model works remarkably well, as evidenced by the ROC curve, which has an area under the curve (AUC) of 0.98 for all classes, showing that the model has a very high capacity to discriminate between positive and negative occurrences. The AUC for both the micro-average and macro-average ROC curves is 0.98, indicating that the model performs consistently across all classes.

6.7 CONCLUSION

In order to distinguish eye blink mistakes from EEG signals, this study evaluates 5 ML classifiers and 12 EEG characteristics. The rate at which eye-blink mistakes are detected essentially determines the selection of appropriate features that can distinguish eye-blink events. Also, a key element of success is selecting the appropriate classifier. In this chapter, the aforementioned issues of selecting the appropriate traits and classifiers for eye blink identification are addressed.

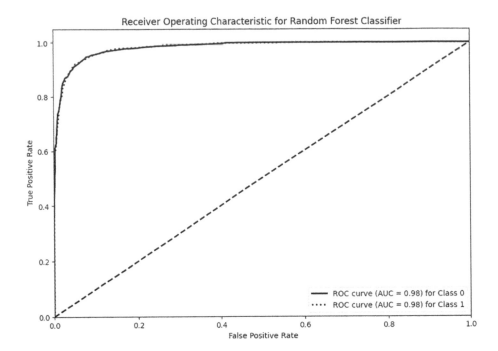

FIGURE 6.10 ROC of random forest classifier.

When it comes to classification, the Random Forest Classifier outperformed other classifiers with an accuracy of 96% and both the Extra Tree Classifier and the Decision Tree Classifier were found to be reliable classifiers. With the help of the mentioned classifier, Blink-error detection became possible.

6.8 FUTURE WORK

In future work, deep neural networks, transfer learning, data augmentation, explainability, and integration with other modalities can be explored to improve the precision, efficacy, and efficiency of deep learning models for predicting eye movements. These findings can contribute to a better understanding of visual perception and attention, with potential applications in psychology, neuroscience, and human-computer interaction.

REFERENCES

1. J. J. Hopp and A. F. Fuchs, "The characteristics and neuronal substrate of saccadic eye movement plasticity," *Progress in Neurobiology*, vol. 72, no. 1, pp. 27–53, 2004.
2. D. Borton, S. Micera, J. del R Millán, and G. Courtine, "Personalized neuroprosthetics," *Science Translational Medicine*, vol. 5, no. 210, p. 210rv2, 2013.
3. F. Chabni, R. Taleb, M. G. Cimoroni, and C. Buccella, "Selective harmonic elimination procedure for uniform step asymmetrical 7-level chb inverter," In *2018 5th International Symposium on Environment-Friendly Energies and Applications (EFEA)*, 2018, pp. 1–6.
4. A. Martin, C. L. Wiggs, L. G. Ungerleider, and J. V. Haxby, "Neural correlates of category-specific knowledge," *Nature*, vol. 379, pp. 649–652, 1996.
5. V. Kumar, T. Rahman, and V. Krovi, "Assistive devices for people with motor disabilities," *Wiley Encyclopedia of Electrical and Electronics Engineering*, vol. 22, 1997.
6. M. Rashida and M. A. Habib, "Quantitative eeg features and machine learning classifiers for eye-blink artifact detection: A comparative study," *Neuroscience Informatics*, vol. 3, no. 1, p. 100115, 2023.

7. J. Zhu, Z. Wang, T. Gong, S. Zeng, X. Li, B. Hu, J. Li, S. Sun, and L. Zhang, "An improved classification model for depression detection using eeg and eye tracking data," *IEEE Transactions on Nanobioscience*, vol. 19, no. 3, pp. 527–537, 2020.

8. S. Tanaka, H. Karibe, Y. Kato, A. Komatsuzaki, T. Sekimoto, and J. Shimomura-Kuroki, "Evaluation of eye movement patterns during reading of mixed dentition panoramic radiographs in dental students," *Pediatric Dental Journal*, 2023. doi: 10.1016/j.pdj.2023.01.002.

9. N. S. K. Meethal, J. Robben, D. Mazumdar, S. Loudon, N. Naus, J. Polling, J. van der Steen, R. George, and J. J. Pel, "Detection of visual field defects using eye movement pediatric perimetry in children with intracranial lesions: feasibility and applicability," *Heliyon*, vol. 8, no. 11, p. e11746, 2022.

10. L. Zhang, X. Liu, Q. Chen, Y. Zhou, and T. Xu, "Eyebox: A toolbox based on python3 for eye movement analysis," *Procedia Computer Science*, vol. 201, pp. 166–173, 2022.

11. J. M. Johnson, S. J. Durrant, G. R. Law, J. Santiago, E. M. Scott, and F. Curtis, "The effect of slow-wave sleep and rapid eye-movement sleep interventions on glycaemic control: A systematic review and meta-analysis of randomised controlled trials," *Sleep Medicine*, vol. 92, pp. 50–58, 2022.

12. P. Raatikainen, J. Hautala, O. Loberg, T. Kärkkäinen, P. Leppänen, and P. Nieminen, "Detection of developmental dyslexia with machine learning using eye movement data," *Array*, vol. 12, p. 100087, 2021.

13. R. Morimoto, H. Kawanaka, Y. Hicks, and R. Setchi, "Development of recreation game for measurement of eye movement using tangram," *Procedia Computer Science*, vol. 192, pp. 4924–4932, 2021.

14. S. Wäldchen, J. Macdonald, S. Hauch, and G. Kutyniok, "The computational complexity of understanding binary classifier decisions," *Journal of Artificial Intelligence Research*, vol. 70, pp. 351–387, 2021.

15. D. Thakur and P. Lalwani, "A cuckoo search-based optimized ensemble model (csoem) for the analysis of human gait," *Journal of Intelligent & Fuzzy Systems*, vol. 45, pp. 1–14, 2023.

16. B. Charbuty and A. Abdulazeez, "Classification based on decision tree algorithm for machine learning," *Journal of Applied Science and Technology Trends*, vol. 2, no. 1, 2021 , pp. 20–28.

17. A. Sharaff and H. Gupta, "Extra-tree classifier with metaheuristics approach for email classification," In *Advances in Computer Com- munication and Computational Sciences: Proceedings of IC4S 2018*. Springer, Bangkok, Thailand, 2019, pp. 189–197.

18. D. Thakur and P. Lalwani, "Human joints analysis system: A machine learning approach," In *2022 IEEE World Conference on Applied Intelligence and Computing (AIC)*. IEEE, Sonbhadra, India, 2022, pp. 410–415

7 Machine Learning Advancements in Polymer Material Creation

Successful Prediction of Glass Transition Temperature

Akshat Rastogi, Divya Thakur, Shubh Gupta, Rupal Mishra, Sandeep Balabantaray, and Meet Bikhani

7.1 INTRODUCTION

One of the physical properties of numerous types of polymers that are covered by experimental data in this collection is the glass transition temperature (T_g), a significant element that regulates the thermal stability of a polymer material. The objective of this project is to build machine learning models that can realistically calculate the melting point (T_g) of a polymer material based on its own molecular makeup and processing conditions. For the creation of new polymer materials with desired thermal properties, accurate (T_g) prediction is essential. In the past, determining (T_g) required laborious and drawn-out experimental techniques that could be expensive and weren't always practical for high-throughput screening of several polymer compounds. Consequently, developing precise and efficient prediction models for (T_g).

We will employ supervised learning [1] to train classification models on the Polymer Dataset in order to accomplish this goal. To find the features that are most important for predicting (T_g), we will investigate several feature engineering and selection strategies. The effectiveness of the algorithms is analyzed using a series of metrics, including accuracy, recall, precision, and f1-score. The findings of this study will give insight on how machine learning algorithms are used to determine polymer (T_g), and this will contribute to the construction of more consistent and cost-effective (T_g) measurement methodologies. The proposed models can also be used to screen new polymer materials for their thermal characteristics, which makes it easier to find new materials with the appropriate thermal characteristics for a variety of applications.

The transition temperature of glass (T_g) is an important property of polymers that affects their thermal stability and processing behavior. (T_g) determines the temperature range over which a polymer will use supervised learning to develop regression models on the Polymer Dataset to do this. We will look into several feature engineering and selection strategies for identifying the traits that are most important for the prediction of transition temperature (T_g). The performance of the models will be assessed using a number of metrics, including accuracy, recall, precision, and f1-score. The findings of this work will help the growth of more accurate and cost-effective (T_g) measuring techniques as well as knowledge about how machine learning algorithms may be utilized to compute polymer T_g. It is simpler to locate novel materials with the right thermal properties for a range of applications by using the proposed models to screen new polymer materials for their thermal properties. The performance as well as longevity of polymer materials can be affected by changes from

DOI: 10.1201/9781003457176-7

a stiff, glassy state to a softer, rubbery one. Therefore, for designing and synthesizing polymers having desired thermal characteristics, (T_g) measurement must be accurate and effective.

In the past, measuring the glass transition temperature (T_g) required time-consuming and expensive experimental methods like dynamic mechanical analysis (DMA) or differential scanning calorimetry (DSC). However, recent computer modeling and machine learning developments have made it possible to forecast T_g based on processing parameters and molecule composition, eliminating the need for extensive experimental testing.

In recent years, machine learning models have garnered substantial attention for their ability to efficiently and cost-effectively forecast glass transition temperature (T_g) compared to traditional experimental methods. To construct a model for T_g prediction based on chemical composition and processing characteristics, regression models are trained using supervised learning, a prominent machine learning technique, with the Polymer Dataset. The Polymer Dataset comprises an extensive repository of data on the physical and chemical attributes of various polymers, with T_g as the target variable for the regression models.

A pivotal aspect of developing accurate machine learning models for T_g prediction is identifying the most pertinent features or input variables contributing to T_g prediction. This study employs various feature engineering and selection strategies to discern the most influential elements. Feature engineering involves the creation of new features by combining existing ones, while feature selection aims to pinpoint the most informative subset of features. The effectiveness of the models is assessed through diverse metrics, including accuracy, recall, precision, and the f1-score.

Implementing machine learning in polymer research encounters challenges primarily due to the demand for extensive and diverse datasets. While substantial, the Polymer Dataset used in this study applies to only a limited subset of polymers and may not fully represent the broad spectrum of polymer materials. To overcome this limitation, efforts are underway to construct more prominent and diversified datasets, which can be utilized to develop machine learning algorithms with enhanced accuracy and robustness.

Another obstacle lies in the interpretability of machine learning algorithms. Comprehending their relationship to the fundamental physical and chemical processes governing polymer behavior can be challenging despite their high predictive accuracy. To address this issue, endeavors are being made to devise more interpretable machine-learning algorithms capable of shedding light on the molecular-level mechanisms underlying polymer behavior.

The subject of polymer science could undergo a revolution if precise and effective machine learning algorithms for forecasting (T_g) are developed. It is possible to correctly forecast (T_g) regarding the molecular composition as well as processing parameters by merging machine learning approaches with experimental data, which eliminates the need for costly and time-consuming experimental methods. The creation of new polymers having specified thermal properties and the thermal property screening of advanced materials can both benefit from the development of reliable (T_g) prediction models.

7.2 PROBLEM DESCRIPTION

The glass transition temperature of a polymer material is one crucial element in determining its thermal stability (T_g). In this collection of various polymers and associated experimental data, it is a significant physical property. The goal of this study is to develop a machine learning algorithm that can accurately predict the transition temperature (T_g) for polymer materials using information about those materials' molecular structure and processing properties as inputs. Creating new polymer materials with particular thermal characteristics depends on accurate T_g prediction. Traditional techniques for measuring T_g were expensive and time-consuming, making them unsuitable for the high-throughput screening of many polymer compounds. Establishing precise and effective prediction models for T_g is therefore highly motivated.

Polymer materials are widely used in various applications, such as packaging, construction, textiles, and electronics. However, their thermal stability is an important factor that affects their performance and lifespan. The glass transition temperature of a polymer material is an important consideration when considering its thermal resistance (T_g). The transitional temperature (T_g) between a polymer's glassy and rubbery states. Several variables, such as manufacturing conditions, chain flexibility, and molecular weight, can affect T_g.

In recent years, polymers' molecular makeup and processing factors have been used to predict the glass transition temperature (T_g) with positive results from machine learning (ML) techniques. ML models help create accurate and effective prediction models for T_g because they are good at analyzing large datasets and identifying complex relationships between input factors and the target variable.

The investigation's findings will be beneficial in understanding how machine learning models may be used to calculate polymer T_g. They will help develop more dependable and affordable T_g testing methods. Furthermore, the suggested models make it easier to screen new polymer materials for thermal characteristics, which would streamline the finding of materials with suitable thermal properties for various applications. This work has the potential to significantly influence the polymer sector by presenting a new instrument for the development of high-performance polymer materials.

7.3 LITERATURE REVIEW

In numerous studies, supervised learning methods have been used to develop machine learning models that estimate the transition temperature (T_g) on the basis of information about polymers.

In reference [2], the conventional methods for discovering and designing new materials encounter limitations in terms of time and resources, necessitating the development of a new approach to expedite the process. In materials research, machine learning has become an up-and-coming technique that may significantly improve the accuracy and efficiency of material property prediction and the discovery of new materials. The author focuses on the critical algorithms involved, the proven methods for applying machine learning to materials science, and the state of the field's current research. While there have been notable strides in this domain, challenges in applying machine learning to materials science persist and are explored within this study, along with potential solutions and future research directions.

In reference [3], the author emphasizes how the Materials Genome Initiative may advance methods of informatics that are data-centric, particularly in the development of novel polymer materials. In this article, the author examines the topic of polymer informatics and introduces a brand-new technique for predicting the characteristics of recently produced polymers using machine learning models. The author also details the creation of Polymer Genome, an easily navigable website that contains these prediction algorithms. In addition, a plan has been put out to gradually expand the chemical and property spaces to increase Polymer Genome's adaptability and applicability across a broader range of technological domains.

In reference [4], the author used ellipsometry to look at how different variables may affect the transition temperature (T_g) on dry polystyrene (PS) brushes. These metrics included thicknesses, molecular masses, and peeling densities. It was discovered that T_g is significantly correlated with the PS brushes' grafting density. T_g rises for high-density brushes as Mn (or brush thickness) declines, but T_g falls for low-density brushes as Mn (or brush thickness) decreases. Surprisingly, the investigation also revealed that T_g is insensitive to Mn or brush thickness in intermediate-density brushes. This is likely because the PS brush shape changes from a mushroom-like structure to a brush configuration.

In reference [5] the combination of graphene and carbon nanotubes (CNTs) in bitumen composites formed 1D-2D hybrid structures with dramatically better mechanical properties, according to the author's research. The inclusion of 0.2 weight percent graphene and 0.8 weight percent of carbon nanotubes showed the most substantial improvements in stiffness, rutting resistance, and low-temperature cracking resistance. The study emphasizes the need of minimizing graphene sheet stacking and CNT aggregation in order to make carbon Nano-filler-reinforced composites more widely applicable.

In reference [6], the author acknowledges the intricacies of developing polymers due to their complex chemical composition and structural attributes. However, the study underscores the significant influence of data-driven methodologies in advancing polymer science and engineering. It places a special emphasis on the use of enormous data resources and the implementation of machine learning methods. The author highlights the emergence of polymer informatics as a valuable tool for predicting polymer performance and optimizing polymer development processes. This progress is made possible by continuous advancements in machine learning algorithms and the augmentation of existing databases. The study provides an insightful overview of the developing field of machine learning-assisted polymer computing, which can be very useful to researchers working in the fields of materials science, machine intelligence, and related fields.

For the purpose of forecasting the transition temperature (T_g) of polymers, in reference [7], the author created a technique called Gaussian process regression (GPR) model. This model made use of molecular characteristics, specifically the molecular average hexadecapolar moment and the molecular traceless quadrupole moment. The model is extremely accurate and reliable, demonstrating GPR's capacity to identify and model the connection between quantum chemical parameters as well as (T_g). This model is also simpler and requires less inputs than other approaches, making it useful for a variety of polymers having (T_g) levels above or below room temperature.

In reference [8], the author did extensive research on oxide glasses, gathering a large quantity of data on glass compositions and glass transition temperatures. They devised an artificial neural network capable of confidently forecasting oxide glasses' glass transition temperature (T_g). Their method of research is flexible and can be adapted to forecast numerous different glass qualities. This predictive technique will be made publicly available as a web tool, with the potential to inspire new ideas and ANN applications in the selection and creation of unique glasses with standout features for cutting-edge applications.

In reference [9], the author emphasizes how polyimides' mechanical and thermal characteristics—a critical class of engineering plastics—are shaped by the glass transition temperature (T_g). To create novel polyimide polymers with desired properties and uses, predicting T_g for polyimides beforehand is essential. The author investigates three approaches to estimate T_g for polyimides, including machine learning methods and all-atom molecular dynamics simulations. The findings suggest that T_g may be accurately calculated by combining a machine-learned mathematical model with the diffusion coefficient for simple gas molecules within a polyimide. This study is critical to accelerate the creation and identification of new polyimide polymers with particular characteristics and uses.

In reference [10], the author has successfully shown that an architecture with a deep convolutional neural network may retrieve pertinent data about the polymer glass transition temperature. Given that it only needs to know the chemical composition of the repeating units and thus does not require experimental measurements or calculations as input, this approach is an essential design tool for material scientists and engineers. The author's work offers a potential direction for further research and has significant ramifications for the field of material science.

In reference [11], according to the author, technological changes and the need for novel polymers necessitate continual study in the design and identification of polymers with specified physical and chemical properties. They emphasize the importance of the glass transition temperature in identifying specific applications and appropriate manufacturing conditions. Polymer complexity makes it challenging to design innovative polymers for specific purposes, and the author emphasizes the benefits of computational tools for learning about the features of developed polymers. In this study, the author investigates the performance of the Graph Attention Network (GAN) and the Convolutional Neural Network (CNN) in predicting the transition temperature of polymers.

In reference [12], The transition temperature (T_g) in thermoset systems may be predicted by the author using only the chemical compositions of resins and hardeners, showing the capability of machine learning (ML). The author gets a good accuracy rate (MAE = 16°C and R2 = 0.86) and effectively predicts T_g for 210 new resin/hardener combinations by training a machine learning ensemble model with 94 resin/hardener groupings. These findings accelerate the development of novel thermosets with desired properties and contribute to sustainability by eliminating trial-and-error methods. Currently, the author is enhancing the model's accuracy by incorporating quantum mechanical features of molecules in the dataset. This work underscores the capacity of machine learning in enhancing efficiency and uncovering new relationships in thermoset development.

In reference [13], virgin and post-consumer recycled (PCR) polymers are in high demand due to their unique characteristics, and the author explores the potential advantages of employing a data-driven approach in polymer design. However, the intricate hierarchical structures of polymers present significant challenges in polymer informatics. To address this challenge, machine learning methods are proposed as cost-effective and scalable solutions for predicting a range of polymer material properties. The author gives a thorough rundown of the essential procedures for integrating machine learning into polymer research, including topics such as polymer design, fingerprinting, representations, open-source databases, and algorithms. In order to enable effective and focused polymer discovery and development, the author emphasizes the significance of continuing research in machine learning applications for PCR polymers in their conclusion.

According to reference [14], material scientists must detect Glass Transition Temperatures with precision and efficiency. The author recognizes that determining the Glass Transition Temperature is difficult since it depends on several polymer's chemical and physical characteristics. Particularly when dealing with polymers that have a wide variety of glass transition temperatures, empirical approaches might be challenging. This Simplified Molecular-Input Line-Entry System (SMILES) arrangement of polymer molecules and a Long Short-Term Memory model are used by the author in a novel approach to estimate glass transition temperature.

In reference [15], according to the author, ML and data-enabled methodologies have brought about substantial changes in materials research. As a result of the formation of this new paradigm, the conventional approach towards materials design but also discovery is going to undergo a significant change. Materials informatics, according to the author, is a fully mature science, and ML algorithms assist in efficient materials property forecasts, materials design, and discovery.

In order to investigate and forecast the phases and transitions of polymers, the author of reference [16] underlines the application of AI and machine learning. The article centers on deep learning methodologies and presents dPOLY, an adaptable artificial intelligence instrument to examine molecular dynamics paths. The ability of such dPOLY framework to forecast critical temperatures of phase transitions across a variety of polymer sizes, along with the spiral into globule transition, exemplifies its adaptability. Additionally, this framework may be expanded to include several other phase transitions including dynamic changes in procedures like polymerization and the synthesis of other soft materials. The author highlights how AI and deep learning techniques have the potential to enhance the forecasting and characterization of polymer phases significantly.

In reference [17], the author acknowledges the limits of traditional analytical and empirical models for forecasting the mechanical properties of concrete mixtures and acknowledges that machine learning (ML) models may be a more efficient alternative. The author appears to promote the use of ML models as a promising strategy to overcoming the limitations of older approaches.

In reference [18], the author highlights the increasing importance of employing big data, collaborative computing, and machine learning in materials research, which supplements traditional theoretical and experimental methods. The talk focuses on how these strategies might speed up polymer design and find novel structure-property connections, as well as the underlying concepts of data-driven techniques and their limitations in polymer research. While machine learning models may not match the precision of first-principles techniques, they can provide reliable approximations of material properties within the range of their initial training data, making them practical for interpolation tasks. The author also delves into amalgamating first-principles methods with advanced optimization techniques for polymer inverse design, resulting in substantial data generation for discovering new correlations. The author emphasizes the need for additional efforts to address difficulties related to setting up high-throughput instrumentation as well as seamlessly incorporating them with optimization as well as machine learning algorithms, even though experiments with elevated setups but also robot-assisted synthesis & design have shown preliminary success.

In reference [19], the author delved into the study of sucrose inversion kinetics in the presence of various acids, revealing that the reaction rate escalated with rising temperatures. The author postulated that the activation energy of the reaction was linked to the energy needed for reactant molecules to surmount the energy barrier and attain the transition state. Subsequently, the author formulated the Arrhenius equation, which elucidates the connection between a reaction's activation energy (E_a), rate constant (k), gas constant (R), and temperature (T):

$$\alpha * e^{\frac{-E_a}{R_T}} = k \tag{7.1}$$

Here, α symbolizes the pre-exponential factor, signifying the collision frequency between reactant molecules, while "exp" designates the exponential function. This equation has become a standard tool for investigating the temperature-dependent behavior of reactions and processes in chemistry and various other domains, including materials science, biology, and engineering. The research outlined in this paper is considered a seminal contribution to the realm of chemical kinetics and has played a pivotal role in shaping the progress of modern chemistry.

7.4 METHODOLOGY

7.4.1 DATA ACQUISITION AND PRE-PROCESSING

This dataset displays measured data on the relationship between various input parameters and a polymer solution's viscosity. The log of viscosity (in cP), polymer concentration (wt.%), Ca^{+2} concentration (wt.%), NaCl concentration (wt.%), and log of shear rate (in s^{-1}) are some of the input parameters (in Celsius). The temperature is the output variable.

There are 420 rows in the dataset, and each row represents a different arrangement of the input parameters. The observations were probably made using a rheometer, a tool for measuring the characteristics of fluid flow (Table 7.1).

The dataset could be helpful for understanding how the polymer solution behaves rheologically under various situations and for adjusting the formulation for particular applications.

TABLE 7.1
Description of Attributes

Title	Description
log of shear rate (in/s)	The shear rate is a measurement of how quickly a fluid shears or deforms when a force or tension is applied.
Polymer concentration (wt %)	It represents the amount of polymer present in the solution.
NaCl concentration (wt %)	It refers to the concentration of sodium chloride (NaCl) in the solution.
Ca^{+2} concentration (wt %)	It speaks of the quantity of calcium ions (Ca^{+2}) present in the solution.
Temperature (in Celsius)	It refers to the temperature of the solution during the rheological measurements, expressed in (°C).
log(viscosity) in cP	The viscosity of polymer solution, measured in centipoise, is referred to as "log(viscosity) in cP." (cP).

You can investigate the connections between the input factors and the outcome variable and learn more about the behavior of the solution by using a variety of quantitative and data visualization tools.

Viscosity, which measures a fluid's resistance to flowing, is a crucial characteristic of polymer solutions in many industrial applications. The polymer concentration, NaCl concentration, and Ca^{+2} concentration are all factors that can affect the viscosity of the solution. The rate at which the fluid is sheared is measured by the log of shear rate, which may also have an impact on the solution's viscosity. Temperature is an important output variable because it can affect the behavior of the polymer solution in various ways, such as by influencing the molecular structure of the polymer chains.

The rheometer is a tool that can be used to measure the rheological properties of fluids, such as viscosity, elasticity, and yield stress. The observations in this dataset were likely made using a rheometer, which is a common tool in the field of polymer science and engineering.

You can learn more about the connections between the input and output variables as well as how the mixture behaves rheologically under various circumstances by studying this dataset using data and mathematical visualization tools. For particular applications, such as the creation of coverings, adhesives, and plastics, this knowledge can be used to formulate the solution in the most effective way possible (Figure 7.1).

1. **Rescaling Data:** A data preprocessing technique called rescaling involves converting a dataset's feature values to a common scale, often between 0 and 1 or −1 and 1. This method prevents the issue of some features predominating others, which can result in biased outcomes in machine learning models. In rescaling, the feature values are converted to have the same range and to have modified values that are proportional to the original values. Min-Max scaling and Standardization are the rescaling methods that are most frequently utilized. When the data range is known and fixed, min-max scaling is employed; however, standardization is employed when the data range is unknown or not fixed.

2. **Mean Removal:** Mean removal is a data preprocessing technique used to center the data by removing the mean value of each feature. This technique is used to eliminate the effect of different mean values across features and allows for the comparison of features with different scales.

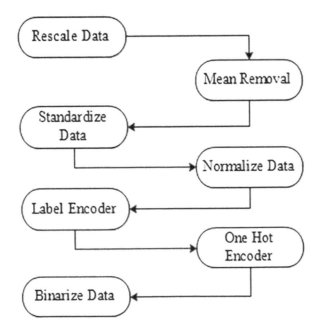

FIGURE 7.1   Data preprocessing steps.

In mean removal, the mean value of each feature is subtracted from each data point. This results in a new dataset with a zero mean for each feature, which is useful for many machine learning algorithms. Mean removal is particularly important when dealing with datasets with a large number of features or when working with high-dimensional data. This technique can help reduce the computational complexity of machine learning models and improve their performance by a large measure. To get the best results, mean removal should be combined with other preprocessing methods like rescaling or normalization, it is vital to highlight.

3. **Standardizing Data:** The obtained features of a dataset are modified using a data preparation method called standardization to have an average of 0 and a sample variance of 1. Using this technique, the data is rescaled to a standard range, which simplifies data analysis and improves the performance of machine learning algorithms. The data is first normalized by subtracting each feature value from its mean and then divided by its confidence interval. In order to facilitate the comparison of traits with different scales, a new sample is built with each characteristic having an average of 0 and sample variance of 1. Classifying data is especially helpful when working with data with various scales and units since it removes the scale influence.

4. **One hot encoding:** A data preparation method called one hot encoding uses a collection of binary variables—one for each potential category—to represent categorical variables. According to this method, each distinct category is given a separate binary variable, whose value is set to 1 if the category is present and 0 otherwise. The dataset that results has a set of binary variables for each category, making categorical data comparison and analysis simple. When working with categorical variables like color or gender that lack an inherent ordering, one hot encoding is especially helpful. It enables categorical data to be used as input for machine learning algorithms, enhancing their efficiency and precision.

5. **Normalizing Data:** Scaling numerical data to a common range is done using the data preprocessing technique known as normalization. The efficiency of machine learning algorithms that use distance-based measures or gradient-based optimization [20] methods can be enhanced by using this technique, which is used to make sure that the numerical values of various features in a dataset have a similar scale. The values of each feature in the dataset are scaled to a range between 0 and 1, or between −1 and 1, as part of the normalization process. This is done by dividing by the feature's range or standard deviation and then subtracting the feature's mean. This procedure makes sure that each feature has a comparable scale, which can facilitate data comparison and analysis.

6. **Label Encoding:** Label encoding is a simple and effective way to prepare categorical features for use in machine learning models. It transforms ordinal and nominal converted into information values that are simple for algorithms to process. However, one potential problem with label encoding is that it introduces an arbitrary order to the categories that may not reflect their true relationship. For example, if "red" is assigned a label of 0 and "green" is assigned a label of 2, this suggests that green is somehow "bigger" or "more important" than red, which may not be true. Therefore, it is important to use label encoding with caution and consider whether the order of the labels is meaningful in the context of the problem at hand. Another limitation of label encoding is that it can lead to overfitting, especially in models with a large number of categories. This is because label encoding creates a new feature for each category, which can increase the dimensionality of the data and make it more difficult for the model to generalize to new examples.

7. **Binarizing Data:** Data preprocessing method called "binarization" is used to translate numerical data into binary values. Setting a threshold value and changing any numbers over it to 1 and any numbers below it to 0 are the steps in this strategy. When working

with numerical data that has distinct thresholds, such as the results of medical tests or the pixel intensities of images, binarizing the data is a valuable technique. Setting the threshold too high or too low could lead to data loss or inaccurate results, therefore it's crucial to select a threshold number that makes sense for the particular situation and dataset.

7.4.2 DISTRIBUTION OF THE DATASET REPRESENTED VISUALLY

The range of temperature readings in the dataset is shown visually in Figure 7.2's histogram plot. By plotting the occurrence of temperature values against their corresponding temperature bins, the plot enables easy identification of the most common temperature values in the dataset, as well as the range of temperatures that occur most frequently. This information can be helpful in understanding the central tendency and spread of temperature data, which is important in many fields such as environmental science, meteorology, and health studies.

The histogram plot not only accurately depicts the temperature data but also provides important information about the temperature distribution's structure. The histogram, for instance, may indicate that the temperature information is routinely distributed if it is about symmetrical. If the histogram has a long tail on one side, it may indicate that the temperature data is skewed. These characteristics of the temperature distribution can inform further analysis and modeling of the data.

The histogram plot is thus a helpful tool for examining and displaying temperature data. It helps in the finding of patterns and themes that might not be immediately apparent from the raw data by providing a succinct and understandable overview of the data. By presenting the data in a graphical format, the histogram plot allows for quick and intuitive comparisons between different datasets or temperature ranges, enabling more effective analysis and decision-making.

7.4.3 BERNOULLINB

The features of the BernoulliNB algorithm are binary, which means they can either be present or not in the document. The existence of the word "spam" in the email, for instance, could be a characteristic for classifying emails as spam or not.

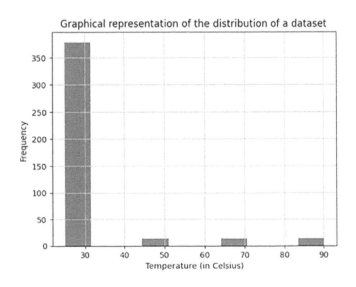

FIGURE 7.2   The distribution of a dataset represented graphically.

Following are the steps the algorithm takes to determine how likely it is that a document refers to the particular class (like spam).:

$$P\left(y|x_1, \ldots, x_n\right) = \frac{P(y)P(x_1, \ldots, x_n)|y}{P(x_1, \ldots, x_n)} \tag{7.2}$$

According to the BernaulliNB algorithm, features can exist without another being present. Therefore, the possibility of the document provided the class can be calculated as the multiplication of the possibilities of each characteristic given the class.:

$$P\left(m_i \mid n\right) = P\left(m_i = 1 \mid b\right)m_i + \left(1 - P\left(m_i = 1 \mid n\right)\right)\left(1 - m_i\right) \tag{7.3}$$

Where, P (m|n) is the probability of noticing a feature given a class. Using maximum likelihood estimation, the probabilities of the characteristics given the class may be calculated from the training data. To prevent zero probability, one can alternatively utilize the Laplace smoothing method.

Therefore, when dealing with binary information, the BernoulliNB algorithm is a straightforward yet efficient technique for text classification applications.

7.4.4 GaussianNB

A variation of the Naive Bayes algorithm used for classification tasks is the Gaussian Naive Bayes (GaussianNB) method. It can handle features with continuous values and makes the assumption that the features have a Gaussian (normal) distribution.

The algorithm determines the probability of the data belonging to a given class as follows:

$$P\left(y \mid x_1, \ldots, x_n\right) = \frac{P(y)P(x_1, \ldots, x_n)|y}{P(x_1, \ldots, x_n)} \tag{7.4}$$

where:

- P (x|y) shows how likely it is that, given the document's characteristics, it belongs to the class.
- $P(x)$ is the prior probability for the class.
- The document's probability, P (y|x), is determined by the class.
- $P(y)$ is the document's evidentiary probability

So, GaussianNB algorithm assumes that the likelihood of the document given the class is a multivariate normal distribution. Hence, given the class, the likelihood of witnessing the document features can be estimated as follows:

$$P\left(x_i \mid y\right) = \frac{1}{\sqrt{2\pi\sigma_y^2}} \exp\left(-\frac{\left(x_i - \mu_y\right)^2}{2\sigma_y^2}\right) \tag{7.5}$$

where:

- π is the mathematical constant pi.
- μ_y is the factor that determines the features' covariance matrix.
- x is the vector of feature values in the document.
- mean is the vector of mean feature values for the class.
- σ_y is the covariance matrix of the features for the class.

You may get the class's likelihood function from the training examples by calculating the percentage of data training set that basically consists. The mean, as well as covariance of a feature for every class, can also be estimated via probabilistic estimation using the training data.

7.4.5 MULTINOMIALNB

The data in the MultinomialNB method are represented by counts, where each feature is a word in the vocabulary and the count denotes how many times that word appears in the document. For example, if we are classifying movie reviews as positive or negative, a feature might be the frequency of the word "great" in the review.

The algorithm computes the possibility of a document belonging to a specific class (e.g., positive) as follows:

$$P\left(y|x_1, \ldots, x_n\right) = \frac{P\left(y\right)P\left(x_1, \ldots, x_n\right)|y}{P\left(x_1, \ldots, x_n\right)} \tag{7.6}$$

where:

- $P\left(x|y\right)$ shows how likely it is that, given the document's characteristics, it belongs to the class.
- $P(x)$ is the prior probability for the class.
- The document's probability, $P\left(y \mid x\right)$, is determined by the class.
- $P(y)$ is the document's evidentiary probability

The following formula can be used to determine the probability of the document given the class:

$$\theta_{yi} = \frac{N_{yi} + \alpha}{N_y + \alpha n} \tag{7.7}$$

where:

- N_{yi} based on the class, what is the likelihood of detecting feature i.
- θ_{yi} is how many features of I are there in the document.

The probabilities of the features given to the class can be estimated from the training data using maximum likelihood estimation or smoothing techniques such as Laplace smoothing.

7.4.6 MLPCLASSIFIER

The MLPClassifier (Multi-Layer Perceptron Classifier) algorithm for classification tasks is a well-known machine learning algorithm. It is a form of artificial neural network composed of numerous layers of nodes, each of which is a simple computational unit that receives input signals and generates an output signal.

By analyzing a collection of training data and labels, the algorithm learns to map input features to output labels. The approach adjusts the biases & weights of the network's node during training to reduce the discrepancy between the expected outcome and the actual label.

The MLPClassifier method produces a probability distribution over all possible classifications. As shown below, a data point's likelihood of belonging to a particular class is calculated.:

$$P\left(y_a = j \mid X_a\right) = \frac{e^{zaj}}{\sum_{k=1}^{K} e^{zak}} \tag{7.8}$$

where:

- y_a is the ath data point's actual label.
- The data point of ath element is X_a.
- j is jth class.
- K is the total number of classes.
- z_{aj} is input to the activation.

A weight value of the output from the layer prior to this is passed through a non-linear activation function to form an activation function for the output layer. The network can learn complex decision limitations because of the activation function's addition of nonlinearity.

To update the weights and biases of the network's nodes, backpropagation is used during training. This involves analyzing the gradient of the gradient descent with appropriate weights and biases and using learning algorithm to update the parameters. For issues related to classification, the loss of cross-entropy function is commonly utilized:

$$L\left(y,\hat{y}\right) = - \sum_{a=1}^{n} \sum_{j=1}^{K} y_{aj} \log\left(\hat{y}_{aj}\right) \tag{7.9}$$

where:

- y_{aj} is the true label of each ath data point for jth class.
- $\hat{y}_{aj}$ is given for the predicted probability of each ath data point for the jth class.
- The overall sample size is n.

The MLPClassifier algorithm is a powerful as well as flexible algorithm that can learn complex decision boundaries and handle high-dimensional input data.

7.4.7 DECISIONTREECLASSIFIER

The decision tree is constructed by recursively separating the data depending on the best attribute that gives the greatest amount of information gain. The information gain quantifies the decrease in entropy or impurity of the data following the split. Every node portrays a potential value or option depending on each node's representation of a feature characteristic.

Information gain is:

$$IG\left(Y,\ A\right) = H\left(Y\right) - H\left(Y \mid A\right) \tag{7.10}$$

where:

- $IG\ (Y, A)$ is attribute A's calculated information gain on data set Y.
- $H(Y)$ is the data set Y's entropy.
- $H\ (Y|A)$ is the data set Y's conditional entropy given attribute A.

The entropy to calculate the Information gain of a set is given by:

$$E\left(S\right) = \sum_{i=1}^{c} - p_i \log_2 p_i \tag{7.11}$$

where:

- S is a collection of samples.
- π is proportion of samples belonging to class i.

As soon as the decision tree is constructed, it can be used to categories fresh data by moving through the tree according to the values of its characteristics until the end is met that correlates to the class label.

7.5   RESULTS

This section describes the simulation setup, performance metrics used for result analysis, and output results.

7.5.1   SIMULATION SETUP

Python was used to run the code on a Jupyter Notebook. The experiment was carried out on a system equipped with an Intel 2.50-GHz, i5 CPU and 8.0-GB RAM. The simulation is run 30 times, and the average results are displayed graphically and tabulated.

7.5.2   PERFORMANCE INDICATORS

This section describes the metrics chosen to evaluate the performance of the suggested methodology.

1. **F1-score performance**: The Predicted accuracy of a Machine Learning model on almost any set of data is assessed using the F-score, also called the F1-score. It is employed to assess the classification issue. Additionally, it is used to assess information retrieval systems, including machine learning models. In essence, it is a method for combining machine learning models' recall and accuracy. It is described mathematically as that of the harmonic average of the recall as well as the accuracy of the machine learning model. The F1 score changes that puts precision before recall or the other way around. To get an F1 score, you must first understand recall and precision.

$$f1 - \text{Score} = 2 * \frac{(\text{Pr} * \text{Rec})}{(\text{Pr} + \text{Rec})} \tag{7.12}$$

2. **Precision performance**: Precision is calculated as the proportion of appropriately significant positive observations to all anticipated positive discoveries. Precision refers to a classifier's capacity to classify data as positive even when they are probably negative.

$$\text{Precision} = \frac{TP}{(TP + FP)} \tag{7.13}$$

   Precision, on the contrary, calculates the percentage of true positive prediction that corresponds to the overall positive class.
3. **Recall performance**: It shows positive predictions obtained from positive examples using connected data collection. Recall is the number of True Positives that our model identifies as Positive (True Positive). Using the same logic, we can argue that when the cost of False Negative is higher, we will use Recall as a model metric to predict our best machine learning model.

$$\text{Recall} = \frac{TP}{(TP + FN)} \tag{7.14}$$

4. **Accuracy performance**: In general, the proportion of correct observations compared to all observations is the most relevant performance metric. Accuracy is an invaluable statistic where the datasets are homogeneous and the number of false positives and negatives are approximately equal.

$$\text{Accuracy} = \frac{(TP + TN)}{(TP + TN + FP + FN)} \tag{7.15}$$

7.6 DESCRIPTION OF OBTAINED RESULTS

Tables 7.2 and 7.3 showcase the results of the proposed models applied, as well as various essential classifiers. It has been discovered that the proposed strategy, which utilizes a DecisionTreeClassifier model, achieves up to 98% accuracy. The F1 score, recall, precision, and accuracy values are shown in Table 7.3.

The information in Figure 7.3 shows the effectiveness measures of various categorization models applied to a dataset. The Recall, Precision, and F1-score values for each model are displayed on the line graph. In this graph, the BernoulliNB, GaussianNB, MLPClassifier, MultinomialNB, and Decision Tree models are contrasted. Metric values are shown on the y-axis, and model names are shown on the x-axis.

As shown in Figure 7.4, the Decision Tree model outperforms all others having precision scores of 0.99, recall scores of 0.98, as well as an F1 score of 0.98. The GaussianNB model likewise performs well, with precision, recall, and F1 scores of 0.98, 0.94, and 0.95, respectively. In comparison to the MultinomialNB model, which used this data, the BernoulliNB model has a precision score of

TABLE 7.2
Different Machine Learning Model's Result

Machine Learning Models	Accuracy Achieved (%)
BernoulliNB	93
GaussianNB	94
MultinomialNB	75
DecisionTreeClassifier	98
MLPClassifier	86

TABLE 7.3
Classification Table of Decision Tree Classifier

Attribute	Precision	Recall	F1 score	Support
25	1.00	0.97	0.99	78
50	0.50	1.00	0.67	2
70	1.00	1.00	1.00	2
90	1.00	1.00	1.00	2
Accuracy			0.98	84
Macro avg	0.88	0.99	0.91	84
Weighted avg	0.99	0.98	0.98	84

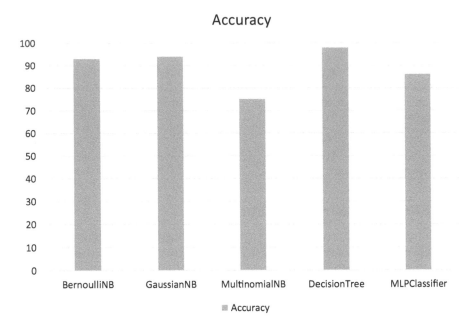

FIGURE 7.3 Comparison graph of accuracy in Percent.

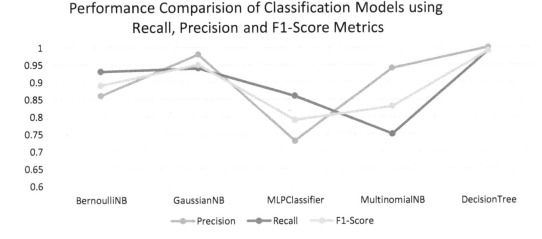

FIGURE 7.4 Precision, recall, and F1-score metrics for performance comparison of classification models.

0.86, a recall score of 0.93, and an F1 score of 0.89. The MLPClassifier technique fared the worst of all models, with precision, recall, and F1 scores of 0.73, 0.86, and 0.79, respectively.

The performance graph shows the values for the DecisionTreeClassifier are shown in a bar graph in Figure 7.5. The model's predictions of true positives are accurate 99% of the time, as shown by the calculated precision value of 0.99. The model correctly detected 98% of the dataset's positive cases, according to its recall value of 0.98. The model appears to be effective at identifying positive occurrences, according to the F1 score of 0.98, which is the harmonic mean of recall and precision.

The bar graph in Figure 7.6 displays the performance metrics of the BernoulliNB classifier, which were evaluated using performance factors. The 0.86-inch-high bar, which represents the classifier's precision, represents the classifier's performance. This demonstrates that 86% of all the occurrences the model identified as positive were in fact true positives. With a recall of 0.93, indicated by the length of the bar, the model was capable of recognizing 93% of the real positive events. The F1 score

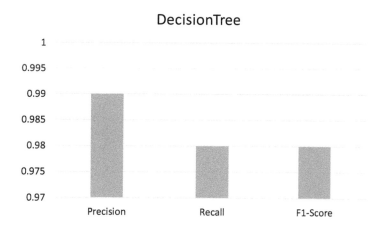

FIGURE 7.5   Graph of decision tree's performance.

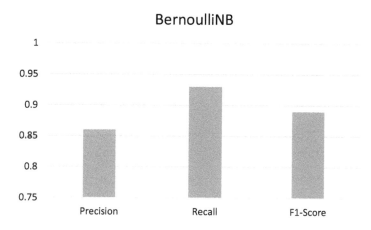

FIGURE 7.6   Bernoulli's performance bar graph.

is 0.89, and it is represented by the length of the green bar. This statistic provides a broad assessment of the model's effectiveness as a weighted harmonic average of recall and precision. An F1-score of 0.89 suggests that the classifier has a decent balance of recall and precision in this case.

The Gaussian Naive Bayes algorithm's performance factor metrics are shown in the bar graph in Figure 7.7. This algorithm has a precision score of 0.98, meaning that it is highly accurate at picking out true positives from all other positive predictions. With a recall score of 0.94, GaussianNB can properly identify a significant portion of true positives among all actual positives. The precision and recall-weighted harmonic mean, or F1-score, is 0.95., indicating excellent ability in forecasting positive events, i.e., the Gaussian Naive Bayes method appears to perform quite well in classification tasks, scoring highly in all three criteria.

Bar graph of Figure 7.8 represents the performance factors for the MultinomialNB classifier. The algorithm's precision score is 0.94, which indicates that 94% of the time when it produces a forecast, it is accurate. Recall is 0.75, which means that 75% of positive samples are correctly identified by the model. The precision and recall components of the F1-score are both 0.83. With this result, the MultinomialNB classifier appears to strike a reasonable compromise between precision and recall for the dataset being used. The graph indicates that the model is significantly biased toward generating false negatives because the accuracy score is higher than the recall score.

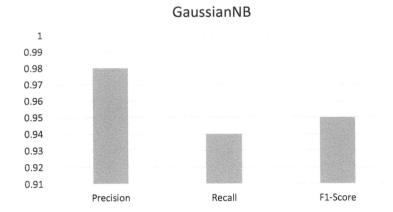

FIGURE 7.7 GaussianNB's performance graph.

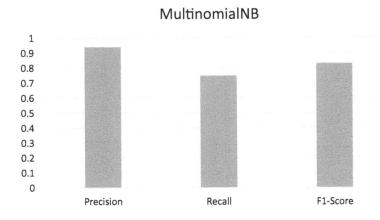

FIGURE 7.8 Multinomial's performance graph.

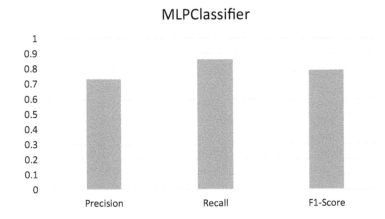

FIGURE 7.9 MLPCLassifier's performance graph.

The Performance Factors for the MLPClassifier model are displayed as bars in Figure 7.9. Recall is 0.86, F1 score is 0.79, and accuracy is 0.73. According to the precision value, 73% of the occurrences that the model identified as positive are indeed positive, while the recall number demonstrates that the model accurately detected 86% of the positive events. The harmonic means of classifiers, known as the F1 score, provides an overall evaluation of the model's performance. These results are shown graphically by a bar graph with the model's performance parameter as the x-axis. The graph shows that MLPClassifier has a relatively lower precision and F1 score compared to the other models in the dataset, indicating that it may not perform as well as other models in predicting the target variable.

7.7 CONCLUSION

According to the evaluation metrics for the Decision Tree Classifier model, the model is effective at forecasting the glass transition (T_g) of polymeric composites. The model achieved high precision, F1 score, and recall of 0.99, 0.98, and 0.98. The model correctly predicted the samples with 98% accuracy. These results demonstrate that (T_g) may be precisely and efficiently predicted using machine learning methods, which can aid in the development of novel polymer materials with desired thermal properties. To enhance the model's functionality and broaden its applicability to various polymer datasets, future research can investigate different feature engineering and selection techniques. As a result, this study contributes to the development of polymer materials and the realm of materials science.

7.8 FUTURE WORK

The accurate prediction of transition temperature is one possible area for machine learning developments in polymer material fabrication (T_g).

A crucial factor that impacts the mechanical, thermal, and physical properties of polymers is the temperature where glass transitions. For the planning and improvement of polymeric composites for numerous applications, including in the automotive, aerospace, and electronics sectors, it is crucial to accurately forecast (T_g).

REFERENCES

1. D. Thakur and P. Lalwani, "Human joints analysis system: A machine learning approach," In *2022 IEEE World Conference on Applied Intelligence and Computing (AIC)*. IEEE, Sonbhadra, 2022, pp. 410–415.
2. Y. Liu, T. Zhao, W. Ju, and S. Shi, "Materials discovery and design using machine learning," *Journal of Materiomics*, vol. 3, no. 3, pp. 159–177, 2017.
3. C. Kim, A. Chandrasekaran, T. D. Huan, D. Das, and R. Ramprasad, "Polymer genome: A data-powered polymer informatics platform for property predictions," *The Journal of Physical Chemistry C*, vol. 122, no. 31, pp. 17575–17585, 2018.
4. B. Zuo, S. Zhang, C. Niu, H. Zhou, S. Sun, and X. Wang, "Grafting density dominant glass transition of dry polystyrene brushes," *Soft Matter*, vol. 13, no. 13, pp. 2426–2436, 2017.
5. Q. Yang, Y. Qian, Z. Fan, J. Lin, D. Wang, J. Zhong, and M. Oeser, "Exploiting the synergetic effects of graphene and carbon nanotubes on the mechanical properties of bitumen composites," *Carbon*, vol. 172, pp. 402–413, 2021.
6. W. Sha, Y. Li, S. Tang, J. Tian, Y. Zhao, Y. Guo, W. Zhang, X. Zhang, S. Lu, Y.-C. Cao et al., "Machine learning in polymer informatics," *InfoMat*, vol. 3, no. 4, pp. 353–361, 2021.
7. Y. Zhang and X. Xu, "Machine learning glass transition temperature of polymers," *Heliyon*, vol. 6, no. 10, p. e05055, 2020.
8. D. R. Cassar, A. C. de Carvalho, and E. D. Zanotto, "Predicting glass transition temperatures using neural networks," *Acta Materialia*, vol. 159, pp. 249–256, 2018.
9. C. Wen, B. Liu, J. Wolfgang, T. E. Long, R. Odle, and S. Cheng, "Determination of glass transition temperature of polyimides from atom- istic molecular dynamics simulations and machine-learning algorithms," *Journal of Polymer Science*, vol. 58, no. 11, pp. 1521–1534, 2020.
10. L. A. Miccio and G. A. Schwartz, "Localizing and quantifying the intra- monomer contributions to the glass transition temperature using artificial neural networks," *Polymer*, vol. 203, p. 122786, 2020.
11. S. Goswami, R. Ghosh, A. Neog, and B. Das, "Deep learning-based approach for prediction of glass transition temperature in polymers," *Materials Today: Proceedings*, vol. 46, pp. 5838–5843, 2021.

12. J. A. Pugar, C. M. Childs, C. Huang, K. W. Haider, and N. R. Washburn, "Elucidating the physicochemical basis of the glass transition temperature in linear polyurethane elastomers with machine learning," *The Journal of Physical Chemistry B*, vol. 124, no. 43, pp. 9722–9733, 2020.
13. N. Andraju, G. W. Curtzwiler, Y. Ji, E. Kozliak, and P. Ranganathan, "Machine-learning-based predictions of polymer and postconsumer re- cycled polymer properties: A comprehensive review," *ACS Applied Materials & Interfaces*, vol. 14, no. 38, pp. 42771–42790, 2022.
14. S. Goswami, R. Ghosh, A. Neog, and B. Das, "Deep learning-based approach for prediction of glass transition temperature in polymers," *Materials Today: Proceedings*, vol. 46, pp. 5838–5843, 2021.
15. G. Pilania, "Machine learning in materials science: From explainable predictions to autonomous design," *Computational Materials Science*, vol. 193, p. 110360, 2021.
16. D. Bhattacharya and T. K. Patra, "dpoly: Deep learning of polymer phases and phase transition," *Macromolecules*, vol. 54, no. 7, pp. 3065–3074, 2021.
17. W. B. Chaabene, M. Flah, and M. L. Nehdi, "Machine learning predic- tion of mechanical properties of concrete: Critical review," *Construction and Building Materials*, vol. 260, p. 119889, 2020.
18. T. K. Patra, "Data-driven methods for accelerating polymer design," *ACS Polymers Au*, vol. 2, no. 1, pp. 8–26, 2021.
19. S. Arrhenius, "Über die reaktionsgeschwindigkeit bei der inversion von rohrzucker durch säuren," Zeitschrift für physikalische Chemie 4(1), 226–248, 1889.
20. D. Thakur and P. Lalwani, "A cuckoo search-based optimized ensemble model (csoem) for the analysis of human gait," *Journal of Intelligent & Fuzzy Systems*, vol. 45, pp. 1–14, 2023.

8 Smart Greenhouse Management System Using AIoT for Sustainable Agriculture

Rupali Pathak, Neha Sharma, and Pragya Ranka

8.1 INTRODUCTION

Agriculture is the foundation of the Indian economy even though the services sector is now contributing more to India's economic growth, which is enabling the nation, to grow at a rate of 7.1% yearly [1,2]. This sector contributes to 13.7% GDP of the total GDP in the Indian economy. It plays a crucial role in creating jobs, maintaining food security, and fostering economic progress while facing the challenges in modernization and sustainability [1,2]. Over half of the population of India, especially in rural areas, is employed in agriculture, making it the major employer in the nation. Millions of farmers, workers, and their families rely on it. The Indian economy has been centered on agriculture, which is still an important aspect of the country's economic structure today. Through its links to other industries like agribusiness, food processing, and retail, agriculture made a significant direct and indirect contribution to India's GDP. But, traditional farming has various disadvantages and restrictions that can impede agricultural production, sustainability, and economic development despite being firmly rooted in many cultures and regions [3]. Adopting technology and clever solutions to improve agricultural productivity and efficiency has become more and more important in recent years. Around the world, efforts are being undertaken to combine traditional practices with cutting-edge farming methods in order to develop more resilient and sustainable farming systems that are good for both farmers and the environment. Implementing smart greenhouse management systems is one area where technology has shown potential. Agricultural industry has changed significantly over time. These transformations are often referred to as different "agricultural revolutions" or "agriculture versions". This transition has been characterized by major technological advances, changing farming methods, and increased productivity. Agriculture 1.0 to Agriculture 4.0 is a transition that shows how agricultural techniques and technology have advanced over time [4]. Each level, from manual labor and simple equipment to highly developed, technologically driven farming practices, illustrates substantial advances in how agriculture is carried out. Here is a summary of each phase as shown in Figure 8.1.

1. **Agriculture 1.0 (Pre-mechanization):**
   - Agriculture 1.0, which dates back thousands of years, is the earliest type of agriculture known to mankind.
   - It was characterized by manual labor, the use of basic hand tools, and a concentration on subsistence farming to supply a family's or community's requirements at the most fundamental level.
   - Traditional knowledge and seasonal cycles were used to guide crop selection and cultivation.
   - The output of this stage was constrained, and it was frequently sensitive to problems with the environment and pests.

DOI: 10.1201/9781003457176-8

FIGURE 8.1   Evolution of architecture.

2. **Agriculture 2.0 (Mechanization):**
   - Mechanization, which started in the 18th and 19th centuries during the Industrial Revolution, was ushered in with Agriculture 2.0.
   - Farming became more productive and efficient because of the use of machinery and mechanization. Human and animal labor was displaced by the use of steam engines, tractors, and mechanical tools.
   - To increase yield, new seed kinds, chemical insecticides, and fertilizers were widely used.
   - It increased agricultural output and created the groundwork for contemporary farming methods.

3. **Agriculture 3.0 (Industrialization):**
   - Emerged during the Green Revolution in the middle of the 20th century.
   - During this era, mass production, standardized practices, improved irrigation, transportation, and infrastructure were introduced in agriculture simultaneously.
   - It regulates the application of high-yield crop varieties, chemical fertilizers, and irrigation systems.
   - The Green Revolution significantly enhanced productivity in agriculture and assisted in addressing the global issue of food scarcity.
   - It also raises concerns about environmental impacts, such as land degradation and water pollution.

4. **Agriculture 4.0 (Digitalization and Automation):**
   - It is a current and emerging phase characterized by the integration of advanced technologies and digital tools in agricultural practices.
   - Agriculture practices now include the use of robotics, big data, IoT, AI, data analytics, drones, and other cutting-edge technologies.
   - Precision agriculture, data-driven decision-making, and environmentally friendly farming methods are highlighted.
   - Farmers can remotely monitor and control various aspects of their operations, using real-time data to improve efficiency, reduce waste, and improve sustainability. It has the potential to revolutionize agriculture by making it more sustainable, more productive, and more capable of facing challenges like resource scarcity and climate change.

- Agriculture 4.0 represents a paradigm shift in agriculture, moving beyond simply increasing productivity to focus on sustainability, resource efficiency, and data-driven decision-making. It provides farmers with tools and information to optimize every aspect of their operations, from planting and irrigation to pest control and harvesting, helping to meet the growing demand for food worldwide. Globally, it minimizes costs and environmental impact.
- Significant improvements are made in the industry through the implementation of Agriculture 4.0, which optimizes resource use, boosts productivity, and addresses sustainability issues.

We propose an AIoT-based futuristic greenhouse management system for the agricultural industry as shown in Figure 8.2. A comprehensive set of tools, technologies, and procedures used to track and manage many elements of greenhouse settings is cumulative as a greenhouse management system. Monitoring and managing environmental parameters, irrigation, and fertilizer availability are necessary to sustain optimal plant growth. Greenhouse management systems are created to provide plants with the optimum, regulated environment and produce at their highest levels.

In Agriculture 4.0, the scope of AIoT is extensive and has enormous potential to change the agriculture sector. The following are some crucial areas in agriculture where AIoT is having a significant impact:

- **Precision Farming:** The AIoT makes it possible to precisely track and oversee agricultural operations. IoT sensors gather information on crop health, soil moisture, temperature, humidity, and nutrient levels [5]. To optimize resource allocation, irrigation scheduling, and pest management, AI systems analyze these data. As a result, the yield improves, input costs are decreased, and the environmental effect is reduced.
- **Smart Irrigation:** AIoT-based irrigation systems continuously track the temperature and soil moisture content. AI systems can use this data to analyze beneficial irrigation plans and adjust water distribution accordingly. By doing so, water resources are conserved and water use efficiency is increased. This also minimizes overwatering and water wastage.
- **Crop Monitoring and Disease Detection:** AIoT systems encourage precise and continuous crop growth and health monitoring. These systems use sensors, cameras, and other IoT devices to collect information on crop health. temperature, humidity, and plant growth [6]. Then, machine learning algorithms are used to examine this data in order to find any indications of irregularity or disease in the crops. Artificial intelligence (AIoT) systems can assist farmers in identifying problems early and taking appropriate measures to stop losses by continually and correctly monitoring crops. So, crop damage can be avoided and treatment plans can be optimized with timely intervention.
- **Supply Chain Optimization:** AIoT contributes in improving agricultural supply chain efficiency. Throughout the whole supply chain, sensors and connected devices monitor the location, quality, and state of agricultural products. To maximize logistics, minimize spoilage, and minimize post-harvest losses, AI systems analyze these data. This makes inventory management easier and guarantees that customers receive high-quality goods.
- **Livestock Monitoring and Management:** AIoT technologies help manage and monitor the health and productivity of cattle. Body temperature, milk production, feeding habits, and animal behavior are just a few of the factors that IoT sensors can monitor. These data are analyzed by AI systems to find health problems, make the best feeding plans, and forecast breeding cycles. This improves overall farm productivity, disease prevention, and animal welfare.
- **Agricultural Robotics:** AIoT makes it possible to integrate robotic technologies into agriculture. Planting, harvesting, and spraying chores can be carried out by autonomous drones, robots, and intelligent gear with AI and IoT capabilities [7]. These robots can

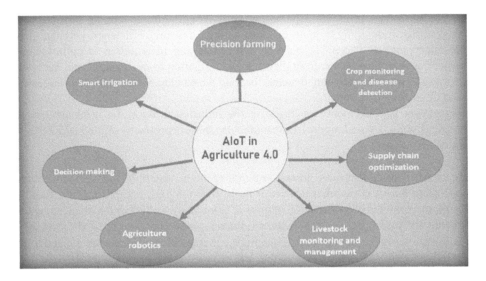

FIGURE 8.2   AIoT in agriculture 4.0.

analyze real-time data, make choices on the fly, and execute precise operations, increasing efficiency and lowering labor costs.

- **Decision-Making Based on Data:** AIoT systems offer farmers and other agricultural stakeholders useful information for making decisions. To develop prediction models, recommend best practices, and assist in strategic planning, AI algorithms analyze both historical and current data. Making educated decisions, lowering risks, and enhancing overall farm management are all facilitated by this data-driven approach.

The adoption of AIoT in greenhouse management offers several benefits and addresses various challenges faced by traditional greenhouse systems. The need for AIoT-based system is needed due to the following reasons:

1. Enhanced resource optimization
2. Real-time monitoring and decision-making
3. Improved crop health and disease management
4. Precision irrigation and nutrition management
5. Climate control and energy efficiency
6. Remote monitoring and automation
7. Data-driven insights and predictive analytics
8. Sustainability and environmental benefits

8.2   LITERATURE SURVEY

The absence of accurate crop damage information hinders integrated pest management (IPM). For informed decision-making, farm managers need knowledge about insect pests and plant diseases. In order to manage pests and diseases wisely and effectively, a system known as IPDM was developed [8]. Edge computing devices were used to locate pest insects in greenhouses and assess environmental conditions. Long-term spatiotemporal insect pest counts and environmental data collection revealed significant annual reductions in insect pest count, up to 50.7%, in greenhouses growing tomatoes and orchids. The ESP8266 Node MCU is a low-cost, effective programmable module that can monitor and regulate a range of greenhouse parameters, including the moisture content of the soil, the amount of light being used, the temperature, and the humidity [9]. With this module, greenhouse conditions may be precisely managed for maximum crop yields through real-time monitoring and automatic control. In this method, sensors collect data, which is processed by the NodeMCU module, and parameters are controlled via water pumps, motors, exhaust systems, and light systems. The module was connected to the wireless internet or IoT platforms to send data to smartphones, enabling remote monitoring. Different types and working principles of humidity sensors and moisture sensors and their applications were explored. With the help of this cutting-edge system, a more effective and sustainable solution can be produced for greenhouse management where the system collects data from various sensors to optimize temperature, humidity, and lighting conditions for plant growth [10]. Multi-sensor data are processed through the improved fuzzy controller to generate accurate data features for neural network training. AIoT, NB-IoT, and 5G technologies applied to intelligent greenhouse control systems and the improvement of fuzzy neural network algorithm enhanced system performance these both Contribute to the development of smart greenhouses [11]. Through the provision of real-time data analysis and remote monitoring capabilities, AIoT, NB-IoT, and 5G technologies are revolutionizing greenhouse management systems. The creation of smart greenhouses with improved automation, precision farming, and crop yield optimization is made possible by these technologies. Fuzzy neural network methods optimize irrigation, temperature, and lighting control, which is a key factor in enhancing system performance [11]. The employment of these technologies in greenhouse operations boosts production, efficiency, and sustainability.

8.3 TRADITIONAL VS AIOT APPROACH FOR GREENHOUSE MANAGEMENT

1. Traditional greenhouse management growers rely on manual monitoring of environmental variables that can be time-consuming and prone to human errors, decisions regarding resource allocation, irrigation schedules, and pest management are often based on individual experience and knowledge as shown in Figure 8.3. Utilizing only manual monitoring could result in inconsistent or inaccurate monitoring of greenhouse conditions, crop health, and resource utilization. By utilizing cutting-edge data analysis methods and technology, greenhouse operations can be greatly improved, and it is able to collect precise, real-time data and acquire thorough insights about greenhouse conditions, crop health, and resource usage [12].

2. By using the AIoT approach, we may achieve real-time data monitoring, data-driven decision-making, proactive management, predictive analysis, automation, and remote control, as well as improved efficiency and productivity with the AIoT approach in greenhouse management.

3. Monitoring of real-time data: AIoT systems continuously gather real-time data from IoT sensors deployed everywhere in the greenhouse as shown in Figure 8.4. This makes it possible to monitor the health of plants and the environment

FIGURE 8.3 Traditional greenhouse management system.

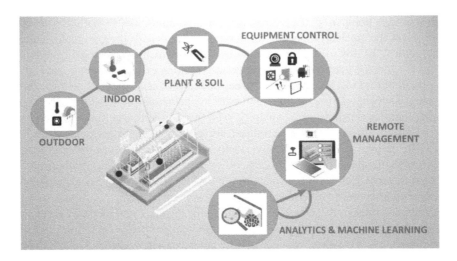

FIGURE 8.4   AIoT based smart greenhouse management system.

4. Making decisions based on data analysis: In order to analyze the collected data and deliver relevant information, AI systems are essential. AI algorithms can be used to process and evaluate the sensor data, which includes environmental variables, in order to derive useful insights and offer greenhouse operators practical recommendations.
5. Proactive management: AIoT offers proactive management by spotting anomalies, foreseeing prospective problems, and automatically initiating responses. This keeps growing conditions at their best while also preventing crop damage and using fewer resources.
6. Predictive analysis: AIoT systems can foresee future conditions and trends by using previous data and predictive analytics. In terms of crop cycles, resource allocation, and market demands, this helps growers to plan and make smart decisions.
7. Automation and remote control: IoT enables automated and remote control of greenhouse activities. Systems like irrigation, lighting, and climate controls can be managed by AI algorithms, requiring less physical labor and enabling remote monitoring and management.
8. Increased productivity and efficiency: AIoT optimizes resource management, minimizes waste, and ensures the most optimal circumstances for growth. This boosts agricultural yields, production of higher quality, and overall productivity.

8.4   WORKING OF AIOT-BASED SMART GREENHOUSE MANAGEMENT SYSTEM

The application of AI and IoT in agriculture has enormous potential for effective and sustainable farming methods. AI-powered smart greenhouses can optimize temperature, humidity, and light levels for optimal growth conditions, while IoT sensors can monitor soil moisture, temperature, and other factors to improve irrigation and fertilization. Following are the many processes that AI and IoT take to operate in smart greenhouse management systems as shown in Figure 8.5.

1. **Data Collection:** In this phase, IoT sensors and devices which are placed all over the greenhouse are used to gather data. Sensors keep an eye on things like CO_2 levels, soil moisture, temperature, humidity, and light levels. IoT gadgets keep track of variables like nutrient and irrigation levels.
2. **Data Transmission:** After the collection of data, IoT devices transmit the collected data to a central data hub or cloud platform, and the data are securely transferred using wireless protocols like Wi-Fi or Zigbee.

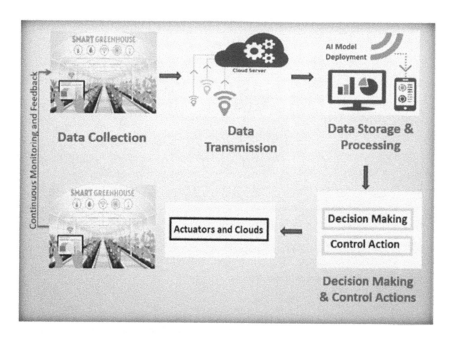

FIGURE 8.5 Working on a smart greenhouse management system.

3. **Data Storage and Processing:** The central data hub or cloud platform stores the collected data. AI algorithms are then applied to this collected data for its processing and analysis. After that, AI models can detect patterns, anomalies, and correlations between different environmental factors.

4. **Decision-Making and Control:** In this step, AI algorithms interpret the data and make intelligent decisions based on predefined rules or machine learning models. Decisions can include adjusting environmental settings, triggering alarms, or activating specific systems.

5. **Actuation and Automation:** Based on decisions made by AI algorithms, control systems are activated to implement the necessary actions. These control systems can regulate temperature, humidity, lighting, irrigation, and nutrient supply. To complete the necessary activities, IoT devices interface with actuators and systems.

6. **Feedback and Continuous Monitoring:** IoT sensors continuously monitor changes performed by the control systems. Data are once more gathered and transmitted to the central hub for evaluation and comments. They can gradually improve their decision-making by creating and modifying AI algorithms.

   Data from this cycle, which is continuously repeated, are used to monitor and optimize the greenhouse environment. The agriculture industry gains a number of advantages from the efficient resource management made possible by the integration of AI systems with IoT technology in greenhouse systems [11].

8.5 ADVANTAGES OF AIOT-BASED GREENHOUSE MANAGEMENT

The AIoT has several advantages for greenhouse management systems as shown in Figure 8.6 and the descriptions are listed below:

1. It enables real-time monitoring and control of a range of environmental variables. The system can automatically modify these parameters using AI algorithms to enhance plant growth and lower energy usage, making the greenhouse operation more sustainable and effective [11].

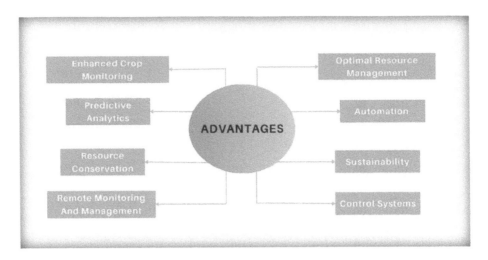

FIGURE 8.6   Advantages of smart greenhouse system.

2. The AIoT strategy also automates routine processes like fertilization and irrigation, which boosts productivity and lowers labor costs.
3. Machine learning algorithms of AIoT analyze previous data to anticipate future plant growth, pest attacks, and disease outbreaks. This aids greenhouse managers in taking preventative steps to avoid production loss and minimize the usage of pesticides, resulting in a more economical and ecologically friendly method of farming.
4. AI systems can examine the accumulated data to offer analyses and prognostications. This supports sustainable practices and lessens the environmental impact of greenhouse operators' decisions regarding resource allocation, pest and disease control, energy use, and others.

8.6   CHALLENGES OF AIOT-BASED GREENHOUSE MANAGEMENT

Despite the many advantages of AIoT-based greenhouse management systems, several challenges exist as shown in Figure 8.7, and these challenges must be resolved.

1. **Data Security and Privacy:** AIoT systems collect and send enormous amounts of data from sensors and devices. The security and privacy of sensitive data must be ensured. Precautions such as encryption, access restrictions, and secure data storage must be put in place to stop unauthorized access or data breaches.
2. **Interoperability and Standards:** It is possible for IoT devices used in greenhouse management to come from different manufacturers and employ various communication protocols. To enable efficient communication and integration across diverse devices and systems, smooth interoperability and standardization of protocols are crucial.
3. **Scalability:** It is more complex to manage and scale the infrastructure as the number of IoT devices and sensors increases. There may be scalability issues that need to be resolved when handling a lot of data, configuring and maintaining equipment, and guaranteeing dependable communication.
4. **Data Complexity and Analysis:** Data collected by IoT sensors can be expensive and complicated. From this data obtaining some meaningful insights and patterns demands high-tech AI Techniques and analytics skills [13]. To handle such complicated data, it might be difficult to develop and apply robust analytics models.

Challenge 1
Data Security and Privacy

Challenge 2
Interoperability & Standards

Challenge 3
Scalability

Challenge 4
Data Complexity & Analysis

Challenge 5
Power Consumption & Energy Efficiency

Challenge 6
Cost and Return on Investment

Challeneg 7
Technical Skills and Knowledge

FIGURE 8.7   Challenges associated with smart greenhouse system.

5. **Power Consumption and Energy Efficiency:** Energy is continuously used by IoT devices and sensors. The need for precise data collection and power usage optimization might be challenging to balance. To ensure the cost-effective and sustainable operation of the AIoT system, energy efficiency plans must be implemented [14].
6. **Cost and Return on Investment (ROI):** Deploying an AIoT-based greenhouse management system may involve significant upfront costs, including investment in IoT devices, sensors, connectivity infrastructure, and AI software platforms. It's crucial to guarantee a profitable return on investment in the form of higher agricultural output, resource savings, and operational improvements.
7. **Technological Skills and Knowledge:** The successful implementation and management of AIoT systems require specialized skills and knowledge in areas such as IoT, AI, data analytics, and cybersecurity. To install and manage these sophisticated systems efficiently, organizations may encounter difficulties finding or developing the requisite skills.

Addressing these challenges through proper planning, robust security measures, system design, and the selection of reliable vendors and partners can help overcome the hurdles associated with AIoT-based greenhouse management systems. Ensuring ongoing monitoring, adaptation, and continuous improvement can lead to successful implementations in the long run.

8.7   GREENHOUSE MANAGEMENT SYSTEM USING IOT AND AIOT

To provide automated farming operations, the IoT-based greenhouse system minimizes manual involvement. It protects plants from unfavorable weather conditions such as wind, hail, UV radiation, insects, and pests. The greenhouse keeps track of important climatic factors like temperature, humidity, light intensity, and soil moisture [15].

The smart greenhouse consists of polyvinyl chloride (PVC) pipes supporting the wooden plywood base that are joined at junctions. The stability and balance of the structure are preserved by steel wires. Except for the foundation, the greenhouse is entirely covered in a transparent plastic sheet as shown in Figure 8.8.

FIGURE 8.8   Model of the greenhouse system.

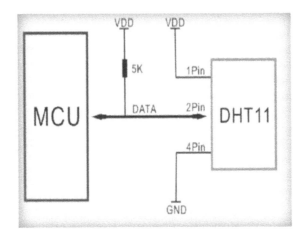

FIGURE 8.9   Interfacing of node MCU with DHT sensor.

IoT-based greenhouse management system consists of two modules, a hardware module and a software module. The hardware module consists of ESP32, Arduino Uno, DHT11 humidity and temperature sensor, light dependent resistor (LDR), soil moisture sensor, humidifier and dehumidifier, relay, and power supply as shown in Figure 8.9, while the software module is ThingSpeak open source program.

After being gathered, sensor data are transmitted to a microcontroller for processing. For internet access, this microcontroller is connected to an ESP-8266 Wi-Fi module. Then, processed data are sent to the cloud platform ThingSpeak to be shown on a customized webpage.

ThingSpeak is used to store and retrieve data from linked devices (things) through the internet or a local area network (LAN) utilizing protocols like Hyper Text Transfer Protocol (HTTP) and Message Queuing Telemetry Transport (MQTT). The popular data analysis and visualization program MATLAB can then be used to analyze and display the ThingSpeak data. Application areas for ThingSpeak include sensor logging, social media logging, and location monitoring [16,17]. The components used to build the hardware module and their respective functions are as follows:

1. **ESP32:** It is a 2.4 GHz frequency band Wi-Fi and Bluetooth combination chip. It offers capabilities including Wi-Fi and Bluetooth connectivity, power management, and others. The interfacing of ESP32 with the water pump is as shown in Figure 8.10.
2. **DHT11 Humidity and Temperature Sensor**: It is a digital temperature and humidity sensor with a data pin that outputs a digital signal. It uses two electrodes with a moisture-holding substrate sandwiched between them to measure the humidity of the air around it as shown in Figure 8.11.
3. **LDR:** LDR is a resistor influenced by the amount of light that strikes its surface. It is sometimes referred to as a photocell, photoresist, or photoconductor. An LDR has a high resistance in the dark and a lower resistance in the light.

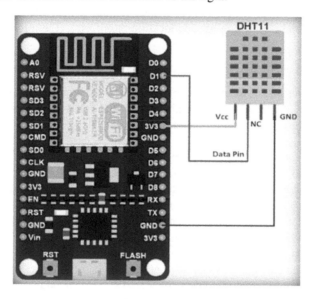

FIGURE 8.10   Interfacing of node MCU with water pump.

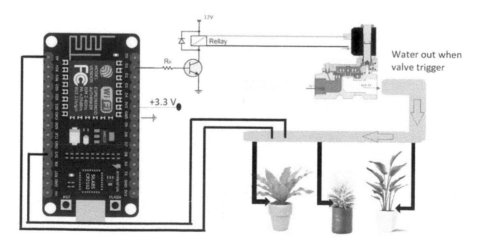

FIGURE 8.11   Interfacing of MCU with DHT sensor.

Interfacing

4. **Humidifier and Dehumidifier:** This works by converting electricity into a temperature difference across a Peltier module via the thermoelectric effect. As a result, there is a temperature difference that can be used to humidify and dehumidify the air. The system consists of a Peltier module, cold- and hot-side heat sinks, a fan, and relays.

5. **Soil Moister Sensor:** It uses capacitance to determine the water content of the soil and then produces a voltage proportional to that water content. It is frequently used in agricultural applications and can function in analog or digital modes.

6. **Arduino Platform:** It is an open-source hardware and software platform for building electronics projects. It offers an Integrated Development Environment (IDE) for microcontroller programming as shown in Figure 8.12.

7. **ThingSpeak:** It is a free, open-source IoT application for storing and retrieving data. For data analysis and visualization, it supports several protocols, including Hyper Text Transfer Protocol (HTTP) and MQTT. It is used for many different purposes, including sensor logging, social media logging, and location monitoring (Figure 8.13).

8.7.1 IoT-Based System to AIoT-Based System

To enhance the capabilities of the existing IoT-based smart greenhouse management system, automated decision-making, and improved crop management, the following strategies are applied and converted into an AIoT-based system as shown in Figure 8.14.

1. To improve the quality of data collection, advanced sensors are used for checking soil quality, plant health, and environmental factors. Since a massive amount of data are generated by advanced sensors, there is a need to set up a powerful data storage system.

2. Data pre-processing is required for accurate AI analysis. To achieve efficient and accurate AI analysis, computer vision, machine learning, and deep learning-based AI models are deployed. These AI models are used to predict diseases of plants, yield optimization, and effective management of resources. After training and learning of AI models from past setup data, real-time data analysis can be done. This is a continuous process to make predictions and recommendations. By using the model's recommendation, automated system can be developed to adjust the temperature and humidity levels of the greenhouse system.

    The feedback loop can be incorporated for taking continuous and regular updates. Using this iterative feedback mechanism, the accuracy of the AI model can be enhanced [18].

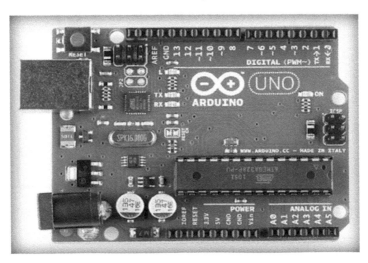

FIGURE 8.12　Arduino uno microcontroller.

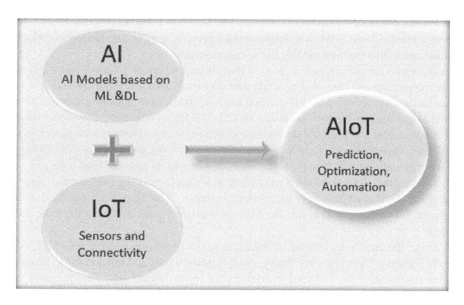

FIGURE 8.13   Combination of AI and IoT.

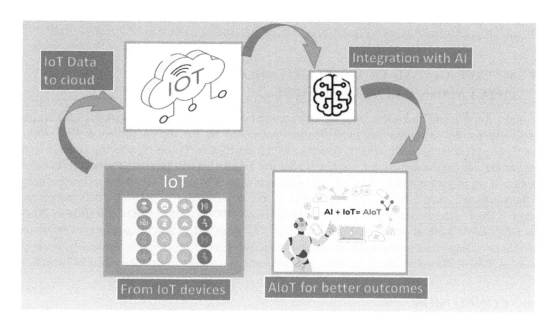

FIGURE 8.14   From IoT to AIoT.

3. To control parameters and continuous monitoring of system performance, a user-friendly interface is required so that managers can monitor and control real-time data remotely [19].

8.8   RECENT ADVANCEMENTS OF AIOT APPLICATION IN SMART GREENHOUSE MANAGEMENT

The integration of multiple technologies has been the focus of recent developments in smart greenhouse systems with the goals of enhancing productivity, sustainability, and agricultural output. Significant advancements in smart greenhouse systems include the following:

- Accurate environmental parameter modification becomes possible by modern automation and control technology. In order to improve plant growth, sensors and actuators collaborate to continuously monitor and modify these circumstances.
- IoT technologies are currently used in smart greenhouses to connect various parts and enable remote monitoring and control. Real-time data on factors like soil moisture, nutrient levels, and air quality are provided by IoT-enabled sensors and devices, enabling growers to make informed decisions to improve plant health [20–22]. Smart greenhouse systems based on AIoT combine data analytics and decision support tools to offer growers with powerful information and suggestions. These technologies can boost crop yields, increase efficiency, and improve crop management techniques by analyzing historical and real-time data.
- Crops can be grown in a controlled environment without soil using hydroponics and vertical farming techniques in smart greenhouse systems. While maintaining ideal growing conditions, this method makes the most use of available space and uses the least amount of water.
- To examine the enormous amount of data that smart greenhouses have gathered, AI and machine learning techniques are being used. Based on past and current data, these technologies can forecast the real-time conditions for crops, improving efficiency, and saving resources.
- Energy is heavily used in greenhouses for lighting, heating, and cooling. Energy-efficient insulation materials, energy-saving lighting systems like LED lights, and the utilization of renewable energy sources like solar power to lower energy costs and environmental effect are all examples of advances in smart greenhouse technology [23–25].

8.9 MARKET ANALYSIS OF SMART GREENHOUSE EFFECT MANAGEMENT USING AIOT

The quest for efficient and sustainable agriculture methods has led to major growth in the smart greenhouse market. This rise has been further accelerated by the incorporation of AIoT technology into greenhouse management systems, which enables real-time monitoring, data-driven decision-making, and automation for optimal resource utilization and increased productivity. The adoption of smart greenhouse technologies is being encouraged by numerous governments throughout the world, which is boosting market expansion. It is expected that in the year 2020, the global market of smart greenhouses will be USD 1.4 billion and will reach up to USD 2.1 billion by 2025 with a CAGR of 9.2% as shown in Figure 8.15 [26,27]. AIoT offers several advantages in smart greenhouse management such as helping in harvesting, improving crop productivity, and optimizing resources [28,29]. Based on the technology and applications, the reports are described in Table 8.1.

8.10 CONCLUSION

This chapter briefly explores the evolution of agriculture from Agriculture 1.0 to Agriculture 4.0. With the use of technologies like AI, IoT, big data, and robotics, Agriculture 4.0 emphasizes data-driven decision-making, precision farming, and environmentally friendly farming methods. Greenhouse management system based on AIoT provides better optimization of resources, real-time analysis, remote monitoring, better decision making, better crop health, disease prediction with its management, precise irrigation, climate control, energy efficiency, automation, data-driven insights, predictive analytics, sustainability, and environmental benefits. This chapter also explains how a smart greenhouse system uses sensors attached to a microcontroller for data collection. The system can access the internet because the microcontroller is also linked to a Wi-Fi module. To show the gathered data on a customized webpage, the processed data are uploaded to the cloud via ThingSpeak. Furthermore, it shows how an IoT-based system can be transformed into an AIoT-based greenhouse management system. Working of a smart greenhouse management system, the benefits, challenges, and applications of AIoT are also discussed in this chapter.

FIGURE 8.15 Market growth of smart greenhouse system.

TABLE 8.1
Reports of AIoT in Agriculture

S. No.	Scenario	Details
1.	Market Size in 2025	USD 2.1 billion
2.	Market Size in 2020	USD 1.4 billion
3.	Growth Rate	CAGR of 9.1%
4.	Segment Included	I. Type Hydroponics and non-hydroponics II. Covering material Polyethylene, polycarbonate, and others Offering hardware, software, and services. III. Components HVAC system, various sensors, controller, LED. IV. End User Retail gardens, education, and research institutes, commercial growers, and others
5.	Geographical Regions	North America, Europe, Asia, Latin America, Middle East & Africa
6.	Company Covered	Nexus corporation-USA, Argus control-Canada, Green Tech. agro-USA, Heliospectra-Sweden, and many more
7.	Technology	Machine Learning, Computer Vision, Predictive Analytics
8.	Crops Cultivated	Vegetables, flowers, and food

REFERENCES

1. U. Pattanayak, M. Mallick, "Agricultural production and economic growth in India: An econometric analysis." *Asian Journal of Multidisciplinary Studies*, 5(3), 62–66, 2017.
2. R. Wagh, A. Dongre, "Agricultural sector: Status, challenges and its role in Indian economy." *Journal of Commerce & Management Thought*, 7(2), 209–218, 2016.
3. B. Sinha, R. Dhanalakshmi, "Recent advancements and challenges of Internet of Things in smart agriculture: A survey." *Future Generation Computer Systems*, 126, 169–184, 2022.
4. N. Sharma, S. Tiwari, A. Khandekar, "Review on applications of industry 4.0 in agriculture sector." *International Journal of Creative Research Thoughts (IJCRT)*, 8(8), 1989–93, 2020.

5. M.M. Abbassy, W.M. Ead, "Intelligent greenhouse management system." *2020 6th International Conference on Advanced Computing and Communication Systems (ICACCS)*. IEEE, Coimbatore, India, 2020.

6. Z. Li, et al. "Design of an intelligent management system for agricultural greenhouses based on the internet of things." *IEEE International Conference on Computational Science and Engineering (CSE) and IEEE International Conference on Embedded and Ubiquitous Computing (EUC)*, vol. 2. IEEE, Guangzhou, China, 2017.

7. S.G. Vougioukas, "Agricultural robotics." *Annual Review of Control, Robotics, and Autonomous Systems*, 2, 365–392, 2019.

8. D.J.A. Rustia, L.Y. Chiu, C.Y. Lu, Y.F. Wu, S.K. Chen, J.Y. Chung, J.C. Hsu, T.T. Lin, "Towards intelligent and integrated pest management through an AIoT-based monitoring system." *Pest Management Science*, 78(10), 4288–4302. doi: 10.1002/ps.7048. Epub 2022 Jul 8. PMID: 35716088,2022.

9. A. Vishwakarma, A.K. Sahu, N.A. Sheikh, P. Payasi, S.K. Rajput, L. Srivastava, "IOT based greenhouse monitoring and controlling system." *IEEE Students Conference on Engineering & Systems (SCES)*, pp. 1–6, Prayagraj, India, 2020.

10. H. Liu, S. Fang, X. Guo, "Research and design of intelligent greenhouse control system based on AIoT fusion technology." *IOP Conference Series: Earth and Environmental Science*. Vol. 474. No. 3. IOP Publishing, 2020.

11. A. Zaguia, "Smart greenhouse management system with cloud-based platform and IoT sensors." *Spatial Information Research*, 31, 1–13, 2023.

12. F. Zhang, X. Wan, T. Zheng, J. Cui, X. Li, Y. Yang, "Smart greenhouse management system based on NB-IoT and smartphone." *17th International Joint Conference on Computer Science and Software Engineering (JCSSE)*, Bangkok, Thailand, pp. 36–41, 2020. doi: 10.1109/JCSSE49651.2020.9268351.

13. H. Li, et al., "Towards automated greenhouse: A state of the art review on greenhouse monitoring methods and technologies based on internet of things." *Computers and Electronics in Agriculture*, 191, 106558, 2021.

14. R. Rayhana, G. Xiao, Z. Liu, "Internet of things empowered smart greenhouse farming." *IEEE Journal of Radio Frequency Identification*, 4(3), 195–211, 2020.

15. A. Badji, A. Benseddik, H. Bensaha, A. Boukhelifa, I. Hasrane, "Design, technology, and management of greenhouse: A review." *Journal of Cleaner Production*, 373, 133753, 2022. ISSN 0959-6526.

16. A.K. Nair, C. John, J. Sahoo. "Implementation of intelligent IoT.", *AI and IoT for Sustainable Development in Emerging Countries: Challenges and Opportunities*. Cham: Springer International Publishing, pp. 27–50, 2022. doi: 10.1007/978-3-030-90618-4_2.

17. A. Vishwakarma, A. Sahu, N. Sheikh, P. Payasi, S.K. Rajput, L. Srivastava, "IOT based greenhouse monitoring and controlling system." *IEEE Students Conference on Engineering & Systems (SCES)*, Prayagraj, India, pp. 1–6, 2020. doi: 10.1109/SCES50439.2020.9236693.

18. Y. Aisha, Y.A. Abass, S. Adeshina, "Greenhouse monitoring and control system with an arduino system." *15th International Conference on Electronics, Computer and Computation (ICECCO)*, pp. 1–6, Abuja, Nigeriay, 2019. doi:10.1109/ICECCO48375.2019.9043188.

19. H.K. Adli, M.A. Remli, K.N.S. Wan Salihin Wong, N.A. Ismail, A. González-Briones, J.M. Corchado, M.S. Mohamad, "Recent advancements and challenges of AIoT application in smart agriculture: A review." *Sensors*, 23(7), 3752, 2023. doi:10.3390/s23073752.

20. A. Chamra, H. Harmanani, "A smart green house control and management system using IoT." In: Latifi, S. (eds.) *17th International Conference on Information Technology-New Generations (ITNG 2020)*. Advances in Intelligent Systems and Computing, vol. 1134. Springer, Cham, 2020. doi: 10.1007/978-3-030-43020-7_86.

21. Z. Xiaoyan, Z. Xiangyang, D. Chen, C. Zhaohui, S. Shangming, Z. Zhaohui, "The design and implementation of the greenhouse monitoring system based on GSM and RF technologies." *2013 International Conference on Computational Problem-Solving (ICCP)*, Jiuzhai, China, pp. 32–35, 2013. doi: 10.1109/ICCPS.2013.6893574.

22. P. Laiolo, et al., "Validation of remote sensing soil moisture products with a distributed continuous hydrological model." *IEEE Geoscience and Remote Sensing Symposium*, Quebec City, QC, Canada, pp. 3319–3322, 2014. doi: 10.1109/IGARSS.2014.6947190.

23. A. Bseiso, B. Abele, S. Ferguson, P. Lusch, K. Mehta, "A decision support tool for greenhouse farmers in low-resource settings." *IEEE Global Humanitarian Technology Conference (GHTC)*, Seattle, WA, pp. 292–297, 2015. doi: 10.1109/GHTC.2015.7343987.

24. K. A. Czyzyk, S. T. Bement, W. F. Dawson, K. Mehta, "Quantifying water savings with greenhouse farming." *IEEE Global Humanitarian Technology Conference (GHTC 2014)*, San Jose, CA, pp. 325–332, 2014. doi: 10.1109/GHTC.2014.6970300.

25. M. Mahdavian, M. B. Poudeh, N. Wattanapongsakorn, "Greenhouse lighting optimization for tomato cultivation considering Real-Time Pricing (RTP) of electricity in the smart grid." *10th International Conference on Electrical Engineering/Electronics, Computer, Telecommunications and Information Technology*, Krabi, Thailand, pp. 1–6, 2013. doi: 10.1109/ECTICon.2013.6559619.

26. J. Zhao, J. Zhang, Y. Feng, J. Guo, "The study and application of the IOT technology in agriculture." *3rd International Conference on Computer Science and Information Technology*, Chengdu, pp. 462–465, 2010. doi: 10.1109/ICCSIT.2010.5565120.

27. Business wire: Global Smart Greenhouse Market Report 2022: "Integration of IoT and AI in Agriculture Practices Drives Growth - Research And Markets.com". https://www.businesswire.com/news/home/20221114005727/en/Global-Smart-Greenhouse-Market-Report-2022-Integration-of-IoT-and-AI-in-Agriculture-Practices-Drives-Growth---ResearchAndMarkets.com.

28. The Future of Smart Greenhouses Empowered by AIoT. https://medium.com/foothill-ventures/the-future-of-smart-greenhouses-empowered-by-aiot-43650dc7fa1b.

29. V. Sorathia, Z. Laliwala, S. Chaudhary, "Towards agricultural marketing reforms: Web services orchestration approach." *IEEE International Conference on Services Computing (SCC'05)*, vol-1, Orlando, FL, pp. 260–267, 2005. doi: 10.1109/SCC.2005.100.

9 CardioSegNet Meets XAI
A Breakthrough in Left Ventricle Delineation within Cardiac Diagnostics

Abhinaya Saravanan, S. David Samuel Azariya, and Nisha Soms

9.1 INTRODUCTION

Cardiovascular ailments remain a predominant health challenge worldwide, accounting for numerous fatalities annually. Prompt and accurate cardiac assessments are pivotal for elevating patient prognosis and alleviating healthcare system strains. Echocardiography stands as a pivotal non-invasive diagnostic tool, offering real-time cardiac insights, tracking disease progression, and gauging therapeutic impacts. However, manual echocardiographic evaluations can be time-consuming, subject to observer variability, and demand specialized acumen. This has spurred interest in harnessing deep learning for echocardiography image automation, aiming for heightened precision, swifter analyses, and reduced human-induced segmentation errors.

This manuscript unveils an innovative preprocessing methodology for echocardiographic imagery, targeting image enhancement and facilitating subsequent analyses. The method integrates noise mitigation, contrast amplification, and standardization, priming images for optimal segmentation. Utilizing the CAMUS dataset, CardioSegNet, a deep learning architecture, is used post-preprocessing to carefully separate the left ventricle (LV) from echocardiographic pictures.

CardioSegNet represents a specialized convolutional neural network (CNN) architecture developed specifically for delineating cardiac structures. It combines many loss function advantages to improve segmentation accuracy. Through metrics such as the Dice coefficient, Tversky loss, and binary cross-entropy loss, CardioSegNet offers a comprehensive evaluation of pixel differentiation and segmentation precision. Additionally, data augmentation strategies, including horizontal and vertical inversions, are employed to bolster model robustness and deter overfitting.

To conclude, this contribution enriches the burgeoning domain of deep learning in cardiac imaging by introducing a distinctive preprocessing strategy and the avant-garde CardioSegNet model. The proposed approach showcases promising results in automated and precise LV segmentation from echocardiographic visuals, signifying potential enhancements in clinical cardiac evaluations' efficiency and reliability.

The integration of Explainable AI (XAI) in our approach provides a transparent understanding of the model's decisions, bridging the gap between high-dimensional data and human interpretability. In the realm of medical imaging, where decisions can have profound implications on patient care, the ability to understand and trust a model's predictions is paramount. In addition to introducing a cutting-edge segmentation model and a novel preprocessing approach, this study highlights the relevance of explainability in AI-driven cardiac assessments.

DOI: 10.1201/9781003457176-9

9.2   LITERATURE REVIEW

The quest for pioneering medical image analysis methodologies has surged, particularly within cardiology. Utilizing deep learning for cardiac structure segmentation in echocardiography has become a focal research area, with numerous studies exploring varied architectures and strategies to enhance segmentation efficiency. This segment offers a literature synopsis, emphasizing echocardiography, the CAMUS dataset, image preprocessing techniques, deep learning-driven cardiac image segmentation, and the CardioSegNet architecture.

9.2.1   Echocardiography

Echocardiography, a non-intrusive imaging modality, employs ultrasonic waves to render cardiac anatomical and functional visuals [1]. It's a cornerstone in diagnosing and monitoring diverse cardiac disorders, such as myocardial infarctions, congenital anomalies, and valve pathologies [2]. Particularly emphasizing the left ventricle (LV), echocardiographic images are crucial for evaluating cardiac functionality [3].

9.2.2   CAMUS Dataset

In 2D echocardiographic images from the publicly available CAMUS dataset, both the left ventricle (LV) and right ventricle (RV) are emphasized across different phases of the cardiac cycle [4]. It amalgamates data from healthy individuals and those with varied cardiac disorders, making it apt for crafting and evaluating segmentation algorithms [5].

9.2.3   Image Preprocessing

Image preprocessing stands as a pivotal phase in medical image analysis, enhancing image clarity and interpretability [6]. Existing literature proposes myriad preprocessing strategies, including intensity standardization, noise mitigation, and data augmentation [7]. In our exploration, we advocate a novel preprocessing paradigm that integrates intensity standardization, trimming, and resizing, aiming to elevate echocardiography image clarity and simplify subsequent segmentation tasks.

9.2.4   Deep Learning for Cardiac Image Segmentation

Deep learning paradigms have emerged as potent tools in cardiac image segmentation, offering automated and meticulous cardiac structure delineation [8]. Convolutional neural networks (CNNs) are predominantly employed due to their prowess in discerning intricate spatial image features [9]. U-Net, a renowned CNN blueprint for medical image segmentation, is celebrated for its symmetric encoder-decoder design and efficient data utilization [10]. Numerous U-Net variants have been proposed to further enhance segmentation efficiency, including the V-Net [11] and Attention U-Net [12].

9.2.5   DeepLabV3+ for Cardiac Image Delineation

DeepLabV3+, conceptualized by Chen et al., is an advanced deep learning model tailored for semantic image segmentation, showcasing exemplary performance across varied applications, including cardiac image delineation [13]. This architecture builds upon the foundational DeepLabV3 design, incorporating a decoder component to enhance the precision of segmentation, particularly around object edges. Using atrous convolutions and Atrous Spatial Pyramid Pooling (ASPP), DeepLabV3+ captures multi-scale contextual information, refining it for the precise delineation of complex cardiac areas such as the LV in echocardiographic images.

9.2.6 Explainable AI (XAI) in Medical Imaging

The surge of deep learning in medical imaging has ushered in remarkable advancements in diagnostic accuracy and efficiency. However, the "black-box" nature of these models, where their decision-making processes remain opaque, has been a point of contention, especially in critical applications like cardiology. Explainable AI (XAI) emerges as a solution, aiming to make AI decisions transparent, interpretable, and trustworthy [17]. In cardiac imaging, XAI can elucidate the model's focus areas, providing cardiologists with insights into regions of interest and potential anomalies, thereby reinforcing their confidence in the model's predictions. Furthermore, XAI can aid in model refinement by highlighting areas where the model might be misinterpreting the data, paving the way for enhanced diagnostic precision [18].

9.2.6.1 Recent Advancements in Cardiac Imaging Using Deep Learning

The advent of deep learning has ushered in a transformative era for cardiac imaging, setting new benchmarks in precision and efficiency for the identification and diagnosis of heart-related ailments. The following are some of the groundbreaking developments in this domain:

Enhanced Cardiac Structure Segmentation: Historically, delineating cardiac structures like the left ventricle, right ventricle, and myocardium demanded significant time and expert oversight. However, with the introduction of convolutional neural networks (CNNs), the segmentation process has been significantly expedited, delivering consistent and precise results.

Detection of Cardiac Anomalies: Advanced deep learning algorithms are now adept at identifying irregularities in cardiac imagery, including myocardial infarctions, cardiomyopathies, and valve malfunctions. These algorithms can rapidly process vast image repositories, highlighting potential concerns for cardiologist evaluation.

Echocardiograms and Time-Series Analysis: The application of Recurrent Neural Networks (RNNs) and Long Short-Term Memory (LSTM) networks to echocardiogram datasets has enhanced the analysis of sequential data. This has been instrumental in forecasting cardiac incidents and comprehending cardiac functionality over durations.

Embracing Transfer Learning: Owing to the scarcity of annotated cardiac images, transfer learning has emerged as a favored technique. Models initially trained on extensive datasets can be subsequently refined using smaller, specialized datasets, amplifying the precision of cardiac imaging algorithms.

Application of Generative Adversarial Networks (GANs): GANs have found utility in cardiac imaging for data augmentation purposes. They can fabricate synthetic images, which are invaluable for training models, especially when genuine datasets are limited.

Incorporating Explainable AI (XAI) in Cardiac Imaging: Given the opaque nature of deep learning models, there's an increasing thrust toward ensuring their decisions are transparent and interpretable. Tools like Grad-CAM and LIME have been integrated with cardiac imaging models to provide visual insights into their focal points within images.

Synergy with Wearable Tech: The surge in wearable devices that track heart metrics has spurred the development of deep learning algorithms tailored to analyze these data in real time. These algorithms provide invaluable insights into cardiac health and might even forecast cardiac events.

In conclusion, the amalgamation of deep learning techniques with cardiac imaging has accelerated diagnostic processes, enabling tailored treatment regimens. As technological innovations persist, it's envisioned that these algorithms will further solidify their position in cardiac healthcare, delivering instantaneous insights and enhancing patient care outcomes.

9.3   METHODOLOGY

Our research delineates a comprehensive strategy for echocardiographic image preprocessing and the application of CardioSegNet for meticulous LV delineation. The methodology encompasses pivotal phases, including image preprocessing, evaluation metrics, data augmentation, and CardioSegNet's deployment. This segment elucidates the techniques and methodologies employed to achieve optimal echocardiography image segmentation.

9.3.1   IMAGE PREPROCESSING

Our echocardiography image preprocessing encompasses three pivotal phases: intensity standardization, trimming, and resizing. Intensity standardization is executed to homogenize pixel intensity values across visuals, ensuring model consistency and insensitivity to brightness and contrast variations [14]. The standardization formula employed is:

$$\text{normalized\_image} = \left(\text{image} - \text{min\_intensity}\right) / \left(\text{max\_intensity} - \text{min\_intensity}\right) \qquad (9.1)$$

Trimming is executed to excise extraneous regions, concentrating solely on the region of interest (ROI) encapsulating the LV. This phase aids in computational efficiency enhancement and model performance optimization by discarding superfluous data [15]. The trimming parameters are derived from the CAMUS dataset's manual annotations.

To visually represent echocardiography visuals and their corresponding masks, Figure 9.1 showcases an original visual juxtaposed with its ground truth mask. The left frame displays the echocardiography visual, capturing the LV and adjacent cardiac structures, while the right frame presents the ground truth mask, emphasizing the LV in the visual.

Lastly, resizing ensures uniform input image dimensions, a prerequisite for deep learning model training. In our study, visuals are resized to a consistent 256×256 pixel dimension using bilinear interpolation, a prevalent image resizing technique preserving the original visual's structure and fluidity [16].

Figure 9.1 displays a graphical depiction of an echocardiographic image alongside its corresponding ground truth mask for left ventricle (LV) segmentation. On the left side of the figure, the echocardiogram image displays the heart's anatomy, prominently featuring the left ventricle. The image demonstrates the complexity of the cardiac anatomy and probable problems in precisely

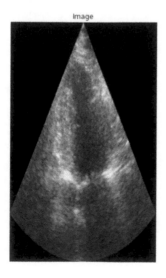

FIGURE 9.1   The ground truth mask (b) and original echocardiogram picture (a) are shown side by side in a single frame for comparison.

segmenting the LV. On the right side of the image, the segmented section is presented in white against a black background, emphasizing the LV in a binary representation. This mask guides the model as it learns the goal segmentation pattern throughout training. Figure 9.1's side-by-side comparison highlights how crucial effective segmentation is to ensure the correct extraction of clinically pertinent information from echocardiogram images.

Figure 9.2 displays a single frame with three pictures to visualize the original, preprocessed echocardiogram images and their related masks. On the left side of the frame, the original echocardiogram image is presented, depicting the left ventricle and adjacent cardiac structures. The center showcases the preprocessed image, emphasizing the enhancements achieved through preprocessing steps like intensity normalization, cropping, and resizing. The preprocessed ground truth mask, which draws attention to the left ventricle in the picture, is seen on the right side.

In Figure 9.3, two echocardiogram images are displayed side by side. The original picture, which depicts the various architecture and features of the heart, is displayed in the left panel. On the

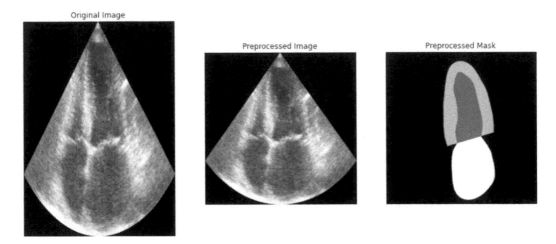

FIGURE 9.2 Original echocardiogram image (a), preprocessed image (b), and preprocessed ground truth mask (c), all exhibited side by side inside a single frame for comparison.

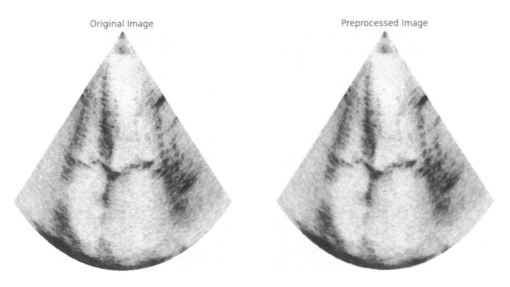

FIGURE 9.3 Using XAI-enhanced visualization, a comparison between the original echocardiography image (a) and its preprocessed version (b).

contrary, the preprocessed version of the identical image is shown in the right panel. Preprocessing improves the image's clarity visually, making it easier to see the cardiac structures.

The picture is made as ready as possible for subsequent analysis through normalization and other preparation procedures. Heatmap visualization is used to highlight the contrasts between original and processed photos, clearly depicting the advantages of preprocessing.

Figure 9.4 thoroughly visualizes the echocardiogram picture and the accompanying mask. The original echocardiogram picture, which depicts the complicated components of the heart, can be seen in the top-left panel. The original mask is shown in the top-right panel next to it, emphasizing the area of interest in the left ventricle. The preprocessed version of the echocardiogram picture is shown in the bottom-left panel. The image's clarity is improved using preprocessing methods, making it easier to see the heart components. Lastly, the bottom-right panel exhibits the preprocessed mask, which aligns with the enhanced details of the preprocessed image. This four-panel visualization provides a holistic view of the transformation and enhancement processes, from the original image and mask to their preprocessed counterparts.

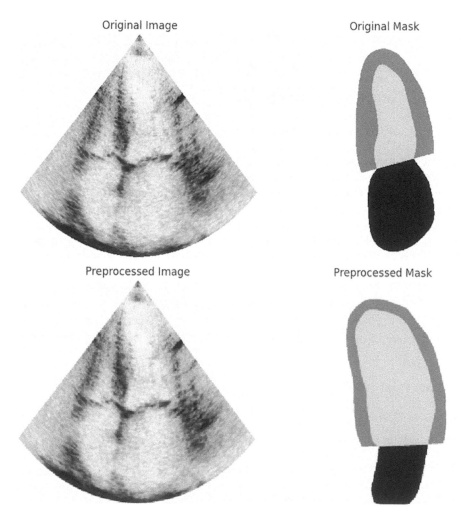

FIGURE 9.4 Comparative visualization of original and preprocessed echocardiography images with corresponding masks.

9.3.2 EVALUATION METRICS

Dice Coefficient (D_c): The Dice metric, sometimes referred to as the Sørensen-Dice similarity measure, evaluates the congruence between the forecasted segmentation overlay and the genuine reference overlay. The following equation is used to calculate the Dice metric:

$$\text{Dice}(X,Y) = (2*|X \cap Y| + \text{smoothing}) / (|X| + |Y| + \text{smoothing} + \text{tiny\_constant}) \qquad (9.2)$$

In cases where smoothing and tiny_constant are small values, dividing by zero is avoided. Higher Dice coefficient values indicate that the model segmented the images more accurately.

Dice Loss (D_l): The Dice coefficient (D_c), the inverse of dice loss, is calculated as follows. The complement of the dice coefficient is used to compute the dice loss:

$$D_l = 1 - D_c \qquad (9.3)$$

Tversky Loss (T_l): Tversky loss is a more inclusive version of Dice loss that considers different weightings of false positives and false negatives. Tversky loss is calculated as follows:

$$T_l = 1 - T_c \qquad (9.4)$$

where the Tversky coefficient (T_c) is described as:

$$T_c = (y_{tp} + s) / (y_{tp} + \alpha * f_p + (1 - \alpha) * f_n + s + t_c) \qquad (9.5)$$

[y true positive(y_{tp}), false positive(f_p), false negative(f_n), tiny constant(t_c), smoothing(s)]

In this context, smooth and epsilon act as minor constants to avoid zero division, whereas alpha is a hyperparameter that determines the relative relevance of false positives and false negatives.

Mixed Loss (M_l): The binary cross-entropy loss (Bcel), dice loss (D_l), and Tversky loss (T_l) are balancedly combined to form the combined loss. This harmonized loss approach aids the model in emphasizing both individual pixel classification and the overall quality of segmentation. The formula for the mixed loss is:

$$M_l = \alpha * B_{cel} + (1 - \alpha) * [\beta * D_l + (1 - \beta) * T_l] \qquad (9.6)$$

Here, α and β are hyperparameters that determine the relative weight of each loss component.

Pseudocode for Data Preprocessing

Algorithm PreprocessData

Input: data_path (path to the dataset)

Output: preprocessed_data

```
function LOAD_DATASET(data_path)
    images, masks ← [], []
    for each file in data_path do
```

```
            image, mask ← LOAD_IMAGE_AND_MASK(file)

            images.APPEND(image)

            masks.APPEND(mask)

        end for

        return images, masks

    end function


    function RESIZE_AND_NORMALIZE(images, masks, desired_size)

        for each image, mask in images, masks do

            image ← RESIZE(image, desired_size)

            mask ← RESIZE(mask, desired_size)

            image ← NORMALIZE(image)

        end for

        return images, masks

    end function

    images, masks ← LOAD_DATASET(data_path)

    images, masks ← RESIZE_AND_NORMALIZE(images, masks, 256x256)


    training_data, validation_data, test_data ← SPLIT_DATA(images,
    masks)


    SAVE_PREPROCESSED_DATA(training_data, validation_data, test_
    data)


    return preprocessed_data
```

9.3.3 DATA AUGMENTATION

We employ data augmentation techniques to expand and diversify the training dataset, thereby boosting the model's adaptability and reducing the risk of overfitting. The subsequent data enhancement methodologies are applied to both input echocardiography visuals and their corresponding ground truth masks: Horizontal and vertical inversions. The visuals and masks undergo horizontal or vertical inversions, generating reflective counterparts of the original data. This augmentation aids the model in discerning cardiac structures from diverse perspectives.

9.3.4 CardioSegNet Model Implementation

The U-Net-based CardioSegNet model used in this study is designed to identify the LV in echo-cardiographic pictures. A variety of convolutional layers, pooling layers, and upsampling layers are used in both the encoding and decoding routes of the model, which has these two components [17]. While decoding focuses on recovering spatial information and creating a segmentation map that adheres to the original image's dimensions, the encoding pathway collects high-level characteristics from the input pictures. The design comprises an encoder, a connecting bridge, and a decoder as illustrated in Figure 9.5.

Encoder: The encoder seizes the characteristics and context of the input image via a sequence of convolutional layers with escalating feature maps (64, 128, 256, and 512). Instance normalization is employed after each convolution to standardize the feature maps, succeeded by ReLU activation. Max-pooling layers are employed to expand the receptive field and reduce the spatial scale.

Bridge: The bridge serves as a link between the encoder and decoder sections of the network. It comprises two convolutional layers, each containing 1,024 feature maps, instance normalization, ReLU activation, and dropout layers to avert overfitting.

Decoder: The decoder reconstructs the segmented image from the features extracted by the encoder and bridge. It upsamples the feature maps using transposed convolutions and concatenates them with the corresponding encoder feature maps.

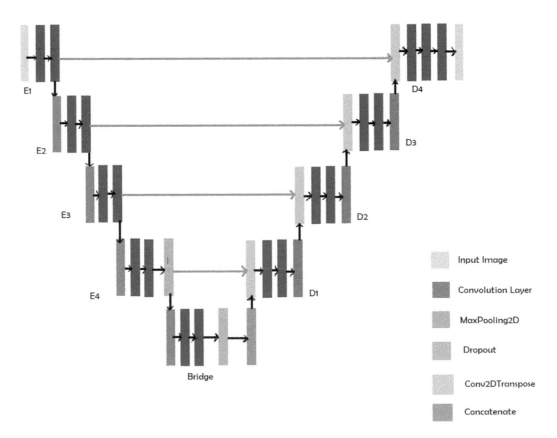

FIGURE 9.5 CardioSegNet model architecture—an illustration of encoder, bridge, and decoder layers for cardiac image segmentation.

The decoder has a symmetrical structure to the encoder, with the same number of feature maps (512, 256, 128, and 64). Following each convolution, instance normalization and ReLU activation are utilized.

Output: A concluding 1×1 convolutional layer, paired with a sigmoid activation mechanism, generates the output mask, producing a single-channel image that displays the delineated region.

To enhance the accuracy of segmentation tasks, the model employs the Adam optimizer with a learning rate set at 1e-4. Additionally, it utilizes a distinctive loss function that merges binary cross-entropy with the Dice coefficient. The model integrates residual connections to streamline information transfer across layers and address the vanishing gradient issue [18]. Leveraging multi-scale feature fusion allows the model to apprehend both local and global context present in the input images, which is crucial for accomplishing accurate segmentation [19].

During the training phase, the model utilizes Dice loss to focus on the overall shape of the segmented region, while binary cross-entropy loss targets pixel-level classification accuracy [20]. By combining these two losses, the model effectively balances both aspects of the segmentation task. Over a span of 100 epochs, the model is trained using the Adam optimizer, set at a learning rate of 1e-4, with batches comprising 8 samples each. To avoid overfitting and guarantee that the best-performing model is kept, early halting and model checkpointing are used.

9.3.5 Explainability in CardioSegNet

To ensure that our model's predictions are not only accurate but also interpretable, we have integrated XAI techniques into CardioSegNet. By visualizing attention maps, we can pinpoint regions in the echocardiographic images that the model deems significant during the segmentation process. These maps serve as a form of real-time feedback, allowing clinicians to understand the model's focus areas and decision rationale.

Furthermore, by juxtaposing these attention maps with the ground truth and the model's predictions, we can gain insights into potential discrepancies and areas of improvement. This not only enhances the model's reliability but also fosters trust among clinicians, ensuring that AI-driven insights align with medical expertise and intuition.

Pseudocode for Model Implementation and Evaluation in the context of Explainable AI(XAI)

Algorithm ModelImplementation

Input: training_data, validation_data

Output: model_evaluation_metrics

```
function DEFINE_UNET_ARCHITECTURE()

    model ← INITIALIZE_U_NET()

    COMPILE(model, loss="binary_crossentropy", optimizer="Adam",
metrics="Dice coefficient")

    return model

end function
```

```
function TRAIN_MODEL(model, training_data, validation_data)
    best_weights ← INITIALIZE_EMPTY()
    for each epoch in epochs do
        TRAIN(model, training_data)
        metrics ← VALIDATE(model, validation_data)
        if metrics ARE BETTER THAN previous_metrics then
            best_weights ← model.GET_WEIGHTS()
        end if
    end for
    model.SET_WEIGHTS(best_weights)
    return model
end function


function GRADCAM_VISUALIZATION(model, test_data)
    // Implementation for visualizing feature importance using
Grad-CAM
end function
function LIME_VISUALIZATION(model, test_data)
    // Implementation for visualizing feature importance using
LIME
end function


BEGIN
    model ← DEFINE_UNET_ARCHITECTURE()
    model ← TRAIN_MODEL(model, training_data, validation_data)

    test_predictions ← model.PREDICT(test_data)
    evaluation_metrics ← COMPUTE_METRICS(test_predictions, test_
data)
    GRADCAM_VISUALIZATION(model, test_data)
     return evaluation_metrics
END
```

9.3.6 MODEL EVALUATION

To gauge the efficacy of the proposed preprocessing technique and the CardioSegNet model, we utilize a suite of metrics commonly adopted in medical image segmentation studies. Key performance indicators include the Dice Similarity Coefficient (DSC), sensitivity (rate of true positives), and specificity (rate of true negatives). The Dice metric, which has values between 0 and 1, assesses the congruence between the predicted segmentation and the actual reference mask. A higher DSC value indicates superior segmentation performance [21]. Sensitivity is determined by the ratio of accurately segmented pixels (true positives), while specificity is gauged by the ratio of correctly identified non-segmented pixels (true negatives), providing a comprehensive evaluation of segmentation quality [22].

The model's performance is assessed using a five-fold cross-validation approach. The dataset is split into five parts of equal size. Four subsets are used as the training data throughout each iteration, and the final subset is used for validation. Each subset serves as the validation set once throughout this method, which is repeated five times. The mean values over all five folds are used to determine the final performance measures.

9.4 EXPERIMENTAL RESULTS, XAI INSIGHTS, AND DISCUSSION

The combined approach of our preprocessing method and CardioSegNet model underwent evaluation on the CAMUS dataset, employing the metrics and cross-validation strategy detailed in Section 9.3. Results indicate that our integrated approach achieves high DSC, sensitivity, and specificity values, signifying precise and consistent left ventricle segmentation in echocardiographic images.

Model Performance with XAI Insights: To gauge the CardioSegNet model's proficiency during training, we computed the Dice coefficient for both training and validation datasets at each epoch. Figure 9.4 showcases the progression of these coefficients throughout training. As depicted, the model's performance escalates over epochs, indicating its growing proficiency in left ventricle segmentation from echocardiography images.

Simultaneously, XAI-driven attention maps highlight areas the model focuses on during its decision-making process. These maps, when juxtaposed with traditional metrics, offer a comprehensive understanding of the model's learning trajectory and its areas of focus.

During the training process, we monitored both the loss values and the Dice coefficient for training and validation. Figure 9.6 graphically represents the loss values for each training epoch. As evidenced by the decreasing trend in loss metrics for both training and validation sets, the CardioSegNet model effectively learns to differentiate the left ventricle in echocardiographic images, demonstrating impressive adaptability to the validation dataset throughout its training.

To further emphasize the capabilities of the CardioSegNet model, a qualitative comparison that includes the input echocardiography image, the reference annotation, and the generated segmentation is presented in Figure 9.7. These images show that the CardioSegNet model is proficient in producing accurate segmentation masks that closely match the ground truth annotations, effectively outlining the boundaries of the left ventricle.

Upon evaluation, the model posted a test loss of 0.2286 and a Dice coefficient of 0.8294. The test loss measures how closely the model's predictions align with the actual data, with a lower value indicating better performance. Conversely, the Dice coefficient serves as a metric to evaluate segmentation accuracy. Conversely, the dice coefficient serves as a metric to evaluate segementation accuracy as illustrated graphically in Figure 9.8. It scales between 0 and 1, where 1 signifies a perfect match and 0 indicates no overlap between the predicted and reference annotations. In this context, a Dice coefficient of 0.8294 suggests commendable segmentation accuracy by the model.

The outcomes illustrate the efficacy of the suggested preprocessing technique in improving the quality and interpretability of echocardiography images. They also showcase the CardioSegNet model's capability to accurately segment the left ventricle. The combination of these techniques

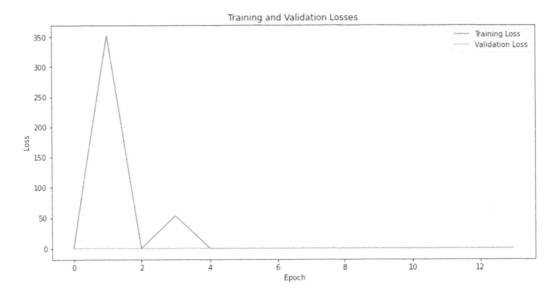

FIGURE 9.6 A graph depicting the training(black) and validation (grey) loss values throughout the course of the training process.

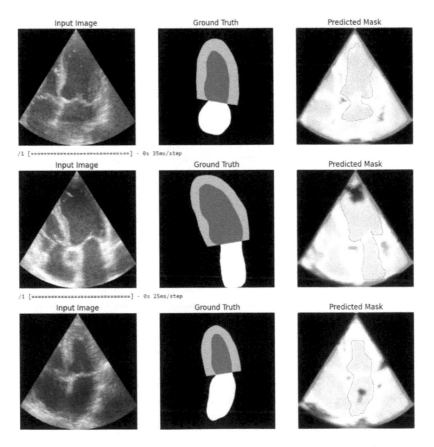

FIGURE 9.7 A visual comparison of the ground truth mask, the predicted mask, and the input echocardiogram picture can be shown on the right.

has the potential to facilitate the development of automated, efficient, and accurate tools for cardiac assessment in clinical settings.

The Figure 9.9 showcases a side-by-side comparison of an echocardiography image and its corresponding Grad-CAM heatmap. On the left, the original image provides a clear view of the cardiac structures. On the right, the Grad-CAM heatmap, overlaid on the original image, highlights the regions that the model deems most crucial for its predictions. The warmer regions in the heatmap indicate areas of higher importance, shedding light on the model's decision-making process and offering insights into its interpretability.

When benchmarked against other leading segmentation models such as V-Net and Attention U-Net, the superior efficacy of the CardioSegNet model in this particular domain becomes even more evident. Future research may examine the applicability of the suggested approach to other

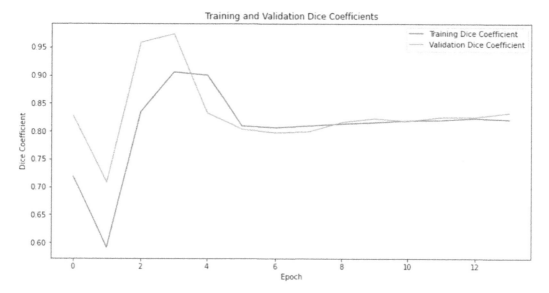

FIGURE 9.8 A chart displaying the training (black) and validation (grey) Dice coefficients during the progression of the training procedure.

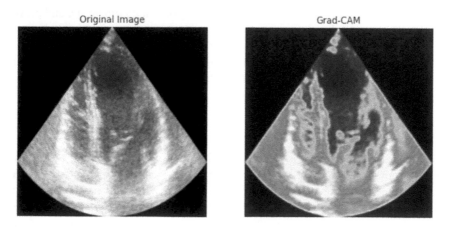

FIGURE 9.9 Original echocardiography image (a) and corresponding grad-CAM heatmap overlay (b) highlighting model's areas of focus.

cardiac structures and imaging modalities, as well as the incorporation of new improvements to optimize segmentation performance and computational effectiveness further.

9.5 FUTURE RESEARCH DIRECTIONS IN CARDIAC IMAGING AND XAI

The rapid evolution of deep learning in cardiac imaging has opened up numerous avenues for exploration and innovation. Here are some potential areas of research that promise to further revolutionize the field:

Generative Adversarial Networks (GANs) for Data Augmentation: The limited availability of labeled cardiac images poses a challenge for training robust models. GANs can be employed to generate synthetic yet realistic cardiac images, enhancing the diversity and volume of training datasets, and thereby potentially improving model accuracy.

Reinforcement Learning for Model Optimization: Reinforcement learning offers a dynamic approach to model training. By continuously adjusting model parameters based on feedback loops, it can optimize performance on cardiac imaging tasks, ensuring models are fine-tuned to the specific nuances of cardiac datasets.

Federated Learning for Data Privacy: Given the sensitive nature of medical data, transferring patient information across networks can raise privacy concerns. Federated learning provides a solution by training models across multiple decentralized devices or servers while keeping the data localized, ensuring patient confidentiality.

Advancements in Explainable AI (XAI): As deep learning models become more complex, understanding their decision-making processes becomes crucial, especially in the medical domain. Advanced XAI techniques can offer clearer insights into model predictions, ensuring they align with medical expertise and are more transparent to clinicians.

Multi-modal Imaging Integration: Different imaging modalities, such as MRI, CT, and echocardiograms, provide varied perspectives of cardiac structures. Integrating insights from these diverse sources using fusion techniques can offer a more comprehensive view, potentially enhancing diagnostic accuracy.

Personalized Treatment Plans with AI: By analyzing a combination of cardiac images, genetic information, and patient history, AI models can assist in crafting personalized treatment strategies, ensuring optimized patient care.

Real-time Monitoring with Wearables: With the rise of wearable health devices, there's an opportunity to develop deep learning models that can analyze cardiac data in real time. Such models can provide immediate feedback, potentially predicting and preventing adverse cardiac events.

The intersection of cardiac imaging and deep learning offers a plethora of research opportunities. By delving deeper into these areas, we can further enhance the accuracy, efficiency, and comprehensiveness of cardiac diagnostics and treatment.

9.6 CONCLUSION

This investigation presents an innovative preprocessing method, coupled with the CardioSegNet architecture, to accurately demarcate the left ventricle in echocardiography captures, drawing on the CAMUS dataset. The preprocessing strategy, which includes intensity normalization, cropping, and resizing, optimizes the input image for the segmentation task. The CardioSegNet model, built upon the U-Net architecture with residual connections and multi-scale feature fusion, outperforms other segmentation methodologies in existing literature.

The study's outcomes hold significant promise for the development of automated cardiac evaluation tools. Precise left ventricle segmentation is pivotal for comprehensive cardiac performance assessment. Future research avenues might delve into transfer learning, pre-trained model utilization, or ensemble methods to further enhance segmentation outcomes. The model's potential application to other cardiac structures or imaging modalities could also be explored, broadening its clinical applicability. Using XAI, the model's predictions are made to be accurate and understandable, building confidence and closing the knowledge gap between AI-driven insights and medical expertise.

REFERENCES

1. Picard M.H., Adams D., Bierig S.M., et al. American society of echocardiography recommendations for quality echocardiography laboratory operations. *J Am Soc Echocardiogr.* 2011;24(1):1–10.
2. Pellikka P.A., Douglas P.S., Miller J.G., et al. American society of echocardiography cardiovascular technology and research summit: A roadmap for 2020. *J Am Soc Echocardiogr.* 2013;26(4):325–338.
3. Smiseth O.A., Torp H., Opdahl A., et al. Myocardial strain imaging: How useful is it in clinical decision making? *Eur Heart J.* 2016;37(15):1196–1207.
4. Leclerc S., Smistad E., Pedrosa J., et al. CAMUS: An open-source multi-vendor, multi-instrument and multi-protocol ultrasound imaging dataset. arXiv:2106.03328 [cs.CV]. 2021.
5. Smistad E., Ostvik A., Haugen B.O., et al. Real-time standard scan plane detection and localisation in 3D freehand echocardiography. In: *Proceedings of the 9th International Workshop on Statistical Atlases and Computational Models of the Heart (STACOM).* 2018.
6. Gonzalez R.C., Woods R.E. *Digital Image Processing.* 3rd ed. London: Pearson Education Inc.; 2008.
7. Pham D.L., Xu C., Prince J.L. Current methods in medical image segmentation. *Annu Rev Biomed Eng.* 2000;2(1):315–337.
8. Litjens G., Kooi T., Bejnordi B.E., et al. A survey on deep learning in medical image analysis. *Med Image Anal.* 2017;42:60–88.
9. LeCun Y., Bengio Y., Hinton G. Deep learning. *Nature.* 2015;521(7553):436–444.
10. Ronneberger O., Fischer P., Brox T. U-Net: Convolutional networks for biomedical image segmentation. In: Navab N., Hornegger J., Wells W., Frangi A., eds. *Medical Image Computing and Computer-Assisted Intervention - MICCAI 2015.* Lecture Notes in Computer Science. Cham: Springer; 2015:234–241.
11. Milletari F., Navab N., Ahmadi S.A. V-Net: Fully convolutional neural networks for volumetric medical image segmentation. In: *2016 Fourth International Conference on 3D Vision (3DV).* Stanford, CA, USA: IEEE; 2016:565–571.
12. Oktay O., Schlemper J., Folgoc L.L., et al. Attention U-Net: Learning Where to Look for the Pancreas. arXiv:1804.03999 [cs.CV]. 2018.
13. Chen L. C., Zhu Y., Papandreou G., Schroff F., Adam H. Encoder-decoder with atrous separable convolution for semantic image segmentation. In: *Proceedings of the European Conference on Computer Vision (ECCV).* 2018.
14. Reinhard E., Adhikhmin M., Gooch B., et al. Color transfer between images. *IEEE Comput Graph Appl.* 2001;21(5):34–41.
15. Pluim J.P.W., Maintz J.B.A., Viergever M.A. Mutual-information-based registration of medical images: A survey. *IEEE Trans Med Imaging.* 2003;22(8):986–1004.
16. Keys R. Cubic convolution interpolation for digital image processing. *IEEE Trans Acoust Speech Signal Process.* 1981;29(6):1153–1160.
17. Çiçek Ö., Abdulkadir A., Lienkamp S.S., et al. 3D U-Net: Learning dense volumetric segmentation from sparse annotation. In: Ourselin S., Joskowicz L., Sabuncu M., Unal G., Wells W., eds. *Medical Image Computing and Computer-Assisted Intervention - MICCAI 2016.* Lecture Notes in Computer Science. Cham: Springer; 2016:424–432.
18. He K, Zhang X, Ren S, and Sun J. Deep residual learning for image recognition. In: *Proceedings of the IEEE Conference on Computer Vision and Pattern Recognition (CVPR)* Las vegas, NV, USA: IEEE; 2016:770–778.

19. Chen L.-C., Papandreou G., Kokkinos I., et al. DeepLab: Semantic image segmentation with deep convolutional nets, atrous convolution, and fully connected CRFs. *IEEE Trans Pattern Anal Mach Intell.* 2018;40(4):834–848.

20. Sudre C.H., Li W., Vercauteren T., et al. Generalised dice overlap as a deep learning loss function for highly unbalanced segmentations. In: Cardoso M.J., Arbel T., Gao F., et al., eds. *Deep Learning in Medical Image Analysis and Multimodal Learning for Clinical Decision Support, DLMIA 2017, ML-CDS 2017.* Lecture Notes in Computer Science. Cham: Springer; 2017:240–248.

21. Dice L.R. Measures of the amount of ecologic association between species. *Ecology.* 1945;26(3):297–302.

22. Powers D.M. Evaluation: From precision, recall and F-measure to ROC, informedness, markedness and correlation. *J Mach Learn Technol.* 2011;2(1):37–63.

10 Artificial Intelligence-Based Techniques for Early Detection of Chiari Malformation

R. Monisha and K. S. Tamilselvan

10.1 INTRODUCTION

Congenital brain abnormalities, alternatively known as congenital brain malformations, encompass a diverse spectrum of deformities or pathologies afflicting the brain during gestation due to developmental disturbances at varying embryonic or fetal stages [1]. The fetal brain undergoes rapid development post-conception, progressing steadily throughout the course of pregnancy, during which millions of neurons traverse a crucial developmental journey culminating in the formation of various brain regions. Brain abnormalities may occur if this process is interrupted in any way, particularly amid the preliminary 12 weeks of pregnancy. Inadequate skull development may also give rise to brain abnormalities. Abnormalities that have been mentioned earlier persist throughout the process of childbirth and become apparent from the time of birth. These abnormalities appear if there are any deviations that occur during the brain formation and development stages. They are classified as disorders that exert an influence on the structure and function of the neurological system. These irregularities manifest as peculiarities in brain features, including their shape, size, morphological, and physiological characteristics. Several regions in the brain like ventricles, cerebellum, etc. show the presence of these abnormalities.

The etiology of this particular malformation may exhibit variation for each case, with the causative factors largely unknown. These irregularities may arise from chromosomal aberrations, infections, physical trauma, or toxins that the mother was subjected to during gestation. Additionally, they could stem from environmental influences, infections, or spontaneous genetic mutations within the developing embryo.

The manifestation and prognosis of congenital brain malformations are subject to variation contingent upon both their type and severity. While certain brain malformations are identifiable at birth, others may remain undetected until adolescence or adulthood. The extent of malformation can range from trivial to severe, and its impact on the individual can vary extensively. Some congenital malformations are minor, whereas others are severe yet correctable through surgery led by experts in the field. The impact of congenital brain malformations on individuals can exhibit a vast spectrum. Certain malformations may cause mild or subtle symptoms that are controllable through appropriate interventions and support. In contrast, more severe malformations can significantly impede an individual's physical and cognitive abilities, resulting in substantial challenges in their daily life, necessitating constant medical care, and rehabilitation.

Figure 10.1 shows the four major categories under which congenital brain malformations fall namely:

Disorders of Dorsal induction: During the gestation period of 3–5 weeks, the neural tube undergoes development and closure through dorsal induction. This process is characterized by two distinct phases, namely, primary neurulation that encompasses neural plate formation and the subsequent neural tube emergence, and secondary neurulation that involves

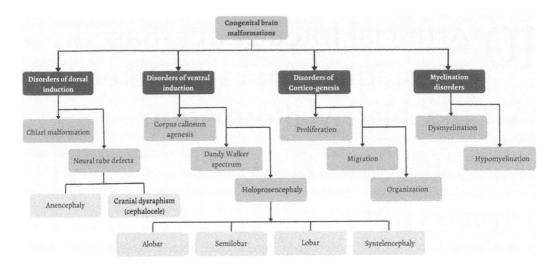

FIGURE 10.1   Classification of congenital brain malformations.

the distal cord, coccygeal segment, and sacral creation. The collapse of dorsal induction may result in several malformations, including but not limited to chiari malformation; neural tube defects: anencephaly, and cephaloceles (cranial dysraphism) [2].

Disorders of Ventral Induction: Another cluster pertaining to congenital malformation is the disorder of ventral induction that arises from the inadequacy in the cleavage of the prosencephalon and consequent midline structure evolution [3]. The severity of the maladies varies widely among affected individuals. Failure in the normal development of the embryonic structure responsible for the forebrain, known as the prosencephalon, leads to the occurrence of ventral induction disorders [3]. Genetic mutations, environmental factors, or a combination of both may contribute to this failure. The ramifications of ventral induction disorders can manifest themselves in a multitude of ways, contingent upon the degree of severity of the malformation. In certain instances, those individuals who are affected may only endure subtle facial irregularities, while in more extreme cases, they may suffer from substantial cognitive impairment, seizures, and other neurological complications. Furthermore, associated anomalies may encompass heart defects, cleft lip and palate, and other atypicalities. In essence, ventral induction disorders can be classified as a collection of congenital malformations that arise owing to the abnormal underdevelopment of the prosencephalon. The consequences of these disorders can be highly diverse, and they may be triggered by genetic mutations, and environmental variables, both in tandem [3].

Disorders of Cortico-Genesis: Cortico-genesis pertains to the intricate process of the cerebral cortex's growth, encompassing the generation, migration, and differentiation of cortical neurons. It is noteworthy that disorders arising from cortico-genesis may manifest as an array of neurological conditions including but not limited to epilepsy, intellectual disability, and autism spectrum disorders. This outcome can be attributed to genetic mutations, the influence of the surroundings, or a collaboration of all causative agents [4].

Myelination disorders: Myelin disorders pertain to pathological conditions that involve myelin, which is the primary component of white matter. The affliction of white matter, inclusive of myelin, glia, blood vessels, and axons, is highly prevalent in central nervous system disorders [5]. Such disorders manifest in the form of tumors, infarcts, infections, and also as a secondary consequence of neuronal and axonal degeneration. Conversely, myelin disorders predominantly and chiefly affect myelin.

A multidisciplinary approach, involving neurologists, neurosurgeons, geneticists, developmental specialists, and other healthcare professionals, is frequently employed. Treatment options may consist of medication to regulate symptoms, surgical interventions to rectify structural abnormalities, rehabilitation therapies to enhance motor function or cognitive skills, and supportive interventions to address associated challenges and optimize quality of life. Similar to many other malformations, congenital brain malformations can also be diagnosed through surplus imaging techniques, such as magnetic resonance imaging (MRI). This image capturing is required for visualization of the rich features in the brain structure and helps in spotting any abnormalities that the human eye finds hard to process. The treatment process relies on the specific type, symptoms, and level of severity.

Chiari malformation, classified under the disorders of the dorsal induction category, corresponds to a neurological condition described by the cerebellum protrusion at the posterior aspect of the skull via a normal aperture where it converges with the spinal canal. This condition leads to the compression of various areas of the spinal cord and brain, giving rise to a spectrum with mild to severe symptoms. Typically, this condition is present from birth and is considered congenital in nature.

Early detection of Chiari malformation enables timely intervention, which in turn mitigates potential complications associated with the condition. Additionally, it facilitates close monitoring by healthcare professionals, ensuring suitable management and preventing further neurological impairments. Regular follow-up visits and imaging assessments may also be necessary to evaluate the effectiveness of treatment and identify any changes to the condition. It is important to acknowledge that each instance of Chiari malformation is unique, and symptoms and severity may vary among individuals. Thus, early detection and a comprehensive evaluation by healthcare professionals specializing in neurology and neurosurgery are essential in determining the most appropriate treatment approach customized in relevance to every patient's unique requirements.

In this chapter, an overview of Chiari malformation as a specific congenital brain abnormality is provided. Next, the diagnostic techniques for Chiari malformation, with a special focus on imaging tests, are highlighted. Then, a brief introduction to artificial intelligence (AI) followed by applications of AI in medical image processing is given. Then, the AI approaches involved in the early detection of Chiari malformation are detailed. Finally, we conclude this chapter by giving some recommendations for future research that can be made in this field.

10.2 OVERVIEW OF CHIARI MALFORMATION

Chiari malformation (CM) falls under the dorsal induction disorders category of congenital brain malformations and is defined as a defect in the structure of the cerebellum. Hans Chiari, an Austrian pathologist who will always be remembered in the neurosurgery field, reported the existence of this condition in 1891, which later came to be known as Chiari malformation in the late 19th century [6]. This neurological condition can mainly be recognized by the downward shift in any one or both of the cerebellar tonsils. It happens via the opening present in the root of the skull, which is also known as the foramen magnum (fm). In situations such as these, it has been observed that the tongues of cerebellar tissue have been found to be significantly and restrictively bound down to the medulla, thereby resulting in an impending intercession to the pathway of the cerebrospinal fluid by way of the fourth ventricle (4th v) roof. This occurrence has the potential to significantly impact the normal functioning and physiological processes of the brain. In the magnetic resonance imaging scan, this downward shift in the cerebellar tonsils should be 5 mm on the far side of the line or stroke of McRae that runs starting in the basion (frontal end) till the opisthion (rear end) along the fm [7]. If the declination is only 3 mm less than the expected value, it can be considered to be mere variations in physiology. Whereas if the declination lies within the 3–5 mm range, then it can be considered to be marginal and warrant the collection of further information or re-evaluate the previous results in case of symptoms related to syringomyelia. Syringomyelia [8] is also a neurological condition, where the cerebrospinal fluid, the watery substance that encloses and shields both the spinal cord

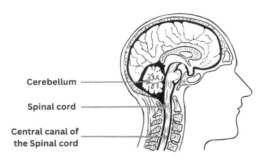

Cerebellum

Spinal cord

Central canal of
the Spinal cord

FIGURE 10.2   Basic structure of the human brain.

and the brain, grows into the spinal cord tissue regions, and forms the syrinx, thus enlarging the central canal. Syrinx is a cyst comprising liquid and it can expand large enough to damage the nerves that pass information to and fro the brain and body. Thus CM can cause various neurological symptoms and complications due to the compression of brain tissue and disruption of cerebrospinal fluid flow [9,10] Figure 10.2 shows the general structure of the human brain.

Some common symptoms of CM include headaches, speech and hearing problems, neck pain, dizziness, vomiting, balancing problems, buzzing or ringing in ears, muscle weakness, numbness of hands and feet, difficulty swallowing and eating, inability to gain weight, insomnia, depression, abnormal heart rhythm and breathing, excessive drooling or gagging, lack of control in motor skills, curvature of the spine (scoliosis) [11].

There are some factors by which we can extend our care to the people affected by this malformation. Clinical trials provide an excellent opportunity for all researchers, practitioners, scientists, and clinicians to explore and understand these types of complications better. For this kind of practice, human volunteers are an asset. These trials rely heavily on our volunteers as the clinicians gain insights thoroughly on the malformation, which can potentially lead to the development of safer detection techniques, the invention of various novel treatment methods, or the establishment of an effective cure/preventive measure for the malformation. It is crucial for the volunteers participating in this research to be from diverse backgrounds to achieve generalization. That is, the study results must apply to a broad range of individuals, such that the research results can be widely used by all categories. Therefore, individuals of all ages, genders, races, and ethnicities, regardless of health status, are encouraged to consider volunteering for clinical trials. We can contribute by considering participating in these types of research for the benefit of medical and general society. A wide range of volunteers are required like people who are healthy and who are not healthy and have disorders or chronic illness; people belonging to a variety of cultures, age groups, races, countries, and genders for the purpose of ensuring safety and generalization of the study findings such that the results obtained can be used for as many as patients as possible effectively. For patients suffering from malformation, these clinical trials might be a golden chance to access new treatments that are not yet available to the general public. This can be helpful to a large majority having Chiari malformation, as there is no cure for the condition, and treatment options are limited in the current. For others, this creates a window of opportunity for improving our understanding of the malformation. Volunteering in a clinical trial can give us a sense of purpose and make us feel like we are making a difference in the lives of others. Clinical trials may offer compensation to participants in some cases, which can be beneficial in offsetting associated costs such as travel expenses, lodging, and lost wages. However, there are also potential risks that should be thoroughly evaluated before deciding to volunteer. It is crucial to carefully consider the risks involved in clinical trials before deciding to participate, as the experimental treatment being tested may have unknown side effects. Additionally, there is no guarantee that the experimental treatment will be effective in treating the specific condition being studied, such as Chiari malformation. Furthermore, the experimental treatment may result in harm to the participant.

It is highly recommended to discuss the risks and potential benefits of participating in clinical trials with your healthcare provider before making any decisions. In order to make an informed decision, it is also crucial to conduct thorough research and choose a clinical trial that is suitable for our individual circumstances. By doing so, you can ensure that you are making a well-informed decision about participating in a clinical trial and that you are aware of any potential risks involved. Overall, while financial compensation may be attractive, it is important to prioritize your health and well-being when considering participating in clinical trials.

10.3 HISTORY

The following paragraph discusses the history of Chiari malformation in a chronological manner, which can be traced back to the late 19th century as shown in Figure 10.3 [11].

In 1829, Jean Cruveilhier (1791–1874) illustrated many cases regarding spina bifida and hydrocephalus mostly pertaining to the sac infection and meningitis [12]. He has also mentioned the 'Arnold - Chiari malformation' accompanied by diastematomyelia briefly. In 1883, a medical case was reported by John Cleland from Edinburgh (1835–1925) detailing an abnormal congenital disorder in the brain stem [13,14]. He illustrated the anomaly spotted on a child in addition to spina bifida and hydrocephalus highlighting the following complications: the stretched medulla, the cervical canal breached by the 4th v, and the distorted posterior vermis. The work, although lacking in clarity and being less discernible, could be considered to be at the forefront of the history of CM. This case came to be known later as 'Chiari II' or 'Arnold–Chiari malformation' in 1907. A few years later, Hans Chiari (1851–1916) presented his research findings in 1891 on the cerebellar tissue ectopia [6,15]. He was a pathologist from Vienna, who lectured at the German University, Prague afterward in Strasbourg. He reported the medical case of an adolescent female who was 17 years old for whom the tonsils sprouted cone-like objects that were jammed into the spinal cord [13]. In 1907, four examples having meningomyelocele and anomalies in the cerebellum and the brain were elaborated by Schwalbe and Gredig, students who learned under Julus Arnold, a German pathologist, thus naming this the now popularly known "Arnold–Chiari" malformations [13].

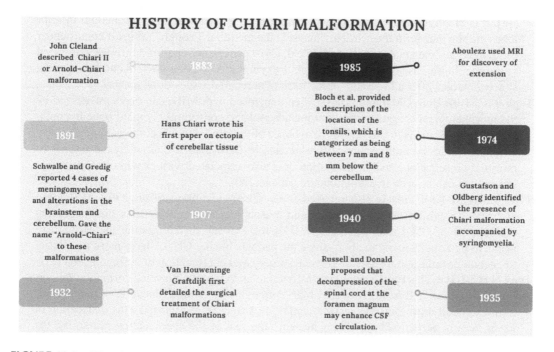

FIGURE 10.3 Historical development of CM.

In 1932, Van Houweninge Graftdijk (1888–1956) identified the surgical treatment for CM, but all the patients who underwent surgery died either due to the surgery or postoperative complications [13]. This event demonstrated progress in the trials made in the treatment of the malformation in its early stages. In 1935, Donald and Russell found that the circulation of cerebrospinal fluid could be enhanced by the spinal cord decompression process at the fm [13]. They came up with this postulate for the purpose of researching the mechanisms involved in cerebrospinal fluid circulation. Five years later, the Gustafson-Oldberg couple in 1940 affiliated with Chicago diagnosed CM with the presence of syringomyelia [11]. The research conducted by these people has been very helpful in illustrating the relationship between CM and syringomyelia. Syringomyelia can be termed to be a chronic disease that occurs in the spinal that is bound to develop gradually [16]. It has a diverse etiology that is caused by any disruption in the regular activities of the cerebrospinal fluid circulation. The lesions that result from this condition can be characterized by the tubular cavity development in the gliosis and gray substance of the spinal cord. The exact cause of this condition is unknown and there are various approaches for treatment of this type of disease. The research made by Gustafson and Oldberg facilitated the comprehension of the pathophysiology of CM. Another significant event was the differentiation of the position of the tonsils, which was calculated to be 7–8 mm distance below the cerebellum [13]. This discovery is considered to be significant because it became the key component in deducing the severity of the malformation. The invention of medical imaging for the diagnosis and treatment of the spinal cord was initially made in 1985 by Aboulezz, who used MRI to detect the extent of the spinal cord.

10.4 TYPES OF CHIARI MALFORMATION

Chiari malformations can be represented within four categories, namely:

Type I (CM-I): Initially Hans Chiari described this type of abnormality to be restricted within the cerebellum, but later researchers introduced a medullary abnormality [17]. It can be further subdivided in correlation with syringomyelia: the presence of syringomyelia comes under CM-I A category and the absence of syringomyelia comes under CM-I B category [18]. It is distinguished by the elongation similar to spike tonsils and cerebellum inferior lobes middle part from the cervical alongside the medulla. Though CM itself comes under the congenital brain malformations subfield, CM-I can also be acquired through some kind of trauma. In the case of being congenital, the symptoms do not appear in childhood and it slowly emerges after a few years in the form of cerebellar issues or headaches.

Type 0 (CM-0): Both CM-I and CM-0, when diagnosed with MRI, can be characterized by the morphological characteristics that include isolated congenital occipital bone hypoplasia and modifications in the various base bones of the skull that affect the volume and posterior cranial fossa configuration [19], whereas CM-0 can also be defined by the absence or minimal presence of tonsillar herniation. It is also associated with or without syringomyelia, which can be seen in asymptomatic patients [20].

Type 1.5 (CM-1.5): This is also referred to as 'Chiari complex'. Similar to CM-0, CH-I and CM-1.5 exhibit some anatomical and morphological characteristics thus becoming the subtype of CM-I malformation. Besides the existing differentiating methods, there needs to be a radiological method, since the patients having CH-1.5 have more possibility to encounter failure in the decompressive surgery and continuation of syringomyelia [21].

Type II (CM-II): This type is popularly referred to as 'Arnold–Chiari malformation' honoring Hans Chiari and Julius Arnold. Chiari defined this type as dislocation of the cerebellum, extended 4th v into the cervical canal [4]. Later, he re-reported it as dislocation of lower vermis parts, medulla oblongata, with the rest of the specification remaining the same. The change or inconsistencies in the above two statements is to highlight the hindbrain displacement as the crucial component of the malformation. In contrast to the subtler tonsillar herniation noticed in CM-I, the cerebellar vermis displacement is more prominent in this type. Tonsillar herniation and lumbosacral myelomeningocele or lumbar are additionally observed below the fm [22].

Type III (CM-III): This type of CM is represented by the absence of a section of tentorium cerebelli, thus resulting in the prolongation of the 4th v in conjunction with the cerebellum to the cervical canal. It is also supplemented by a hydromyelic cavity which is in interaction with the 4th v.

Type IV (CM-IV): Primary cerebellar agenesis is a condition marked by inadequate development of the cerebellum [22]. This results in the brainstem and the cerebellum being situated in the posterior fossa, without any connection to the fm. This lack of cerebellar development is equivalent to the condition of cerebellar agenesis [23].

10.5   DIAGNOSIS OF CHIARI MALFORMATION

Diagnosis of CM is done by combining the history of the patient, the results from a professional neurological examination by a clinician, and the medical reports obtained through imaging techniques [24]. The end result we expect from medical diagnostics is the determination of the problem cause and the proposition of a viable solution or treatment method. Imaging techniques for diagnosis in practice vary such as X-rays, CT, MRI, ultrasounds, etc. In addition to the above-mentioned objectives, medical diagnostics are used for the wholesome management process of monitoring a medical condition, evaluating the results of the treatment, and also deducing other serious issues before they reach a critical stage beyond rescue. The most common methods when it comes to imagery for diagnosis are CT (computerized tomography) and MRI (magnetic resonance imaging) scans. CT scans are similar to regular X-rays as they can show the structures present in our body. It generates cross-sectional scans of the body employing X-rays. But, it is more advanced than normal X-rays as it can detect a broad spectrum of surfaces or structures like tumors, bone fractures, internal injuries, brain structures, COVID cases, etc. [23]. It is a trustworthy and minimally meddlesome medical imaging method. After initial diagnosis and confirmation of certain diseases through CT scans, we can proceed with the clinical treatments pertaining to surgeries, chemotherapies, radiation therapies, etc. [25]. CT can take pictures of bones, brains, organs, blood vessels, tissues, and muscles. They provide a more correct and clearer view of the texture, density, shape, and size of the human body. Although CT and CT myelography have better qualities, they still fall short in characterizing syringomyelia and also other neurological disorders due to their limitations in resolution. After which MRI, a medical imaging technique, was introduced and it felt suitable for Chiari malformation.

Magnetic resonance imaging (MRI) is both non-aggressive and non-radiative and has demonstrated significant value in the detection and treatment of a variety of disorders, as noted in the literature [26]. MRI, as an in vivo biomedical imaging tool, has played a critical role in current developments in medical and biological sciences [27]. In terms of offering impeccable contrast of the soft tissue, MRI proves to be superior to other imaging modalities. It is a highly versatile diagnostic tool that possesses extensive applicability in a broad range of research and clinical applications. This imaging modality enables the visualization of anatomical structures with exceptional resolution and facilitates the measurement of several biophysical functions. Furthermore, it provides a means to assess the permeation and diffusion of soft organs and soft tissues with weighted microscopic structures, thereby opening up new avenues for non-invasive diagnostic imaging. MRI has thus become a key tool in the diagnosis and treatment of numerous medical conditions and is expected to continue to be a valuable resource in the future. The utilization of MRI has become increasingly popular due to the need for lesser imaging time periods and better image quality. However, this demand has resulted in a decrease in the signal-to-noise ratio for MRI, leading to the emergence of image artifacts caused by the motion of the object of interest and distortion of the scanned image. These challenges have made it difficult to post-process MRI images. Nevertheless, it is crucial to note that the correction of subject movement is a fundamental aspect of image enhancement in MRI, as any movement or motion can significantly impair the accuracy and reliability of the final image output. Among these techniques, the process of denoising involves the removal of noise from images to increase clarity and eliminate unwanted visual distortions. Furthermore, geometric distortion correction techniques aim to rectify any deformities or discrepancies that may have occurred during the image acquisition process, thereby further enhancing the overall quality of the image. Additionally, it cannot be overstated that the correction of subject movement is a fundamental aspect of image enhancement in MRI, as any sort of movement or motion can significantly compromise the accuracy and reliability of the final image output. Early works in this field have already demonstrated substantial improvements in image quality, showing the great potential of this approach in the field of MRI. Prenatal diagnosis of CM-II can be done through ultrasound [28].

Despite this, the emergence of artificial intelligence & machine learning, particularly deep learning, presents a significant opportunity for further advancement in identifying Chiari malformation.

10.6 ARTIFICIAL INTELLIGENCE

Artificial intelligence (AI) has become a widespread phrase being used repeatedly in numerous domains over the past few years. Nevertheless, it is quite fascinating that this concept was first introduced and established a long way back in the 1940s. John McCarthy, an esteemed American scholar in the fields of computer science and cognitive studies, is credited with coining the term "artificial intelligence" in the year 1956. He is one of the founders of the AI discipline. AI is essentially a subfield in computer science that involves the development of algorithms that can replicate human-like behaviors like learning processes and solving problems. The recent affluence of AI is largely attributed to the significant advancements in computational power and data availability. Notably, machine learning (ML) and deep learning (DL) algorithms implemented in AI applications have made unprecedented breakthroughs in computer vision dynamics over the past decade. These developments have been groundbreaking and have opened up new avenues for research in the field of AI.

AI has emerged as a ubiquitous term particularly when concerned with image processing and analysis [29]. In the medical field, faculties like radiology, pathology, and oncology, where images hold a significant place, have capitalized on the opportunity, and significant R&D efforts have been undertaken for the translation of AI prospects into clinical establishments. The medical field has been able to utilize remarkable advancements in technology to create AI applications that optimize medical images, automate various aspects of clinical practice, and offer support for clinical decisions. Numerous studies that incorporate AI and ML techniques have reported encouraging outcomes in various clinical applications. Diagnosing disorders, segmenting images, and forecasting outputs are currently under the hot category in the midst of unprecedented changes owing to the recent developments in AI. In recent times, AI tools have reached a level of maturity that satisfies clinical requirements, resulting in clinical teams, laboratories, and also companies, collaborating for research.

Although AI is becoming more and more common for conventional medical image analytic activities such as sectioning, screening, and categorizing, ensuring the secure and effective utilization of AI in practice is greatly dependent on expert users. Therefore, it is imperative that medical professionals become familiar with the basics of AI as it has the potential to change the practice of medicine till now. By doing so, they can ensure that they remain at the forefront of innovation and are equipped to provide the best possible care to their patients.

Assisting the medical physics community in obtaining a comprehensive foundational understanding of AI, inclusive of their progression and present contemporaries, will undoubtedly lead to an increase in quality research, expedite the initial stages for budding scholars in the field, and encourage innovative problem statements with future directions. The AI domain advances fast, with novel techniques being published frequently. Nevertheless, there are only a minimal number of pivotal concepts that have been firmly established.

AI algorithms enhance the prediction accuracy, speed, and efficiency of a diagnostic process. One of the most prominent ways AI assists healthcare providers is by analyzing medical images from X-rays, CT, MRI, ultrasounds, etc. Additionally, AI analyzes a vast range of documents including personal data, patients' health charts, medical history, biosignals, vital signs, and lab test results. By doing so, AI can aid the decision-making process and deliver precise results, thereby enhancing the overall quality of medical diagnostics.

With this, healthcare providers can benefit from making more informed decisions about their patients' care. The utilization of data fusion offers an ideal solution to enable diagnosis decisions from different findings, including text, signal, and image representations. The diversity of the patient's data can assist in providing a thorough understanding of their health condition. This can effectively reduce the likelihood of misdiagnosis and improve the accuracy of diagnosis. Continuous monitoring of the patient's health condition can help in analyzing or pointing out any discrepancies in their treatment process. Over time, the patient's treatment progress can be assessed. This enables healthcare providers to manage and treat chronic diseases more effectively. Overall, the integration of multimodal data in healthcare can assist in enhancing patient care by providing more accurate diagnoses and enabling more effective treatment plans.

10.7 FUNDAMENTAL CONCEPTS OF AI

Machine learning, a subdivision of AI and computer science, can be used to solve a problem by building algorithms or models that rely on the dataset or previous similar examples of the concerned activity. The major steps involved in solving a machine learning problem are to gather a dataset and to build an ML model to solve the problem algorithmically. In a general context, a dataset could be separated as train, test, and validation set. Figure 10.4 shows the outline classification of a machine learning model.

According to Figure 10.4, there are four broad divisions of machine learning.

10.7.1 SUPERVISED LEARNING

Supervised learning, a method of ML, in which the training dataset as mentioned above in the ML paragraph, collected would be labeled for every sample. The model is supplied with this labeled training data for the learning process and the model adjusts its weights appropriately. Cross-validation is integral to this process, as it ensures that the model does not underfit or overfit our problem.

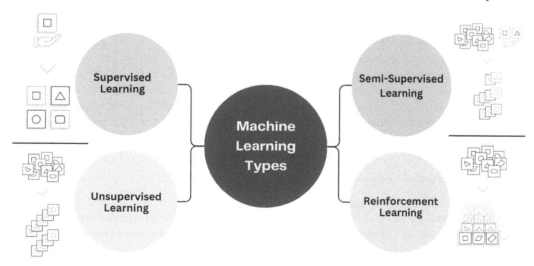

FIGURE 10.4 Classification of ML.

By using supervised learning, entities can address numerous real-world problems, like classifying livestock on a farm. To accomplish this, various methods including naïve Bayes, random forest, linear & logistic regression, and support vector machines are used. With its ability to harness the power of labeled data, supervised learning is a powerful tool for data scientists and organizations alike. Mathematically, the dataset can be denoted as $\{(a_i, b_i)\}$; $1 <= i <= N$; N denotes the total samples in numbers; i denotes features in the dataset. The model inputs the feature vector a and outputs the label or class to which the input image belongs. For example, a disease detection model takes the abnormalities in a person as input and produces the disease which those symptoms fall under.

10.7.2 UNSUPERVISED LEARNING

Unsupervised learning supports ML algorithms where the model categorizes input data that are void of any labeling. The algorithms used in this approach reveal latent patterns or data clusters without requiring any human intervention. The capacity of the technique to identify alikeness and discrepancies in information renders is well-suited for conducting exploratory analysis of data, devising cross & up-selling strategies, implementing client segmentation, and performing pattern, visuals, and video recognition. Machine learning models have numerous applications across various domains, such as clustering, dimensionality reduction, and outlier detection. In clustering, the model identifies the cluster for each feature vector in the dataset. On the other hand, in dimensionality reduction, the model generates a feature vector with a smaller number of features than the input x. Lastly, in outlier detection, the model produces a real number that signifies how x differs from the normal data points in the dataset. These outputs serve as crucial inputs for further analysis and decision-making processes. Furthermore, it is often applied to decrease the model features by engaging in dimensionality-reducing processes. Singular value decomposition & principal component analysis are two widely utilized methods that enable this form of reduction. Overall, unsupervised learning helps in analyzing and making sense of datasets whose characteristics are not immediately apparent.

10.7.3 SEMI-SUPERVISED LEARNING

Semi-supervised learning has emerged as one of the promising approaches that bridge the gap between supervised and unsupervised learning. Its key advantage lies in the utilization of a dataset with only a few samples having been labeled to steer the feature extraction & classification processes from a set of unlabeled samples during the training phase. This technique has proven to be effective in addressing the issue of inadequate labeled data that poses a significant challenge for supervised learning algorithms. Furthermore, it can also be employed to mitigate the high cost associated with labeling a vast amount of data, which makes it a feasible option for many real-world applications. In summary, semi-supervised learning has been widely recognized as a valuable strategy that can enhance the performance of machine learning models, particularly in scenarios where labeled data are scarce or expensive to obtain. Therefore, it is crucial to explore its potential and limitations in different domains and applications. This is similar to supervised learning with the concept that using a few labeled samples can help the model learn better.

10.7.4 REINFORCEMENT LEARNING

Reinforcement Learning constitutes a science of decision-making, which involves the acquisition of optimal behavior in an environment to gain the maximum reward. In order to achieve this goal, interactions with the environment are necessary, as well as observations of the environment's response to such interactions. This process is comparable to children exploring the world around them and learning the actions that prove conducive to their goals. Reinforcement learning is particularly well-suited to sequential decision-making and is therefore highly useful in numerous fields, including game playing, robotics, resource management, and logistics. These are all areas where long-term goals are paramount, and effective decision-making is essential to success. Therefore, reinforcement learning is a critical tool for success in these areas.

10.7.5 Deep Learning

Another subfield of AI, currently in the focus is the deep learning field. In order to know what deep learning is, first we have to delve into neural networks. A neural network is a technique that is employed in the field of artificial intelligence to enable data processing by computers in a manner comparable to that of the human brain. These networks, also known as deep learning, comprise interconnected nodes or neurons that are arranged in a layered structure, akin to the human brain. By employing such a network, an adaptive system is created that enables computers to learn from their errors and improve consistently. Consequently, artificial neural networks endeavor to resolve intricate problems, such as facial recognition or document summarization, with greater precision and efficiency. In essence, the purpose of neural networks is to replicate the learning process of the human brain, thereby enhancing the capabilities of computers in a variety of fields.

The neural network architecture is influenced by the intricacies of the human mind, which comprises neurons that form a complex and highly interlinked network. These neurons transmit electrical signals to each other, thereby facilitating the processing of information by the human brain. Similarly, an artificial neural network is composed of artificial neurons that work in tandem to resolve a given problem. These artificial neurons are essentially software modules termed nodes, and the neural networks represent software programs or algorithms that employ computing systems to solve mathematical calculations at their core. In essence, neural network architecture attempts to replicate the functioning of the human brain, albeit through the use of software modules and algorithms that simulate the complex processes that occur within the human brain. Therefore, the neural network architecture represents a vital tool in the development of artificial intelligence and possesses enormous capability to change the manner in which we process, analyze, and interpret information. Similar to Figure 10.5, every neural network must possess three indisputable layers: the input layer, the hidden layer, and the output layer. Input that is sourced externally enters an artificial neural network through its input layer. The data are then processed and categorized by the

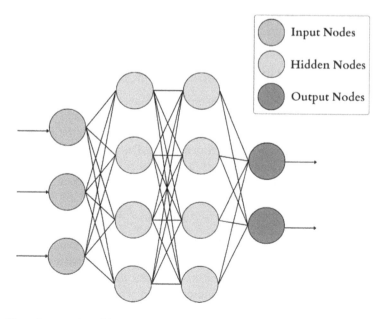

FIGURE 10.5   Neural network architecture.

input nodes, after which they are transferred to the next layer in the network. Hidden layers within the network obtain their input from the input layer or from other hidden layers. It is possible for an artificial neural network to have a vast number of hidden layers. Each hidden layer analyzes the results of the previous layer, processes them further, and then transfers them onto the next layer. The output layer of the network is responsible for providing the ultimate outcome of all data processing conducted within the network. It can consist of a single or multiple nodes. In the case of a binary (yes/no) classification problem, the output layer will contain a solitary output node which will deliver a result of either 1 or 0. On the other hand, for a multi-class classification problem, the output layer may comprise more than one output node.

Deep learning networks, also known as deep neural networks, comprise multiple hidden layers with interrelated artificial neurons, numbering more than millions. These neurons are linked by a numerical value called weight, which signifies the connection between one node and another. The weight can be either positive, indicating excitation between nodes, or negative, representing suppression between nodes. Nodes with higher weight values exert greater influence on the other nodes in the network.

Theoretically, deep neural networks possess the capability of mapping any input type to any output type. However, they require significantly more training compared to other machine learning methods. In contrast to simpler networks that may require just hundreds or thousands of examples of training data, deep neural networks require millions. This is due to the complex nature of these networks and their ability to learn intricate patterns and relationships. With the exponential growth of data, deep neural networks have become increasingly popular in various fields such as disease recognition, medical report processing, and even drug discovery. One of the key issues is the issue of interpretability, as the inner workings of deep neural networks are often opaque and difficult to interpret. Moreover, the training of deep neural networks is a computationally intensive task, requiring significant amounts of computational resources. This has led to the development of specialized hardware like Graphics Processing Units and Tensor Processing Units to accelerate the training process.

In conclusion, deep neural networks are a powerful tool for solving complex problems and have shown remarkable performance in various domains. However, their training requires significant amounts of data and computational resources, and the issue of interpretability remains a major challenge. Despite these challenges, deep neural networks continue to hold great promise for advancing the field of artificial intelligence. They can be trained similarly to ML algorithms as mentioned above.

10.8   AI FOR CHIARI MALFORMATION

In reference [30], the authors have used morphometric measures that allow the discernment of structural posterior cranial fossa to classify and discern patients having CM-0, CM-1.5, and CM-I. It was a comparative study in finding the best classifiers among the seven different supervised classification ML algorithms including Naive Bayes, Decision tree, k-NN, Logistic regression, Linear and quadrant discriminant analysis, and Support vector machine for their problem. ML technology has been able to effectively identify specific morphometric measurements. These measurements are capable of distinguishing between various types of CM. Specifically, the technology can differentiate between classic CM-I, which has a thickness of over 5 mm, and other variations such as CM-I with medium thickness & CM-1.5. The accuracy of the technology is quite high, 87% independent of the thickness criterion. However, it is lower in patients suffering from CM-0. Later, reference [31] also relied on morphometric measures to identify the CM's existence. Demon image registration was used to associate the subject in the feature of interest onto other images, in parallel with adjustment in head size differences. A kernelized SVM was utilized to extract distinct features that highlight the contrast in the deformation of images between disease groups and control groups. Statistical analysis was used to evaluate the quality of classification and estimate sensitivity and specificity. In reference [32], two supervised ML approaches: unbiased recursive partitioning technique conditional inference tree plus multiple logistic regression were used. Instead of classifying or identifying the types of CM, patients with CM-I or 1.5 who are at risk of having sleep-related breathing disorders are predicted. The utilization of the MLR model involved the employment of the general linear model (glm) in R, with the binomial family serving to segregate the relationship between predictors and resultant variables. The introduction of preselected input variables into the model facilitated the identification of statistically significant variables, while those that failed to meet this criterion were eliminated. On the other hand, the URP-CTREE model was executed through the use of the ctree function, which is an integral component of the partykit R package. In carrying out its operations, the model conducted a comprehensive examination of every potential partition of all input variables and subsequently identified the covariables that exhibited the most optimal split. This procedure enabled the model to generate reliable outcomes that were indicative of the correlation between the variables and the resultant variable. Reference [33] puts forward a novel approach to determine the optimal surgical assistance CM-I based on morphometric parameters of the cerebellum, brain, and posterior fossa which are calculated by analyzing MRIs. Furthermore, the estimation of the region boundaries is refined by active contour employing a third-party force that drives the area boundary towards darker regions. Once the regions have been accurately estimated, morphometrics are measured to quantify the relevant parameters. Finally, a classifier is used to identify the patients who require surgical intervention, and a second classifier is used to determine the severity of the condition (mild or severe), thereby enabling the nomination of appropriate surgical assistance. In summary, their fully automated method represents a notable accomplishment in the field of medical image analysis and can also improve the accuracy of surgical intervention for patients with CM-I. Supervised ML models including XGBoost, Stochastic Gradient Boosting, Bagged CART, Random Forest, and Logistic Regression were implemented in reference [34] using R Studio for the diagnosis of CM. Reference [35] suggested a technique utilizing SVM classification in machine learning, which is employed to distinguish patients with an elevated likelihood of syringomyelia and clinical decline, through the use of a variety of morphometric indices derived from sagittal MRI and patient data. Reference [36] reviewed CM over the years and summarized the following points. The requirement for more descriptive and pathogenic terminology for Chiari malformation has arisen due to the expanded classification systems, and recent MRI advances have disclosed more sustenance and existence of CM-1 in persons who are unrelated to classic characteristics as deduced by Hans Chiari, making it crucial to establish a terminology that accurately reflects the diverse presentations and underlying causes of these conditions. Retrospective MRI datasets consisting of individuals found to have CM-I and healthy people having normal brain scans were utilized for training convolutional neural network (CNN) models from January 2010 to May 2020 [37]. In order to differentiate between images as CM-I and normal, VGG-19 and ResNet-50 models were trained. For improving model accuracy, isotropic volume transformation, image cropping, skull stripping, and data augmentation techniques were applied. Model performance was evaluated using k-fold cross-validation to calculate specificity, sensitivity, and the area under the receiver operating characteristic curve (AUC). VGG-19 exhibited a 97.1% sensitivity; 97.4% specificity; 0.99 AUC. In contrast, the ResNet50 model showed a 94.0% sensitivity; 94.4% specificity; 0.98 AUC. The application of ImageNet pre-trained weights during the CNN model initialization facilitated transfer learning and further improved model accuracy. To optimize diagnostic performance, various hyperparameter tuning was done in the CNN, and input data were tested. The integration of CNNs in the analysis and automated diagnosis of CM-I has the potential to develop machine-aided clinical decision tools for diverse aspects of CM-I management. This study showcases the effectiveness of CNN models in the classification of CM-I and normal brain MRIs. The results obtained from this study highlight the potential of CNNs in improving diagnostic capabilities and clinical decision-making for CM-I. The use of CNNs in medical image analysis is rapidly gaining prominence and this study contributes to the growing body of literature on the subject. The success obtained from this study may pave the way for future research and clinical applications of CNNs in the diagnosis and management of CM-I. Their research encompassed a cohort of 148 patients who were diagnosed with CM-I at the host institution. Furthermore, 205 healthy controls were also included in [38]. The analysis was conducted using T1-weighted sagittal magnetic resonance imaging images. To train and validate the convolutional neural network models, 220 and 355 slices were acquired from 98 CMI patients and 155 HCs, respectively. Additionally, median sagittal images obtained from 50 CM-I patients and 50 HCs for testing the models were selected. To train the CI- and CVI-based CNN models, they employed original cervical MRI images (CI) and images of the posterior cranial fossa and craniocervical junction area (CVI). They utilized transfer learning and data augmentation for model construction and each model was retrained ten times.

10.9 PROPOSED METHODOLOGY

In this section, we briefly skim over the feasibility of a proposed deep learning model used for differentiating between the types of Chiari malformation from MRI radiology images. Here we apply a vision transformer-based model for image processing applications in order to classify the CM – (I–III, and 1.5) types.

10.9.1 DATASET

The dataset used for this problem contains around 90 images in total. The folders in the dataset contain four common types of Chiari malformation. When using the dataset in our model, we split it into two sections: the training dataset and the test dataset. They are split in the ratio of 70%–30%. The dataset initially obtained is raw without any form of pre-processing being done to reduce image complications.

10.9.2 ATTENTION MECHANISM

The concept of self-attention was introduced mainly for Natural language processing, as an attempt to improve the quality of Recurrent Neural Networks for managing long sentences and sequences. Their general focal point indirectly is the scaling of the network. Subsequently, a tremendous appreciation was provided for the successful implementation of self-attention as a deployable model [39]. Figure 10.6 shows a typical attention layer in a transformer architecture. Then over a few years later, this attention was applied to images as the initial work extended to language analysis [40]. This finding revolutionized the workings of attention for image processing without making use of skip connections, convolutions, and recursions concepts. This is considered to be a pioneer in leading the deep learning field in a direction without parasitizing convolutional layers.

In the case of deep learning, we aim to replicate the actions of the human brain using machines. Similar to this concept, the attention mechanism also aims to recognize the action of providing importance to only things that are relevant to us all the while ignoring the other unnecessary information. Note that in a normal attention model, all the inputs are treated with the same priority.

10.9.3 GLOBAL AND LOCAL ATTENTION

They were terms introduced in 2015 in correspondence with hard and soft attention. Global attention is where all the images formed from the dataset are given equal importance with zero partiality whereas local attention is where a single image is attended to at a time. From this concept, we can derive self-attention as "a mechanism through which the deployable model itself contemplates and decides which patch of image should it give more attention" in accordance with the image processing context.

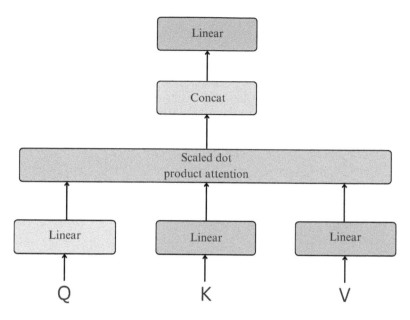

FIGURE 10.6   Attention layers in the transformer.

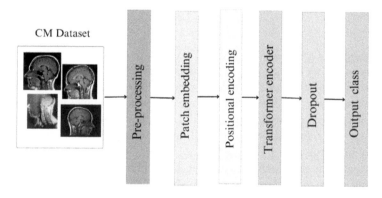

FIGURE 10.7   Workflow of the method proposed.

10.9.4 METHOD

We explore the feasibility of using a vision transformer for the classification of various types of Chiari malformation (I–III, and 1.5) as mentioned previously.

Figure 10.7 depicts the overall work planning done in the proposed methodology. The dataset is first made to undergo the augmentation process, so as to increase the variations and count of the samples present in the dataset. The background color is removed as the next step and also they are resized such that all images were in 128×128 pixels. After which every input image is divided into a number of patches of order 16 and they are flattened into 1D tensors, since most of the workings of the neural networks tend to be with tensors. These flattened vectors are now encoded with a positional embed because when the patch enters the encoder it does not have an order and follows a non-sequential manner. Finally, these patches enter the encoder which consists of a typical feed-forward neural network alongside a self-attention layer. The outline of the self-attention layer is given in Figure 10.6. The output is the class to which the input belongs to is made possible through the attention mechanism head in every transformer. Before the last step where we acquire

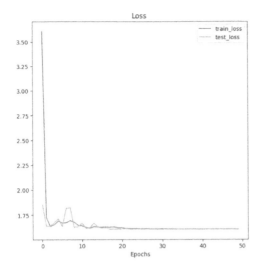
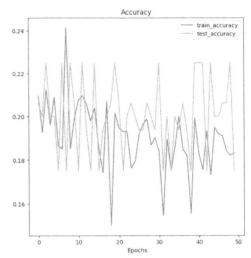

FIGURE 10.8   Loss and accuracy graph.

the classification results, a dropout layer is introduced. This is a type of regularization technique that helps in reducing the computational complexity of the model.

10.9.5   RESULTS

The training and validation graph was plotted and is shown in Figure 10.8. From the graph we can infer certain points including but not limited to: the number of epochs trained may be very low to achieve finite results; the most important keynote is the lack of a heavy dataset. On this note, generally we know neural networks perform well with large numbers of samples and vice versa. But there have also been efforts in having small to very small dataset that may or may not contain more than one image to be used for model learning. So overall the performance of our model heavily relies on the sample quantity in a dataset.

Another key takeaway is the overfitting concept. From Figure 10.8 we can see that there is no overfitting occurring which is good news as this condition can spoil the credibility of a deployable model.

Our ultimate aim is to create a deployable vision transformer. In that case, we should have a lightweight model that can be implemented as a mobile app or a widget. Considering the parameters shown in Figure 10.9, this solution can be a little heavy-weight to be practical, but not impossible. To overcome this, we need to develop a light model with less number of parameters in the future.

10.10   CONCLUSION

Chiari malformation comes under the congenital brain malformation – disorders of the dorsal induction category. Modern medical imaging techniques are used for the preliminary diagnosis and confirmation of the malformation. CT scans and MRI scans are the major techniques through which the malformation is identified albeit few diagnoses are done using ultrasound. Artificial intelligence as prospective as it is for other applications can also be applied to medical image analysis and research. Various initiatives include machine learning and deep learning being the identification tools for CM. More research using deep learning or hybrid approaches in this area would be appreciated as there are only a finite number of studies undertaken so far. This under-explored branch of neurology has tremendous potential to be studied in the future.

```
Out[23]: ================================================================================
======
Layer (type (var_name))                    Input Shape      Output Shape      Param #        Trainable
================================================================================
======
TransformerEncoderBlock (TransformerEncoderBlock) [1, 197, 768]   [1, 197, 768]     --             True
├─MultiheadSelfAttentionBlock (msa_block)  [1, 197, 768]    [1, 197, 768]     --             True
│    └─LayerNorm (layer_norm)              [1, 197, 768]    [1, 197, 768]     1,536          True
│    └─MultiheadAttention (multihead_attn) --               [1, 197, 768]     2,362,368      True
├─MLPBlock (mlp_block)                      [1, 197, 768]    [1, 197, 768]     --             True
│    └─LayerNorm (layer_norm)              [1, 197, 768]    [1, 197, 768]     1,536          True
│    └─Sequential (mlp)                    [1, 197, 768]    [1, 197, 768]     --             True
│    │    └─Linear (0)                     [1, 197, 768]    [1, 197, 3072]    2,362,368      True
│    │    └─GELU (1)                       [1, 197, 3072]   [1, 197, 3072]    --             --
│    │    └─Dropout (2)                    [1, 197, 3072]   [1, 197, 3072]    --             --
│    │    └─Linear (3)                     [1, 197, 3072]   [1, 197, 768]     2,360,064      True
│    │    └─Dropout (4)                    [1, 197, 768]    [1, 197, 768]     --             --
================================================================================
======
Total params: 7,087,872
Trainable params: 7,087,872
Non-trainable params: 0
Total mult-adds (M): 4.73
================================================================================
======
Input size (MB): 0.61
Forward/backward pass size (MB): 8.47
Params size (MB): 18.90
Estimated Total Size (MB): 27.98
================================================================================
======
```

FIGURE 10.9 Computational complexity of the proposed model.

REFERENCES

1. Chaudhari, B.P. and Ho, M.L. Congenital brain malformations: An integrated diagnostic approach. *Seminars in Pediatric Neurology*, 42, 100973, 2022.
2. Anand, C.V. and Mahmoud, H.E.S. A 4-week-old infant with scalp swelling in the parietal region. *Pediatric Annals*, 44, 312–314, 2015.
3. Calloni, S.F., Caschera, L. and Triulzi, F.M. Disorders of ventral induction/spectrum of holoprosencephaly. *Neuroimaging Clinics*, 29, 411–421, 2019.
4. Montero-Pedrazuela, A., Grijota-Martínez, C., Ausó, E., Bárez-López, S. and Guadaño-Ferraz, A., Endocrine aspects of development. Thyroid hormone actions in neurological processes during brain development. *Diagnosis, Management and Modeling of Neurodevelopmental Disorders*, 85–97, 2021. doi: 10.1016/B978-0-12-817988-8.00008-7.
5. van der Knaap, M.S. and Valk, J., Classification of myelin disorders. *Magnetic Resonance of Myelination and Myelin Disorders*, 20–24, 2005. doi: 10.1007/3-540-27660-2_2.
6. Chiari, H., Ueber veränderungen des kleinhirns infolge von hydrocephalie des grosshirns1. *DMW-Deutsche Medizinische Wochenschrift*, 17, 1172–1175, 1891.
7. Massimi, L., Peretta, P., Erbetta, A., Solari, A., Farinotti, M., Ciaramitaro, P., Saletti, V., Caldarelli, M., Canheu, A.C., Celada, C. and Chiapparini, L., Diagnosis and treatment of Chiari malformation type 1 in children: The international consensus document. *Neurological Sciences*, 43, 1311–1326, 2022.
8. Williams, B., Syringomyelia. *Neurosurgery Clinics of North America*, 1, 653–685, 1990.
9. Gad, K.A. and Yousem, D.M., Syringohydromyelia in patients with Chiari I malformation: A retrospective analysis. *American Journal of Neuroradiology*, 38, 1833–1838, 2017.
10. Bordes, S., Jenkins, S. and Tubbs, R.S., Defining, diagnosing, clarifying, and classifying the Chiari I malformations. *Child's Nervous System*, 35, 1785–1792, 2019.
11. Chiari malformation. (n.d.). In Wikipedia. (2023, May 17) https://en.wikipedia.org/wiki/Chiari_malformation.
12. Cruveilhier, J., Anatomie pathologique du corps humain; ou, Descriptions, avec figures lithographiées et coloriées, des diverses altérations morbides dont le corps humain est susceptible. Paris: Chez JB Baillière, City, 1842.
13. Schijman, E., History, anatomic forms, and pathogenesis of Chiari I malformations. *Child's Nervous System*, 20, 323–328, 2004.
14. Carmel, P. W., and Markesbery, W. R., Early descriptions of the Arnold-Chiari malformation: The contribution of John Cleland. *Journal of Neurosurgery*, 37, 543–547, 1972.
15. Pearce, J.M.S., Arnold chiari, or "Cruveilhier cleland Chiari" malformation. *Journal of Neurology, Neurosurgery & Psychiatry*, 68, 13–13, 2000.

16. Wu, J., Ji, S., Niu, P., Zhang, B., Shao, D., Li, Y., Xie, S. and Jiang, Z., Knowledge mapping of syringo-myelia from 2003 to 2022: A bibliometric analysis. *Journal of Clinical Neuroscience*, 110, 63–70, 2023.

17. Chiari H. Concerning alterations in the cerebellum resulting from cerebral hydrocephalus. *Pediatric Neurosurgery* 13(1), 3–8, 1987.

18. Hiremath, S.B., Fitsiori, A., Boto, J., Torres, C., Zakhari, N., Dietemann, J.L., Meling, T.R. and Vargas, M.I., The perplexity surrounding chiari malformations-are we any wiser now? *American Journal of Neuroradiology*, 41, 1975–1981, 2020.

19. Bogdanov, E.I., Faizutdinova, A.T. and Heiss, J.D., The small posterior cranial fossa syndrome and Chiari malformation type 0. *Journal of Clinical Medicine*, 11, 5472, 2022.

20. Mesin, L., Ponzio, F., Carlino, C.F., Lenge, M., Noris, A., Leo, M.C., Sica, M., McGreevy, K., Fabrik, E.L.A. and Giordano, F., A machine learning approach to support treatment identification for Chiari I malformation. *Applied Sciences*, 12, 9039, 2022.

21. Bogdanov, E.I., Faizutdinova, A.T. and Heiss, J.D., Posterior cranial fossa and cervical spine morpho-metric abnormalities in symptomatic Chiari type 0 and Chiari type 1 malformation patients with and without syringomyelia. *Acta Neurochirurgica*, 163, 3051–3064, 2021.

22. Yu, F., Jiang, Q.J., Sun, X.Y. and Zhang, R.W., A new case of complete primary cerebellar agenesis: Clinical and imaging findings in a living patient. *Brain*, 138, e353–e353, 2015.

23. Kulathilake, K.S.H., Abdullah, N.A., Sabri, A.Q.M. and Lai, K.W., A review on deep learning approaches for low-dose computed tomography restoration. *Complex & Intelligent Systems*, 9, 2713–2745, 2023.

24. Al-Antari, M.A., 2023. Artificial intelligence for medical diagnostics-existing and future AI technol-ogy! *Diagnostics*, 13, 688, 2023.

25. Kaur, R., Juneja, M., and Mandal, A. K., A comprehensive review of denoising techniques for abdomi-nal CT images. *Multimedia Tools and Applications*, 77, 22735–22770, 2018.

26. Zhang, Y. and Yu, J., The role of MRI in the diagnosis and treatment of gastric cancer. *Diagnostic and Interventional Radiology*, 26(3), 176, 2020.

27. Chen, Z., Pawar, K., Ekanayake, M., Pain, C., Zhong, S. and Egan, G.F., Deep learning for image enhancement and correction in magnetic resonance imaging-state-of-the-art and challenges. *Journal of Digital Imaging*, 36, 204–230, 2023.

28. Masse, O., Kraft, E., Ahmad, E., Rollins, C.K., Velasco-Annis, C., Yang, E., Warfield, S.K., Shamshirsaz, A.A., Gholipour, A., Feldman, H.A. and Estroff, J., Abnormal prenatal brain development in Chiari II malformation. *Frontiers in Neuroanatomy*, 17, 1116948, 2023.

29. Barragán-Montero, A., Javaid, U., Valdés, G., Nguyen, D., Desbordes, P., Macq, B., Willems, S., Vandewinckele, L., Holmström, M., Löfman, F. and Michiels, S., Artificial intelligence and machine learning for medical imaging: A technology review. *Physica Medica*, 83, 242–256, 2021.

30. Urbizu, A., Martin, B.A., Moncho, D., Rovira, A., Poca, M.A., Sahuquillo, J., Macaya, A. and Español, M.I., Machine learning applied to neuroimaging for diagnosis of adult classic Chiari malformation: role of the basion as a key morphometric indicator. *Journal of Neurosurgery*, 129, 779–791, 2017.

31. Spiteri, M., Knowler, S.P., Rusbridge, C. and Wells, K., Using machine learning to understand neuro-morphological change and image-based biomarker identification in Cavalier King Charles Spaniels with Chiari-like malformation-associated pain and syringomyelia. *Journal of Veterinary Internal Medicine*, 33, 2665–2674, 2019.

32. Ferré, Á., Poca, M.A., De La Calzada, M.D., Moncho, D., Urbizu, A., Romero, O., Sampol, G. and Sahuquillo, J., A conditional inference tree model for predicting sleep-related breathing disorders in patients with Chiari malformation type 1: Description and external validation. *Journal of Clinical Sleep Medicine*, 15, 89–99, 2019.

33. Mesin, L., Mokabberi, F. and Carlino, C.F., Automated morphological measurements of brain struc-tures and identification of optimal surgical intervention for Chiari I malformation. *IEEE Journal of Biomedical and Health Informatics*, 24, 3144–3153, 2020.

34. Tetik, B., Mert Doğan, G., Paşahan, R., Durak, M.A., Güldoğan, E., Saraç, K., Önal, Ç. and Yıldırım, İ.O., Multi-parameter-based radiological diagnosis of Chiari malformation using machine learning technology. *International Journal of Clinical Practice*, 75, 14746, 2021.

35. Mesin, L., Ponzio, F., Carlino, C.F., Lenge, M., Noris, A., Leo, M.C., Sica, M., McGreevy, K., Fabrik, E.L.A. and Giordano, F., A machine learning approach to support treatment identification for Chiari I malformation. *Applied Sciences*, 12, 9039, 2022.

36. Sahuquillo, J., Moncho, D., Ferré, A., López-Bermeo, D., Sahuquillo-Muxi, A. and Poca, M.A., A criti-cal update of the classification of Chiari and Chiari-like malformations. *Journal of Clinical Medicine*, 12, 4626, 2023.

37. Tanaka, K.W., Russo, C., Liu, S., Stoodley, M.A. and Di Ieva, A., Use of deep learning in the MRI diagnosis of Chiari malformation type I. *Neuroradiology*, 64, 1585–1592, 2022.

38. Lin, W.W., Liu, T.J., Dai, W.L., Wang, Q.W., Hu, X.B., Gu, Z.W. and Zhu, Y.J., Diagnostic performance evaluation of adult Chiari malformation type I based on convolutional neural networks. *European Journal of Radiology*, 151, 110287, 2022.

39. Vaswani, A., Shazeer, N., Parmar, N., Uszkoreit, J., Jones, L., Gomez, A.N., Kaiser, Ł. and Polosukhin, I., Attention is all you need. 31st Conference on *Advances in Neural Information Processing Systems* (NIPS 2017), 30, Long Beach, CA, USA, 2017.

40. Dosovitskiy, A., Beyer, L., Kolesnikov, A., Weissenborn, D., Zhai, X., Unterthiner, T., Dehghani, M., Minderer, M., Heigold, G., Gelly, S. and Uszkoreit, J., An image is worth 16×16 words: Transformers for image recognition at scale. *arXiv preprint arXiv:2010.11929*, 2020.

11 AI-Driven Restoration
Enhancing Biodiversity Conservation and Ecosystem Resilience

Jayanthi J. and Arun Kumar K

11.1 INTRODUCTION

Developing nations like India have huge demographic pressure[1]; however, rich natural resources provide habitat to millions of species. To sustain the nutritional needs of 1.8 billion individuals, significant and excessive exploitation of natural resources is occurring, resulting in the depletion of habitats and adversely impacting countless species at a physiological level. Many of these species now teeter on the brink of extinction. Adding to this, the pressing issues of poaching, alterations in agricultural land usage, and the swift expansion of industrialization are significant drivers accelerating the loss of biodiversity. The global scale of biodiversity loss has prompted both national and international bodies to establish policies at various intervals. However, the coordination between the implementation of these policies and the oversight of conservation strategies has often been lacking synchronization between the national and international levels.[2] Only 15% of priority areas were identified for conservation strategies, and most of the land use changes were overlooked.[3] Given India's varied climatic conditions, the country hosts a multitude of habitats that support a wide array of species. In such a context, even a minor alteration in these habitats can potentially result in substantial biodiversity depletion. Therefore, it is imperative to maintain continuous vigilance and surveillance to mitigate this risk.[4] In developing nations, where a significant portion of the population faces limited socioeconomic resources, dependence on the natural ecosystem becomes vital for livelihood sustenance. In such circumstances, where the primary focus is on ensuring food security rather than prioritizing biodiversity preservation, the rapid and irreparable decline of species and ecosystems becomes an alarming issue.[5] The leading contributor to biodiversity decline is the deforestation carried out for agricultural purposes. This is particularly impactful as many habitats rely heavily on tree canopies, and their clearance leads to a substantial loss of biodiversity. This transition from dense tree-covered habitats to agriculturally exploited areas marked by heavy agrochemical use and eventually to barren lands signifies a progressive erosion of biodiversity. This transformation of habitats encompasses a series of detrimental impacts, including the overexploitation of natural resources, the proliferation of invasive species, pollution, and the eventual loss of habitat for numerous species. India boasts two significant biodiversity hotspots—the Eastern Himalayas and the Western Ghats. Unfortunately, the conservation efforts within these areas have shown limited effectiveness. A more concerning aspect is that within these biodiversity-rich hotspots, deforestation for agricultural purposes is occurring, posing a threat to biodiversity.[6] The pace of climate change has escalated, resulting in severe repercussions for various species. Many of these species are compelled to alter their natural habitats, adjust their phenological cycles, or undergo genetic modifications to cope with the changing environment. Research has substantiated that climate change has a profound impact on a broad spectrum of India's flora and fauna. Given this scenario, it is imperative for the nation to respond promptly. Developing strategies for

DOI: 10.1201/9781003457176-11

ecological restoration and the augmentation or rehabilitation of habitats becomes an urgent necessity to alleviate the substantial biotic and abiotic stress currently affecting countless species.[7] According to the Intergovernmental Science-Policy Platform on Biodiversity and Ecosystem Services (IPBES), there is an alarming trend of extensive ecosystem degradation. This distressing situation has placed nearly ten million species on the precipice of extinction. Adding to the concern, the aftermath of the COVID pandemic has seen a significant influx of resources directed toward medical healthcare and food security, overshadowing the allocation for vital conservation initiatives.[8] Despite covering just 2.3% of the Earth's total land area, India boasts a remarkably rich biodiversity owing to its diverse climatic gradients, providing a habitat for approximately 8% of the world's biodiversity.[9] India bears witness to one of the highest rates of land use change and habitat conversion. Although the government has embarked on a tree plantation mission, an overlooked aspect is the prevalent practice of monocropping or the cultivation of a single plant species that can readily adapt to the environment. Unfortunately, this approach leads to a homogenous condition, posing a significant menace to biodiversity.Research indicates that a substantial proportion, roughly 33%, of India's angiosperm plants exhibit endemism, rendering them uniquely vulnerable to the perils posed by climate change. This predicament raises pressing concerns regarding the imperative to safeguard and diligently oversee these species. As evident from studies, climate change has the potential to significantly disrupt the natural habitats of these plants, underscoring the necessity for fostering heterozygous conditions as a crucial mechanism for the survival and sustenance of these distinctive endemic plant species.[10]

Historically, one-third of Earth's landscape was typically adorned with the verdant cloak of forest cover, a critical foundation that sustains an impressive 80% of terrestrial biodiversity. This lush expanse of trees not only contributes immensely to our ecological heritage but also plays the pivotal role of rendering numerous ecosystem services.[11] In the pursuit of effective biodiversity restoration, forests emerge as highly auspicious target sites. They hold the potential to serve as reparative havens, capable of mending habitats and providing conducive environments for the flourishing growth and proliferation of myriad species. Typically, two prevalent paradigms of restoration strategies exist: the first isthe community approach, wherein emphasis rests upon the biological interactions among diverse organisms; the second is the ecosystem-based restoration approach, which operates on a grander scale encompassing primary production and bio-geochemical cycles. However, these methodologies share a common limitation: a certain lack of precision in their efforts to conserve, mend habitats, and reintegrate species affected by the perturbations inflicted by human-induced changes in the environment.

11.2 BACKGROUNDS

11.2.1 Systematic Conservation Planning

Systematic conservation planning constitutes a pivotal array of methodologies, enabling conservation biologists to meticulously curate lists of species imbued with paramount priority and profound conservation worth (Figure 11.1). This strategic framework operates seamlessly across a spectrum ranging from individual species to entire ecosystems and intricate biological communities. Consequently, it presents a finely honed mechanism for tailoring the precise composition of species within designated target locales.[12] At its essence, this approach adheres to the complementarity principle, whereby the selection of species is guided by the objective of attaining a harmonious blend that optimizes the preservation of biodiversity. Of notable significance within this framework are keystone species, which are accorded elevated priority, recognizing their pivotal roles in ecosystem functionality and stability.The foundational tenets of systematic conservation planning encompass the essential pillars of complementarity, adequacy, efficiency, and spatial compactness. These principles have been judiciously employed in developed nations, yielding elevated species richness and heightened biodiversity diversity.[13] Nonetheless, the adoption of such methodologies in developing nations has proven to be less effective, resulting in a disconcerting pattern of haphazard

Scope and Costing of Planning Process

Identifying and involving stakeholders

Planned Conservation Area Descriptions

Identifying conservation goals

Identified area socio- economical variables and threat identification

Biodiversity and Natural Resource Availability Data Collection

Setting conservation objectives

Review current achievements of objectives

Selecting additional conservation area

Apply conservation actions to selected areas

Maintaining and Monitoring conservation area

FIGURE 11.1   Systematic conservation planning approach.

land use alterations that subsequently pave the way for the unfortunate occurrence of biodiversity loss.Systematic conservation planning (SCP) operates as a structured and meticulously designed approach, characterized by its discernible objectives and a collaborative framework that involves the insights of a diverse array of experts, often extending to policymakers. This strategic process is anchored in the establishment of quantifiable goals, encompassing the preservation of diverse elements such as vegetation, flora, and fauna within the ambit of conservation.[14] At its core, SCP is underpinned by a comprehensive and cautious decision-making process, drawing upon the expertise of biodiversity and conservation biologists. A prominent tool that has gained widespread recognition for the implementation of SCP is the Marxan software package, introduced in 2011 (available at https://marxansolutions.org/). This software serves as a potent instrument, facilitating the systematic design of conservation planning endeavors. By embracing SCP, conservation biologists are equipped with a decision-making compass that not only aids in the protection of species but also embraces the multifunctionality and heterogeneity of landscapes. This approach fosters a cohesive integration of diverse ecological components, empowering practitioners to make well-informed and effective choices in the pursuit of species conservation.[15]

11.2.2 MARXAN, SCP, AND AI

Marxan stands as the preeminent conservation planning software globally, renowned for its prowess in addressing intricate conservation conundrums within various landscapes. The Marxan suite of software has been meticulously crafted to serve as a valuable tool in systematic reserve design within conservation planning (Figure 11.2). Employing the prowess of stochastic optimization techniques, specifically Simulated Annealing, MARXAN facilitates the creation of spatial reserve systems. These systems are ingeniously designed to fulfill specific objectives of biodiversity representation, all while maintaining a commendable level of optimization.Simultaneously, the advent of systematic conservation planning introduced a paradigm shift by offering a lucid, replicable, and quantifiable methodology. This approach, marked by transparency and precision, effectively determines optimal conservation focal points that are both economically viable and efficacious.[16]

In the pursuit of sustainability and the enduring provision of essential ecosystem services, a heightened degree of systematic methodology becomes imperative. It becomes apparent that conventional conservation endeavors, though significant, might fall short of adequately addressing the

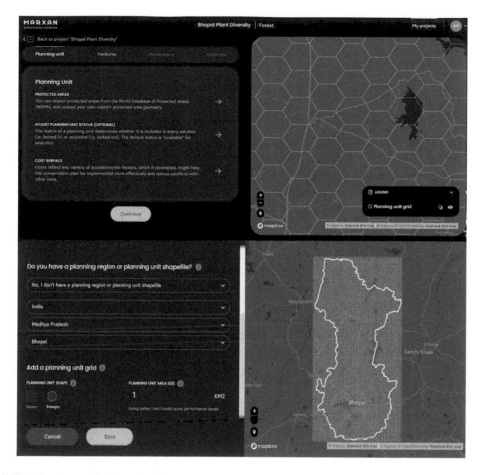

FIGURE 11.2 Target site identification via Marxan.

mounting challenges. With the constant escalation of demographic pressures, the demand for natural resources surges in tandem, underscoring the urgency of the situation.Systematic conservation planning approach (SCPA) manages and regulates landscapes for the protection and productivity of ecosystem services.[17] Systematic conservation approach allows the stakeholders to compile the list of conservation-required species and further use specified algorithms for prioritization of species distribution.[18] The variability in land use poses numerous challenges for species conservation within a specific landscape. However, employing a systematic conservation planning approach enables users to establish both short and long-term goals, fostering the creation of effective habitats within protected areas.[13] Silvestro et al.[19] introduced CAPTAIN, an innovative approach for conservation area prioritization utilizing Artificial Intelligence (AI) technology. CAPTAIN, which stands for Conservation Area Prioritization Through AI and Reinforcement Learning, not only assesses the impact of human activities on land use but also forecasts the potential consequences of exploitation. These methods play a crucial role in systematic conservation efforts and contribute significantly to biodiversity restoration. Likewise, for effective conservation strategies and planning, the utilization of smaller area selection, coupled with the identification of pertinent plant and animal species, along with robust conservation algorithms,[20] offers advanced AI-based technology. This technology is capable of analyzing and suggesting comparable sites for the protection of both plants and animals, enhancing the efficiency of conservation efforts.

To address this intricate landscape, a multifaceted strategy emerges as a requisite. The amalgamation of restoration and afforestation approaches holds promise as a formidable solution.

However, this alone might not suffice. The introduction of systematic restoration planning assumes paramount significance. This holistic approach, synergizing afforestation and meticulous planning, stands poised to tackle the complexities of our current predicament effectively.

11.3 PROPOSED WORK

11.3.1 Systematic Biodiversity Restoration Approach (SBRA)

We propose a comprehensive approach to systematically rejuvenate ecosystems that have fallen into a state of degradation. This entails the deliberate introduction of species that possess the inherent capacity to thrive within the ecosystem's existing environment, all while harmoniously coexisting with the resident species. This strategic interplay ensures that the restoration process not only takes root but also results in the augmentation of species richness within the once-degraded ecosystem. Parallel to the introduction of species, we advocate for the enrichment of these ecosystems with natural resources that have been depleted due to degradation. This deliberate infusion of vital elements further fortifies the restoration process, facilitating the recovery of the ecosystem's functionality and vigor. However, the endeavor doesn't conclude with these actions alone. An indispensable facet of our proposal lies in the continuous monitoring of the revitalized ecosystem's functions. This vigilant oversight serves as a safeguard, ensuring that the restored ecosystem remains on a trajectory of recovery and sustains its renewed vitality over time (Figure 11.3).

Accurate determination of canopy height within forested areas serves as a valuable resource, furnishing crucial data for the identification of tree species. This information, in turn, holds immense significance in pinpointing specific target sites for conservation efforts. For instance, the utilization of LiDAR imagery facilitates the detection of potential habitat fragmentation. These segmented and disjointed areas emerge as prime candidates for the application of a systematic approach to biodiversity restoration planning. Incorporating this approach, areas characterized by habitat fragmentation present a distinct opportunity. By leveraging such discontiguous and fragmented lands, a proactive approach to afforestation can be undertaken. This strategic endeavor not only endeavors to ameliorate the fragmented landscape but also strives to foster the enrichment of biodiversity within the designated zone. Through this multifaceted approach, canopy height estimation serves as a pivotal stepping stone toward the meticulous and effective planning of biodiversity restoration efforts.

Canopy height estimation is a meticulous procedure that involves determining the vertical distance from the ground to the uppermost layer of vegetation. Cutting-edge techniques like drone imaging and remote sensing are harnessed to construct sophisticated models, facilitating the precise

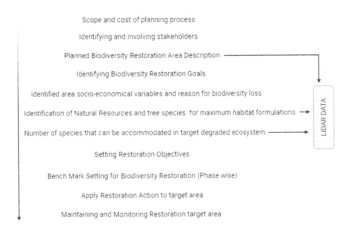

FIGURE 11.3 Proposed systematic biodiversity restoration planning approach.

measurement of canopy height. This pivotal information transcends multiple domains, encompassing forestry, agriculture, ecology, and urban planning. The process itself demands the abstraction of intricate forest structures into streamlined mathematical representations. The gamut of remote sensing techniques, including but not limited to LiDAR and radar, are harnessed to capture the requisite data for this abstraction process. Employing remote sensing methodologies, canopy height estimation entails data manipulation and model creation. These models can vary depending on the remote sensing modality employed, such as LiDAR or photogrammetry. Throughout this process, data points are meticulously collected, each representing the height of the canopy at distinct locations within the forest.

Sophisticated algorithms like LiDAR, along with approaches like Canopy Height Model (CHM) and statistical methods, are brought to bear in the meticulous analysis of the amassed data, culminating in the calculation of the average canopy height. LiDAR, for instance, employs laser pulses to gauge distances between the sensor and both ground surfaces and objects, thus forming a highly detailed point cloud. The discernment of ground points within the LiDAR dataset paves the way for the creation of a Digital Terrain Model (DTM), which characterizes the earth's surface. By subtracting the DTM from the initial LiDAR point cloud, a Canopy Height Model (CHM) emerges, offering insight into vegetation height relative to the ground.

These ingenious algorithms encapsulate the intricate nuances of individual trees within overarching canopy height values, thereby facilitating a more comprehensive understanding of forest dynamics. In summation, the endeavor of canopy height estimation utilizing drone imaging necessitates meticulous planning, data acquisition, sophisticated data processing, and a rigorous analytical approach. This method, in essence, redefines our capacity to comprehend and effectively manage the intricate dynamics of vegetation across diverse environments.

The estimation of canopy height holds paramount importance in unraveling the intricacies of ecosystem dynamics and orchestrating well-informed conservation strategies. Despite the process's abstraction, it yields invaluable insights into forest structure without necessitating the physical measurement of every individual tree's height. Particularly pertinent within India's context, canopy height estimation emerges as a pivotal endeavor due to the nation's diverse and ecologically significant landscapes. India, renowned as one of the world's biodiversity hotspots, boasts a kaleidoscope of ecosystems and species that warrant vigilant monitoring and preservation.

This practice is instrumental in safeguarding the assorted habitats and their indigenous flora and fauna. In regions prone to natural calamities such as floods, landslides, and forest fires, canopy height estimation plays an integral role in prognosticating and mitigating the ramifications of these events. The ascendancy of drone-based imagery has gained traction in canopy height estimation, a testament to the manifold advantages it proffers over conventional methodologies. Drones, lauded for their adaptability, seamlessly navigate various terrains and environments, including challenging landscapes like rugged or otherwise inaccessible areas. Their utility is further pronounced in reaching remote locations, including densely forested regions, precipitous slopes, or wetlands, where on-ground measurements prove arduous. As such, we employ drone-based imaging for canopy height estimation, forsaking traditional techniques such as Clinometer and Hypsometer.

Beyond its relevance to forest ecosystems, canopy height estimation significantly intersects with agricultural practices, furnishing invaluable insights into crop vitality, development, and overall management. The canopy height becomes a palpable gauge of crop growth and robustness. The continuous monitoring of canopy height fluctuations empowers farmers to gauge the trajectory of their crops, enabling prompt decisions concerning irrigation, fertilization, and other agronomic inputs. Beyond this, the correlation between canopy height and crop yield potential is pivotal. Accurate estimation empowers farmers to foresee potential harvest yields and strategize for storage, distribution, and marketing endeavors.

The utility of canopy height estimation extends to detecting anomalies in crop health. Unhealthy or stressed crops often reflect deviations in canopy height, an early indicator of diseases, nutrient deficiencies, or pest incursions. The judicious timing of harvesting is another facet influenced by canopy height. This knowledge ensures crops are reaped at their zenith yield and quality, circumventing premature or belated harvests.

Beyond these tangible impacts, the distribution of canopy height within a field streamlines resource allocation, allowing farmers to calibrate irrigation, fertilization, and pesticide application rates with precision. These data, in concert with other remote sensing and sensor inputs, fashion a panoramic comprehension of field conditions, underpinning judicious decision-making to optimize operations and augment profits. In essence, the estimation of canopy height in agriculture underpins a holistic comprehension of crop dynamics, well-being, and growth. It arms farmers with the discernment needed to navigate modern agricultural practices with sagacity, fortifying crop yields, resource utilization, and overall sustainability.

In recent years, a plethora of studies and research endeavors have been dedicated to harnessing the potential of drone-based imaging for the estimation of canopy height. Leveraging drone imagery, researchers have adeptly employed Structure from Motion (SfM) and photogrammetry techniques to craft intricate 3D models of vegetative landscapes. These models serve as the canvas upon which canopy height estimation is rendered, achieved by juxtaposing the surface model against a reference digital terrain model.

The exploration of texture-based attributes extracted from drone images constitutes another avenue of inquiry in the quest for accurate canopy height estimation. These attributes encapsulate variations in color and texture, attributed to disparities in vegetation density and elevation. A notable advantage lies in the employment of drones outfitted with cameras or LiDAR sensors, which present a judicious and efficient modality for data acquisition over expansive tracts. This automation expedites data-gathering processes, enabling more frequent updates and insights.

However, the veracity of drone-based canopy height estimations hinges on robust validation. Consequently, researchers have been tirelessly devising methodologies for ground-truthing and validation, often entailing field measurements and ground-based LiDAR systems. The machine learning algorithms have also been tapped into with convolutional neural networks (CNN) showcasing tremendous potential in autonomously inferring canopy height from drone imagery. The training of models on substantial datasets encompassing drone images and corresponding canopy height information has emerged as a conduit for precise predictions.

The synergy of data from various sensors, including LiDAR, RGB cameras, and multispectral sensors, ushers in a new era of comprehensive analysis. Such amalgamation endows the estimation process with heightened accuracy and a more granular understanding. Research endeavors in this domain frequently spotlight specific applications, such as forestry management, environmental monitoring, and precision agriculture. This approach aligns with the evolving trend of tailoring methodologies to suit the nuanced requisites of these distinct applications.

11.3.2 LiDAR -Light Detection and Ranging for Conservation

LiDAR is a remote sensing method that uses laser light to measure distances and create detailed 3D representations of objects and landscapes. It works by emitting laser pulses and measuring the time it takes for the light to bounce off objects and return to the sensor. This information is used to create accurate point cloud data, which represents the 3D coordinates of various surfaces, including the ground, vegetation, buildings, and more.[21-25]

The working principle of LiDAR involves measuring the time it takes for a laser pulse to travel to a surface and back to the sensor. This time is then used to calculate the distance between the LiDAR sensor and the surface. Here's a simple mathematical derivation of how LiDAR works:

Speed of Light Equation:
The speed of light in a vacuum is a constant denoted by "c," approximately 299,792,458 meters per second (m/s).

Time of Flight Calculation:

Let's assume that a LiDAR sensor emits a laser pulse that travels to a surface and then reflects to the sensor. The total time it takes for this round-trip journey is the "time of flight," denoted as "t."

Distance Calculation:

The distance "d" between the LiDAR sensor and the surface can be calculated using the formula for distance traveled by light in a given time:

$$\text{Distance} = \text{Speed} \times \text{Time} \qquad (11.1)$$

Substituting the speed of light "c" for the speed and the time of flight "t" for the time:

$$d = c \times t \qquad (11.2)$$

However, since the laser pulse travels to the surface and back, the actual distance is half of the total distance traveled by the light pulse:

$$\text{Actual Distance} = d/2 = (c \times t)/2 \qquad (11.3)$$

This equation represents the basic principle of LiDAR working: measuring the time it takes for a laser pulse to travel to a surface and back. By knowing the speed of light and the time of flight, the LiDAR sensor can calculate the distance to the surface.

In practical applications, the LiDAR sensor emits a series of laser pulses and measures the time it takes for each pulse to return. These time measurements are then used to create a point cloud, which represents the distances to different surfaces. The point cloud data can be further processed to create 3D models, generate terrain information, and estimate features like canopy height.

LiDAR data processing refers to the various steps involved in handling and extracting information from the raw LiDAR point cloud data. This includes tasks such as filtering noise, classifying points into different categories (ground, vegetation, buildings, etc.), generating digital terrain models (DTMs) and digital surface models (DSMs), and extracting features such as canopy height, building heights, and terrain elevation. LiDAR data processing often involves using specialized software and algorithms to manipulate and analyze the point cloud data to extract meaningful information.[26-29]

Calculate Canopy Height Model (CHM):

The canopy height[30-32] at a particular location can be calculated as the difference between the elevation value in the DSM and the elevation value in the DTM at the same location:

$$\text{Canopy Height (CH)} = \text{DSM Elevation - DTM Elevation} \qquad (11.4)$$

This equation gives you the canopy height at a specific point.

11.3.2.1 Rasterization and Interpolation

In LiDAR data analysis, the data are conventionally presented as a point cloud. To facilitate visualization and analysis, this point cloud requires conversion into a raster format. Various interpolation techniques, including bilinear or cubic interpolation, can be applied to bridge the gaps between individual LiDAR points. These methods enable the creation of a seamless and continuous canopy height surface for comprehensive analysis.[33,34]

11.3.2.2 Bilinear Interpolation

Bilinear interpolation[35] is commonly used to estimate values in a 2D space between four known neighboring points. It assumes a linear relationship between the values of adjacent points.

Given four points with their associated values:

$$A(x_0, y_0, \text{value}_0)$$

$$B(x_1, y_0, \text{value}_1)$$

$$C(x_0, y_1, \text{value}_2)$$

$$D(x_1, y_1, \text{value}_3) \tag{11.5}$$

The interpolated value at a point (x, y) within the range of $x_0 \leq x \leq x_1$ and $y_0 \leq y \leq y_1$ can be calculated using the following formula:

$$\text{Interpolated Value} = (1-\alpha)(1-\beta) * \text{value}_0 + \alpha(1-\beta) * \text{value}_1 + (1-\alpha)\beta * \text{value}_2 + \alpha\beta * \text{value}_3 \tag{11.6}$$

where:
$\alpha = (x-x_0)/(x_1-x_0)$
$\beta = (y-x_0)/(y_1-y_0)$

11.3.2.3 Cubic Interpolation

Cubic interpolation is a sophisticated technique employing cubic polynomials to estimate values by considering adjacent data points. This method yields smoother outcomes compared to bilinear interpolation.

Given four neighboring points:

$$A(x_0, \text{value}_0)$$

$$B(x_1, \text{value}_1)$$

$$C(x_2, \text{value}_2)$$

$$D(x_3, \text{value}_3) \tag{11.7}$$

The interpolated value at a point x between x_1 and x_2 can be calculated using the cubic interpolation formula, which involves solving a system of equations based on the cubic polynomial:

$$\text{Interpolated Value} = f(x) = a * x^3 + b * x^2 + c * x + d \tag{11.8}$$

The coefficients a, b, c, and d are determined using the values of the neighboring points and the derivatives at those points.

11.3.2.4 Spatial Analysis

Once you have the canopy height model[36] in raster format, you can perform spatial analysis to extract valuable information, such as the maximum canopy height in a specific area, the average canopy height across a region, or identifying areas with significant vegetation.

11.3.2.5 Validation and Ground Truthing

It's important to validate the accuracy of the derived canopy height model. Ground Truthing[37] involves collecting field measurements at specific locations to compare with the estimated canopy height values. This helps ensure the reliability of the model.

11.3.3 Proposed Sample Experimental Result

In this example, we're generating random LiDAR points with *X*, *Y*, and *Z* coordinates and assuming we already separated ground points. We calculate canopy heights by subtracting the ground elevation from the *Z* coordinate of each point. Finally, we visualize the distribution of canopy heights using a histogram (Figures 11.4 and 11.5).

---

a. Psudocode

  ➤ Imports necessary libraries.
  ➤ Reads a LiDAR data file (LAS format) using the laspy library.
  ➤ Extracts and prints dimension names and classifications from the data.
  ➤ Retrieves the X, Y, Z, and intensity values from the LiDAR data.
  ➤ Visualizes the LiDAR data using the geemap library.
  ➤ Prepares the data for machine learning:
  ➤ Combines X, Y, Z, and intensity into features.
  ➤ Sets the target variable as the canopy height (z).
  ➤ Splits the data into training and testing sets.
  ➤ Normalizes the features using StandardScaler.
  ➤ Trains a K-nearest neighbors (KNN) regression model with K=5.
  ➤ Evaluates the model using R2 score for both the training and testing data.
  ➤ Make s a sample prediction on canopy height using the trained model.

b. Output of sample data

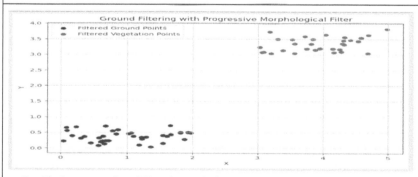

c. Graphical representation of filtered groundpoints and filterered vegetation points

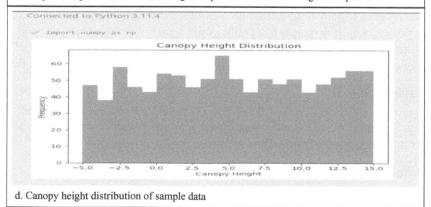

d. Canopy height distribution of sample data

FIGURE 11.4 Filtered ground points and filtered vegetation points visualization.

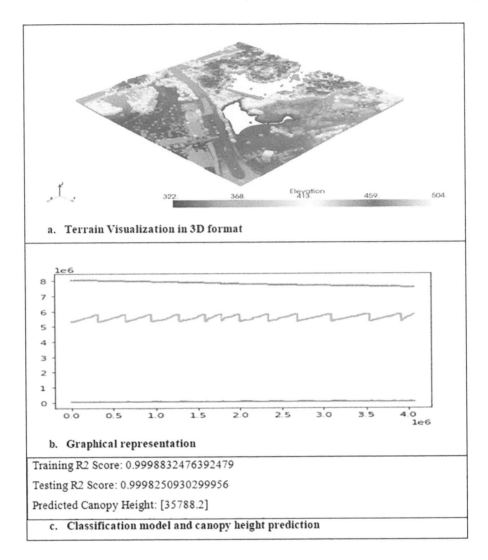

a. Terrain Visualization in 3D format

b. Graphical representation

Training R2 Score: 0.9998832476392479

Testing R2 Score: 0.9998250930299956

Predicted Canopy Height: [35788.2]

c. Classification model and canopy height prediction

FIGURE 11.5   Classification model and 3D visualization.

Minimizing noise in canopy height estimation from LiDAR data is essential to ensure precise results. Noise can encompass diverse artifacts like outliers, incorrect measurements, and vegetation reflections, all of which can significantly influence the accuracy of canopy height estimation. The following techniques and strategies can be employed to mitigate noise in canopy height estimation:

11.3.3.1   Outlier Removal

Detect and eliminate outliers within the LiDAR point cloud data. Outliers have a notable impact on result accuracy. Statistical methods or distance-based approaches can be employed to identify and exclude points that deviate significantly from the anticipated distribution.[38,39]

11.3.3.2   Ground Filtering

Precise ground filtering is vital to distinguish ground points from vegetation points. Utilizing algorithms like progressive morphological filters can assist in classifying ground points, minimizing interference from ground features.[40]

11.4 CONCLUSION

In conclusion, the utilization of drone-based imagery for canopy height estimation stands as a promising and impactful technique that transcends ecosystem boundaries. The integration of drones equipped with cutting-edge remote sensing technologies, including LiDAR and high-resolution cameras, has unveiled possibilities for capturing intricate insights into the vertical intricacies of vegetation.

Undoubtedly, this innovative approach has orchestrated a paradigm shift in the arenas of forestry and environmental monitoring. The marriage of high-resolution imagery and three-dimensional capabilities has bestowed fresh vantage points upon the landscape, empowering researchers, land managers, and conservationists with a profound understanding of vegetation structure. Such knowledge fosters the formulation of data-driven decisions that steer resource management strategies toward sustainability and fortify the foundations of biodiversity conservation. Nonetheless, while the strides made are commendable, the journey toward the full realization of drone-based canopy height estimation's potential demands unwavering dedication to continued research and technological advancement. As the ecological landscape evolves, addressing challenges and refining methodologies remain imperative. Only through the concerted efforts of scientists, practitioners, and technological innovators can we unlock the full spectrum of possibilities that drone-based canopy height estimation holds across a myriad of ecological applications. In parallel, another essential facet of holistic ecosystem restoration and conservation is systematic restoration planning. The integration of species capable of harmonizing with their environment, coupled with strategic habitat enrichment and vigilant ecosystem monitoring, offers a comprehensive framework for rejuvenating degraded ecosystems. Through deliberate planning and diligent execution, we can ensure the sustained vitality of these ecosystems and pave the way for a thriving coexistence of diverse species within them.

ACKNOWLEDGMENT

The authors express gratitude to the VIT Bhopal University for providing the necessary support.

DISCLOSURE STATEMENT

The authors declare no conflicts of interest.

DATA AVAILABILITY STATEMENT

The authors affirm that the data supporting the conclusions of this study can be found within the chapter.

REFERENCES

1. Kumar, A.; Sahu, S. K.; Jayanthi, J. Developing nation's soil microbial community shifts and diversity loss: Leading towards major ecological threat. *Environment Conservation Journal*2021, 22(3), 117–121. https://doi.org/10.36953/ECJ.2021.22314.
2. Sharma, P.; Batish, D. R. Reasons of biodiversity loss in India. In *Biodiversity in India: Status, Issues and Challenges*;Springer Nature Singapore: Singapore, 2022; pp. 555–567.
3. Srivathsa, A.; Vasudev, D.; Nair, T.; Chakrabarti, S.; Chanchani, P.; DeFries, R.; Nayak, R. Prioritizing India's landscapes for biodiversity, ecosystem services and human well-being. *Nature Sustainability* 2023, 6, 568.
4. Iyer, A.; Srinivasan, S.Role of biodiversity and ecological consequences in India. *Applied Science & Engineering Journal for Advanced Research* 2022, 1, 2583–2468.
5. Shanker, K.; Hiremath, A.; Bawa, K. Linking biodiversity conservation and livelihoods in India. *PLoS Biology* 2005, 3(11), e394.

6. Anil, M. N.; Kumari, K.; Wate, S. R. Loss of biodiversity and conservation strategies: An outlook of Indian scenario. *Asian Journal of Conservation Biology* 2014, 3(2), 105–114.

7. Behera, M. D.; Behera, S. K.; Sharma, S. Recent advances in biodiversity and climate change studies in India. *Biodiversity and Conservation* 2019, 28, 1943–1951.

8. Bawa, K. S.; Nawn, N.; Chellam, R.; Krishnaswamy, J.; Mathur, V.; Olsson, S. B.; Shankar, D. Envisioning a biodiversity science for sustaining human well-being. *Proceedings of the National Academy of Sciences* 2020, 117(42), 25951–25955.

9. Khoshoo, T. N. Census of India's biodiversity: Tasks ahead. *Current Science* 1995, 69, 14–17.

10. Chitale, V. S.; Behera, M. D.; Roy, P. S. Future of endemic flora of biodiversity hotspots in India. *PLoS One* 2014, 9(12), e115264.

11. Aerts, R.; Honnay, O. Forest restoration, biodiversity and ecosystem functioning. *BMC Ecology* 2011, 11(1), 29.

12. Boulton, A. J.; Bichuette, M. E.; Korbel, K.; Stoch, F.; Niemiller, M. L.; Hose, G. C.; Linke, S. Recent concepts and approaches for conserving groundwater biodiversity. *Groundwater Ecology and Evolution* 2023, 525–550. doi: 10.1016/B978-0-12-819119-4.00001-9.

13. Boulad, N.; Al Shogoor, S.; Sahwan, W.; Al-Ouran, N.; Schütt, B. Systematic conservation planning as a tool for the assessment of protected areas network in Jordan. *Land* 2021, 11(1), 56.

14. McIntosh, E. J.; Chapman, S.; Kearney, S. G.; Williams, B.; Althor, G.; Thorn, J. P.; Grenyer, R. Absence of evidence for the conservation outcomes of systematic conservation planning around the globe: A systematic map. *Environmental Evidence* 2018, 7(1), 1–23.

15. Cimon-Morin, J.; Goyette, J. O.; Mendes, P.; Pellerin, S.; Poulin, M. A systematic conservation planning approach to maintaining ecosystem service provision in working landscapes. *FACETS* 2021, 6(1), 1570–1600.

16. Nielsen, E. S.; Hanson, J. O.; Carvalho, S. B.; Beger, M.; Henriques, R.; Kershaw, F.; Von der Heyden, S. Molecular ecology meets systematic conservation planning. *Trends in Ecology & Evolution* 2022, 38, 143–155.

17. Margules, C. R.; Pressey, R. L. Systematic conservation planning. *Nature* 2000, 405(6783), 243–253.

18. Boulton, A. J.; Bichuette, M. E.; Korbel, K.; Stoch, F.; Niemiller, M. L.; Hose, G. C.; Linke, S. Recent concepts and approaches for conserving groundwater biodiversity. *Groundwater Ecology and Evolution* 2023, 525–550. doi: 10.1016/B978-0-12-819119-4.00001-9.

19. Boulad, N.; Al Shogoor, S.; Sahwan, W.; Al-Ouran, N.; Schütt, B. Systematic conservation planning as a tool for the assessment of protected areas network in Jordan. *Land* 2021, 11(1), 56.

20. Silvestro, D.; Goria, S.; Sterner, T.; Antonelli, A. Improving biodiversity protection through artificial intelligence. *Nature Sustainability* 2022, 5(5), 415–424.

21. Mehri, A.; Salmanmahiny, A.; Mirkarimi, S. H.; Rezaei, H. R. Use of optimization algorithms to prioritize protected areas in Mazandaran Province of Iran. *Journal for Nature Conservation* 2014, 22(5), 462–470.

22. Anderson, K.; Gaston, K. J.; Warren, P. H. Can drone-based image data aid the assessment of vegetation height for wildlife conservation? *Remote Sensing in Ecology and Conservation* 2017, 3(3), 144–155.

23. Chen, Q.; Feng, Q.; Cheng, G.; Liu, J. A new method for individual tree crown delineation from drone-based RGB imagery. *ISPRS Journal of Photographer and Remote Sensing* 2018, 144, 56–67.

24. Coops, N. C.; Zahawi, R. A. Using drone-based imaging for canopy height estimation. *Remote Sensing* 2014, 6(10), 10279–10293.

25. Dandois, J. P.; Ellis, E. C. Remote sensing of vegetation structure using computer vision. *Remote Sensing* 2010, 2(4), 1157–1176.

26. Hill, M. J.; Woodhouse, I. H.; Mackin, S. A comparison of consumer-grade cameras for photogrammetric purposes in forest inventory. *Forestry* 2016, 89(1), 69–81.

27. Hu, T.; Yao, W. Individual tree crown delineation and tree species classification using UAV-based photogrammetric point clouds and hyperspectral data. *Remote Sensing* 2017, 9(1), 36.

28. Kattenborn, T.; Heurich, M.; Förster, M. UAV-based monitoring of large areas-the impact of spatial resolution on the assessment of forest properties. *Forestry* 2018, 91(3), 315–329.

29. Lin, Y.; Shen, H.; Zhu, X.; Yang, G.; Cao, Q. A novel method for tree height estimation from unmanned aerial vehicle (UAV) point clouds. *ISPRS Journal of Photogrammetry and Remote Sensing* 2018, 144, 41–55.

30. Lisein, J.; Linchant, J.; Lejeune, P.; Bouché, P.; Vermeulen, C. Unmanned aerial survey of elephants. *PLoS One* 2015, 10(10), e0139244.

31. Lucieer, A.; Harvey, K. Improving small object detection using UAV-based hyper-temporal RGB imagery and deep learning for ecological applications. *Remote Sensing* 2018, 10(4), 619.

32. Ma, H.; Li, H.; Li, X.; Shi, Q. Canopy height estimation of large-scale forest areas using UAV LiDAR data and object-based image analysis. *Remote Sensing* 2020, 12(14), 2323.

33. Messinger, M.; Asner, G. P.; Silman, M.; Knapp, D. E. Unmanned aerial systems for monitoring tropical forests. Oxford Research Encyclopedia of Environmental Science 2016.

34. Mou, W.; Zhang, J.; Tan, X.; Liu, S.; Zhou, G.; Liu, J. A review of remote sensing of forest change. *Forest Ecology and Management* 2018, 422, 62–75.

35. Puletti, N.; Calders, K.; Burt, A.; Coomes, D. A. Beyond canopy height: Incorporating individual tree structure into large-scale forest modelling with UAV-derived photogrammetric point clouds. *Journal of Applied Ecology* 2018, 55(1), 281–293.

36. Rango, A.; Laliberte, A. Semi-automated object-based extraction of shrubs in a desert riparian ecosystem. *Journal of Arid Environments* 2010, 74(8), 955–964.

37. Wallace, L.; Lucieer, A.; Watson, C. Evaluating tree detection and segmentation routines on very high resolution UAV LiDAR data. *IEEE Transactions on Geo science and Remote Sensing* 2012, 50(6), 2186–2198.

38. Wallace, L.; Lucieer, A.; Malenovský, Z.; Turner, D. Assessment of forest structure using two UAV techniques: A comparison of airborne laser scanning and structure from motion (SfM) point clouds. *Forests* 2016, 7(3), 62.

39. Wang, L.; Sousa, W. P.; Gong, P. Integration of object-based and pixel-based classification for mapping mangroves with IKONOS imagery. *International Journal of Remote Sensing* 2004, 25(24), 5655–5668.

40. Zhang, C.; Kovacs, J. M.; Flores-Anderson, A. Remote sensing canopy height estimation and change detection for a mixed temperate forest using UAV Lidar data. *Remote Sensing* 2018, 10(5), 716.

12 Improvised DenseNet and Faster RCNN for Assisting Agriculture 4.0

*Sharmila A., K.S. Tamilselvan, R. Monisha,
and Dhivya Priya E. L.*

12.1 INTRODUCTION

In recent years, demands for food and food products have been gradually increasing owing to an increase in population. Due to urbanization and industrialization, the agronomists practicing agriculture keep on reducing. Agriculture 4.0, the recent revolution in agriculture, proffers more assistance to the farmers with less requirements and human needs with the recently developed technologies. Agriculture 4.0 increases productivity with minimal resources and assists in staying away from wasting food and food products, pesticides, and chemical fertilizers, and should accept the climate interchange and occurrence of natural calamities. As of record, the agronomists have to satisfy the food requirements of about 10 billion in the upcoming years. In order to meet the food demands of the drastically growing population, the average productivity has to be increased by an average of about 70% from now. In inclusion, agronomists have to face the challenges offered by nature and its disasters as they immensely influence the productivity of the crops. The challenges such as floods, droughts, soil erosion, underground water scarcity, geographical area of cultivation, and availability of resources for practicing agriculture. The temperature, humidity, dosage of the fertilizers, timely irrigation, harvests [1], disease detection in its initial stages, preventing the crops from pests [2], removing the weeds, selection of crops suitable for the geographical area [3] are to be taken at most care in order to increase the productivity. The above-mentioned parameters vary from crop to crop and from reason to reason. Plant diseases lead to 20%–40% of loss in the production of crops [4]. Earlier diagnosis of the disease can prevent the loss to an expected extent. Preventing diseases manually is the traditional practice in agriculture. Due to the outbreak of new diseases and pest attacks, there will be the possibility for the wrong prediction results in the usage of unrelated pesticides and fertilizers leading to some other problems [5]. Automation is a vital thing for agriculture as there are increasing demands for human resources and a lack of proper knowledge for practicing agriculture. Deploying deep learning techniques in the processors can be employed to detect diseases in real time [6]. The processors can be connected to the cloud in order to send the results to the agronomists and lessen the human requirements in crop monitoring processes. The work done in reference [6] analyzes the requirements and difficulties in deploying lightweight deep learning models in the processors [7]. Agriculture 4.0 aims to increase productivity by employing automation in each and every aspect of agriculture. The emerging technologies require the farmers to do less with the least resources and get more. In order to increase productivity with minimal requirements, Agriculture 4.0 adopts the Artificial Internet of Things AIOT [8,9]. The increasing demand for human resources in agriculture can be compensated by engaging the robots [10] for harvesting purposes by incorporating the artificial Internet of Things in controllers like jetson nano, an edge-embedded device with various algorithms, and analyzing the difficulties in deploying the deep learning techniques to the processors [10,11]. Incorporating artificial intelligence techniques in the greenhouse [12] to monitor and improve crop yield, reduce

DOI: 10.1201/9781003457176-12

the pest, effectively utilize the fertilizers, timely irrigation, and detection of diseases increases the productivity of the crops. IOT and AIOT analyze various wireless communication techniques for the effective practice of agriculture [12,13]. Agriculture 4.0 aims to computerize the activities in agriculture [14–16] to increase the yields with the least resources, prevent food waste, and able to withstand the climate conditions by employing emerging and recently evolving techniques such as artificial intelligence, Internet of Things, and cloud computing. Artificial Internet of Things employs deep learning techniques for disease detection and fertilizer suggestion for a particular variety of diseases.

The proposed work employs deep convolutional neural networks in predicting the diseases in crops. The backbone of the network is the dense net architecture followed by the head which is the Faster RCNN. The dense net architecture in the proposed work is employed with the following improvisations:

1. The proposed dense net architecture comprises CNN layers convolution pooling followed by the dense block layer.
2. Three dense block layers comprise 6, 12, and 6 convolution layers. Each layer is connected with every other layer to resolve the problem of vanishing gradients.
3. The self-attention layer is included in the dense net architecture so as to focus only on the required features and reduce the computational complexity.
4. The Faster RCNN is employed to classify and detect the disease with the bounding boxes.

Region proposal network in which the activation function in the convolution layer is replaced by the LeakyReLU to increase the accuracy of the proposed model.

12.2 RELATED WORKS

The productivity of crops is effected by various factors. The occurrence of diseases and pests is greatly influencing the yields of crops. Pests are not visible in the earlier stages as they stay beneath the surface of the leaves in the daytime to safeguard themselves and appear only at nighttime. Because of this the pests are difficult to identify even in the drone captured images. The system gathers the dataset from unmanned aerial vehicles and mobile phones [2]. The dataset before feeding into the deep learning model to recognize the presence of pests and the location of pests in the leaves underwent preprocessing techniques such as image enhancement and edge detection. The YOLO 3 You Only Looked Once object detection model is used in locating the pests, and the environmental parameters like temperature, intensity of light, and humidity are collected from the sensors [2]. The presence of pests and the parameters related to crops responsible for degradation in productivity are sent to the mobile phones of the agronomists to prevent the outbreak of infections through pests.

The need for the Artificial Internet of Things in Agriculture 4.0 and the provocation in implementing AIOT in Agriculture 4.0 are discussed in the work done in reference [1]. The proposed systems incorporate these techniques that assist in overcoming the difficulties in practicing traditional farming such as disease detection in the early stages, pest detection, post- and pre-harvesting issues. IOT in general employs wireless sensor networks to collect the parameters required for increasing productivity with the help of communication protocols and microcontrollers, and actuators to take appropriate action upon the irregularities in the parameters measured by the sensors [1]. The reviews done in the paper focus on weed detection, crop disease prediction, parameters answerable for automatic irrigation system, and categorize the fruit based on its color and texture by continuous monitoring through video observations. Numerous deep learning and machine learning techniques, such as SVM support vector machine classifier, k-Nearest Neighbor, and distinct architectures of convolutional neural networks, and by combining the desired features of the algorithms such as region-based convolution neural networks to the object classification models are incorporated in the previous works to predict the variety of parameters promotes enhancement in productivity. The status of irrigation, crop disease, and pest detection is informed to the farmers through mobile applications. The integration of artificial intelligence and Internet of Things immensely enhances agriculture practices, improves the productivity of crops with cost-effective solutions, and lessens the requirements of human resources in practicing agriculture.

Smart farming increases the productivity of crops and the quality of food products by engaging the emerging techniques in weed detection to disease and pest detection [3]. Selection of crops appropriate to the farmlands plays a crucial role in improving the quantity as well as the quality of yields. The proposed work suggests a suitable crop for the selected farm field by the ecofriendly crop guidance technique. The technique gathers the details of temperature and the average rainfall of the target location and recommends the preferable crop by enrolling in the artificial Internet of Things (AIOT) techniques [3]. These techniques lessen the need for human resources in the crop recommendation system and at the same time improve the crop yields to a great extent.

Dense net architecture 41 combined with the faster RCNN to recognize the handwritten digits is proposed in reference [17]. Dense net 41 is used as a backbone to draw out the attributes from the input image. The extracted features are fed into the Faster RCNN for recognizing and detecting the handwritten digits.

The Faster RCNN has the region proposal networks that generate the proposals of the region. The proposals of the region are offered as input to the Region of Interest pooling, which in turn resizes the proposals to the same size and engages the maximum pooling to draw the required proposals [17] and skip the remaining proposals to gain accuracy in classification and detection of hand written digits. Densenet along with the mask RCNN for road damage detection is proposed in [18]. It offers notable accuracy in classification by combining the Densenet and mask RCNN.

Combination of Densenet and Faster RCNN is employed to detect glaucoma in [19]. The proposed work with the region of proposals proffers remarkable accuracy than the Densenet architecture.

Object detection model with the hybrid dilated model an improved version of VGG 16 [20] and the faster RCNN to procure the extensive accuracy. The proposed work employs the LeakyReLU as an activation function instead of ReLU as it considers the negative input values. Positive output close to zero is considered as zero [20]. Spatial pyramid network is engaged to resolve the issue of requirement of fixed-size images. The system proffers high accuracy than the existing VGG16 and the Faster RCNN with the reduced training time.

Improved dense net with the squeeze and excitation attention mechanism to detect and highlight the portion with the presence of pneumonia [21]. The proposed system employs four dense blocks and three transition layers. The average pooling in the third transition layer is supplanted with the maximum pooling layers. The data augmentation by the rotation, horizontal, and vertical flipping is systematized before being fed into the dense net architecture. The activation function engaged is the parametric Rectified Linear Unit to overcome the issues with the dying ReLU [6]. Glaucoma is detected in the earlier stages by engaging the dense net architecture and the Faster RCNN for finding the optic disc and CDR ratio to analyze the stages of glaucoma [22].

Enhancing productivity in agriculture is done through the incorporation of recent technologies such as Internet of Things and Artificial Internet of Things [23] by monitoring the various parameters to predict the presence of diseases and pests.

Damage in roads can be predicted by employing deep learning models in hybrid mode [24]. The dense net architecture engages itself as a backbone to extract the vital features proceeded by the mask RCNN for classifying and detecting the locale of the damage in roads. Features are drawn out from the dense layer of the backbone architecture. The extracted attributes serve as an input to the feature pyramid network (FPN) for integrating the features taken out. Region proposal networks to create the region proposals. Region of Interest made use of the desired proposals and fed to the fully connected layers for precise prediction [24]. It provides three outputs: object classification, detection, and mask for the output. Mask RCNN predicts the finer details by offering the mask for the output.

Incorporating unmanned aerial vehicles for field monitoring keeps on increasing, and it greatly assists farmers in the present day in improving yields. The datasets extracted from the drones are analyzed using deep learning techniques. The ResNet 101 is employed as a backbone network for the purpose of extracting the attributes from the input image. The Mask RCNN is employed as a head for detecting and locating the diseases in crops. The FPN, RPN, and ROI heads are employed to get the classification of diseases, bounding boxes, and the mask for the output to get the faultless prediction of diseases.

Artificial Internet of Things is used for monitoring the fish farm in real time [25]. The deep learning model employed detects the number of fishes, their weight, health status, and environmental conditions of the fish farm and automates the process of feeding by employing embedded devices such as controllers, sensors, and actuators. The fish monitoring by deep learning techniques from sonar images and the stereo camera to detect the weight, height, and health conditions of fishes in the underwater tanks [26]. Planting mint in the office and monitored by deploying small-scale agriculture with the Artificial Internet of Things to monitor its growth status [27] and the growing environment is taken care of by the sensors embedded with the controllers. The status of the growth at numerous stages is monitored by incorporating AIOT technologies.

Agronomists face immense difficulties in practicing agriculture to attain reasonable productivity: rotation in climatic conditions, non-availability of adequate resources, drastic growth in the population, labor cost, diseases in crops, incorporating recent technologies to increase production, and assurance for food safety [3]. Employing automation for agricultural practices with the integration of Internet of Things and Artificial Intelligence has a significant impact on increasing production despite its requirements for the data for training purposes and network connectivity. AIOT will adapt itself to the recent advancements in deep learning techniques and promote sustainable agriculture.

Integration of Internet of Things and Artificial Intelligence has paved the way for engaging techniques to predict the happenings of the future and can take decision on its own devoid of the need for human suggestions [28]. Edge computing overcomes the challenges faced by Artificial Internet of Things including the huge amount of data requirements and networking facilities. Edge computing in addition to Artificial Internet of Things immensely assists in improving productivity [29]. The proposed work demonstrates the implementation of Artificial Internet of Things in real-time applications.

Artificial Internet of Things analyzes numerous factors responsible for improving productivity in agriculture. Real-time monitoring of soil is performed to predict suitable crops, disease detection in crops, and identify effective irrigation facilities by incorporating sprinkler and drip watering techniques to promote precision agriculture [30]. The system offers solutions for practicing agriculture upon analyzing the climatic conditions. The proposed work enhances the productivity of crops with optimal energy utilization.

To promote smart farming, artificial intelligence integrates itself with robotics, Internet of Things and multifunctional algorithms [31,32]. The sensor technologies combined with Artificial Intelligence perform real-time monitoring and gathering of data related to growth conditions [33] and disease detection and perform appropriate actions.

Precision agriculture is made possible by employing deep learning techniques. The system focuses on all the parameters such as disease prediction, presence of weeds and pests in farm fields, and various nutrients of the soil responsible for increasing yields [34]. Numerous deep learning techniques are analyzed for accuracy in predicting the diseases in leaves, weeds, and pests to enhance smart farming [35].

12.3 PROPOSED WORK

The proposed Deep Learning architectures are supervised learning models as they employ remote data to classify the type of diseases. In the dataset, about 70% of data are engaged for training and 30% of data are engaged for testing the accuracy of the system. Preprocessing is the initial step to be performed in deep learning in which the images are subjected to the prescribed size as to lessen the computational time.

12.3.1 LAYERS OF DEEP LEARNING ARCHITECTURES

1. Convolution Layer
2. Pooling Layers
3. Fully connected layers
4. Batch normalization
5. Transition layer
6. Dense block layer

The layers of the CNN model are shown in Figure 12.1. The second step is the attribute drawn out. It extracts the vital attributes from the images. The pivotal attributes are mandatory to classify the type of disease in the given image. Feature extraction involves the convolution and pooling layers. The convolution layers are filters to draw out the important attributes from the given input image. It also involves the activation function that decides which attributes to pass on to the next layer and avoids the repetition of information. The convolutional layer is followed by the pooling layer.

Maximum pooling layer is preferable for extracting the immense attributes from the images. The striding and padding are occupied so as not to miss out the required attributes in the image data. The workflow of CNN model is shown in Figure 12.2. Once the attributes are extracted, the model enters into the classification stage. Flattening layer is employed to reduce the dimension of the image to a single dimension before the information is loaded to the classification layer. It assists in increasing the computational speed of the CNN model. The classification layer will be the fully connected layer or dense block layer. The classification layer in turn occupied the softmax activation function to classify the type of the disease in the given image data. This mechanism is called feed-forward neural network. After which the losses can be calculated by the cross entropy loss function. The Adam optimizer with the loss function is to renovate the weights by propagating backward from the output layer. This process of reducing the error rate is known as backpropagation. It improves the performance of the model. The layers vary from architecture to architecture.

The accuracy of the model needs to be predicted using True Positive, True Negative, False Positive, and False Negative values. The Accuracy, Precision, Recall, and F1 Scores can be predicted for all the models of CNN to evaluate their performance.

12.3.2 DATASET DESCRIPTION

The Plant village dataset for the training and testing of the proposed improvised dense net architecture with Faster RCNN. Totally, there are 54,303 images in the plant village dataset with healthy and diseased leaves of the plants. The dataset comprises 38 distinct diseases of various plants.

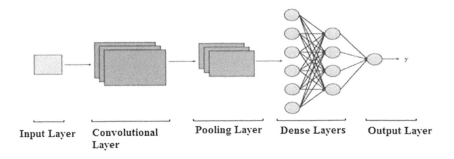

Input Layer   Convolutional   Pooling Layer   Dense Layers   Output Layer
                  Layer

FIGURE 12.1 Layers of CNN Models.

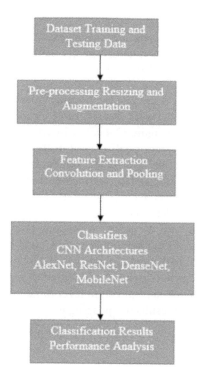

FIGURE 12.2 Overview of the proposed system.

12.3.3 DENSENET ARCHITECTURE

The proposed work detects the diseases in potato plant by collecting the datasets of the healthy and the infected leaves of the plant as most of the diseases occur in the leaves of the plants. The dataset comprises distinct diseases of potato plants. The major diseases prone to the degradation in the production of potato plants are the early and the late blight diseases.

The proposed system engages the improved dense net architecture with the self-attention layers proceeded by the faster region-based convolution neural networks. The dense net architecture with the attention layers offers high accuracy in the classification of the diseased and the healthy leaves and in distinguishing the variety of diseases. Faster region-based convolution neural network is engaged to locate the infected region of the leaves.

12.3.4 IMPROVED DENSE NET MODEL

The dense net architecture in turn offers a reasonable accuracy in comparison with the existing architectures. It completely overcomes the problem of vanishing gradients which is due to the deeper layers of convolution neural networks.

The attributes will be lost in the training phase when propagating through the large number of the layers between the input and output. While updating errors through backpropagation, there is a possibility for the value of the gradient to become zero. The dense net architecture overcomes the problem of vanishing gradients by utilizing the dense block layers where all the layers are connected with every other layer so that there is no possibility of losing the attributes required for classification.

The densenet architecture comprises of convolution layer, pooling layer, three dense block layers followed by the transition layer, average pooling, and the fully connected layer.

The densenet architecture is improvised by including the self-attention layers. The self-attention layer is included after the last dense block layer. There are three dense block layers in the improved dense net architecture. The transitional layer is removed in the architecture as there is no down-sampling required. The self-attention layers are encompassed in the dense net architectures to reduce the computational complexity and to remember the attributes for a long time. It permits the input attributes to collaborate with one and all. Self-attention decides which attribute of the input the model should reimburse more attentiveness to get more accuracy in classification. It focuses only on the required attributes and in turn decreases the training time and lessens the inconsequential features so as to reduce testing time. The work slow of the proposed model is shown in Figure 12.3.

Dense net 121 architecture shown in Figure 12.4 comprises of convolutional layer, pooling layers, dense block layers, transition layer, average pooling layer, fully connected layer. In the improvised dense net121 architecture a self-attention layer is incorporated in between the transition, average pooling layer followed by average pooling and the fully connected layer to enhance the performance of prevailing dense net architecture as shown in Figure 12.5. 121 in dense net architecture indicates the number of layers employed in the dense net architecture.

Convolution layer which is fed with the input image comprises of batch normalization layer, convolution layers with filters of size 7×7, Rectified Linear Unit as an activation function and drop out layer to extract the attributes from the input image with the 64 filters with the stride of two. The stride represents the number of steps the convolution filter has to move over the image so as to prevent the losses in the attributes. Batch normalization layer in general is connected before or after activation layer to get the appropriate results by speeding up the process of training. The activation

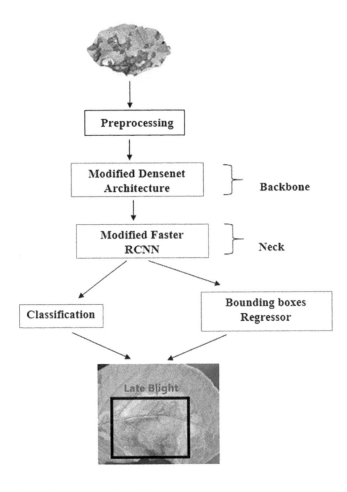

FIGURE 12.3 Workflow of the proposed model.

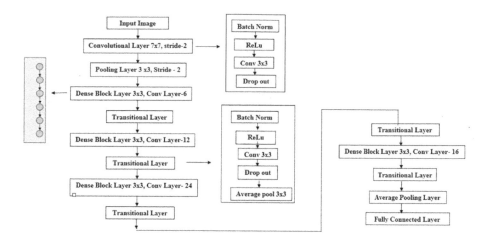

FIGURE 12.4 Dense net architecture.

layer allows only the prescribed attributes to pass through the neurons. The second layer in the architecture is the pooling layer. It is to extract the maximum and the most significant attributes of the images. Pooling is followed by the dense block layer. It comprises six convolution layers. Each layer in the dense block layer is connected to every other layer so as to prevent the problem of fading gradients. Each layer should be of the same dimension as they are interconnected with one another.

Transition layer is to reduce the proportions of the attributes to shrink the statistical complexity. It encompasses of average pooling layer and the convolutional layer to reduce the overall proportions of the attributes. There are three consecutive layers of dense block and transitional layers to solve the issue of fading gradients, proceeded by the average pooling and the fully connected layers. In the modified dense net architecture, the pre-trained self-attention layers are incorporated to improve the performance of the model and to reduce the time required for training by focusing only on the desired attributes of the images. The model outperforms the existing architecture of dense net in terms of accuracy and computational time.

12.3.5 Faster RCNN

The proposed work engages the dense net architecture for object classification and Faster RCNN for object detection is shown in Figure 12.6. The output obtained from the average pooling layer of the dense net architecture is fed as an input to the Faster RCNN. In general, the Faster RCNN which is the integration of Fast RCNN and the regional proposal network.

Object detection plays a vital role in computer vision. Able to detect objects in the camera or from the video surveillances. Fast and Faster RCNN are the enhancement over the existing region-based convolutional neural networks. Fast RCNN employs Region of Interest and FC layers for the detection of object with the bounding boxes.

12.3.5.1 Region of Interest (RoI)

Input image passes through the convolutional layer, maximum pooling layers to extract beneficial attributes from an image. The features drawn out from the layers are given as an input to the Region of Interest (RoI) to get the feature vector for the drawn out features. The other input to the RoI is from the region proposal network, and it receives the attributes from the convolution and pooling layers to generate the proposed regions.

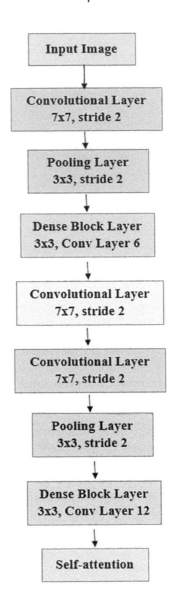

FIGURE 12.5 Proposed dense net architecture.

12.3.5.2 Regions of Proposals

To generate the proposed regions, the filter is moved smoothly along the features. A set of pre-defined bounding boxes of various aspects of width and height are placed on the center of the filter to acquire the scale and the aspect ratio. Aspect ratio is the ratio between the width and the height called resolution, enlargement suitable for pixels to be visible on the entire screen. Based on the number of feature maps and the bounding boxes, there are a large number of proposals generated with the stride of about 16. Considering all the proposals is not an easy task. In this case, region proposal arranges the proposal with the highest order of proposal first, followed by the remaining proposals. The region proposal Network comprises of convolution layer and the fully connected layers. The convolution layer comprises filters and the activation function. The activation function

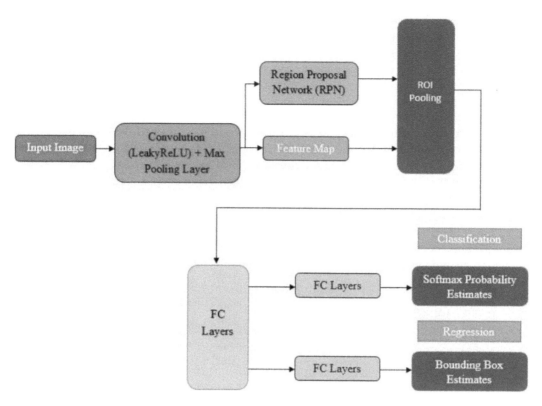

FIGURE 12.6   Faster RCNN.

employed in the proposed work is LeakyReLU instead of ReLU to lessen the problem of dying ReLU and to improve the performance of the model. The proposed activation function focuses not only on the positive values but also on the negative slopes.

12.3.5.3   Non-Max Suppression

The RPN engages non-max suppression to remove the unimportant proposal and keep the one with high information required for object detection. It is an algorithm that combines the predictions belonging to a similar object in an image. Some of the anchors may contain similar information. Such anchor boxes can be removed by the non-max suppression. There is a threshold value required to be employed to decide whether to remove or continue with the anchor boxes with their scores. The suppression technique immensely helps to reduce the number of unwanted proposals.

12.3.5.4   Loss Function

The anchors are assigned labels upon the IOU overlap between the anchor boxes. If the intersection over Union is found to be greater than 0.7, then the anchor box is given a positive label. If the IOU score is less than 0.7, then the anchor is offered with the negative label. The overall loss is considered to be the addition of classification and reverting loss.

12.3.5.5   RoI Pooling

The proposals from the region proposal network are of various sizes. To process the proposals further they are requiring being of similar size. The RoI pooling generates proposals of the same size.

It divides the proposals into a number of same size regions and then applies the maximum pooling to obtain the required attributes to be fed into the fully connected layers.

The output from the RoI is fed to the fully connected layers for object detection with the bounding boxes. The fully connected layers proffer the classification result of the bounding boxes to project the object in the input image with the softmax activation function and offset of the bounding box. The plant diseases are detected with the locale with the Faster RCNN. The region proposal networks outperformed the selective search in the fast RCNN.

The proposed work combines the modified dense net and the Faster RCNN to gain accuracy in the prediction of the plant disease shown in Figure 12.7. The attributes from the last transition layer are directly fed as input to the Region Proposal Network of the Faster RCNN. The Faster RCNN proffers expected accuracy with the modified dense net as a backbone for attribute prediction.

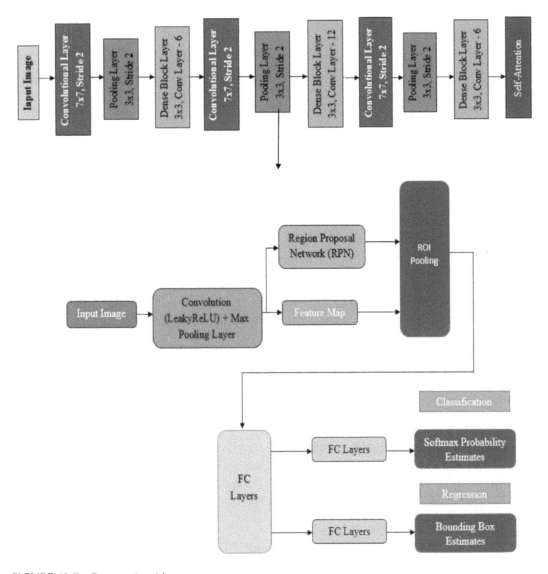

FIGURE 12.7 Proposed architecture.

12.4 RESULTS AND DISCUSSION

The accuracy and the training loss of the proposed model are shown in the figure. The training and validation loss decreases with the increase in accuracy. The accuracy of the existing dense net model is shown in Figure 12.8. The accuracy of the proposed model is demonstrated in Figure 12.9.

The detection of disease in the crops using the improvised dense net and faster RCNN is shown in the figure. The model classifies the type of disease that occurred with the bounding boxes to locate the diseased portion of the leaf. The accuracy, F1 score, precision, and recall of the proposed work in comparison with the existing work are shown in Table 12.1.

```
Epoch 1/10
54/54 [==============================] - 235s 4s/step - loss: 0.8461 - accuracy: 0.5330 - val_loss: 0.7139 - val_accuracy: 0.6615
Epoch 2/10
54/54 [==============================] - 232s 4s/step - loss: 0.5819 - accuracy: 0.7454 - val_loss: 0.4536 - val_accuracy: 0.7865
Epoch 3/10
54/54 [==============================] - 237s 4s/step - loss: 0.3952 - accuracy: 0.8304 - val_loss: 0.3509 - val_accuracy: 0.8594
Epoch 4/10
54/54 [==============================] - 232s 4s/step - loss: 0.4164 - accuracy: 0.8241 - val_loss: 0.3923 - val_accuracy: 0.8594
Epoch 5/10
54/54 [==============================] - 235s 4s/step - loss: 0.2911 - accuracy: 0.8912 - val_loss: 0.3005 - val_accuracy: 0.8958
Epoch 6/10
54/54 [==============================] - 233s 4s/step - loss: 0.2319 - accuracy: 0.9097 - val_loss: 0.3728 - val_accuracy: 0.8646
Epoch 7/10
54/54 [==============================] - 228s 4s/step - loss: 0.2337 - accuracy: 0.9039 - val_loss: 0.1841 - val_accuracy: 0.9219
Epoch 8/10
54/54 [==============================] - 228s 4s/step - loss: 0.1829 - accuracy: 0.9334 - val_loss: 0.2077 - val_accuracy: 0.9219
Epoch 9/10
54/54 [==============================] - 224s 4s/step - loss: 0.1979 - accuracy: 0.9294 - val_loss: 0.1531 - val_accuracy: 0.9479
Epoch 10/10
54/54 [==============================] - 234s 4s/step - loss: 0.1738 - accuracy: 0.9306 - val_loss: 0.1268 - val_accuracy: 0.9531
```

FIGURE 12.8 Results obtained from the densenet architecture.

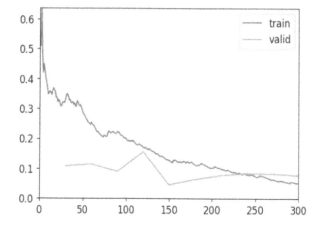

FIGURE 12.9 Training and validation loss of the proposed densenet.

TABLE 12.1

Comparison of Accuracy Recall Precision and F1 Score

Model	Recall	F1 Score	Precision	Accuracy
Proposed model	0.98	0.985	0.97	98
DenseNet	0.97	0.96	0.95	95

The proposed model proffers an accuracy of 98% in detecting diseases in crops. The disease detection in potato leaves is demonstrated in Figure 12.10 with the bounding boxes to localize the images in the result from the application with the accuracy and time required to predict the health status of crops. Figure 12.11 shows the accuracy in the prediction of leaf diseases with the

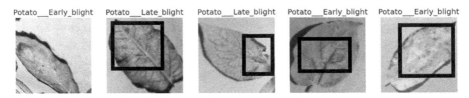

FIGURE 12.10 Disease detection in the crops with the proposed model.

FIGURE 12.11 Improvised dense net with accuracy.

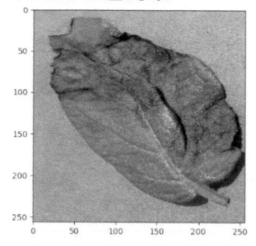

FIGURE 12.12   Disease detection with time step.

FIGURE 12.13   Confidence score.

improvised dense net architecture. A comparison of the actual and the extracted output with the time step required for the prediction of the diseases in the potato leaves is shown in Figure 12.12. Training and validation accuracy, and training and validation losses plotted by the proposed work are shown in Figure 12.13 and Figure 12.14.

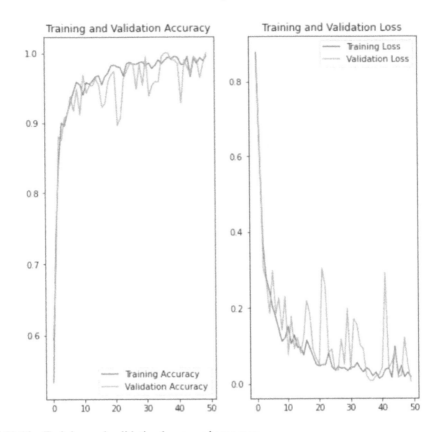

FIGURE 12.14 Training and validation losses and accuracy.

REFERENCES

1. H.K. Adli, M.A. Remli, K.N.S. Wan Salihin Wong, N.A. Ismail, A. González-Briones, J.M. Corchado and M.S. Mohamad, Recent advancements and challenges of AIoT application in smart agriculture: A review. *Sensors*, 23(7), 3752, 2023. doi: 10.3390/s23073752.
2. C.-J. Chen, Y.-Y. Huang, Y.-S. Li, C.-Y. Chang and Y.-M. Huang, An AIoT based smart agricultural system for pests detection. *IEEE Access*, 8, 180750–180761, 2020. doi: 10.1109/ACCESS.2020.3024891.
3. Y.M. Leong, E.H. Lim, N.F.B. Subri and N.B.A. Jalil, "Transforming agriculture: navigating the challenges and embracing the opportunities of artificial intelligence of things," In: *2023 IEEE International Conference on Agrosystem Engineering, Technology & Applications (AGRETA)*, Shah Alam, Malaysia, 2023, pp. 142–147. doi: 10.1109/AGRETA57740.2023.10262747.
4. N. Ghatwary, M. Zolgharni and X. Ye, "GFD faster R-CNN: Gabor fractal DenseNet faster R-CNN for automatic detection of esophageal abnormalities in endoscopic images," In: *Machine Learning in Medical Imaging*, vol. 11861, 2019. doi: 10.1007/978-3-030-32692-0_11.
5. A.A. Ahmed and G.H. Reddy, A mobile-based system for detecting plant leaf diseases using deep learning. *AgriEngineering*, 3(3), 478–493, 2021. doi: 10.3390/agriengineering3030032.
6. Crop Protection Network. 2021.
7. H.-H. Ku, C.-H. Liu and W.-C. Wang, Design of an artificial intelligence of things based indoor planting model for mentha spicata. *Processes*, 10(1), 116, 2022. doi: 10.3390/pr10010116.
8. R. Budjac, M. Barton, P. Schreiber and M. Skovajsa, "Analyzing embedded AIoT devices for deep learning purposes," In: Silhavy, R. (eds.) *Artificial Intelligence Trends in Systems. CSOC 2022*. Lecture Notes in Networks and Systems, vol. 502, 2022. Springer, Cham. doi: 10.1007/978-3-031-09076-9_39.
9. C.-C. Chang, N.A. Ubina, S.-C. Cheng, H.-Y. Lan, K.-C. Chen and C.-C. Huang, A two-mode underwater smart sensor object for precision aquaculture based on AIoT technology. *Sensors*, 22(19), 7603, 2022. doi: 10.3390/s22197603.

10. N.A. Ubina, H.-Y. Lan, S.-C. Cheng, C.-C. Chang, S.-S. Lin, K.-X. Zhang, H.-Y. Lu, C.-Y. Cheng and Y.-Z. Hsieh, Digital twin-based intelligent fish farming with artificial intelligence internet of things (AIoT). *Smart Agricultural Technology*, 5, 100285, 2023. doi: 10.1016/j.atech.2023.100285.

11. M. Rahmouni, M. Hanifi, C. Savaglio, G. Fortino and M. Ghogho, "An AIoT framework for precision agriculture," In: *2022 IEEE Intl Conf on Dependable, Autonomic and Secure Computing, Intl Conf on Pervasive Intelligence and Computing, Intl Conf on Cloud and Big Data Computing, Intl Conf on Cyber Science and Technology Congress (DASC/PiCom/CBDCom/CyberSciTech)*, Falerna, Italy, 2022, pp. 1–6. doi: 10.1109/DASC/PiCom/CBDCom/Cy55231.2022.9927989.

12. C.-C. Chiu, T.-L. Liao, C.-H. Chen and S.-E. Kao, AIoT precision feeding management system. *Electronics*, 11(20), 3358, 2022. doi: 10.3390/electronics11203358.

13. K.M. Hou, X. Diao, H. Shi, H. Ding, H. Zhou and C. de Vaulx, Trends and challenges in AIoT/IIoT/IoT implementation. *Sensors*, 23(11), 5074, 2023. doi: 10.3390/s23115074.

14. K. Sun, X. Wang and Q. Zhao. A Review of AIoT-based Edge Devices and Lightweight Deployment. TechRxiv. May 31, 2023. DOI: 10.36227/techrxiv. 21687248.v2.

15. K. El Moutaouakil, B. Jabir and N. Falih, "Agriculture 4.0: Literature review and application challenges in the "Beni Mellal-Khenifra" region," In: *2022 8th International Conference on Optimization and Applications (ICOA)*, Genoa, Italy, 2022, pp. 1–6. doi: 10.1109/ICOA55659.2022.9934114.

16. N. Kansal, B. Bhushan and S. Sharma, "Architecture, security vulnerabilities, and the proposed countermeasures in agriculture-internet-of-things (AIoT) systems," In: Prasant Kumar Pattnaik, Raghvendra Kumar, Souvik Pal (eds.) *Internet of Things and Analytics for Agriculture*, vol. 3, 2022. ISBN: 978-981-16-6209-6. doi: 10.1007/978-981-16-6210-2_16.

17. D. Muhammed, E. Ahvar, S. Ahvar and M. Trocan, "A user-friendly AIoT-based crop recommendation system (UACR): Concept and architecture," In: *2022 16th International Conference on Signal-Image Technology & Internet-Based Systems (SITIS)*, Dijon, France, 2022, pp. 569–576. doi: 10.1109/SITIS57111.2022.00091.

18. Q. Chen, X. Gan, W. Huang, J. Feng and H. Shim, Road damage detection and classification using mask R-CNN with DenseNet backbone. *Computers, Materials & Continua*, 65(3), 2201–2215, 2020.

19. M. Aljazaeri, Y. Bazi, H. AlMubarak and N. Alajlan, "Faster R-CNN and DenseNet regression for glaucoma detection in retinal fundus images," In: *2020 2nd International Conference on Computer and Information Sciences (ICCIS)*, Sakaka, Saudi Arabia, 2020, pp. 1–4. doi: 10.1109/ICCIS49240.2020.9257680.

20. S. Albahli, M. Nawaz, A. Javed, et al. An improved faster-RCNN model for handwritten character recognition. *Arabian Journal for Science and Engineering*, 46, 8509–8523, 2021. doi: 10.1007/s13369-021-05471-4.

21. F. Xin, H. Zhang and H. Pan, Hybrid dilated multilayer faster RCNN for object detection. *Visual Computer*, 2023. doi: 10.1007/s00371-023-02789-y.

22. M. Javaid, A. Haleem, R.P. Singh and R. Suman, Enhancing smart farming through the applications of Agriculture 4.0 technologies. *International Journal of Intelligent Networks*, 3, 150–164, 2022. doi: 10.1016/j.ijin.2022.09.004.

23. K. Wang, P. Jiang, J. Meng and X. Jiang, Attention-based densenet for pneumonia classification. *IRBM*, 43(5), 479–485, 2022. doi: 10.1016/j.irbm.2021.12.004.

24. J.A. Sosa-Herrera, N. Alvarez-Jarquin, N.M. Cid-Garcia, D.J. López-Araujo and M.R. Vallejo-Pérez, Automated health estimation of capsicum annuum L. crops by means of deep learning and RGB aerial images. *Remote Sensing*, 14(19), 4943, 2022. doi: 10.3390/rs14194943.

25. K.S. Mohamed, "Deep learning for IoT "Artificial Intelligence of Things (AIoT)," In: *Deep Learning-Powered Technologies*. Synthesis Lectures on Engineering, Science, and Technology, 2023. Springer, Cham. doi: 10.1007/978-3-031-35737-4_3.

26. L.-B. Chen, X.-R. Huang and W.-H. Chen, Design and implementation of an artificial intelligence of things-based autonomous mobile robot system for pitaya harvesting. *IEEE Sensors Journal*, 23(12), 13220–13235, 2023. doi: 10.1109/JSEN.2023.3270844.

27. C. Maraveas, Incorporating artificial intelligence technology in smart greenhouses: Current state of the art. *Applied Sciences*, 13(1), 14, 2023. doi: 10.3390/app13010014.

28. Z. Chang, S. Liu, X. Xiong, Z. Cai and G. Tu, A survey of recent advances in edge-computing-powered artificial intelligence of things. *IEEE Internet of Things Journal*, 8(18), 13849–13875, 2021. doi: 10.1109/JIOT.2021.3088875.

29. X. Zhang, Z. Cao and W. Dong, Overview of edge computing in the agricultural internet of things: Key technologies, applications, challenges. *IEEE Access*, 8, 141748–141761, 2020. doi: 10.1109/ACCESS.2020.3013005.

30. R.S. Muthu, Agricultural internet of things: Challenges and future research directions. *International Journal of New Media Studies: International Peer Reviewed Scholarly Indexed Journal*, 9(2), 36–41, 2022.

31. B. Kaur and C.S. Mukhopadhyay, "Artificial intelligence-driven, IoT-based technologies in agriculture: A review," In: Mukhopadhyay, C. S., Choudhary, R. K., Panwar, H., Malik, Y. S. (eds.) *Biotechnological Interventions Augmenting Livestock Health and Production. Livestock Diseases and Management*, 2023. Springer, Singapore. doi: 10.1007/978-981-99-2209-3_22.

32. W. Wei and S. H. Ahmed, Guest editorial: Advanced collaborative technologies for artificial intelligence of things. *IEEE Transactions on Industrial Informatics*, 18(2), 1197–1199, 2022. doi: 10.1109/TII.2021.3105564.

33. L.-B. Chen, G.-Z. Huang, X.-R. Huang and W.-C. Wang, A self-supervised learning-based intelligent greenhouse orchid growth inspection system for precision agriculture. *IEEE Sensors Journal*, 22(24), 24567–24577, 2022. doi: 10.1109/JSEN.2022.3221960.

34. T. Saranya, C. Deisy, S. Sridevi and K.S.M. Anbananthen, A comparative study of deep learning and Internet of Things for precision agriculture. *Engineering Applications of Artificial Intelligence*, 122, 106034, 2023. doi: 10.1016/j.engappai.2023.106034.

35. M.S. Anari, A hybrid model for leaf diseases classification based on the modified deep transfer learning and ensemble approach for agricultural AIoT-based monitoring. *Advances in Computational Intelligence Techniques for Next Generation Internet of Things*, 2022, 2022. Article ID 6504616. doi: 10.1155/2022/6504616.

13 Libraries for Explainable Artificial Intelligence (EXAI) *Python*

A. Helen Victoria, Ravi Shekhar Tiwari, and Ayaan Khadir Ghulam

13.1 INTRODUCTION

AI has a huge impact on flourishing human life and in almost every industry. It helps in enhancing human intelligence along with artificial intelligence. It has rapid progress right from daily life applications to high-end mission-critical applications. Experts say that AI has the potential to change the world even more than the greatest inventions of all time. Nowadays, the sophistication of this technology has emerged, hence eliminating the need for human intervention for design and deployment. There are certain applications like healthcare and defense where the decisions of these systems have a direct impact on the lives of human beings. Many researchers strive on building a stronger AI that can outsmart humans at all levels of tasks. Hence, there is a need for more validation and explanation of the decisions or outcomes obtained by these smart systems. In order to bring more transparency, understanding, and reasoning to the AI algorithms, a widely acknowledged field, Explainable AI (XAI) has been framed. XAI has a suite of techniques to address the limitations of AI methods in terms of understanding the predictions, feature extraction, and the significance of characteristics that are considered by the model while selecting decisions. These techniques will help in assuring the trustworthiness of the models deployed in real-time applications. Adding interpretability and explanation to the model helps to satisfy the target audience with different profiles like End Users, Domain Experts, Product Developers, Data Scientists, and Researchers.

The main need for Explainable AI is

1. To assure building trustworthy AI algorithms to manage the emerging need of the technology in different aspects.
2. To bring in more transparency to the deep learning models that adapt the black-box approach.
3. To add more explainability for the results obtained without degrading the learning ability and performance of the models.
4. To imbibe more contextual meaning to the machine learning models with the suite of XAI techniques (Figure 13.1).

13.2 TERMINOLOGIES

To avoid confusion because of the jargon used in this chapter, let's have an insight about them so that we can have an in-depth understanding of the concepts.

Algorithms: It is defined as the set of rules that machine follows in order to accomplish its goal/aim. It can be considered as a well-defined step which has well-defined input as well as output and the procedures to process the input in order to get desired output.

DOI: 10.1201/9781003457176-13

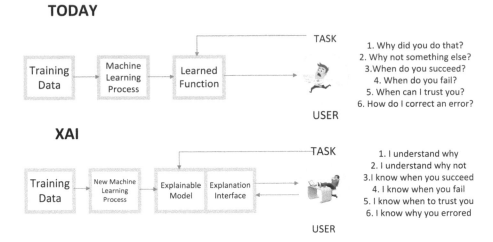

FIGURE 13.1   Traditional AI and XAI.

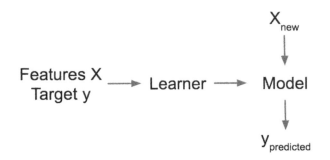

FIGURE 13.2   AI algorithm.

Artificial Intelligence: AI is referred as the process by which machine learns from examples, i.e., datasets, i.e., try to learn the underlying features from the dataset and implement this ability to make prediction in real-world data. There is an assortment of AI strategies, which include supervised learning, unsupervised learning, and reinforcement learning. AI is a change in perspective from "typical programming" where all guidelines should be unequivocally given to the PC to "backhanded programming" that happens through giving information.

Machine Learning Algorithm/Learner: It is the set program that implements algorithms that enable machines to learn from the dataset and predict the unseen data.

    (e.g., Decision trees, Linear Regression) (Figure 13.2).

Black Box Model: It is described as a system that is incomprehensible to human, i.e., humans can use it but they cannot decrypt the functional mechanism of this system, which is similar to deep neural networks.

Interpretable Machine Learning: It is referred to the machine learning algorithms that are understandable by humans, i.e., humans can justify the decision made by the algorithms as per the algorithm perspective.

Dataset: It is a collection of huge number of samples by which models learn to predict unseen data by extracting the underlying features from these samples. It can be divided into two parts: dependent variable Y, i.e., output we want from the model, and independent variables or features X, i.e., input to these models. Instance is a term referred to one row from the dataset.

13.3 WHY INTERPRETABILITY?

When an ML/a DL model performs as per our expectation, then why do we doubt the model's capabilities to make decisions in real time on a real dataset? The problem is with the metric – unable to make descriptions in real-world scenarios, we used to train the model and underlying relation with the dataset and noises present in it. When it comes to prediction from a model, we always must make some trade-off. The most common is bias-variance trade-off. We do not want to know just the prediction from the model; instead, we want to know the prediction as well as the reason why the model predicted what is the reason and how the features (individual as well as well as collectively) present in the datasets interact with the dependent variable. In some cases, we do not want to get the idea behind the model prediction, but in most cases, we always want to know the intuition of the model behind its prediction. It gives us the idea of interaction and relationship between dependent and independent variables as well as various scenarios on which our trained model can fail.

As we all know some models are implemented in low-risk scenarios so they will not lead to any disaster when their predictions are incorrect but when some models are deployed in high-risk scenarios, if they predict False Positive or True Negative that can be catastrophic for us. Hence, it is very important for certain problems which are being solved by employing machine learning models to explain it intuition along with their prediction because prediction solves only half of the problem. Also, the dataset can be biased toward some objects and there have been experimental results where we have seen when black people in the USA were wrongly predicted as felonies, biased toward men and women which can be catastrophic in real-world scenarios. The following are the reasons for the need of the interpretability of the machine learning models:

1. Human curiosity and learning
2. To find meaning and sustain in world scenarios
3. To gain knowledge – goal of science
4. As a safety measure and testing
5. To detect bias
6. Increase in social acceptance
7. Debug and auditing

13.4 HOW XAI ADDRESSES THE LIMITATIONS OF AI MODELS

XAI gives the opportunity to build trust and confidence in machine learning and deep learning algorithms. Incorrect predictions may cause serious issues. Hence, there is a need to assure the trustworthiness and integrity of the applications in which it is deployed. This helps to justify the reasoning for the results obtained. Explaining the results will be more helpful for applications like healthcare and other critical applications.

XAI has a lot of libraries and tools to explain the predictive results. Deep Neural Networks exhibit complex architecture and XAI acts as a tool to unveil the intermediate results of the DL Algorithms. As there will be more AI-based tools in the future, it is highly recommended to explain the transparency in the architecture. Visualization techniques act as proof for the applications, improve the understanding of the bias, and show the fairness of the model enhancing the robustness of the model.

13.5 SCOPE OF XAI

In ML or DL, we train algorithms that are dependent on their datasets and their implementation. The training of these algorithms is a complex step that involves several steps, i.e., from data-pre-processing, modeling the algorithm, optimization, and many other steps. These steps are always examined in terms of transparency or interpretability of the respective algorithms, so they are not in the black box. We will talk about the many aspects of the XAI scope in this part.

13.5.1 Transparency of Algorithm

Algorithm transparency refers to how an algorithm/model learns from the dataset and hidden relationships hence it can recognize the class associated with the datapoints. If we employ Convolutional Neural Networks (CNN) for image classification, then we can explain that the algorithm learns to detect the edges (vertical and horizontal) along with the different visual features depending upon the filters we are employing to extract the feature maps.

This understanding of the model can be used to explain the functioning of the specific algorithm, but for the specific datapoint or dataset, we cannot explain how the model came to this specific prediction for respective datapoints. The requirement of algorithm transparency is to explain the functioning of the algorithms, not the relationship learned from the dataset. One of the metrics is the Root Mean Square Error (RMSE) algorithm by which we access how well the model performs on test, training, and evaluation datasets—these algorithms are fully analyzed by the researchers before using them in real-world applications; hence, they have a high degree of expandability and interpretability. DL is less well understood because the parameters grow exponentially as the number of layers increases. Hence, we are not able to describe the model's operation in relation to the dataset or datapoints; therefore, it is called black box models; the inner mechanism of these models is the center of attention for the researchers because they are similar to the black box.

We have a variety of models which we can train and predict on the respective dataset. Some of the models are self-explanatory, i.e., they are easy to understand and explain because they have less parameters – easy to track and easy to understand, whereas there are some models that are complex, and hence, it is not manually possible to keep track of all the parameters. As a result, these models become Black box models: We only understand the model's predictions; we are unsure of how the model arrived at these results and the reason behind the model prediction. Due to insufficient or no explanation, we don't see the real-world implementation of the complex model as compared to the simpler model though there is a huge variance in the model performance (Figure 13.3).

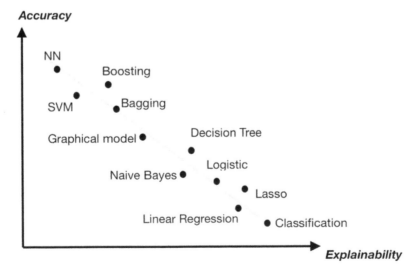

FIGURE 13.3 Accuracy vs Explainability.

13.5.2   Local Interpretability – Single Prediction

We can concentrate on one datapoint and examine it for the model prediction for the specific data-point and we can explain why the model came to this conclusion with the respective datapoint. If we analyze the individual prediction by the model the prediction by the complex model will be more accurate when compared to the simple model. For one datapoint, i.e., locally the dependent may be linearly or monotonically dependent on the independent features instead of having a complex relationship with the independent variables. For instance, the price of a car may depend non-linearly on its dimensions. But if you're seeing just boot space, i.e., one feature from the datapoint, then there's a chance for that the subset of the datapoint that our model's prediction is linearly dependent on the dimensions of the car. Since we are concentrating on one feature from a single instance of the data-sets, local explanations are much more helpful than global explanations. By simulating, we may discover how the projected price changes after the dimensions are increased or decreased by 10-cm m^2.

13.5.3   Local Interpretability – Group of Prediction

When a model predicts multiple datapoints, we can explain it with the help of the global model interpretation functions or with the help of individual instances. Most of the time, by treating these datapoints as a group of datapoints, the global function may be applied to them, i.e., treating them as a group of datapoints and using a global function with these datapoints. We can also use the individual explanation methods for each of the datapoints, and we can take the average for the whole group.

13.6   WHY INTERPRETABILITY IN HEALTHCARE?

As we know that there is a significant rise in the application of AI in every sector, similarly in the field of healthcare also AI is now taking baby steps by predicting the disease beforehand, and hence, valuable human life can be saved. During COVID-19, we have seen that many sectors such as healthcare and banking were relying on AI product. Healthcare sector is one of the most crucial sectors we have seen during COVID-19 pandemic, and a lot of lives were saved but unfortunately a lot of lives were also lost. In advanced countries, such as the USA and Canada, healthcare system was utilizing the power of AI to detect COVID-19 infection in humans and treat them before the situation becomes uncontrollable. Although many products were developed and employed to achieve the goal and the products saved millions of lives, there was a lack of transparency in the model prediction. The reason behind the model prediction was not clear and the healthcare personnel were hesitant to trust the model prediction. By implementing AI, we have reduced human intervention but we have to always keep an eye on the model prediction because still we don't have any insight about why the model predicted this, so we have to cross-check the machine decision. So, XAI has a very crucial role when we will or we want to implement ML or DL algorithms.

AI is applicable in almost all sections such as aerospace, ship building, construction, healthcare, and many more which we can imagine. If we rely only on the model prediction, there is a possibility that the model can be biased, or it can give an incorrect prediction, but the model does not give us any explanation about its prediction, i.e., trust deficiency. We have many models, and some of them are explainable, for example, Regression (Linear/Multiple), Decision Trees, Random Forest though we have to compromise the accuracy of these models since they are not able to fully extract the underlying features of the datasets. On the contrary, we have black box model whose accuracy is outstanding but we have no idea how the model is coming to its prediction. In healthcare, there is no space for error, and if error occurs, then the result will be catastrophic. In order to implement the ML/DL algorithms and to avoid any catastrophe we have to know the model perspective with respect to its prediction, i.e., Explainable Artificial Intelligence.

13.7 XAI EVALUATION

There is currently no consensus among scholars regarding what interpretability in ML means. Also, there is no method on how we can measure the interpretability of ML models. There is little research in this formula to evaluate the interpretability of the models which are described below.

13.7.1 APPLICATION-LEVEL EVALUATION

It is a simple task where we embed the reason in the merchandise/application, and the resulted product is tested by the end user extensively. For example, we can imagine a cancer detection application with a machine/deep learning algorithm that can identify and highlight cancerous tissue from the CT scans. Now if we see from the application level, the respective end user will extensively test and evaluate the model with explanation, which is embedded in the application, and it is totally dependent on the expertise of the end user on how he explains the equivalent outcome.

13.7.2 HUMAN-LEVEL EVALUATION

Human-level evaluation is a similar process to application-level evaluation; the only difference is that it doesn't need an expert to oversee it; any random person, who may or may not have domain knowledge, can do it, which reduces the cost of experiments and allows us to test a wide range of people.

13.7.3 FUNCTION-LEVEL EVALUATION

Function-level evaluation doesn't require humans to intervene. It performs up to the mark when the model category has been evaluated by some person during human-level evaluation. For example, if the end users fully understand regression algorithms in this instance, the depth of the tree may also serve as a stand-in for explanation. Shorter trees would have a much higher explainability rating. The requirement that the tree's prediction performance stays strong and doesn't decline noticeably in comparison to a bigger tree may be added to the feature set.

13.8 XAI ALGORITHMS

In the above sections, we have seen how XAI can empower us to deploy complex ML and DL models; in this section, we will have deep insight about the various algorithms which explains the model's decision, local and global, with respect to the dataset.

13.8.1 PERMUTATION FEATURE IMPORTANCE

ML models' performance is dependent on the dataset's features. If features have a high correlation, then models will perform outstanding; however, we have to keep an eye on the multicollinearity. Features play a huge role in every aspect of the model, especially when we need to demystify the black box model.

ML models are trained on the datasets which can consist of several columns, where each column contributes to the prediction from the model according to their correlation with the dependent variable. In Permutation Feature Importance, we determine how significant the independent variable features in the dataset are by measuring the increase of the overall errors from the models by permuting or shuffling the features/column from the dataset. If the feature is not considered important by the model while making the prediction, and if the feature is valued highly by the models, then the permuted feature set will result in a low measurement of errors; otherwise, the measurement of the error will be minimal or remain the same. This algorithm was initially proposed by Breiman [21] with respect to Random Forest. Later, an alternative version of model-agnostics called model reliance was introduced by Fisher, Rudin, and Dominici [22]. The below pseudo code explains the working of the Permutation Feature Importance:

Let us assume that we have trained a M model on D dataset which consists of F features where the target vector is Y and the error is $L(Y, M)$

$$eorig\ (Original\ model\ error) = L(Y, M(F)) \tag{13.1}$$

For i in range (0, F):

a. *Generate permutation feature matrix D(perm) by shuffling or permuting the feature/ independent i in the dataset D. This breaks the association between feature i and true outcome Y.*

b. *Estimate error eperm = L(Y, f(Xperm)) based on the predictions of the permuted data.*

c. *Calculate permutation feature importance FIj = eperm/eorig. Alternatively, the difference can be used: FIj = eperm – eorig Sort the feature descending by Fi.*

Example:

The below example will help you to understand the Permutation Feature Importance more clearly. Let us assume we have a dataset with the following format as shown in Figure 13.4.

We want to predict the person's height using the Socks owned at age 10 along with their height when they were 10 years old. Since Permutation Feature importance is calculated after the model is fully trained, we will not change any parameter of the model while getting insight about the feature importance. Since our dataset consists of many columns for the sake of simplicity, we will select only one column, i.e., height at 10 and shuffle/permutate the data as shown in Figure 13.5.

Height at age 20 (cm)	Height at age 10 (cm)	...	Socks owned at age 10
182	155	...	20
175	147	...	10
...	...	...	...
156	142	...	8
153	130	...	24

FIGURE 13.4 Sample dataset.

Height at age 20 (cm)	Height at age 10 (cm)	...	Socks owned at age 10
182	155	...	20
175	147	...	10
...	...	...	...
156	142	...	8
153	130	...	24

FIGURE 13.5 Permuted column-sample dataset.

Now we have two datasets: one is the original dataset and one is the permuted dataset in which we have permuted the height at age 10 feature. Since we have trained our model on the original dataset and calculated the error, i.e., original model error, and we repeated the same step for calculating the error for permuted dataset, i.e., permuted model error. We must do this for all features, and then, we can measure the importance of features for each of the features present in the dataset.

Pros	Cons
Easy to interpret.	Discrepancy between the use of algorithm, i.e., with training or test data.
Provides compressed and global insight in the model behavior.	Linked to the model's error, so we have to train and optimize the model first.
It is comparable across all different problems.	Multicollinearity and collinearity can affect the feature's importance.
It takes account of all features interaction in the model.	Model dependent so results can vary from model to model.
Does not require retraining.	

13.8.2 Partial Dependence Plot (PDP)

PDP refers to Partial Dependence Plot that was invented by J.H. Friedman [16]. In essence, it is a visualization of the features that are present in the dataset that shows the typical marginal impact of the features on the model prediction. Partial Dependence Plot also specifies the type of relationship linear, monotonic, or complex between the dependent and independent variables. In context of the Linear Model such as Regression (Single or Multiple), Partial Dependence Plot always shows a linear relationship between dependent and independent variables. PDP is very helpful in answering the below-mentioned questions:

1. By considering all features in the house dataset as constant, what impact does location have on home prices? In simple words, what will be the cost of house of the same features but at different locations?

The below formulae depict the partial Dependence Plot equation for the regression models:

$$f_x s = E_{xc}\left[f\left(x_c, x_s\right)\right] = \int \left(xS, xC\right) dP\left(xC\right) \tag{13.2}$$

where:

$x =$ *features set/independent variable,*
$x_s \subseteq x$
$n\{xS\} = 1$ or $2,$
$x_c \subseteq x$
$x_c \bigcup x_s = x,$

Where xS is the features that must be plotted for are represented by a subset of the characteristics in the dataset of Partial Dependence Plot and xC is a subset of the dataset's features that shows the additional features used to train the ML algorithm and the model.

$f_x s(x_s)$ represents the model that has been trained on the entire dataset for prediction. Generally, these are one or two feature sets (S) that represent the features which we want to know the result on the prediction, if we take the union of these two subsets, we will get the entire feature set of independent variables, i.e., x. In Partial Dependence Plot, we keep all the other features, i.e., xC constant, and we predict using the model fxs (xs) after training on x features over n-epochs but we change the values of the features present in xS set which is generally one or two features, by strictly keeping xC constant to get the intuition how the feature present in the xS effect the model prediction and to the relationship between xS and the model prediction. We marginalize the features over the other features, we get a function that is strictly dependent on the feature set xS while including other features set also xS. Finally, we calculate the partition function which is depicted in Equation (13.3):

$$fxS(xs) = \frac{1}{n} \sum nf\left(xS, s_c^{\{i\}}\right) \tag{13.3}$$

Equation (13.3) shows the partial function that tells us the relationship and the marginal effect of the feature xS on the predictions from the model, $f_{xs}(x)_s$. In Equation (13.3), $x^{\{i\}}_c$ are the real features from the present in the dataset for the provisions which we are not intrigued to get their effect on the model expectation and n is the quantity of tests in the dataset on which model is prepared. A suspicion of the PDP is that the provisions in xC are not connected with the elements in xS. On the off chance that this supposition that is abused, the midpoints determined considering that the halfway reliance plot will have informational themes that are unlikely or even inconceivable. The fractional dependence plot shows the likelihood for a particular class given various attributes for feature(s) in xS for characterization where the AI model produces probabilities. Creating a single border or plot for each class is an easy way to manage many classes.

Pros	Cons
PDP is intuitive	Heterogeneous effect might be hidden.
Easy to implement	Assumption of Independence.
Interpretation is clear	Do not show feature Distribution
It is causal interpretation	Model dependent so result can vary from model to model.
No retraining of model is required	Maximum number of Feature in PDP is two.

Example:

Assume that the dataset we are using contains information about the players' passes, shots, goals, and other actions. Using a single row from the relevant dataset, we will calculate the PDP. The feature has the values shown below, for illustration: a team that possessed the ball for 50% of the time, completed 100 passes, attempted 10 shots, and scored 1 goal.

Let's assume that we have trained the model to forecast the likelihood that the specific player would be named the man of the match for the specific football match. The trained model, split, and feature with Gini coefficient are shown in the Figure 13.6.

Since we have trained the model and it is ready to predict we select one feature, i.e., Goal Scored and keep all the other features constant and alter the value of the selected feature to know its relationship with the prediction from the model output. We apply the partial function to calculate the effect and plot it on the graph which is shown in Figure 13.7.

Interpretation of the graph:

The X-axis in the graph above shows the xS feature we want to observe the relationship for, and the Y-axis represents the prediction from the model, i.e., decision tree in our case and feature set xc is constant. As the goal scored is increased, and it is between 0 and 1.5, the probability of the player to win the man of the match also increases but after 1.5, it becomes constant. Analyzing this graph, we can observe that the likelihood of scoring a goal significantly raises your odds of being named "Man of The Match." But further goals beyond that seem to have little effect on forecasts.

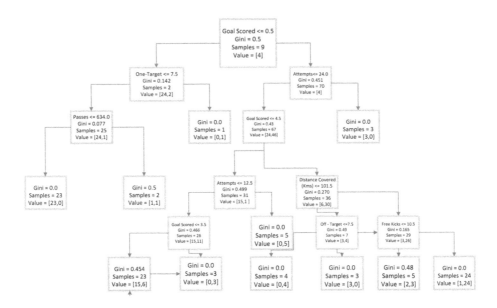

FIGURE 13.6 Decision tree fitted on the dataset.

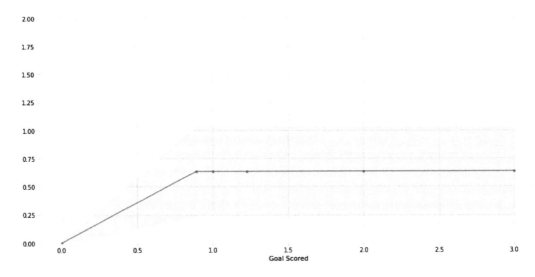

FIGURE 13.7 PDP for goal-scored feature.

13.8.3 LIME – LOCAL INTERPRETABLE MODEL-AGNOSTIC EXPLANATIONS

Deep Learning Models give useful predictions to many applications, but the developer is not aware of the reason for some correct predictions or mispredictions. These outcomes obtained from the model are used in some critical applications, where misprediction might end in vain. Hence, it is always necessary to understand the reason behind the outcome of the model. Since ML and DL algorithms adapt black box approach, we need some surrogate model to interpret the outcomes of AI-based models.

Local interpretable model-independent explanations (LIME) is one such substitute model, similar to how a person might explain their decision-making process.

Individual predictions are explained using this interpretable model. LIME is based on two simple properties, namely:

13.8.3.1   Agnosticism to All the Models

This property claims that it can give explanations to any supervised learning models. All the models that come under the category of black box approach can be addressed by LIME.

13.8.3.2   Local Fidelity

LIME can give explanations locally based on the data samples that are chosen in the data set. The explanations will be bound to the vicinity of the data instance being experimented on. Figure 13.8 explains the role of LIME in interpreting the model.

13.8.3.3   Working of LIME

LIME aims to give an explanation for each data sample that is present in the dataset in terms of its feature contribution and its underlying meanings or explanations. This is achieved by training these models in such a way to understand the predictions approximately.

13.8.3.4   Building a Surrogate Dataset

Individual predictions are interpreted which makes the overall model as an acceptable one. The ultimate goal of LIME is to study about the predictions when the data is varied. Hence, in LIME, a dataset with chosen or altered samples is created, and this dataset is used to train the model. This approach helps us to achieve the local approximation rather than focusing on global approximation.

13.8.3.5   Importance of Features in Surrogate Dataset

LIME understands the importance of every feature that contributes to the prediction for every sample. It captures the most contributing feature that impacts the prediction of that particular sample. With regression analysis, it checks the weightage of each sample to overall samples. It uses feature selection techniques to obtain the most important features. LIME API's can give explanations to image related, text and tabular datasets (Figure 13.9 shows a sample outcome).

Similar behaviors to those of the original predictive model should be displayed by the surrogate model. This guarantees the applicability of the derived features.

The following is a list of the Surrogate Model's workflow.

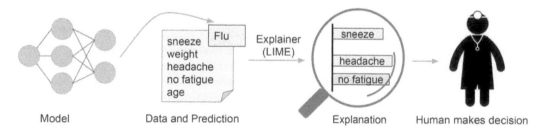

FIGURE 13.8   LIME explainer.

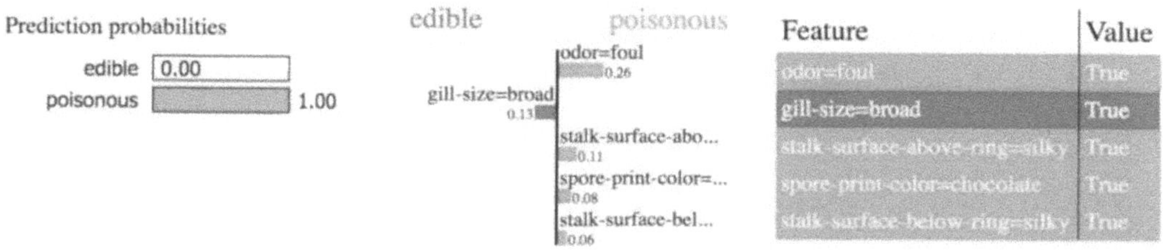

FIGURE 13.9   Single datapoint lime explanation.

1. Select the samples that are not easily understood by the black box approach requiring further explanations.
2. Black box predictions are made for these newly procured and perturbed samples.
3. The new samples are weighted according to the proximity of the interested samples.
4. Train the weighted Model
5. Make interpretations by making variations in the local model.
6. Give explanations for the obtained predictions by interpreting the results of the trained local model.

Pros	Cons
Sampling is done to obtain the interpretation of most important predictions	Sampling and simple perturbations might be misleading at times as it may introduce bias into the model.
Local interpretation could pave the way for better global approximation	When complicated, non-interpretable models are required for a dataset, non-linearity at local areas occurs. An important problem is that LIME cannot be used in these situations.
Explaining the most important features that contribute to the predictions of the actual model.	

13.8.4 INDIVIDUAL CONDITIONAL EXPECTATION (ICE)

When we adjust the feature value, ICE, or individual conditional expectation, visualizes one datapoint prediction per line. It is a global approach that is comparable to the Partial Dependence Plot, which depicts the average of the feature effect on the prediction from the model.

Instead of concentrating on the individual data points, PDP averages the impact on model prediction.

Individual Conditional Expectation as its name suggests it is considered the individual datapoint instance and works in the same way as PDP works. ICE was invented by Goldstein et al. [24]. ICE plots visualized the dependence of the feature present in the dataset for each row/datapoint with the model prediction separately which results is depicted in the graph as one line per instant. A PDP is created by averaging the lines in an ICE plot that correspond to the feature that we are most interested. The value of the instance/datapoint (one instance) is calculated as same as PDP i.e., we select one feature - which we want to see its effect on the model prediction and strictly we treat other features as constant, and finally, we predict these variants on these datapoints/instances by manipulating the selected feature. The outcome is a collection of points for a particular occurrence that includes the feature value from the grid and the accompanying predictions. The ICE graphs are represented by the equations below:

$$f \, xS = E_{xc}\left[f\left(x_c, x_s\right)\right] = \int (xS, xC)dP(xC) \qquad (13.4)$$

where:

$x = $ *features set/independent variable,*

$x_s \subseteq x,$

$n\{xS\} = 1 \text{ or } 2,$

$x_c \subseteq x,$

$x_c \cup x_s = x$

Where xS is the subset of the features that must be plotted for each unique. Conditional Expectation is represented by a subset of the features in the dataset. The dataset's Plot and xC feature subset represents the different features that were used to train the ML model. f_xs (xs) represents the model which has been trained on the entire dataset for prediction. Generally, these are one or two feature set (S), which represent the features that we want to know the result of the prediction; if we take the union of these two subsets, we will get the entire feature set of independent variables, i.e., x. In Partial Dependence Plot, we keep all the other features, i.e., xC constant, and we predict using the model fxs (xs) after training on x features over n-epochs but we change the values of the features present in xS set, which is generally one or two features, by strictly keeping xC constant to get the intuition how the feature present in the xS effects the model prediction and to the relationship between xS and the model prediction. We marginalize the features over the other features; we get a function that is strictly dependent on the feature set xS while including other features set also xS. Finally, we calculate the partition function which is depicted in Equation (13.4):

$$f_{xs}(x)_S = \sum nf\left(xS, x^{\{i\}}{}_c\right)$$
(13.5)

Equation (13.5) shows the partial function which tells us the relationship and the marginal effect of the feature xS on the predictions from the model $f_{xs}(x)_S$. In Equation (13.5), $x^{\{i\}}{}_c$ is the actual feature value from the current dataset for the features in which we are not interested in evaluating their influence on model prediction, and n is the number of samples in the dataset on which the model is trained. The PDP plot shows the likelihood for a particular class given various features in xS for classification, where the AI model calculates probabilities.

One boundary or plot per class can be defined as an easy way to manage many classes. The heterogeneous relationship produced by the interaction between the dependent and independent variables can be hidden using PDP, which makes ICE Plots independent. PDP displays the typical correlation between a characteristic and the intended variable. It only works when there are weak interactions between the other features and the features for which the PDP is calculated. The ICE plot will provide much more justification for interactions.

Pros	Cons
More intuitive to understand	Plot can become overcrowded
Easy to understand	It can only display one feature meaningfully and plots is crowded
No need of re training the model	Certain lines' points could contain data points with inaccurate values.

13.8.5 GRAD-CAM

Visualization exhibits the actual learnings of the model to validate the predictions. One such visualization technique is Gradient Class Activation Map (Grad-CAM). Deep Learning has been extensively used for computer vision, image segmentation, and object detection-based applications.

13.8.5.1 Dimensions of Interpretability

Interpretability is based on a data model for representing and learning about the data and explanations or reasoning for the model prediction. Grad-CAM gives the reasoning and major features or the pattern pertaining to each image. Class Activation Map (CAM) uses feature maps that catch the important regions of all the targets of the models. Hence for example, in the feature map, the patterns of both cat and dog are shown without highlighting the individual class features.

Grad-CAM records the course localization map in order to draw attention to the key feature areas in the image that provide the justification for the prediction of a specific target or image. This is done by using the gradient values of the target, the values that are passed on to the last convolutional layer. This brings in transparency and helps in visualizing the areas of interesting features in each image. Grad-CAM identifies the important pixel features corresponding to the class of interest. The gradient

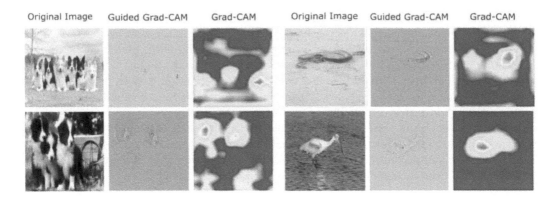

FIGURE 13.10   Grad-CAM.

for the vital intended class in relation to the feature maps of the previous convolutional layer is calculated. Class discriminative localization is obtained. The equation for the Grad-CAM is given by

$$a_k^c = \frac{1}{Z}\left(\sum_j i\left(\delta Y \wedge c / \delta A\_i_l^k\right)\right)$$ (13.6)

Global average pooling is applied to the obtained gradients with respect to the image. This identifies the most important and contributing feature of that class. Grad-CAM visualizations are a more effective method of explaining class localization. Grad-CAM visualization is low even though it highlights the relevant features but still fails to identify the fine-grained details from the image. Guided Grad-CAM aims to leverage the positive gradients from the previous feature map. In guided Grad-CAM the negative gradients are set to zero. It takes only the intersecting pixel points from the backward pass and deconvolution, so the most unique feature of each class will be retrieved. This helps to give more intact explanation and reasoning to each class compared to Grad-CAM. It is mainly used in order to finalize the fine-grained details of the image. In Figure 13.10, the original, Grad-CAM and Guided Grad-CAM images are given.

Grad-CAM is applicable mainly to deep learning models, namely, Convolutional Neural Networks with the following specifications:

1. CNN with connected layers
2. CNN with structured outputs
3. CNN with multimodal tasks
4. Simple Reinforcement Learning without the need for any retraining or architectural changes

13.8.6   Shapley Additive Explanation (SHAP)

Lundberg and Lee [30] developed the SHAP (Shapley Additive explanations) method to explain specific forecasts. The fictitious ideal Shapley Values of the game determine SHAP. The first choice that the KernelSHAP designers put up was a piece-based assessment method for Shapley esteems supported by neighboring proxy models. They also put forth TreeSHAP as a productive evaluation method for models that use trees as their foundation. Second, based on total Shapley esteems, SHAP supports a number of international translation options. In this section, we will have SHAP as a feature importance and summary plots. SHAP is helpful in clarifying below questions:

1. According to a model, a bank shouldn't provide someone cash, and the bank is legally required to give an explanation for every advance rejection.
2. A medical services supplier needs to distinguish what components are driving every understanding's danger of some sickness so they can straightforwardly address those danger factors with designated well-being mediations

By logging each element's commitment to the forecast, SHAP aims to clarify what can be expected in instance x. The coalitional game hypothesis is processed via the SHAP clarification strategy. The benefits of an informational occurrence take the shape of alliance members. We can distribute the "payout" (also known as the anticipation) among the components in a reasonable manner by using Shapley esteems. A player can be a unique aspect of regard, such as for event information. A group of component values can also represent a player. Super pixels are groups of pixels that can be used to send expectations among one another to clarify a picture. One advancement that SHAP offers, along with the attribution approach, a straight model, is the Shapley esteem clarification, which is discussed as an additional substance. The clarification, according to SHAP, is:

$$g(z') = \phi 0 + M \sum j = 1 \phi j z' \tag{13.7}$$

where g is the explanatory model, $z' \in \{0,1\}^M$ is the coalition vector, M is the maximum coalition size, and $\phi j \in R$ is the feature attribution for a feature j, or the Shapley values, for a feature j. What I refer to as "coalition vector" is referred to as "simplified features" in the SHAP study. I believe that this word was coined because, for instance, in picture data, images are aggregated to super pixels rather than being represented at the pixel level. Think of the z's as describing coalitions, in my opinion, to make sense of them: A 1 indicates that the associated feature value is "present" in the coalition vector, whereas a 0 indicates that it is "absent." If you are aware of Shapley values, this ought to sound familiar to you. Shapley values are calculated by simulating the playback of some feature values (called "present") while other features (called "absent") are not. A method used in the computation of the ϕ's is to represent coalitions as a linear model. The coalition vector x', for instance, x is a vector of all 1, indicating that all feature values are "present", for instance, x is the object of interest. The equation is reduced to:

$$(x') = \phi 0 + M \sum j = 1 \phi \tag{13.8}$$

An arrangement with a Shapley value as its principal component meets the efficiency, symmetry, dummy, and additivity requirements. Given that SHAP calculates the Shapley value, it also satisfies these requirements. Inconsistencies between Shapley characteristics and SHAP qualities can be found in the SHAP article. The next three positive features, Local precision, Missingness, and Consistency, are all shown by SHAP.

13.8.6.1 SHAP as Feature Importance

Following is the main notion supporting the significance of the SHAP highlight: It is crucial to have features with high absolute Shapley values. We total the Shapley esteems per inclusion across the data because we need to know the overall significance:

$$Ij = n \sum i = 1 |\phi(i)| \tag{13.9}$$

The provisions are then mapped out and arranged in decreasing order of significance. The accompanying image highlights the SHAP's applicability to the arbitrary timberland that was built beforehand for spotting the onset of cervical cancer (Figure 13.11).

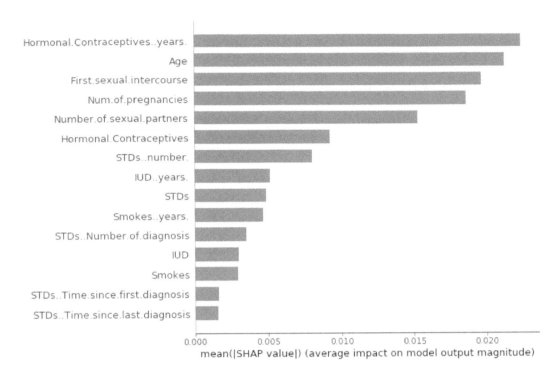

FIGURE 13.11 Importance of features – SHAP.

In contrast to stage includes significance, SHAP highlight significance as an alternative. Both significance measures differ significantly in the following ways: The decline in model execution determines the relevance of permutation highlights. SHAP is influenced by component attribution size. Although useful, the element significance plot just shows the significance.

13.8.6.2 SHAP Summary Plots

Because permutation generates straightforward numerical metrics to determine which characteristics of a model matter most, it is crucial. It makes it simple for users to compare features, and non-technical audiences may easily understand them when presented as graphs. It does not, however, explain the significance of each trait. A characteristic may have a significant impact on a small subset of predictions while having minimal overall impact, or it may have a moderate impact on all predictions if it has a feature of moderate permutation significance. SHAP summary graphs offer a top-down perspective of feature importance and the factors affecting it. For the aforementioned football data, here is an example plot to lead you through (Figure 13.12).

Numerous dots make up this layout. Each dot possesses the following three qualities:

1. The vertical axis identifies the representing feature.
2. A feature's color indicates whether it was important or not for that particular row with respect to the dataset.
3. If that number has a positive or negative impact on the projection, it is shown by horizontal placement.

When, for example, the point in the top left represented a team that scored few goals, the prediction was reduced by 0.25.

1. The following items should be simple for you to choose from:
2. The Red and Yellow & Red features were not taken into account by the model.

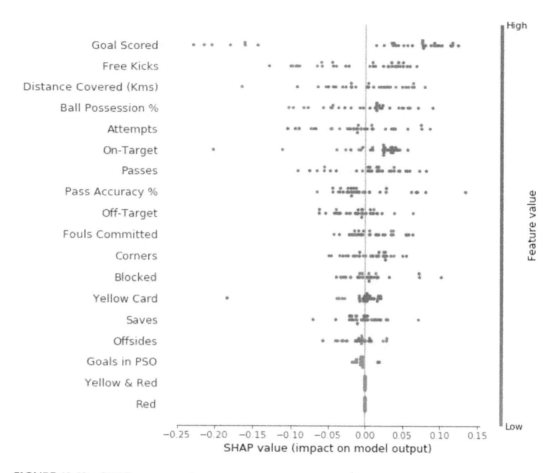

FIGURE 13.12 SHAP-summary plots.

3. Typically, a Yellow Card has minimal effect on the prediction. but in one rare instance, a high value resulted in a significantly lower projection.
4. Higher forecasts were made when higher goals were scored, and lower predictions were made when lower goals were scored.

Pros	Cons
Solid theoretical foundation and fairly Distributed	KernelSHAP is slow.
Connects LIME and Shapley values	KernelSHAP ignores feature dependence.
Tree-based models with quick implementation.	Inexplicable feature attributions can be generated via TreeSHAP.
For the interpretations of the global model, it is necessary	TreeSHAP has a tendency to yield illogical feature attributions.

13.8.7 GLOBAL SURROGATE

An interpretable model that has been created to approximate the predictions of a discovery model is known as a surrogate model. Deciphering the proxy model allows us to draw conclusions about the discovery model, i.e., how to improve AI interpretability by including more AI. In addition, developing surrogate models involves: Considerably, a modest and rapid alternative model of the result can be used if a valuable result is expensive, time-consuming, or in any event difficult to evaluate (for instance, because it derives from a complex virtual experience). The main difference between the Surrogate models used for designing and in interpretable AI is that the core model is an AI model (not a replication), and the proxy model should be comprehensible. The goal of (interpretable) proxy models is to simultaneously be interpretable and to infer the core model's predictions as accurately as possible. Many names are used to refer to the potential of surrogate models: Metamodel, response surface model, and emulator are examples of approximate models. As it relates to the theory: To understand surrogate models, there isn't really much hypothesis expected. If the alternative model expectation work g is comprehensible, we may want to compare our recorder forecast work to it as closely as possible. Any interpretable model is frequently used to assess capacity, for example:

Linear model as surrogate model:

$$g(x) = \beta 0 + \beta 1 x 1 + \cdots + \beta p x \qquad (13.10)$$

Since the process of creating a replacement model only requires access to information and doesn't require any knowledge of the black box model's internal workings, it may be considered a model-agnostic technique. In this way, the prediction function is important. You'll still use the proxy strategy even if the default AI model has been replaced with a different one. The selection of the discovery model and the substitute model sort are independent decisions. I've included a reference to the steps for making the replacement model below:

1. *Select a dataset X. This can be the same dataset that was used for training the black box model or a new dataset from the same distribution. You could even select a subset of the data or a grid of points, depending on your application.*
2. *For the selected dataset X, get the predictions of the black box model.*
3. *Select an interpretable model type (linear model, decision tree, …).*
4. *Train the interpretable model on the dataset X and its predictions. You now have a surrogate model. Measure how well the surrogate model replicates the predictions of the black box model.*
5. *Interpret the surrogate model.*

Pros	Cons
	This makes assumptions about the model rather than the data used to train it.
It is intuitive to understand	
Flexible and easy to understand	Cut-off for R-squared
	Need of re-training the model

13.9 XAI FRAMEWORKS

In previous sections, we have discussed about the different XAI algorithms that demystify the neural network model from black box to white box theoretically, but we have to pay our attention and get acclimatized to various libraries which gives us immense power to implement various XAI algorithms. Nowadays, every IT giant has one of their XAI libraries which offers us a myriad of choices as per our requirement for model explanation. In order to deduce the inference as per neural network perspective and have substantial reason about the prediction/decision of the model from the dataset, these framework/libraries enable the user to justify its model prediction and prevent biases that may get embedded with the model because of the dataset imbalance or bias in our society and increase the trust in AI. Below we have mentioned various XAI frameworks that are widely used in the industries and by researchers to demystify the black box model.

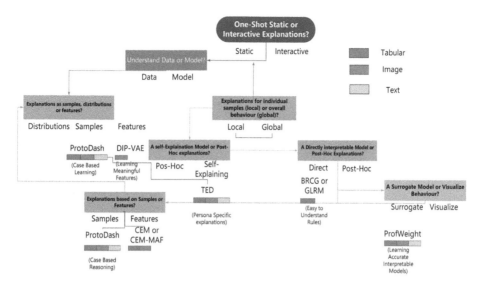

FIGURE 13.13   AIX360.

13.9.1   AIX360

AIX360 or AI Explainability is a toolkit developed by IBM, not just Python package. It has a huge caliber to describe any ML model with interactive user experience along with the introduction of concepts. It is an open-source toolkit that encourages researchers and innovators from all over the world to contribute to this package and make models that can help in uplifting humanity. It has eight different algorithms that explain the model well such as Contrastive, ProtoDash, DIP-VAE, LIME, Metrics, Pro Weight, RBM, TED, and SHAP. These algorithms are developed with the mindset to take into consideration the local and explaining the dataset's global features for the ML algorithm. A direct interpretable or postdoc model as well as the surrogate of the model explains the model behavior and model visualization. Figure 13.13 succinctly explains the AIX360 toolkit.

13.9.2   WHAT-IF TOOL

What-If tool is an ML explainability tool developed by Google, and it is only compatible with TensorFlow and libraries associated with it. Since it is not enough to train the model and walk away rather it is need of the time to become an investigator and investigate the model thoroughly according to dataset as well as the model perspective. One of the scenarios is by changing the threshold in each of the feature set but that is also not enough as it takes a lot of programming skills which is practically a tremendous task for non-programmers. What-If tool is a no-code tensor board web-based application, which allows users to analyze the ML model with the help of one click. This tool is composed of a large feature set as well as the dataset set visualization using facets. It is available in Jupyter, Collaboratory and Cloud AI platform notebooks, it can be used with dataset that includes Image, Text data, and Tabular data as well. The set of features offered by What-If tool to explain the models are as follows:

1. Automatic Visualization of dataset using Facets.
2. Visualizing the model result by changing individual features to get the intuition of Feature Importance of the dataset.
3. The option where we can manually select the examples from the dataset and can analyze the effect in real time (Figure 13.14).

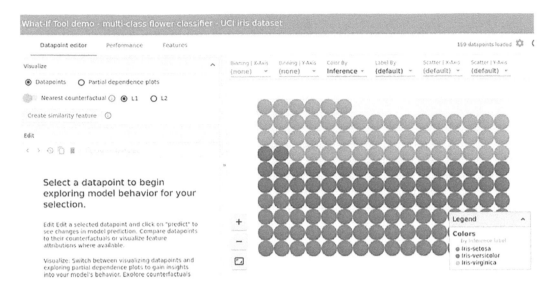

FIGURE 13.14   What-If tool.

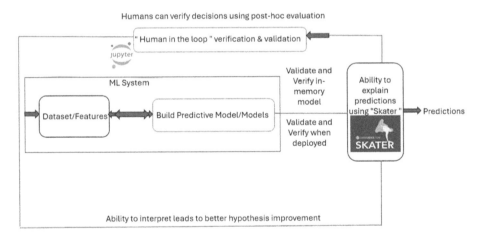

FIGURE 13.15   Skater.

13.9.3 Skater

Skater is a free, open-source model interpretation framework created for all models to develop a comprehensible ML model. It is a Python library which was designed to demystify the learned structure by the dataset in the black box model by globally referencing the dataset as well as by locally referencing the dataset. It implements LIME to validate the model decision policies for the single prediction, which uses the surrogate models to assess our model. It is a post hoc model interpretation algorithm. Skater can help to explain the model in the following way:

1. To evaluate the model's behaviors on a complete dataset as well as single datapoint.
2. To identify the variable interaction and gain knowledge in specific domain.
3. It can also measure the difference in model performance in developments and deployment environments (Figure 13.15).

13.9.4 ELI5

ELI5 is an open-source Python Unified Library, which is compatible with many deep learning frameworks that include Keras, CatBoost, LightGBM, XGBoost, Scikit-learn, and sklearn-crfsuite. It is based on Permutation Importance for explaining local and global interpretation of dataset and depends on LIME for interpreting and analyzing black-box models.

BIBLIOGRAPHY

1. Friedman, J., T. Hastie, and R. Tibshirani, "The elements of statistical learning." www.web.stanford. edu/~hastie/ElemStatLearn/ (2009).
2. "Definition of Algorithm." https://www.merriam-webster.com/dictionary/algorithm (2017).
3. Miller, T., "Explanation in artificial intelligence: Insights from the social sciences." arXiv preprint arXiv:1706.07269 (2017).
4. Kim, B., R. Khanna, and O.O. Koyejo, Examples are not enough, learn to criticize! Criticism for inter-pretability. In: *Advances in Neural Information Processing Systems* 29 (2016). 30th Conference on Neural Information Processing Systems (NIPS 2016), Barcelona, Spain.
5. Murdoch, W.J., C. Singh, K. Kumbier, R. Abbasi-Asl, and B. Yu, Definitions, methods, and applications in interpretable machine learning. *Proceedings of the National Academy of Sciences*, 116(44), 22071–22080 (2019).
6. Doshi-Velez, F., and B. Kim, "Towards a rigorous science of interpretable machine learning." no. Ml: 1–13. arXiv preprint arXiv:1702.08608 (2017).
7. Heider, F., and M. Simmel, An experimental study of apparent behavior. *The American Journal of Psychology*, 57(2), 243–259 (1944).
8. Lipton, Z.C., "The mythos of model interpretability." arXiv preprint arXiv:1606.03490 (2016).
9. Robnik-Sikonja, M., and M. Bohanec, Perturbation-based explanations of prediction models. In: Zhou, J., and Chen, F. (eds.) *Human and Machine Learning*. Springer, Cham, pp. 159–175 (2018).
10. Lipton, P., Contrastive explanation. *Royal Institute of Philosophy Supplements*, 27, 247–266 (1990).
11. Kahneman, D., and A. Tversky, "The Simulation Heuristic." Stanford Univ CA Dept of Psychology (1981).
12. Štrumbelj, E., and I. Kononenko, A general method for visualizing and explaining black-box regression models. In: *International Conference on Adaptive and Natural Computing Algorithms*. Springer, pp. 21–30 (2011). doi: 10.1007/978-3-642-20267-4_3.
13. Nickerson, R.S., Confirmation Bias: A ubiquitous phenomenon in many guises. *Review of General Psychology*, 2(2), 175 (1998).
14. Ribeiro, M.T., S. Singh, and C. Guestrin, Model-agnostic interpretability of machine learning. In: *ICML Workshop on Human Interpretability in Machine Learning* (WHI 2016), New York, NY (2016). arXiv preprint: 1606.05386.
15. Aamodt, A., and E. Plaza, Case-based reasoning: Foundational issues, methodological variations, and system approaches. *AI Communications*, 7(1), 39–59 (1994).
16. Friedman, J.H., Greedy function approximation: A gradient boosting machine. *Annals of Statistics*, 29, 1189–1232 (2001).
17. Greenwell, B.M., B.C. Boehmke, and A.J. McCarthy, "A simple and effective model-based variable importance measure." arXiv preprint arXiv:1805.04755 (2018).
18. Zhao, Q., and T. Hastie, Causal interpretations of black-box models. *Journal of Business & Economic Statistics* 39(1), 272–281 (2021). https://doi.org/10.1080/07350015.2019.1624293.
19. Apley, D.W., and J. Zhu, Visualizing the effects of predictor variables in black box supervised learning models. *Journal of the Royal Statistical Society: Series B (Statistical Methodology)*, 82(4), 1059–1086 (2020).
20. Grömping, U., "Model-agnostic effects plots for interpreting machine learning models." Reports in Mathematics, Physics and Chemistry: Department II, Beuth University of Applied Sciences Berlin. Report 1/2020 (2020).
21. Breiman, L., Random Forests. *Machine Learning*, 45(1), 5–32 (2001).
22. Fisher, A., C. Rudin, and F. Dominici, "All models are wrong, but many are useful: Learning a variable's importance by studying an entire class of prediction models simultaneously." arXiv preprint arXiv:1801.01489 (2018).

23. Wei, P., Z. Lu, and J. Song, Variable importance analysis: A comprehensive review. *Reliability Engineering & System Safety*, 142, 399–432 (2015).

24. Goldstein, A., et al., Peeking inside the black box: Visualizing statistical learning with plots of individual conditional expectation. *Journal of Computational and Graphical Statistics*, 24(1), 44–65 (2015).

25. Ribeiro, M.T., S. Singh, and C. Guestrin, Why should I trust you? Explaining the predictions of any classifier. In: *Proceedings of the 22nd ACM SIGKDD International Conference on Knowledge Discovery and Data Mining.* ACM (2016).

26. Alvarez-Melis, D., and T.S. Jaakkola, "On the robustness of interpretability methods." arXiv preprint arXiv:1806.08049 (2018).

27. Slack, D., et al., Fooling lime and shap: Adversarial attacks on post hoc explanation methods. In: *Proceedings of the AAAI/ACM Conference on AI, Ethics, and Society* (AIES '20), February 7–8, 2020, New York, NY, USA. (2020).

28. Shapley, L.S., A value for n-person games. *Contributions to the Theory of Games*, 2(28), 307–317 (1953).

29. Štrumbelj, E., and I. Kononenko, Explaining prediction models and individual predictions with feature contributions. *Knowledge and Information Systems*, 41(3), 647–665 (2014).

30. Lundberg, S.M., and S.-I. Lee, A unified approach to interpreting model predictions. In: *Advances in Neural Information Processing Systems*, 31st Conference on Neural Information Processing Systems (NIPS 2017), Long Beach, CA, USA (2017).

31. Sundararajan, M., and A. Najmi, "The many Shapley values for model explanation." arXiv preprint arXiv:1908.08474 (2019).

32. Janzing, D., L. Minorics, and P. Blöbaum, Feature relevance quantification in explainable AI: A causal problem. In: *International Conference on Artificial Intelligence and Statistics.* PMLR, Proceedings of the 23rd International Conference on Artificial Intelligence and Statistics (AISTATS) 2020, Palermo, Italy (2020).

33. Selvaraju, R.R., M. Cogswell, A. Das, R. Vedantam, D. Parikh and D. Batra, Grad - CAM: Visual explanations from deep networks via gradient-based localization. In: *2017 IEEE International Conference on Computer Vision (ICCV)*, pp. 618–626 (2017). doi: 10.1109/ICCV.2017.74.

34. Chattopadhay, A., A. Sarkar, P. Howlader, and V.N. BalaSubramanian, Grad-CAM++: Generalized gradient-based visual explanations for deep convolutional networks. In: *2018 IEEE Winter Conference on Applications of Computer Vision (WACV)*, Lake Tahoe, NV, USA, pp. 839–847. IEEE, (2018).

35. Selvaraju, R.R., A. Das, R. Vedantam, M. Cogswell, D. Parikh, and D. Batra, "Grad-CAM: Why did you say that? Visual Explanations from Deep Networks via Gradient-based Localization." arXiv preprint arXiv:1610.02391 (2016).

36. Yang, C., A. Rangarajan, and S. Ranka, Visual explanations from deep 3D convolutional neural networks for Alzheimer's disease classification. In: *AMIA Annual Symposium Proceedings 2018*, pp. 1571–1580 (2018).

37. Kim, I., S. Rajaraman, and S. Antani, Visual interpretation of convolutional neural network predictions in classifying medical image modalities. *Diagnostics*, 9, 38 (2019). doi: 10.3390/diagnostics9020038.

38. Staniak, M., and P. Biecek. "Explanations of model predictions with live and breakDown packages." arXiv preprint arXiv:1804.01955 (2018).

14 Trends and Advancements of AI and XAI in Drug Discovery

Tanisha Chandak, Jayashree J., and Vijayashree J.

14.1 INTRODUCTION

The drug discovery landscape stands at the crossroads of a revolutionary transformation, catalysed by the synergistic advancements of Artificial Intelligence (AI) and Explainable AI (XAI). These cutting-edge technologies have not only reshaped the conventional contours of drug development but have also offered unprecedented insights into the enigmatic world of molecular interactions. In this opening section, we embark on a journey into the intricate realm of AI and XAI in drug discovery, unveiling their profound significance and the compelling reasons for their integration.

14.1.1 UNVEILING THE POTENTIAL OF AI AND XAI

The convergence of AI and XAI emerges as an epoch-making paradigm shift, redefining the contours of how new therapeutic agents are identified and designed. Within this subsection, we navigate the multifaceted landscape of AI-driven drug discovery. From analysing complex biological data to orchestrating intricate predictive models, the amalgamation of AI and XAI has set forth an array of innovative tools that empower researchers to venture beyond the limitations of traditional methodologies. Through comprehensive data mining and pattern recognition, AI elucidates hidden correlations and patterns that were hitherto concealed, illuminating promising avenues for therapeutic interventions.

14.1.2 CONFRONTING CHALLENGES OF TRADITIONAL APPROACHES

Beneath the surface of conventional drug discovery methods lies a series of challenges that have hindered progress for decades. The labyrinthine process of identifying potential drug candidates, coupled with the extensive timeframes and exorbitant costs involved, has cast a shadow over the pharmaceutical industry. In this subsection, we delve deep into these challenges, unravelling the intricacies of traditional approaches that necessitate a transformative leap. As we navigate through these hurdles, it becomes evident that the integration of AI and XAI has been fuelled by a resounding call to address the shortcomings of the past and embark on an era defined by innovation and efficiency.

14.2 AI APPLICATIONS IN DRUG DISCOVERY: TRANSFORMING THE DISCOVERY PROCESS

The fusion of Artificial Intelligence (AI) and drug discovery has unfurled a tapestry of transformation, weaving innovation into the very fabric of pharmaceutical research. This section embarks on a comprehensive journey through the multifaceted applications of AI, each a testament to its profound impact on the discovery process. From unravelling the complexities of biological networks to predicting the attributes of lead compounds, AI traverses every phase of drug discovery with unwavering precision and potential. As we navigate through these applications, the depth of AI's influence comes to light, promising to reshape the landscape of drug discovery fundamentally.

14.2.1 Target Identification: Deciphering Biological Networks with AI

At the heart of the drug discovery process lies the pivotal juncture of identifying potential drug targets. Traditionally, this phase has been characterized by a labyrinthine complexity, with researchers sifting through a deluge of biological data to discern the most promising candidates. AI emerges as a beacon of innovation in this context, wielding computational prowess to dissect intricate biological networks. These networks, a convergence of genomics, proteomics, and chemical structures, encapsulate the intricate machinery of life itself. Through AI's lens, these networks transform into landscapes of opportunity, harbouring clues to disease mechanisms and potential intervention points (Figure 14.1).

Within these networks, AI's algorithms operate as intrepid explorers, deciphering the intricate interactions that dictate cellular processes. They navigate the molecular highways and byways, identifying nodes that hold the promise of being viable drug targets. As AI unravels hidden relationships and correlations, the landscape of drug discovery undergoes a seismic shift. What was once a daunting task involving years of trial and error is now expedited through AI's ability to unveil potential drug targets with pinpoint accuracy (Figure 14.2).

14.2.2 Lead Optimization: Predictive Power of Machine Learning

Transitioning from target identification to lead optimization marks a critical juncture in the drug discovery journey. Historically, this phase has been riddled with challenges, as researchers navigate the arduous path of refining potential lead compounds to ensure efficacy and safety. This is where AI emerges as a formidable ally, wielding the predictive power of machine learning to revolutionize the optimization process.

AI-driven machine learning algorithms, honed through the assimilation of vast datasets, possess the ability to predict the behaviour of lead compounds with remarkable accuracy. Attributes such as binding affinity, pharmacokinetics, and toxicity, which once required a cascade of experiments, are now at the fingertips of researchers through predictive modelling. The implications are profound—a significant reduction in the time and resources expended in trial-and-error iterations.

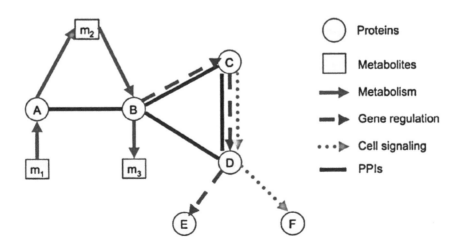

FIGURE 14.1   Network analysis visualization to identify potential drug targets.

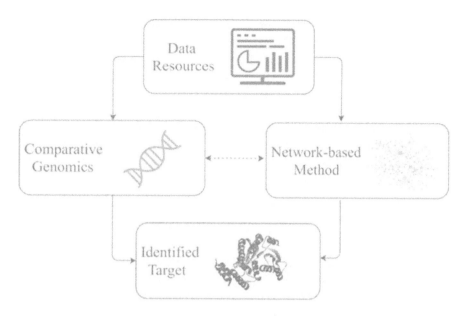

FIGURE 14.2 Cycle for identifying potential drug targets.

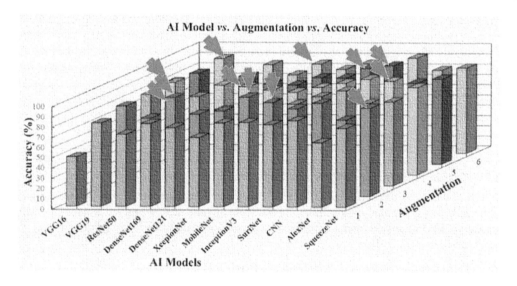

FIGURE 14.3 Graph of comparative analysis of predictive accuracy.

14.2.2.1 Graph – Comparative Analysis of Predictive Accuracy

Consider a bar graph that compares the predictive accuracy of AI-driven models with the outcomes of traditional experimental methods. Each bar could represent a specific attribute (binding affinity, pharmacokinetics, toxicity) and depict how AI predictions closely align with experimental data. The visual alignment of bars underscores AI's efficacy in predictive lead optimization (Figure 14.3).

14.2.3 VIRTUAL SCREENING AND DE NOVO DRUG DESIGN: AI'S INTELLIGENT SCREENING

The digital age has ushered in a new dimension in drug discovery—virtual screening and de novo drug design, both fuelled by the prowess of AI. Here, AI's ability to decipher complex molecular

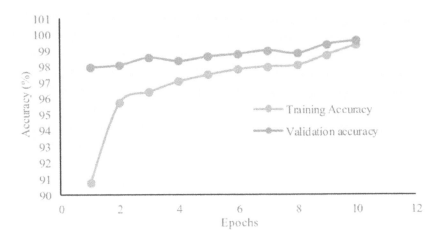

FIGURE 14.4 Performance metrics of CNN and RNN.

interactions and patterns comes to the forefront. Convolutional neural networks (CNNs) and recurrent neural networks (RNNs) stand as stalwart tools, armed with the capability to sift through massive chemical libraries in search of potential drug candidates.

Virtual screening, a process akin to a digital fishing expedition, involves subjecting vast databases of chemical compounds to AI's analytical prowess. AI-powered algorithms swiftly filter through these compounds, identifying those that exhibit promising interactions with target molecules. This method expedites the identification of potential drug candidates, significantly shortening the time it takes to move from screening to experimental validation.

De novo drug design takes the innovation a step further, empowering AI to generate entirely new molecules with desired properties. This capability is revolutionary, introducing an element of creativity into the drug discovery process. AI-generated compounds are not limited by pre-existing chemical structures, opening the door to novel therapeutic avenues.

14.2.3.1   Graph: Performance Metrics of CNN and RNN

A line chart that depicts the performance metrics (accuracy, precision, recall) of CNNs and RNNs in virtual screening tasks can vividly illustrate their effectiveness. The upward trajectory of these lines emphasizes AI's capacity to discern potential drug candidates accurately (Figure 14.4).

14.2.4   Drug Repurposing: AI's Keen Eye on Existing Drugs

One of the most tantalizing applications of AI in drug discovery lies in the realm of drug repurposing. The notion of breathing new life into existing drugs for novel therapeutic indications is both resource-efficient and strategically sound. AI's prowess in pattern recognition finds a harmonious synergy with this approach, uncovering hidden correlations and connections that may have been overlooked through conventional methods.

AI scours extensive datasets, seeking patterns that hint at alternative uses for existing drugs. By analysing vast biological, chemical, and clinical information, AI identifies compounds that could potentially address unmet medical needs. This approach not only bypasses much of the time and expense associated with traditional drug development but also unlocks a treasure trove of therapeutic possibilities.

14.2.4.1   Graph: Success Rate of Repurposing Strategies

See Figure 14.5.

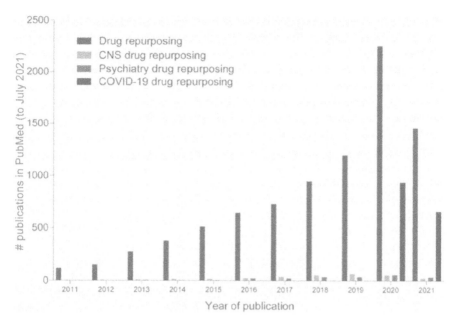

FIGURE 14.5 Graph of the success rate of repurposing strategies.

14.3 THE IMPORTANCE OF EXPLAINABLE ARTIFICIAL INTELLIGENCE (XAI) IN DRUG DISCOVERY: ILLUMINATING THE BLACK BOX

The marriage of Artificial Intelligence (AI) and drug discovery has illuminated pathways previously obscured by complexity. While AI's transformative potential is undeniable, the enigmatic nature of AI models has sparked a vital conversation around their transparency and decision-making mechanisms. In this section, we delve deep into the indispensable role of Explainable Artificial Intelligence (XAI) in the context of drug discovery. XAI serves as a beacon, casting light into the "black box" of AI and fostering a deeper understanding, trust, and accountability.

14.3.1 UNRAVELLING THE BLACK BOX: THE CHALLENGE OF AI's OPACITY

AI models often function as modern-day oracles, providing predictions that drive crucial decisions. However, these predictions are often delivered with a veil of opacity, leaving researchers and stakeholders grappling with a central question—how are these predictions made? This inherent "black box" nature of AI has led to a sense of uncertainty. Within the realm of drug discovery, where decisions have profound implications, this opacity poses both scientific and ethical challenges.

The complexity of AI models, particularly those rooted in deep learning, makes it challenging to dissect their inner workings. While the outcomes are commendable, the inability to understand the underlying rationale introduces a sense of unease. The fear of unexpected biases or errors lurking within the shadows of AI's decision-making process further magnifies the need for transparency.

14.3.2 XAI: ILLUMINATING AI's DECISION-MAKING PROCESS

Enter Explainable Artificial Intelligence (XAI), a realm of techniques designed to bridge the gap between AI's complexity and human understanding. XAI aims to make the intricate machinery of

AI comprehensible by generating explanations for its predictions. In essence, XAI acts as a translator, transforming the cryptic language of AI into insights that can be grasped by researchers, clinicians, and regulators alike.

By elucidating the decision-making process, XAI empowers researchers to comprehend why AI arrived at a specific prediction. This newfound clarity not only instils confidence but also equips researchers to identify potential pitfalls or biases within the model. XAI, in essence, transforms the black box into an open book, ushering in a new era of informed decision-making.

14.3.3 Techniques in XAI: From Granularity to Global Insights

XAI techniques span a spectrum, catering to various levels of interpretability. At the local level, techniques like LIME (Local Interpretable Model-Agnostic Explanations) generate surrogate models for individual predictions. These surrogate models, though simplified, capture the essence of AI's reasoning, providing human-readable insights into specific predictions. This local interpretability enables researchers to scrutinize AI's decision-making on a case-by-case basis.

On a broader scale, global interpretability techniques dive deep into the patterns encoded within AI models. One prominent approach is SHAP (SHapley Additive exPlanations), a game theory-inspired technique. SHAP quantifies the contribution of each feature to a prediction, offering a panoramic view of how different factors influence AI's outputs. Techniques like SHAP help researchers discern overarching trends and relationships that shape AI's decision landscape.

14.3.4 Trust and Accountability: The Essence of XAI

In the realm of drug discovery, trust and accountability are non-negotiable. Regulatory bodies, clinicians, patients, and stakeholders demand a transparent and comprehensible decision-making process. XAI rises to the occasion by offering a window into AI's inner workings. By understanding the "why" behind predictions, stakeholders can assess the reliability and relevance of AI's recommendations.

Moreover, XAI empowers researchers to validate AI's predictions against their domain expertise. This interactive validation process fosters a symbiotic relationship between AI and human intelligence, culminating in more robust and dependable results. The newfound transparency not only enhances trust in AI but also fuels informed conversations about its limitations and potential biases.

14.3.5 Bias Detection and Mitigation: Proactive Ethical Considerations

The issue of bias within AI models has garnered significant attention, underscoring the urgency of responsible AI deployment. XAI emerges as a pivotal tool in detecting and mitigating biases within AI systems. By dissecting the factors contributing to predictions, XAI empowers researchers to identify potential biases rooted in training data or model architecture. This proactive stance not only minimizes the risk of biased outcomes but also aligns with ethical considerations, especially in healthcare where biases could lead to disparate treatment outcomes.

14.3.6 Ethical Considerations and Responsible AI: A Unified Front

The integration of AI and XAI is inherently intertwined with ethical considerations. While AI promises efficiency and innovation, these advantages must be coupled with ethical awareness. XAI, operating in tandem with AI, ensures that decisions are transparent, accountable, and devoid of hidden agendas. In the realm of drug discovery, where lives are at stake, responsible AI takes on a heightened significance. The ability to understand, validate, and, if necessary, challenge AI's predictions is pivotal for the safety and well-being of patients.

14.3.7 XAI's Role in the Future of Drug Discovery

The synergy of AI and XAI charts a transformative course for the future of drug discovery. As AI continues to evolve and permeate every facet of research and healthcare, XAI evolves alongside, promising innovative techniques that amplify transparency. This partnership promises a future where AI's predictions are not just accepted but understood and embraced.

XAI is not a panacea; it's a means to an end—a future where AI augments human intelligence and decision-making. The trailblazing potential of AI harmoniously converges with the illuminating power of XAI, forging a path towards responsible, transparent, and ethical drug discovery. This synergy carries the promise of breakthroughs that are not only scientifically remarkable but also ethically conscientious—a beacon of hope for a healthcare landscape characterized by informed choices and improved patient outcomes.

SHAP Value Calculation

One of the central techniques in XAI, SHAP (SHapley Additive exPlanations), employs a mathematical formulation to calculate the contribution of each feature to a prediction. The SHAP value for a feature "i" in a prediction "x" is given by:

$$SHAP(i, x) = \Sigma\ [\Phi(x) - \Phi(z)] / N$$

where:

$\Phi(x)$ represents the model's output for prediction "x"
$\Phi(z)$ represents the model's output for a reference prediction "z"
N is the total number of permutations

Imagine a bar graph illustrating the SHAP values for different features in a prediction. Each bar represents a feature, and the height of the bar indicates the extent to which the feature contributed positively or negatively to the prediction. This graph is illustrated in Figure 14.6.

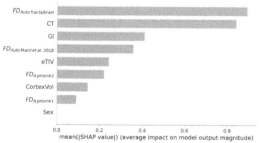
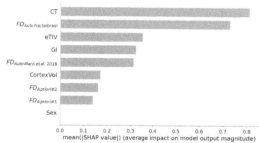

FIGURE 14.6 Graph of SHAP feature contributions.

14.4 SYNERGIZING AI AND XAI WITH EMERGING TECHNOLOGIES: ACCELERATING DRUG DISCOVERY THROUGH INNOVATION

The amalgamation of Artificial Intelligence (AI) and Explainable Artificial Intelligence (XAI) has catalysed a transformation within the realm of drug discovery. However, their impact doesn't exist in isolation. This section delves into the captivating synergy between AI, XAI, and emerging technologies, crafting a narrative of innovation that accelerates drug discovery to unprecedented heights. From high-throughput screening to AI-driven robotics, this intricate interplay reshapes traditional paradigms, forging a path towards efficient, reliable, and forward-looking drug discovery methodologies.

14.4.1 HIGH-THROUGHPUT SCREENING REINVENTED: AI's GUIDING HAND

High-throughput screening (HTS) has long been a cornerstone of drug discovery, enabling the rapid screening of vast compound libraries. The infusion of AI breathes new life into this process, supercharging it with predictive power and efficiency. AI's ability to analyse and make sense of complex datasets empowers HTS to evolve from a shotgun approach to a targeted expedition.

The integration of AI augments HTS in multiple dimensions. AI algorithms meticulously analyse compound structures and biological interactions, enabling the identification of candidates with the highest likelihood of success. This strategic targeting not only conserves resources but also expedites the identification of potential drug candidates. Moreover, AI learns from iterative screenings, honing its predictions with each round, which ultimately leads to a more refined and selective approach to compound selection.

QSAR (Quantitative Structure-Activity Relationship) models serve as the backbone of AI-guided HTS. These models correlate molecular structures with biological activities, facilitating predictive compound selection.

QSAR Models: Quantitative Structure-Activity Relationship (QSAR) models are mathematical models that establish a quantitative link between the structural attributes of molecules (such as molecular weight, chemical properties, and 3D structure) and their corresponding biological activities or properties. These models are based on the principle that the molecular structure of a compound influences its interaction with biological targets.

Correlate Molecular Structures with Biological Activities: The core function of QSAR models is to correlate the unique characteristics of a compound's molecular structure with its observed biological activities. In other words, QSAR models analyse how specific structural features contribute to the compound's effectiveness in binding to a target protein or producing a desired biological effect.

Facilitating Predictive Compound Selection: The derived relationships in QSAR models enable researchers to predict the biological activity of new or untested compounds. By inputting the molecular descriptors (structural attributes) of a compound into the QSAR model, researchers can obtain an estimate of the compound's potential activity. This predictive capability is a crucial aspect of QSAR models, as it allows for informed decisions on whether a compound is worth further experimental testing.

Context of AI-Guided High-Throughput Screening (HTS): In the context of AI-guided HTS, QSAR models are integrated with advanced artificial intelligence techniques. This integration enhances the efficiency and accuracy of the compound screening process. Instead of physically testing every compound in a high-throughput manner, AI-driven QSAR models help identify compounds with a higher likelihood of showing the desired activity. This virtual screening process saves time, resources, and costs by narrowing down the list of compounds that need to be experimentally tested.

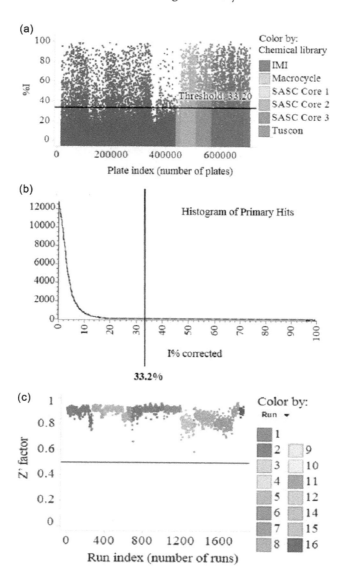

FIGURE 14.7 Graph of the hit rate of compounds identified through traditional HTS and AI-guided HTS.

Imagine a bar graph comparing the hit rate of compounds identified through traditional HTS and AI-guided HTS. The latter's higher hit rate showcases AI's power in narrowing down candidates (Figure 14.7).

14.4.2 Robotic Revolution: AI-Driven Automation in Drug Discovery

Automation has redefined industries, and drug discovery is no exception. AI-driven robotics emerge as protagonists in this narrative, propelling drug discovery towards unprecedented efficiency and throughput. Robots, guided by AI algorithms, perform intricate tasks ranging from compound synthesis to assays, ensuring accuracy, reproducibility, and speed.

The fusion of AI and robotics streamlines the experimental pipeline. Repetitive tasks that once consumed valuable researcher time are now executed swiftly and tirelessly by robotic counterparts.

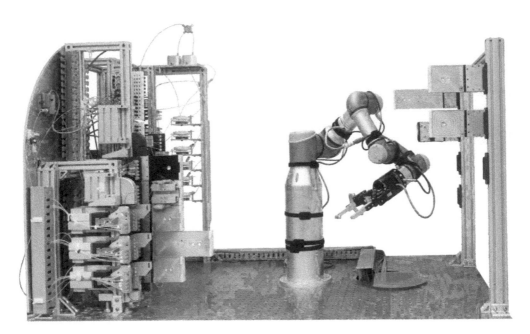

FIGURE 14.8   A robotic arm.

AI's predictive capabilities guide robots in selecting compounds for experimentation, further optimizing the process. This convergence results in a seismic shift, as drug discovery pipelines become more agile, enabling researchers to explore a broader spectrum of possibilities in a shorter timeframe (Figure 14.8).

Above is a figure depicting a robotic arm executing precise pipetting operations under the guidance of AI algorithms, capturing the essence of AI-driven automation in drug discovery laboratories.

14.4.3   Revolutionizing Data Interpretation: AI and XAI in Symbiosis

AI's data analysis prowess, when coupled with XAI's interpretability, heralds a new era in data-driven drug discovery. The deluge of data emanating from genomics, proteomics, and chemical studies holds a treasure trove of insights, but its sheer volume can be overwhelming. AI steps in as the discerning lens, extracting meaningful patterns and correlations from this data labyrinth.

XAI complements AI by adding a layer of understanding to these patterns. As AI deciphers intricate relationships, XAI elucidates the significance of these discoveries in a comprehensible manner. Together, they transform raw data into actionable knowledge. For instance, AI might uncover a potential biomarker, while XAI unravels the biological context and implications of this discovery. This dynamic synergy ensures that data-driven insights are not only accurate but also interpretable, empowering researchers to make informed decisions.

Principal Component Analysis (PCA), a common AI technique, reduces multidimensional data into interpretable components. XAI techniques then unravel the impact of these components on predictions.

> **Principal Component Analysis (PCA)**: Principal Component Analysis is a dimensionality reduction technique used in data analysis and machine learning. It works by transforming high-dimensional data into a new coordinate system, where each axis (principal component) captures the most variance in the data. In other words, PCA identifies the key patterns and relationships within complex datasets.

Reduces Multidimensional Data: One of the primary goals of PCA is to simplify complex datasets with numerous variables (dimensions) into a reduced set of principal components. These components are linear combinations of the original variables and are ordered by the amount of variance they capture in the data. By doing so, PCA transforms the data into a lower-dimensional representation while retaining as much important information as possible.

Interpretable Components: The concept of "interpretable components" refers to the idea that each principal component represents a distinct pattern or relationship within the data. These components are linear combinations of the original variables, making them easier to understand and interpret than the original multidimensional data.

XAI Techniques: Explainable Artificial Intelligence (XAI) techniques are methodologies that enhance the transparency and interpretability of complex AI models. These techniques provide insights into how AI models arrive at their decisions, allowing humans to understand the factors that influence predictions.

Unravel the Impact of Components on Predictions: In the context of PCA integrated with XAI, the focus is on understanding how the identified principal components contribute to the predictions made by AI models. XAI techniques help unravel the influence of these interpretable components on the outcome of predictions, shedding light on the underlying patterns and relationships that the model has learned (Figure 14.9).

Graph: A scatter plot depicting PCA-transformed data points, color-coded based on different classes. Overlay SHAP values on the plot to demonstrate XAI's role in understanding feature contributions.

14.4.4 PERSONALIZED MEDICINE UNLEASHED: AI'S PRECISION IN TREATMENT

Personalized medicine—a paradigm where treatments are tailored to an individual's unique genetic makeup—is a frontier that AI and XAI are poised to conquer. The intricate interplay between genetics,

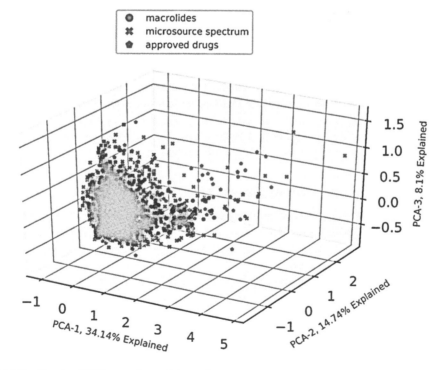

FIGURE 14.9 Graph of PCA-transformed datapoints.

biomarkers, and drug responses demands a level of precision that AI is uniquely equipped to provide. AI's ability to process and analyse massive datasets enables the identification of genetic markers that dictate drug efficacy and potential side effects.

XAI further enhances this personalized medicine revolution by demystifying AI's treatment recommendations. Patients and clinicians can understand the rationale behind treatment decisions, fostering a partnership between human expertise and AI's analytical power. This alliance not only ensures the best possible treatment outcomes but also empowers patients to actively participate in their healthcare journey.

Formula: Genetic algorithms optimize treatment regimens based on patient-specific genetic markers and AI-predicted drug responses, creating personalized therapeutic plans.

Genetic Algorithms (GAs): Genetic algorithms are optimization techniques inspired by the process of natural selection. They involve the iterative generation and evaluation of potential solutions (individuals or "chromosomes") to find the optimal solution to a problem. GAs simulate the principles of evolution, such as selection, crossover, and mutation, to converge towards the best possible solution.

Optimize Treatment Regimens: In the context of personalized medicine, genetic algorithms are employed to optimize treatment regimens. These algorithms explore a range of possible therapeutic options, adjusting drug doses, combinations, and schedules to find the regimen that yields the most favourable outcomes for a specific patient.

Patient-Specific Genetic Markers: Genetic markers are specific variations in a person's DNA sequence that can influence their response to treatments. These markers may indicate susceptibility to certain diseases, potential adverse reactions, or variations in drug metabolism. Integrating patient-specific genetic markers into the treatment optimization process tailors the therapeutic plan to the individual's genetic profile.

AI-Predicted Drug Responses: Artificial Intelligence (AI), particularly machine learning models, can predict how a patient's body will respond to different drugs based on their genetic markers and other clinical data. These predictions are derived from analysing large datasets of genetic and clinical information, enabling the identification of drug candidates that are likely to be effective for a specific patient.

Personalized Therapeutic Plans: The synergy between genetic algorithms, patient-specific genetic markers, and AI-predicted drug responses results in the creation of personalized therapeutic plans. These plans are finely tuned to the patient's genetic makeup, ensuring that the selected treatments have a higher probability of efficacy and minimal adverse effects.

Below is a schematic depicting the workflow of personalized medicine: genetic data input, AI analysis, XAI-driven explanation, and personalized treatment recommendation.

14.4.5 Ethical Considerations in AI-Driven Drug Discovery

As AI and emerging technologies propel drug discovery forward, ethical considerations loom large. The data-driven nature of AI requires meticulous attention to data privacy and security. Ensuring that patient data remains confidential while contributing to the advancement of science is a delicate balance that AI and XAI must navigate.

Moreover, the potential for unintended consequences requires continuous vigilance. Bias detection and mitigation, a cornerstone of responsible AI, gain even greater significance in this intricate interplay. XAI's role in revealing potential biases becomes instrumental in maintaining ethical standards and avoiding harmful outcomes.

Below is a Venn diagram, where one circle represents AI, the other XAI, and the overlapping region symbolizes ethical AI deployment. This visual encapsulates their interconnected roles (Figure 14.10).

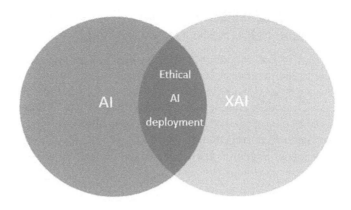

FIGURE 14.10   Venn diagram of AI and XAI.

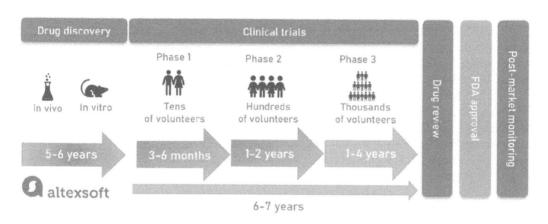

FIGURE 14.11   A timeline of drug discovery methods.

14.4.6   A Glimpse into the Future: A Holistic Approach

The synergy between AI, XAI, and emerging technologies forms the blueprint for the future of drug discovery—a future where efficiency, accuracy, and ethics harmoniously coexist. This holistic approach transforms drug discovery from a laborious process into a dynamic journey of discovery and innovation. The convergence of AI's predictive prowess, XAI's transparency, and emerging technologies' efficiency propels drug discovery towards uncharted horizons.

As AI continues to evolve, guided by XAI and propelled by emerging technologies, the possibilities become limitless. Drug discovery not only becomes more efficient but also more meaningful, yielding therapies that are not just scientifically sound but ethically responsible. This symbiotic synergy is a testament to human ingenuity, as it navigates the intricate nexus of innovation, ethics, and patient well-being

The graph below illustrates a timeline that traces the evolution of drug discovery methods, showcasing how AI, XAI, and emerging technologies influence each stage, leading to improved outcomes (Figure 14.11).

14.5   DEEP LEARNING UNLEASHED: REVOLUTIONIZING DRUG DISCOVERY THROUGH ADVANCED NEURAL NETWORKS

In the rapidly evolving landscape of drug discovery, the synthesis of Artificial Intelligence (AI) and pharmaceutical research has led to monumental breakthroughs. At the forefront of this transformative union is the burgeoning field of Deep Learning, a subset of AI that mimics the human brain's intricate neural networks. Deep Learning has reshaped the fundamental pillars of drug discovery, and this section delves into its unprecedented impact. From Convolutional Neural Networks (CNNs) redefining virtual screening to Recurrent Neural Networks (RNNs) revolutionizing de novo drug design, these advanced neural architectures are driving a seismic shift in how drugs are discovered, designed, and optimized.

14.5.1   Convolutional Neural Networks (CNNs): Redefining Virtual Screening

Virtual screening, a cornerstone of modern drug discovery, involves computational methods to predict the binding affinity of small molecules to target proteins. This step drastically reduces the number of compounds that need to be experimentally tested. Traditional methods relied heavily on simplified molecular representations, which often led to inaccuracies due to the complex nature of molecular structures.

The advent of Convolutional Neural Networks (CNNs) has revolutionized virtual screening by introducing a data-driven and highly accurate approach. CNNs, inspired by the human visual system, are capable of automatically learning features and patterns from complex data, such as images. When applied to molecular structures, CNNs analyse the intricate three-dimensional arrangement of atoms, identifying critical binding sites and interactions.

This new paradigm allows CNNs to predict binding affinities with exceptional precision. The network learns from a large dataset of known binding affinities and molecular structures, developing an intricate understanding of the relationship between structure and activity. As a result, virtual screening powered by CNNs expedites the identification of potential drug candidates, greatly accelerating the drug discovery process (Figure 14.12).

14.5.2   Advancing De Novo Drug Design: Recurrent Neural Networks (RNNs)

The concept of de novo drug design, where novel compounds are generated from scratch to meet specific therapeutic requirements, has historically been an arduous and iterative process. The emergence of Recurrent Neural Networks (RNNs) has reshaped this landscape by enabling the generation of molecular structures in a sequential manner.

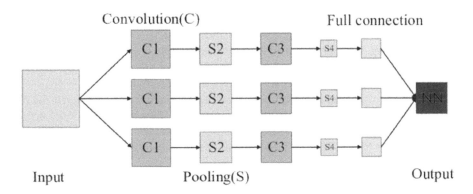

FIGURE 14.12   Input and output of pooling.

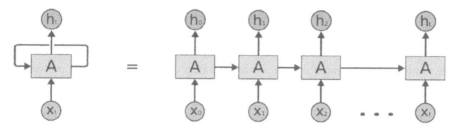

FIGURE 14.13 RNN stages.

RNNs are uniquely suited to handle sequential data, making them ideal for modelling molecular structures, which can be represented as sequences of atoms. The architecture's ability to capture dependencies among sequential elements allows it to predict the next atom based on the previous ones. This sequential generation of molecular structures empowers researchers to tailor compounds with desired properties, such as optimized binding affinity and solubility.

The iterative nature of RNN-driven de novo drug design streamlines the process of generating compounds with specific characteristics. Researchers can iteratively refine and optimize structures based on RNN predictions, significantly reducing the time and resources required for experimental synthesis and testing (Figure 14.13).

14.5.3 Drug Repurposing Reshaped: Graph Neural Networks (GNNs)

Drug repurposing, the practice of identifying new therapeutic applications for existing drugs, is a strategy that capitalizes on the wealth of existing clinical and pharmacological data. The integration of Graph Neural Networks (GNNs) into drug repurposing endeavours has unlocked a new dimension of analysis, leveraging complex molecular interactions and relationships.

GNNs are tailored to handle graph-structured data, where entities (nodes) are connected by edges that represent relationships. In the context of drug repurposing, GNNs analyse intricate molecular graphs, uncovering hidden patterns of interaction between compounds, genes, proteins, and diseases. By capturing nuanced relationships, GNNs unveil potential new applications for existing drugs, offering a data-driven approach to repurposing.

This innovation in drug repurposing transforms it from an intuition-based process to a systematic and informed endeavour. GNNs widen the spectrum of possibilities by unveiling connections that were previously hidden in the vast landscape of molecular interactions.

14.5.4 Quantum Machine Learning: Pioneering Quantum Chemistry

Quantum Mechanics, with its ability to accurately describe the behaviour of molecules at the atomic level, has long been a foundational pillar of drug discovery. The fusion of Quantum Mechanics with Machine Learning gives birth to Quantum Machine Learning (QML), a paradigm that holds immense potential for precise drug design.

QML models leverage the principles of quantum calculations to predict molecular properties and behaviours with unprecedented accuracy. By integrating quantum features into machine learning algorithms, QML transcends the limitations of classical computational approaches. This quantum advantage allows QML models to predict properties such as binding energies, electronic structures, and reaction pathways with remarkable precision.

The integration of QML into drug discovery augments our understanding of molecular interactions and properties, enabling the design of molecules with desired functionalities. The collaboration between Quantum Mechanics and Machine Learning marks a significant leap in our ability to harness the power of the subatomic world for therapeutic advancements.

14.5.5   ADDRESSING CHALLENGES WITH AI: LIMITED DATA AND INTERPRETABILITY

Despite the promise of advanced neural networks, challenges persist in their adoption. Limited availability of high-quality data poses a hurdle, as these models thrive on large and diverse datasets. Generative models, including Variational Autoencoders (VAEs), offer a solution by generating synthetic data that complements real-world datasets

VAEs are part of a family of generative models that learn the underlying distribution of the data. By mapping data points to a lower-dimensional space (latent space), VAEs capture the essence of the dataset. This latent space can then be used to generate new data points that closely resemble the original dataset, effectively expanding the pool of available training data

Furthermore, the black-box nature of deep learning models raises concerns about their interpretability. This is particularly important in drug discovery, where understanding the rationale behind predictions is crucial for validation and decision-making. Techniques like Layer-wise Relevance Propagation (LRP) shed light on the contribution of individual features to model predictions, enhancing interpretability.

14.5.6   ETHICAL CONSIDERATIONS IN DEEP LEARNING

As AI-driven approaches become more integrated into drug discovery pipelines, ethical considerations come to the forefront. Ensuring that these models are fair, unbiased, and transparent is paramount. Graph-based techniques, such as Graph Attention Networks (GATs), have been developed to uncover biases within complex datasets and models.

GATs focus on graph-structured data, analysing relationships between entities. They highlight areas of potential bias by emphasizing nodes that contribute disproportionately to predictions. By identifying and mitigating biases, GATs enhance the ethical deployment of AI in drug discovery, ensuring that underrepresented groups are not overlooked.

Additionally, Explainable AI (XAI) methodologies play a pivotal role in addressing ethical concerns. XAI techniques provide insights into how AI models arrive at their decisions, making the decision-making process transparent and understandable for human experts.

14.5.7   THE UNCHARTED HORIZON: AI-ENHANCED DRUG DISCOVERY

The emergence of advanced neural networks in drug discovery marks a pivotal juncture in pharmaceutical research. These networks, fuelled by the synergy between AI and drug discovery expertise, are reshaping traditional paradigms. The continuous evolution of neural network architectures, guided by ethical considerations and driven by the thirst for innovation, paves the way for an exciting future.

As neural networks advance, they redefine the boundaries of drug discovery methodologies, pushing the envelope of predictive accuracy, efficiency, and ethical responsibility. The integration of Convolutional Neural Networks (CNNs), Recurrent Neural Networks (RNNs), Graph Neural Networks (GNNs), Quantum Machine Learning (QML), Generative Models, and Graph Attention Networks (GATs) collectively propels drug discovery into a new era of scientific discovery and therapeutic breakthroughs. The future holds the promise of AI-augmented drug discovery unlocking unprecedented insights and transforming the healthcare landscape.

14.6   ETHICAL CONSIDERATIONS IN AI-DRIVEN DRUG DISCOVERY: NAVIGATING BIAS, TRANSPARENCY, AND ACCOUNTABILITY

The infusion of Artificial Intelligence (AI) into drug discovery has orchestrated a paradigm shift, propelling scientific progress to unprecedented heights. However, this rapid advancement has not occurred without ethical intricacies. As AI permeates various facets of drug development, it raises a host of ethical considerations that necessitate careful contemplation and conscientious navigation. This section undertakes a comprehensive exploration of the ethical dimensions intrinsic to AI-driven drug discovery, encompassing matters of bias, transparency, accountability, privacy, equity, and collaborative frameworks.

14.6.1 THE VEIL OF BIAS: UNCOVERING AND MITIGATING ETHICAL DILEMMAS

AI models are only as accurate as the data on which they are trained, and therein lies a potential ethical quandary: the presence of bias within datasets. Biased data can inadvertently perpetuate societal inequalities, with consequences that extend to healthcare and medical research. To address this, the field has seen the emergence of fairness-aware machine learning—a methodology that strives to detect and rectify bias in AI predictions.

Fairness-aware machine learning operates on the premise of incorporating fairness constraints during the training process of AI models. This strategy aims to ensure that predictions are equitable across various demographic groups. By penalizing instances where predictions disproportionately favour one group over another, fairness-aware models strive to minimize bias and promote fairness in decision-making.

14.6.2 UNMASKING THE BLACK BOX: ENHANCING MODEL INTERPRETABILITY

A distinctive characteristic of AI models is their opacity—often referred to as the "black box" problem. While these models can make accurate predictions, understanding the rationale behind these predictions remains elusive. This opacity becomes a significant ethical concern in domains such as drug discovery, where insights into the decision-making process are essential for validation and trust.

Explainable AI (XAI) techniques rise to the challenge by providing means to unravel the intricacies of AI models. One such technique is Layer-wise Relevance Propagation (LRP), which aims to shed light on the significance of individual features in contributing to predictions. By tracing the importance of features through the layers of a neural network, LRP offers a pathway to translating complex model outputs into comprehensible insights, thereby enhancing transparency and trust.

An illustration depicts the process of Layer-wise Relevance Propagation (LRP), showing how feature importance is propagated back through the layers of a neural network to explain model predictions (Figure 14.14).

14.6.3 ACCOUNTABILITY IN AUTONOMOUS DECISION-MAKING

AI-driven drug discovery often involves phases where AI systems autonomously make pivotal decisions, potentially altering the trajectory of research and development. However, the autonomy of AI systems raises pertinent questions regarding accountability when unanticipated outcomes transpire.

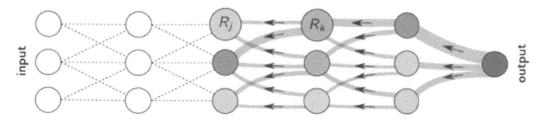

FIGURE 14.14 Layer-wise relevance propagation (LRP).

Algorithmic accountability emerges as a key principle to address this challenge. The essence of algorithmic accountability is rooted in ensuring that the decision-making process of AI models is traceable and understandable. Implementing transparency measures and regulatory frameworks serves as a means to hold stakeholders accountable for the choices made by AI systems.

14.6.4 Privacy and Data Security: Safeguarding Patient Information

The potency of AI stems from its capacity to learn from vast datasets, which often encompass sensitive patient information. The ethical dimension of data privacy and security becomes paramount, particularly in healthcare settings. Data anonymization and encryption techniques materialize as pivotal safeguards to uphold patient confidentiality and stave off unauthorized access to sensitive medical data. By transforming identifiable information into anonymous data points, these methods help strike a balance between the benefits of AI-driven insights and the imperative of data protection.

14.6.5 Ensuring Equity and Fairness: Implications for Healthcare Disparities

AI-driven drug discovery, while promising transformative breakthroughs, bears the risk of exacerbating existing healthcare disparities if not ethically managed. The challenge lies in ensuring that AI models do not perpetuate or amplify inequities but rather contribute to equitable healthcare outcomes. Ethical considerations related to equity and fairness entail a proactive approach to minimize bias in AI predictions. By calibrating models to provide balanced and equitable outputs across diverse patient populations, the goal is to establish a level playing field where healthcare benefits are accessible to all.

14.6.6 Collaborative Ethical Frameworks: Multi-stakeholder Engagement

Ethical challenges cannot be effectively addressed in isolation. The multifaceted nature of ethical considerations in AI-driven drug discovery demands a collaborative approach, involving a diverse spectrum of stakeholders ranging from researchers and clinicians to patients, ethicists, and regulatory bodies.

This collaboration manifests in the formulation of ethical frameworks that provide guidelines for responsible AI implementation. By engaging in inclusive discussions and incorporating diverse perspectives, these frameworks aim to create a comprehensive ethical roadmap that steers AI-driven drug discovery towards ethical excellence.

14.6.7 Guiding Principles for Ethical AI-Driven Drug Discovery

To navigate the intricate ethical landscape that accompanies AI-driven drug discovery, it becomes imperative to establish guiding principles that underscore ethical integrity.

At the heart of ethical considerations lie principles emphasizing fairness, transparency, accountability, patient privacy, and equity. Upholding these guiding tenets ensures that AI-driven drug discovery progresses responsibly and ethically, forging a harmonious synthesis between scientific advancements and ethical imperatives.

In sum, this section has traversed the ethical terrain that accompanies AI-driven drug discovery. Bias, transparency, accountability, privacy, equity, and collaborative frameworks have been intricately examined, spotlighting the ethical intricacies that permeate this groundbreaking convergence of technology and healthcare. By weaving ethical considerations into the fabric of AI-driven drug discovery, a harmonious coexistence of scientific progress and ethical integrity can be fostered, paving the way for transformative healthcare advancements.

14.7 FUTURE PROSPECTS AND IMPLICATIONS: SHAPING THE EVOLUTION OF AI-DRIVEN DRUG DISCOVERY

The evolution of Artificial Intelligence (AI) and its integration into drug discovery has catalysed transformative shifts in research paradigms, redefining the boundaries of what's possible in the quest for novel therapeutics. Heading into the future, the potential and implications of AI-driven drug discovery are poised to reshape the landscape of healthcare and pharmaceutical innovation. This section delves into the future prospects and implications of this dynamic synergy, spanning technological advancements, therapeutic breakthroughs, regulatory considerations, and the societal impact of AI in drug discovery.

14.7.1 TECHNOLOGICAL ADVANCEMENTS: PUSHING THE BOUNDARIES OF POSSIBILITY

The trajectory of AI-driven drug discovery is inexorably intertwined with technological innovations that continue to push the boundaries of scientific exploration. Deep Learning, a cornerstone of AI, has witnessed remarkable progress, paving the way for advanced neural architectures such as Generative Adversarial Networks (GANs) and Transformer models. These innovations enable the generation of novel molecular structures, prediction of protein structures with unprecedented accuracy, and the rapid optimization of drug candidates.

14.7.2 THERAPEUTIC BREAKTHROUGHS: ACCELERATING DRUG DISCOVERY TIMELINES

One of the most profound impacts of AI-driven drug discovery lies in its potential to accelerate the drug development process. By harnessing AI's predictive capabilities, researchers can rapidly identify potential drug candidates, predict their interactions with biological targets, and assess their safety profiles. This acceleration not only reduces the time and cost associated with drug discovery but also expedites the translation of scientific discoveries into clinical applications.

An illustrative image depicts the streamlined drug discovery process facilitated by AI, showcasing the rapid progression from target identification to clinical application.

14.7.3 REGULATORY CONSIDERATIONS: NAVIGATING NOVEL APPROACHES

As AI-driven drug discovery introduces novel methodologies and approaches, regulatory frameworks must adapt to ensure the safety and efficacy of developed therapeutics. Regulators are faced with the challenge of evaluating AI-generated data, assessing the reliability of AI models, and establishing guidelines for the integration of AI into the drug approval process.

Graph: A graph portrays the regulatory considerations surrounding AI-driven drug discovery, highlighting the interplay between technological innovation, regulatory frameworks, and drug development timelines.

14.7.4 ETHICAL AND SOCIETAL IMPLICATIONS: BALANCING INNOVATION AND RESPONSIBILITY

The proliferation of AI in drug discovery comes with profound ethical and societal implications. The potential for AI to exacerbate biases, erode privacy, and alter traditional roles in healthcare necessitates a delicate balance between innovation and ethical responsibility. Transparency, accountability, and equitable access to AI-driven healthcare are critical facets that must be addressed to ensure that advancements are ethically and socially responsible.

14.7.5 DEMOCRATIZATION OF DRUG DISCOVERY: EMPOWERING RESEARCHERS

AI-driven drug discovery has the potential to democratize the field by democratizing access to powerful tools and methodologies. Small research teams and even individual researchers can harness

AI platforms to design experiments, analyse data, and make informed decisions. This democratization fosters innovation and inclusivity in drug discovery, expanding the pool of talent and ideas that contribute to scientific advancements.

14.7.6   Collaboration and Data Sharing: Catalysing Collective Knowledge

The AI-driven paradigm emphasizes collaboration and data sharing across academia and industry. Open-access datasets, collaborative platforms, and shared model architectures enable researchers to build upon each other's work and collectively accelerate drug discovery efforts. This collaborative spirit not only expedites progress but also cultivates a culture of knowledge exchange and innovation.

14.7.7   Environmental Impact: Towards Sustainable Drug Discovery

As AI-driven drug discovery leads to an upsurge in computational experiments, the environmental implications of increased energy consumption come to the fore. Striking a balance between technological advancement and environmental sustainability is crucial. Researchers and developers are exploring energy-efficient AI algorithms and sustainable computing practices to mitigate the ecological footprint of AI-driven drug discovery.

14.8   CONCLUSION: THE CONVERGENCE OF AI AND DRUG DISCOVERY - PAVING THE PATH FORWARD

The synthesis of Artificial Intelligence (AI) and drug discovery stands as a testament to the boundless potential of technology to reshape the contours of scientific inquiry. As we stand at the juncture of these two formidable domains, this section offers a comprehensive conclusion that encapsulates the overarching themes, profound insights, and the roadmap that guides the future trajectory of this dynamic convergence.

14.8.1   The Synergy Unveiled: AI as a Catalyst for Discovery

The synergy between AI and drug discovery transcends mere collaboration; it embodies a transformative alliance that holds the promise of revolutionizing healthcare and therapeutic innovation. AI has transcended the role of a supplementary tool, morphing into a catalytic force that propels drug discovery into uncharted territories. By augmenting efficiency, accelerating timelines, and amplifying predictive capabilities, AI has ushered in a new era of exploration in the realm of therapeutics. It seamlessly integrates itself into each phase of the drug discovery process, from target identification and compound screening to lead optimization and therapeutic prediction. In this convergence, AI emerges as a catalyst, altering not only the processes but the very fabric of drug discovery.

An illustrative image captures the dynamic synergy between AI and drug discovery, illustrating AI's role as a transformative catalyst that accelerates and enhances the discovery process.

14.8.2   Trailblazing Technological Frontiers: Deep Learning and Beyond

The journey of AI-driven drug discovery is inseparable from the technological frontiers it traverses. The hallmark of AI's prowess lies in the exponential progress of deep learning techniques. From the foundational Convolutional Neural Networks (CNNs) that revolutionized image analysis to the sophistication of Recurrent Neural Networks (RNNs) that excel in sequence prediction, AI's ascent is a testament to the ceaseless pursuit of innovation. The advent of advanced architectures such as Generative Adversarial Networks (GANs) and Transformer models further extends the horizons of

AI-driven drug discovery. GANs facilitate the generation of molecular structures, a critical task in drug design, while Transformer models revolutionize protein structure prediction and facilitate the development of novel therapeutics through de novo drug design.

14.8.3 THE CRUCIAL ETHICAL COMPASS: NAVIGATING AI's MORAL IMPERATIVES

Integrating AI into drug discovery propels us beyond technological prowess into the realm of ethical considerations. The omnipresence of bias within data, the opacity of AI models, the accountability in autonomous decision-making, and the imperative to safeguard patient privacy underscore the ethical dimensions that require diligent navigation. Explainable AI (XAI) stands as a beacon of transparency, illuminating the decision-making processes of complex AI models. Algorithmic accountability, which holds decision-makers responsible for AI-driven choices, reinforces the principle of transparency. Collaborative ethical frameworks ensure the convergence of technological advancement and ethical responsibility. These ethical considerations crystallize the essence of responsible AI-driven drug discovery, where innovation flourishes under the vigilant gaze of ethical stewardship.

14.8.4 A GLIMPSE INTO TOMORROW: TRANSFORMATIVE POTENTIAL AND SOCIETAL IMPACT

Gazing into the future, the transformative potential of AI-driven drug discovery extends beyond the confines of laboratories and research institutions. The promise of accelerated drug development timelines, the democratization of research tools, collaborative knowledge exchange, and equitable access to healthcare beckons. Yet, these prospects intertwine with ethical dilemmas, regulatory adaptations, and the delicate balance between scientific innovation and ethical responsibility. The confluence of innovation and responsibility serves as the cornerstone of AI's future impact on drug discovery and healthcare.

14.8.5 THE UNFINISHED SYMPHONY: CHALLENGES AND OPPORTUNITIES AHEAD

The journey of AI and drug discovery thrives on the interplay between challenges and opportunities. While data quality and model robustness pose challenges, they also stimulate innovation in areas like data augmentation and transfer learning. Regulatory harmonization, while complex, nurtures the environment for AI-driven therapeutics to flourish. Environmental sustainability becomes imperative, inviting the exploration of energy-efficient AI algorithms and sustainable computing practices. These challenges, in all their complexity, serve as crucibles for the birth of innovative solutions, driving collaboration, and shaping the trajectory of AI-driven drug discovery.

14.8.6 THE ODYSSEY CONTINUES: NAVIGATING UNCHARTED TERRITORIES

The odyssey of AI-driven drug discovery is an ongoing saga characterized by the intertwining threads of scientific exploration, ethical deliberation, and relentless innovation. Guided by the compass of scientific curiosity, ethical integrity, and a commitment to societal well-being, this journey propels us forward. As we continue to navigate uncharted territories, the integration of AI and drug discovery promises to be a beacon that guides us towards an era of unprecedented therapeutic breakthroughs and ethical excellence.

14.8.7 BEYOND THE HORIZON: A HARMONIOUS COEXISTENCE

The narrative of AI and drug discovery culminates in a harmonious coexistence—a saga where technological prowess converges with ethical responsibility, where innovation aligns with equitable access, and where scientific excellence coalesces with societal impact. The future unfolds as AI and drug discovery converge, weaving a tapestry rich with threads of innovation, collaboration, and ethical stewardship.

In summation, the synthesis of AI and drug discovery represents the dawn of a new era in scientific exploration. This convergence not only amplifies the capabilities of drug discovery but also introduces a paradigm where technology and ethics harmonize to usher in transformative change. The narrative of AI-driven drug discovery is one of inspiration, aspiration, and realization—a story that will undoubtedly reshape healthcare, expand the boundaries of therapeutic innovation, and reaffirm the potency of ethical stewardship in the realm of scientific progress. As the curtains close on this chapter, the story of AI and drug discovery extends an invitation to envision a future where technology and humanity coalesce for the betterment of mankind.

BIBILIOGRAPHY

1. Chen, Z., Liu, X., Hogan, W., Shenkman, E., & Bian, J. (2021). Applications of artificial intelligence in drug development using real-world data. *Drug Discovery Today*, 26(5), 1256–1264.
2. Holzinger, A., Keiblinger, K., Holub, P., Zatloukal, K., & Müller, H. (2023). AI for life: Trends in artificial intelligence for biotechnology. *New Biotechnology*, 74, 16–24.
3. Vijayan, R. S. K., Kihlberg, J., Cross, J. B., & Poongavanam, V. (2022). Enhancing preclinical drug discovery with artificial intelligence. *Drug Discovery Today*, 27(4), 967–984.
4. Askr, H., Elgeldawi, E., Aboul Ella, H., Elshaier, Y. A., Gomaa, M. M., & Hassanien, A. E. (2023). Deep learning in drug discovery: An integrative review and future challenges. *Artificial Intelligence Review*, 56(7), 5975–6037.
5. Blanco-Gonzalez, A., Cabezon, A., Seco-Gonzalez, A., Conde-Torres, D., Antelo-Riveiro, P., Pineiro, A., & Garcia-Fandino, R. (2023). The role of ai in drug discovery: Challenges, opportunities, and strategies. *Pharmaceuticals*, 16(6), 891.
6. Bajorath, J. (2022). Artificial intelligence in interdisciplinary life science and drug discovery research. *Future Science OA*, 8(4), FSO792.
7. Öztürk, H., Özgür, A., Schwaller, P., Laino, T., & Ozkirimli, E. (2020). Exploring chemical space using natural language processing methodologies for drug discovery. *Drug Discovery Today*, 25(4), 689–705.
8. Bess, A., Berglind, F., Mukhopadhyay, S., Brylinski, M., Griggs, N., Cho, T., ... & Wasan, K. M. (2022). Artificial intelligence for the discovery of novel antimicrobial agents for emerging infectious diseases. *Drug Discovery Today*, 27(4), 1099–1107.
9. Obrezanova, O. (2023). Artificial intelligence for compound pharmacokinetics prediction. *Current Opinion in Structural Biology*, 79, 102546.
10. Kırboğa, K. K., Abbasi, S., & Küçüksille, E. U. (2023). Explainability and white box in drug discovery. *Chemical Biology & Drug Design*, 102, 217–233.
11. Karger, E., & Kureljusic, M. (2022). Using artificial intelligence for drug discovery: A Bibliometric study and future research agenda. *Pharmaceuticals*, 15(12), 1492.
12. Brown, P., Merritt, A., Skerratt, S., & Swarbrick, M. E. (2023). Recent trends in medicinal chemistry and enabling technologies. Highlights from the society for medicines research conference. *Drugs of the Future*, 48(3), 211–219.
13. Gillani, I. S., Shahzad, M., Mobin, A., Munawar, M. R., Awan, M. U., & Asif, M. (2022, September). Explainable AI in drug sensitivity prediction on cancer cell lines. In *2022 International Conference on Emerging Trends in Smart Technologies (ICETST)* (pp. 1–5). IEEE.
14. Sahoo, A., & Dar, G. M. (2021). A comprehensive review on the application of artificial intelligence in drug discovery. *The Applied Biology & Chemistry Journal (TABCJ)*, 2(2), 34–48.
15. Baran, S., & Henstock, P. (2022). Pathways for Successful AI Adoption in Drug Development. Available at SSRN 4305068.
16. Kannappan, B., Maria Navin, J. R., Sridevi, N., & Suresh, P. (2022, November). Recent advances of artificial intelligence in drug discovery process. In *2022 International Interdisciplinary Humanitarian Conference for Sustainability (IIHC)* (pp. 245–249). IEEE.
17. Adadi, A., & Berrada, M. (2020). Explainable AI for healthcare: From black box to interpretable models. In *Embedded Systems and Artificial Intelligence: Proceedings of ESAI 2019*, Fez, Morocco (pp. 327–337). Springer Singapore.
18. Gill, S. S., Xu, M., Ottaviani, C., Patros, P., Bahsoon, R., Shaghaghi, A., ... & Uhlig, S. (2022). AI for next generation computing: Emerging trends and future directions. *Internet of Things*, 19, 100514.

19. Adadi, A., & Berrada, M. (2018). Peeking inside the black-box: A survey on explainable artificial intelligence (XAI). *IEEE Access*, *6*, 52138–52160.
20. Stergiou, K. D., Minopoulos, G. M., Memos, V. A., Stergiou, C. L., Koidou, M. P., & Psannis, K. E. (2022). A machine learning-based model for epidemic forecasting and faster drug discovery. *Applied Sciences*, *12*(21), 10766.
21. Sharma, V. K., & Bharatam, P. V. (2022). Artificial Intelligence in Drug Discovery (AIDD). *Current Research & Information on Pharmaceutical Sciences*, *16*(1), 3–7.
22. Kavasidis, I., Salanitri, F. P., Palazzo, S., & Spampinato, C. (2023). History of AI in clinical medicine. In: Michael F. Byrne, Nasim Parsa, Alexandra T. Greenhill, Daljeet Chahal, Omer Ahmad, Ulas Bagci (eds.) *AI in Clinical Medicine: A Practical Guide for Healthcare Professionals*, 39–48.
23. Kim, I., Kang, K., Song, Y., & Kim, T. J. (2022). Application of artificial intelligence in pathology: Trends and challenges. *Diagnostics*, *12*(11), 2794.
24. Fellous, J. M., Sapiro, G., Rossi, A., Mayberg, H., & Ferrante, M. (2019). Explainable artificial intelligence for neuroscience: Behavioral neurostimulation. *Frontiers in Neuroscience*, *13*, 1346.
25. Holzinger, A., Kieseberg, P., Weippl, E., & Tjoa, A. M. (2018). Current advances, trends and challenges of machine learning and knowledge extraction: From machine learning to explainable AI. In *Machine Learning and Knowledge Extraction: Second IFIP TC 5, TC 8/WG 8.4, 8.9, TC 12/WG 12.9 International Cross-Domain Conference, CD-MAKE 2018*, Hamburg, Germany, August 27–30, 2018, Proceedings 2 (pp. 1–8). Springer International Publishing.
26. Górriz, J. M., Ramírez, J., Ortíz, A., Martinez-Murcia, F. J., Segovia, F., Suckling, J., ... & Ferrandez, J. M. (2020). Artificial intelligence within the interplay between natural and artificial computation: Advances in data science, trends and applications. *Neurocomputing*, *410*, 237–270.
27. Hamamoto, R., Suvarna, K., Yamada, M., Kobayashi, K., Shinkai, N., Miyake, M., ... & Kaneko, S. (2020). Application of artificial intelligence technology in oncology: Towards the establishment of precision medicine. *Cancers*, *12*(12), 3532.
28. Qureshi, R., Irfan, M., Gondal, T. M., Khan, S., Wu, J., Hadi, M. U., ... & Alam, T. (2023). AI in drug discovery and its clinical relevance. *Heliyon*, *9*, e17575.
29. Ding, W., Abdel-Basset, M., Hawash, H., & Ali, A. M. (2022). Explainability of artificial intelligence methods, applications and challenges: A comprehensive survey. *Information Sciences*, *615*, 238–292.
30. Antoniadi, A. M., Du, Y., Guendouz, Y., Wei, L., Mazo, C., Becker, B. A., & Mooney, C. (2021). Current challenges and future opportunities for XAI in machine learning-based clinical decision support systems: A systematic review. *Applied Sciences*, *11*(11), 5088.
31. Albahri, A. S., Duhaim, A. M., Fadhel, M. A., Alnoor, A., Baqer, N. S., Alzubaidi, L., ... & Deveci, M. (2023). A systematic review of trustworthy and explainable artificial intelligence in healthcare: Assessment of quality, bias risk, and data fusion. *Information Fusion*, *96*, 156–191.
32. Zhong, Z., Barkova, A., & Mottin, D. (2023). Knowledge-augmented graph machine learning for drug discovery: A survey from precision to interpretability. arXiv preprint arXiv:2302.08261.
33. Rachha, A., & Seyam, M. (2023). Explainable AI in education: Current trends, challenges, and opportunities. *SoutheastCon*, 2023, 232–239.
34. Payrovnaziri, S. N., Chen, Z., Rengifo-Moreno, P., Miller, T., Bian, J., Chen, J. H., ... & He, Z. (2020). Explainable artificial intelligence models using real-world electronic health record data: A systematic scoping review. *Journal of the American Medical Informatics Association*, *27*(7), 1173–1185.
35. Dhanorkar, S., Wolf, C. T., Qian, K., Xu, A., Popa, L., & Li, Y. (2021, June). Who needs to know what, when? Broadening the Explainable AI (XAI) design space by looking at explanations across the AI lifecycle. In *Designing Interactive Systems Conference 2021*, USA. (pp. 1591–1602).
36. Ahmed, I., Jeon, G., & Piccialli, F. (2022). From artificial intelligence to explainable artificial intelligence in industry 4.0: A survey on what, how, and where. *IEEE Transactions on Industrial Informatics*, *18*(8), 5031–5042.
37. Sharma, M., Goel, A. K., & Singhal, P. (2022). Explainable AI driven applications for patient care and treatment. In *Explainable AI: Foundations, Methodologies and Applications* (pp. 135–156). Cham: Springer International Publishing. doi: 10.1007/978-3-031-12807-3_7.
38. Yang, G., Ye, Q., & Xia, J. (2022). Unbox the black-box for the medical explainable AI via multi-modal and multi-centre data fusion: A mini-review, two showcases and beyond. *Information Fusion*, *77*, 29–52.
39. Santosh, K. C., Gaur, L., Santosh, K. C., & Gaur, L. (2021). Introduction to AI in public health. In *Artificial Intelligence and Machine Learning in Public Healthcare: Opportunities and Societal Impact* (pp. 1–10). doi: 10.1007/978-981-16-6768-8_1.
40. Arrieta, A. B., Díaz-Rodríguez, N., Del Ser, J., Bennetot, A., Tabik, S., Barbado, A., ... & Herrera, F. (2020). Explainable Artificial Intelligence (XAI): Concepts, taxonomies, opportunities and challenges toward responsible AI. *Information Fusion*, *58*, 82–115.

15 An In-Depth Analysis of the Potential of AIoT to Improve Agricultural Productivity and Long-Term Sustainability

Upinder Kaur and Shallu Sehgal

15.1 INTRODUCTION

The global food security concept of agriculture encompasses a wide range of challenges, including increasing yields, optimizing resource use, and ensuring environmental sustainability. It is important to recognize that these challenges are compounded by persistent issues such as plant diseases, pest outbreaks, and a lack of labor. In order to resolve these multifaceted issues, we need to adopt revolutionary approaches, especially considering that the population is estimated to rise ten billion by 2050.

During the Fourth Industrial Revolution (IR4.0), the AIoT technology suite emerges as a game-changing technology suite with profound implications for agriculture amidst the transformative landscape of the Fourth Industrial Revolution (IR4.0). AIoT is the confluence of AI technologies with the IoT technology. The IoT approach helps to collecting, analyzing, and querying about refining actionable insights in real time, thereby enhancing productivity levels and advancing sustainability initiatives at the same time. The implementation of AIoT in agriculture is at an early stage, despite countries such as the United States and South Korea taking pioneering steps.

A critical examination of AIoT's untapped potential within the agricultural ecosystem is presented in this paper. By incorporating AI and IoT, it reimagines conventional agricultural techniques and transforms yields and sustainability at the same time. Adaptive resource management and precision agriculture are among the AIoT applications investigated in this study. Furthermore, this study analyzes the hurdles, limitations, and future possibilities of AIoT incorporation into agriculture.

The objective of this analysis is to present a holistic perspective of AIoT's capabilities through a rigorous exploration of case studies, empirical findings, and contemporary trends. AIoT technology can be a linchpin for both environmental stewardship and global food security, thereby providing a solution to urgent challenges associated with agriculture.

15.2 AIOT IN SUSTAINABLE AGRICULTURE: A LAYERED APPROACH FOR DATA-DRIVEN DECISION-MAKING

In the future, one of the most potent forces will be the Artificial Intelligence of Things (AIoT). Using interdisciplinary methods in agriculture offers unmatched chances to increase yields, fix inefficiencies, and advance sustainability. This paper investigated why AIoT might be useful for changing agricultural landscapes by examining aspects designed for contemporary agriculture and presenting a multi-layered architectural argument. The AIoT paradigm is being adopted; it is not just a technology development in the agriculture industry. Data-driven, autonomous, and sustainable

DOI: 10.1201/9781003457176-15

farming techniques are being embraced. This framework is hierarchical in nature and is composed of hierarchical layers that serve various yet linked roles, such as data sources and actuation mechanisms. This research provided a systematic dissection of these to evaluate the theoretical and practical implications of AIoT in contemporary agriculture. The detailed layered approach is presented in Figure 15.1a, and the step-by-step working in different layers is shown in Figure 15.1b.

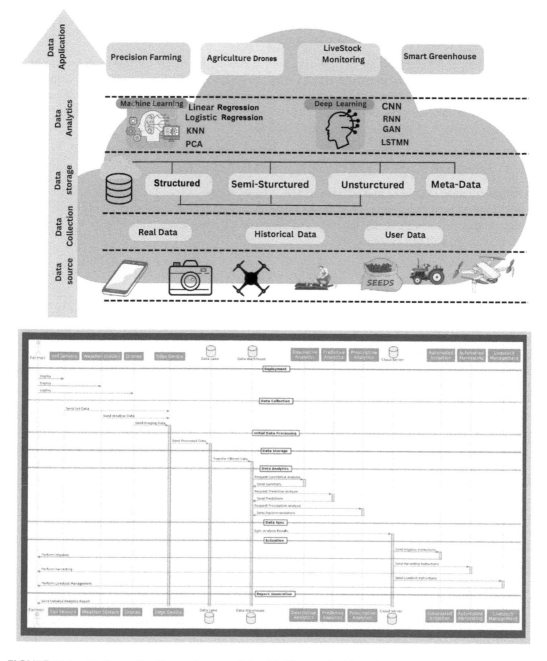

FIGURE 15.1 (a) Generalized layered approach for AIoT in sustainable agriculture. (b) Step-by-step working of AIoT model for sustainable agriculture.

15.2.1 Deployment: A Pattern of Dynamic Data Integration

AIoT's successful implementation depends on the systematic deployment of a variety of sensors (soils, climates, moistures), weather monitoring stations, and unmanned aerial vehicles equipped with advanced imaging capabilities. These instruments provide high-resolution, real-time data, which can be used as raw material for downstream analyses. There are usually three factors guiding the deployment phase: topological considerations, the target problem domain, and existing infrastructure constraints.

15.2.2 Data Collecting and Edge Computing

For aggregating and preprocessing preliminary data at this point, the AIoT framework uses edge computing architectures. Data transfer latency and network bandwidth are optimized with these edge devices strategically placed within the farming ecosystem. Furthermore, edge computing devices mitigate data degradation by conducting localized analytics, ensuring only clean, consistent, and actionable data is forwarded to deeper analysis.

15.2.3 From Data Lakes to Data Warehouses: Managing Data

A Data Lake, which is flexible and schema-less, is used to store multiple data types after initial processing. Integrating, normalizing, and transforming downstream data is critical to this phase. Data is then systematically categorized, indexed, and prepared for complex queries after being stored as preliminary data in a Data Warehouse.

15.2.4 Advanced Analytical Layers with a Trifold Approach

The AIoT framework centers on the analytics layer, which consists of a triad of descriptive, predictive, and prescriptive methodologies. Statistics are used to summarize the current state of the agrarian system through descriptive analytics. Agricultural predictive analytics use a combination of historical data and real-time inputs to forecast future agricultural conditions. A prescriptive analytics approach employs optimization algorithms and decision models to generate recommendations that are actionable and precise based on the context of the analysis.

15.2.5 Adaptive Actions and Interventions: The Actuation Paradigm

By controlling irrigation systems, harvesting equipment, precision farming, agriculture drones, smart greenhouse, and livestock management interfaces using cloud-connected actuators, the analytical insights become real-world interventions. The integration of IoT technologies with AI-based cloud services allows for more informed and responsive real-time decisions to be made and adaptive adjustments to be made, shutting down the feedback loop and realizing the full potential of IoT in agriculture.

15.3 METHODOLOGY

15.3.1 Objective

The research aimed to provide an in-depth analysis of current developments and application of Artificial Intelligence to Things (AIoT) in this smart/sustainable agriculture. Further, we aim to uncover research gaps and latent potentials associated with the deployment of AIoT technology. Research in our group focuses primarily on AIoT's deep learning applications, video surveillance technologies, and computer vision technologies. A structured framework for our study is presented

TABLE 15.1
Question for Research for SLA

Q-ID	Question for Research	Reasoning
Q1	What's the most recent domains in which AIoT has found application?	By exploring this, we contextualize and analyze the evolving landscape of AIoT subject areas.
Q2	Which specific deep learning (DL) models dominate AIoT in smart agriculture?	This inquiry uncovers widely used DL models, providing insights into their comparative efficacy.
Q3	What novel and established technologies are prevalent in AIoT for agriculture? Are there unexplored technologies for the same context?	Addressing this query offers a comprehensive overview of current and potential AIoT technologies.
Q4	How has the number of studies in similar AIoT applications trended over time?	Examining this trajectory adds a temporal dimension to our understanding of AIoT's evolving influence.

in Table 15.1, providing a framework for our research questions. Table 15.1 shows the research-based question followed in this systematic literature analysis (SLA).

15.3.2 DATABASE SEARCH AND RESEARCH INITIATION

As a first step in our research journey, we launched a comprehensive automated database search on 1 August 2023. In order to successfully search for relevant literature, we employed strategic keywords, such as "AIoT in Agriculture" and "Artificial Internet of Things or AIoT." The dynamic search explored prestigious and widely recognized databases, including IEEE Xplore, Scopus, and WoS. In Table 15.2, we have captured the breadth of our data exploration in an elegant manner, providing further insights into this research initiation process.

15.3.3 ARTICLE SELECTION CRITERIA

When selecting articles, we must ensure that the selected literature resonates with the essence of our research. The inclusion and exclusion criteria in this phase are crafted meticulously to suit the unique nature of databases. We search for insightful content in accordance with the criteria outlined in the preceding Figure 15.2.

15.3.4 EVALUATION OF QUALITY AND DATA EXTRACTION

In order to assess each article's relevance and reliability, we conducted a comprehensive quality assessment. The evaluation was composed of five questions, each with a score (yes: 1.0, partially: 0.5, no: 0). Those articles that exceeded a predetermined threshold were then included based on their cumulative score. As shown in Table 15.3, the study's objectives are aligned with the quality evaluation results shown in Table 15.4, which provide insight into the significance of these articles.

TABLE 15.2
Data Extracted Based on Keywords

Keywords	WOS	IEEE	SCOPUS
"AIoT" or "Artificial Internet of Things"	443	324	230
Artificial Internet of Things & Agriculture	27	114	70

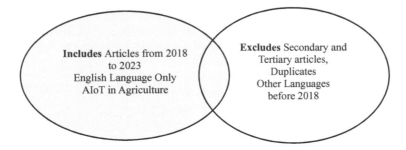

FIGURE 15.2   Inclusion and exclusion criteria for article selection.

TABLE 15.3
Article Quality Evaluation Criteria

QID	Article Evaluation Criteria
A.	Does the study specify its goals in detail?
B.	Do the research articles questionnaire get clearly reported?
C.	Is the article's use of ML/DL/AI/Hybrid algorithms effective?
D.	Is the experiment reported in a well-structured manner?
E.	Do the findings validate the study's pertinent aspects?

TABLE 15.4
Quality Evaluation of Selected Research Articles

ID	Scope	Score	Reference
1	Edge Computing platform to predict low temperatures in agriculture using deep learning	3.5	[1]
2	AIoT based Smart Agriculture for Pest Detection	5.0	[2]
3	Smart Aquaculture farm management using IoT & AI	3.5	[3]
4	Agriculture IoT applications	3.0	[4]
5	AIoT based Smart Live-stock surveillance using Deep Networks	4.5	[5]
6	AIoT for Tea Plant	4.0	[6]
7	AIoT based Indoor Planting Model	3.5	[7]
8	AIoT for Precision Agriculture	4.0	[8]
9	AIoT based crop recommendation	4.5	[9]
10	AIoT based Plant Growth Inspection	4.5	[10]
11	AIoT based Smart Irrigation	4.0	[11]

There are a total of five points awarded to each article based on the sum of the values derived from the responses. When a study's objectives and the results are aligned, it is considered to be a score of 1.0, while when a score is 0.0, it is considered a score of 0.0. The threshold score was set at 0.5 in order to maintain equilibrium. Therefore, this study only included articles that exceeded this threshold.

It is anticipated that these meticulously curated articles will play a fundamental role in the subsequent phases of our research in examining AIoT applications in smart agriculture. There is no doubt that this deliberate selection contributes to an improved understanding of the revolutionary nature of the technology that is reshaping the future landscape of agriculture in ways that we have never seen before.

15.3.5 TOP KEYWORDS ANALYSIS

Technology is rapidly reshaping industries around the world, and several profound keywords have emerged as pivotal drivers for innovation and transformation. At the forefront of these keywords is IoT, a platform that enables the interchange of results, enables remote monitoring, and enables seamless interconnection of devices and systems. As the IoT matures, AIoT becomes more sophisticated through the integration of AI technologies. Both have evolved along with sensors, which provide a platform for real-time data acquisition and seamless connection to IoT systems, which can then be analyzed for insights. Edge computing emerged because of the proliferation of data from these interconnected devices. With this approach, not only is latency reduced, but network bandwidth is also optimized, resulting in more efficient analysis and decisions. Privacy preservation is a paramount concern amidst these remarkable technological advances. It has become increasingly important to ensure robust privacy measures as more and more devices collect and share personal information. Technology and framework advancements that preserve privacy are essential to safeguarding sensitive data and establishing user trust. After a thorough exploration, we found 161 unique keywords grouped into 12 clusters, further enriching the landscape. Smart cities, energy efficiency, and wireless sensor networks are among the topics covered by Cluster 1, which consists of 19 items. Meanwhile, Cluster 2, containing 17 elements, covers areas such as machine learning, data analytics, and cloud computing. With each cluster representing a niche within the broader ecosystem, the intricate interplay of these clusters highlights the multifaceted nature of the technological landscape. Through the fusion of IoT, artificial intelligence, sensors, edge computing, and privacy considerations, connected systems and smart technologies will not only drive innovation but also establish ethical, regulatory, and societal frameworks that will govern the future of connected systems and intelligent technologies. The outcomes are given in Figure 15.3.

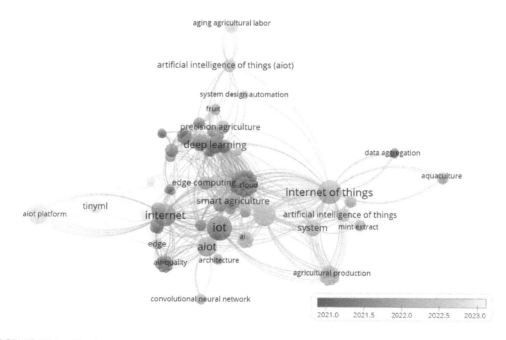

FIGURE 15.3 Top keywords analysis using VOSviewer.

15.4 ML/DL/AI APPROACHES IN AIOT IN AGRICULTURE

In modern agriculture, the confluence of machine learning and deep learning solutions and combined approaches has sparked a transformational revolution. These innovative approaches serve agricultural businesses in a variety of ways, each of which fosters innovation and efficiency through their distinct capabilities.

15.4.1 Machine Learning Techniques

Convolutional neural networks (CNNs) exemplify the highly advanced machine learning techniques of this revolution. Agribusiness innovation has been driven by networks based on AlexNet, VGG16, and InceptionV3. Applications such as Plant Disease Classification, Seed Classification, Crop Classification, Weed Identification, and Land Cover Classification utilize CNNs to uncover intricate patterns in visual data. In addition, Support Vector Machines (SVMs), Naïve-Bayes, and K-Nearest Neighbors are applicable to a wide variety of disciplines, including Soil Moisture Estimation, Stress Detection, and Disease Identification, addressing linear and non-linear data scenarios. With ML techniques, farmers are able to make informed decisions, develop precise agricultural practices, and maximize their productivity through informed decisions [4,12,13].

15.4.2 Deep Learning Approaches

Deep learning is paving the way for a paradigm shift in the agricultural sector, as it thrives in applications that require predictive abilities. Land Cover Classification, Agricultural Yield and Price Forecasting, Disease Localization, and Nutrient Analysis are all examples of applications of Networks of Recurrent Neural Networks (RNNs) and Long-Short-Term Memory (LSTM) in Time Series Analysis and Forecasting. Agribusiness benefits from improved resource allocation, strategic planning, and risk mitigation through this predictive capability. A wide range of neural networks, including Neural Networks (NNs), Deep networks (DNNs), and Convolutional Networks (CNNs), are revolutionizing Weed Control through plant identification, image recognition, and weed management. Neural Networks, Robotics, Machine Learning, and Cloud Computing are driving agricultural efficiency and data-driven decisions with Neural Networks, Robotics, Machine Learning, and Cloud Computing [2,14–17]. Further the author in [18] worked in the reliable crop prediction using the AI.

15.4.3 Hybrid Approaches

Combining the strength of ML/DL paradigms, Hybrid Strategies tackle multifaceted agricultural production challenges in a seamless way. Weed Control, Advanced Crop Management, and Robotic Harvesting can be improved by combining Convolutional Networks (CNNs) and Recurrent Networks (RNNs), which facilitates superior feature extraction and sequential data analysis. For climate prediction, examples include Empirical Mode Decomposition (EMD) coupled with Gated Recurrent Units (GRUs), which bridge the gap between ML and DL. Transformative solutions are created when these approaches are effectively combined [1,11,14,16].

15.4.4 AIoT Approaches in Sustainable Agriculture

There are five primary domains in which AIoT can be utilized to advance agriculture: disease detection and tracking, farm mechanization, live monitoring, weather predictions, crop suggestions, and livestock supervision. Table 15.5 provides further details.

TABLE 15.5

Summary of Research Paper Selected for under AIoT in Agriculture

Year	Techniques Based on AI/ML/DL	Application Domain	Key Findings	Ref
2017	AIoT	Precision Agriculture	Efficient resource management and scheduling for AIoT in agriculture.	[19]
2017	AI - Open Grid Services Architecture (OGSA)	Application	Utilizing service-oriented grid methods for efficient AIoT applications.	
2020	DL - YOLOv3, Long Short-Term Memory (LSTM)	Smart Agricultural	AIoT-based pest detection using deep learning for improved agriculture.	[2]
2020	AI - Routing with Energy Awareness Using a Grid-based Data Aggregation Scheme (EGDAS-RPL)	Agriculture	Energy-aware data aggregation for efficient IoT in agriculture.	[20]
2021	AIoT/IoT	Application	Exploration of AIoT applications and progress in various agriculture domains.	[4]
2021	DL/AIoT	Smart Livestock	Integrating deep networks for robust and semantic-aware livestock monitoring.	[16]
2021	AI - Blockchain and Security	Secure Approach	Secure authentication using blockchain for AIoT based agriculture applications.	[21]
2021	ML - Leaf based detection model presented for Rice crop	Disease Detection	ML algorithms for rice leaf disease detection in agriculture.	[13]
2021	AIoT/ IoT	Application	AIoT applications in particulate matter monitoring and control.	[8]
2021	AI Systems for Industrial Automation Control (IACS), and Systems for Agricultural Automation Control (AACS)	Application, Agriculture	Security assessment of AIoT applications in industrial and agriculture sectors.	[22]
2022	AIoT/IoT	Precision Agriculture	Framework for AIoT in precision agriculture for enhanced operations.	[1]
2022	Ml/DL - Crop recommendation system	Application	Utilizing ML/DL for effective crop recommendation in agriculture.	[9]
2022	AIoT	Smart applications	Robotic transcription of drums based on the AIoT and employing convolutional neural networks.	[23]
2022	AIoT/IoT	Application	Integrated AIoT environment for river flood prevention.	[24]
2022	AIoT/IoT	Precision Agriculture	For intelligent greenhouse orchid growth observation, apply self-supervised learning.	[15]
2022	AI - Case-Based Reasoning (CBR)	Indoor Planting	AI-based indoor planting model for *Mentha spicata*.	[7]
2022	AI and IoT	System Design Automation	Automating the design of IoT systems using AI methods.	[25]
2022	AIoT	aquaculture farm	IoT and AI development for smart aquaculture farm management.	[3]

(Continued)

TABLE 15.5 (*Continued*)
Summary of Research Paper Selected for under AIoT in Agriculture

Year	Techniques Based on AI/ML/DL	Application Domain	Key Findings	Ref
2022	AIoT	Smart Agriculture	Design and implementation of AIoT for tea plantation management.	[6]
2023	AIoT	Smart Agriculture	Recent advancements and challenges in AIoT applications for smart agriculture.	[26]
2023	AIoT/IIoT/IoT	smart agriculture	Trends and challenges in implementing AIoT in smart agriculture.	[14]
2023	AI - Agricultural Resource Hierarchy Model (ARHM)	Agriculture	Design and optimization of AIoT platform for agricultural applications.	[27]
2023	AI - autonomous mobile robot (AMR)	Agriculture	Autonomous mobile robot system for collecting pitayas using the Internet of Things.	[28]
2023	AIoT based on low power consumption devices to manage Smart GreenHouse	Sustainable Agriculture	Assessment of low-power electronics for the creation of smart greenhouses.	[29]
2023	ML - Hybrid optimised approach for monitoring the soil moisture content using SVM and optimization	Soil Monitoring	Soil moisture content prediction using optimized SVM for tea plantation.	[12]

15.4.4.1   In Accordance with Sustainable Agriculture, AIoT Technology Can Be Applied to Identify Diseases and Monitor Plant Health

Through deep learning algorithms and crop imagery, farmers and researchers can detect the first signs of infection quickly, enabling them to take action quickly. Crop inspections using AI technology are far more efficient than previous approaches, like manual inspections, which are often laborious and inaccurate due to their limited efficiency. Using this approach, early detection of diseases is made possible, allowing farmers to respond promptly and effectively to problems that arise due to the early detection of disease. A crop's output can be significantly boosted with AIoT, while chemical intervention has a less harmful impact on the environment as a result.

15.4.4.2   The Automation of Farm Equipment Based on AIoT Offers Great Potential for Sustainability in Agriculture

These innovative machines can plant, weed, and harvest crops independently. Agricultural machines are trained to navigate complex agricultural terrain with the help of deep learning algorithms. As a result, they are able to operate autonomously based on this principle. Real-time sensor data used by autonomous machines can reach conclusions based on current data. An efficient and more effective use of resources may have a number of benefits associated with it: reduced labor costs, higher operational efficiency, and better use of resources. Investing heavily in autonomous robotic technology will enable modern farms to increase their productivity, which in turn will contribute to the sustainability of agricultural practices and thereby increase their profitability.

15.4.4.3 Improving the Efficiency of Agricultural Data Analysis: AIoT-Driven Data Analysis Is an Integral Part of Advancing Sustainable Agriculture

Deep learning algorithms can predict several critical aspects of crop management with high accuracy. Sensor data can be used to predict crop quality, soil health, and agricultural production. Through these predictive capabilities, irrigation schedules can be optimized, fertilizer applied judiciously, and crop production can be more efficient. Furthermore, AI-driven data analysis allows proactive intervention by identifying crop disorders and pests in real time. Sustainable agriculture is advanced through the use of this wealth of information, enhancing crop selection and strategic marketing.

15.4.4.4 Achieving Quality Agriculture Using Weather Forecasting Systems: AIoT Has a Profound Impact on Enhancing Weather Forecasting Capabilities

Forecasting weather patterns and meteorological events with AIoT assists farmers in making informed decisions. Data from weather stations and satellite sources are used by farmers to optimize planting, irrigation, and harvesting strategies. It is possible to schedule irrigation more efficiently and allocate resources more efficiently thanks to the predictive capability. Farmers can also adapt to climate change by using connected farms, which will improve weather forecast accuracy. Resilient, sustainable agriculture promotes crop growth and minimizes stress on crops.

15.4.4.5 Managing Livestock: A Crucial Area of Smart/Sustainable Agriculture, Livestock Management, Benefits Greatly from AIoT

Real-time tracking of livestock health and well-being is possible with sensors and wearable devices integrated with IoT. The technology also allows early detection of diseases as well as prompt intervention and prevention of disease spread within herds. The AIoT also reduces waste and conserves resources by optimizing the distribution of livestock feed. Increasing resource efficiency and ensuring animal welfare are the cornerstones of sustainable livestock farming.

This will enhance the management of livestock and sustainable agriculture. Applications such as these illustrate AIoT's role in resource stewardship, reducing environmental impact, and improving efficiency. With the seamless integration of AIoT into agricultural and livestock practices, we can secure food security and the planet's well-being for future generations through a transition to sustainable food production and environmental stewardship.

15.5 CASE STUDY: MONITORING OF SOIL HEALTH AND NUTRIENT MANAGEMENT USING AIOT

For long-term productivity and environmental conservation, sustainable agriculture requires healthy soil ecosystems. An AIoT case study presented in this section illustrates how AIoT can contribute to sustainable agricultural practices through soil health monitoring and nutrient management. The detailed working of this is presented in Figure 15.4.

15.5.1 It Is Often Difficult to Capture the Dynamic Nature of Soil Conditions Using Traditional Soil Health Assessment Methods, Which Lack Real-Time Insights

Reduced crop yields and environmental degradation can result from soil nutrient imbalances. Using AIoT technologies, this case study creates a nutrient management system and soil health monitoring system to address these challenges.

15.5.2 Implementation

To implement the project, a network of IoT sensors was placed across a farmland area to monitor key soil parameters, such as pH levels, moisture levels, temperature, and nutrient concentrations. Continuous data collection from these sensors was transmitted to a cloud-based AI platform for analysis.

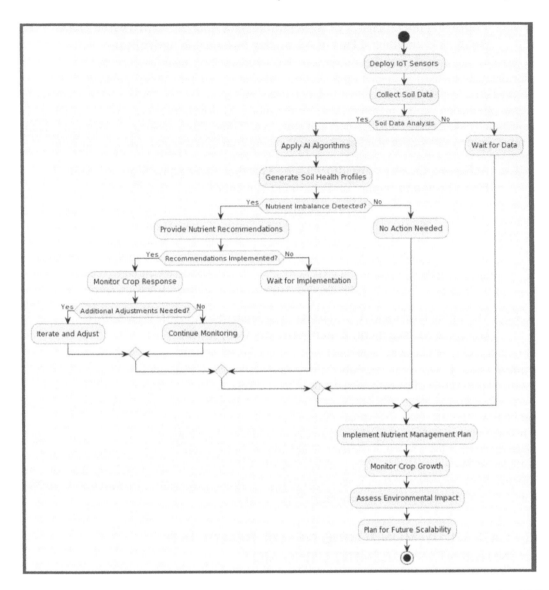

FIGURE 15.4 Flowchart for the case study: Monitoring of soil health and nutrient management using AIoT.

15.5.3 INTELLIGENT SOIL ANALYSIS

Using the AI algorithms that have been integrated into the system, the system generates soil health profiles based on the collected data. An artificial intelligence model has been trained to recognize patterns of nutrient deficiencies and imbalances in order to detect them earlier and provide precise recommendations based on them.

15.5.4 NUTRIENT MANAGEMENT

The system provides farmers with customized nutrient management recommendations based on AI-generated soil health profiles that are generated by the system. Among these recommendations were optimal fertilization schedules and specific nutrient formulations that were tailored to fit the specific needs of each soil area, allowing for optimum crop growth while reducing the need for excessive fertilization.

15.5.5 Impact on the Environment

The AIoT-enabled approach reduces the risk of nutrient runoff into water bodies by ensuring that nutrient applications are aligned with the actual soil requirements. Consequently, water quality will be improved and ecological disturbances will be reduced.

15.5.6 Implications: This Innovative Case Study Opens Doors for Further Development

The analysis of soil health may be refined by incorporating satellite data in future iterations. Moreover, AI-powered predictive models could predict soil health trends and provide proactive recommendations.

The AIoT-enabled soil health monitoring and nutrient management case study demonstrates the potential of combining AI and IoT to address critical sustainability challenges. The beneficial effects of this innovative approach include cultivating healthier soils, optimizing nutrient use, and contributing to sustainable agricultural practices by offering real-time insights and precise recommendations.

Working: Through AIoT-enabled processes, soil health and nutrient management are optimized for sustainable agriculture. An IoT sensor is deployed to collect crucial data from the soil at the beginning of the flowchart. Based on the available data, the AI algorithms generate soil health profiles, revealing vital information about soil health. Following this, nutrient imbalances are detected and tailored recommendations are made for nutrient management. Monitoring crop responses is crucial once these recommendations have been implemented. An iterative approach ensures optimal crop growth and health by refining the nutrient management plan as necessary. The waiting period is factored in when recommendations aren't implemented right away. The process shifts from detection to anticipation and readiness if no nutrient imbalances are detected or soil data are not available. Monitoring crop growth and assessing the environmental impact of nutrient management take center stage. Toward the end of the process, scalability of the AIoT-enabled system is considered, including plans to improve soil health monitoring and nutrient management. The flowchart depicts an overall picture of how informed decision-making is emphasized, iterative adjustments are made, and sustainable agricultural practices are implemented over time.

15.6 OPEN ISSUES AND CHALLENGES

15.6.1 Security, Privacy, and Interoperability

With AIoT, data-rich devices combine with intelligent algorithms, putting data privacy and security at risk. To ensure unauthorized access and cyber threats are thwarted, these devices gather intricate agricultural data. Furthermore, different communication protocols and data formats used by different devices make seamless data exchange difficult. Data interoperability and stronger security can only be achieved by establishing standardized communication protocols.

15.6.2 Agrarian Landscape and Energy Efficiency

Access to the internet is often intermittent in remote pockets of the agrarian landscape. For consistent and resilient internet access, substantial investments in network infrastructure are required. Furthermore, AIoT devices should emphasize energy efficiency in order to minimize their ecological footprint. A symbiotic strategy for reducing environmental impact and extending device operation combines renewable energy with energy efficiency.

15.6.3 An AIoT Solution's Adaptability, Scalability, and Accessibility

The field of agriculture spans a variety of practices, geographic conditions, and crop varieties, making it necessary for AIoT solutions to adapt to these conditions. To ensure relevance across heterogeneous farming methods and ecological conditions, solutions must be both flexible and robust in scalability. For resource-constrained farmers and regions, it is essential to develop AIoT solutions that are accessible. Affordable solutions that are tailored to farmers' needs encourage a broader adoption of agriculture.

15.6.4 EMPOWERING SKILLS AND FINDING ETHICAL SOLUTIONS

AIoT technologies introduce ethical considerations such as data ownership, consent, and disruptions to traditional agricultural operations. Frameworks that define ethical pathways for data use need to be articulated well. Additionally, farmers need to be trained to operate and maintain AIoT devices proficiently in order to facilitate successful integration. In order to strengthen the link between technology and practical application, comprehensive training initiatives are necessary.

15.6.5 DATA QUALITY & ACTIONABLE INSIGHTS IN AIoT

In order to make informed decisions with AIoT devices, it is vital to have a high-quality dataset. In order for insights to be fidelity-oriented, sensor data must be precise, noise interference must be managed, and outliers must be handled adeptly. Agricultural productivity is enhanced when farmers make well-informed decisions regarding irrigation, fertilization, and other pivotal practices.

15.6.6 AFFORDABILITY AND SUSTAINABILITY

Despite AIoT's transformative potential, its financial viability depends on its affordability, especially among smaller farmers. Financial barriers can be overcome by crafting economical solutions that integrate renewable energy. Achieving long-term sustainability of AIoT within the agriculture domain can also be enhanced by embedding energy-efficient practices and technologies.

15.6.7 AIoT REGULATION AND RESPONSIBLE INNOVATION

It is vital for regulatory frameworks to be designed with data sharing, privacy protections, safety benchmarks, and environmental considerations in mind when navigating the extremely complex field of AIoT in agriculture. For the adoption of AIoT to be ethical and responsible, it is imperative that we achieve the delicate balance between fostering innovation and cultivating a robust regulatory environment.

For successful AIoT integration into sustainable agriculture, a holistic approach, combining technological prowess, ethical clarity, and regulatory foresight, is key. Through judicious navigation, the union of AI and IoT technologies can reshape farming practices while upholding privacy, ensuring security, and ushering in a new era of responsible innovation.

Top of Form

15.7 CONCLUSION

As a final reflection, this study emphasizes how AIoT continues to evoke interest and fusion across numerous sectors, with a particular focus on its application in smart agriculture. This technological fusion has gained accelerated momentum in recent years as evidenced by the exponential rise in research articles on AIoT's utility in agriculture. AIoT engenders a sophisticated paradigm for agriculture by symbiotically combining the concept of artificial intelligence with that of IoT. Data-driven discernment combines real-time data assimilation, fluid automation, and data-driven analytics for the potential to reinvent classical agricultural paradigms. This comprehensive exploration highlights a number of advantages, but challenges remain. AIoT can be difficult to integrate unless comprehensive frameworks and cogent mechanisms are established to guide its seamless adoption. As well as the daunting technological challenges, there are also a plethora of challenges surrounding data privacy, security imperatives, and the need to ensure a solid infrastructure. There are many challenges that face AIot as it evolves rapidly, but a concerted approach to addressing these challenges is crucial to unlocking its latent potential to usher in sustainable and efficacious agricultural practices, allowing technology and agriculture to work harmoniously together.

REFERENCES

1. M. A. Guillen et al., "Performance evaluation of edge-computing platforms for the prediction of low temperatures in agriculture using deep learning," *J. Supercomput.*, vol. 77, no. 1, pp. 818–840, 2021, doi: 10.1007/s11227-020-03288-w.
2. C. J. Chen, Y. Y. Huang, Y. S. Li, C. Y. Chang, and Y. M. Huang, "An AIoT based smart agricultural system for pests detection," *IEEE Access*, vol. 8, pp. 180750–180761, 2020, doi: 10.1109/ACCESS.2020.3024891.
3. M. C. Chiu, W. M. Yan, S. A. Bhat, and N. F. Huang, "Development of smart aquaculture farm management system using IoT and AI-based surrogate models," *J. Agric. Food Res.*, vol. 9, 2022, doi: 10.1016/j.jafr.2022.100357.
4. C. T. Yang, H. W. Chen, E. J. Chang, E. Kristiani, K. L. P. Nguyen, and J. S. Chang, "Current advances and future challenges of AIoT applications in particulate matters (PM) monitoring and control," *J. Hazard. Mater.*, vol. 419, 2021, doi: 10.1016/j.jhazmat.2021.126442.
5. W.-T. Su, L.-Y. Jiang, T.-H. O, Y.-C. Lin, M.-H. Hung, and C.-C. Chen, "AIoT-Cloud-integrated smart livestock surveillance via assembling deep networks with considering robustness and semantics availability," *IEEE Robot. Autom. Lett.*, vol. 6, no. 4, pp. 6140–6147, 2021, doi: 10.1109/LRA.2021.3090453.
6. C. L. Chang, C. C. Huang, and H. W. Chen, "Design and implementation of artificial intelligence of things for tea (Camellia sinensis L.) grown in a plant factory," *Agronomy-Basel*, vol. 12, no. 10, 2022, doi: 10.3390/agronomy12102384.
7. H. H. Ku, C. H. Liu, and W. C. Wang, "Design of an artificial intelligence of things based indoor planting model for mentha spicata," *Processes*, vol. 10, no. 1, 2022, doi: 10.3390/pr10010116.
8. D. Murugan, A. Garg, and D. Singh, "Development of an adaptive approach for precision agriculture monitoring with drone and satellite data," *IEEE J. Sel. Top. Appl. Earth Obs. Remote Sens.*, vol. 10, no. 12, pp. 5322–5328, 2017, doi: 10.1109/JSTARS.2017.2746185.
9. D. Muhammed, E. Ahvar, S. Ahvar, and M. Trocan, "A user-friendly AIoT-based crop recommendation system (UACR): Concept and architecture," *2022 16th International Conference on Signal-Image Technology and Internet-Based Systems (SITIS)*. ISEP, Paris, France, pp. 569–576, 2022, doi: 10.1109/SITIS57111.2022.00091.
10. L.-B. Chen, G.-Z. Huang, X.-R. Huang, and W.-C. Wang, "A self-supervised learning-based intelligent greenhouse orchid growth inspection system for precision agriculture," *IEEE Sens. J.*, vol. 22, no. 24, pp. 24567–24577, 2022, doi: 10.1109/JSEN.2022.3221960.
11. M. Rath, S. S. Tripathy, N. Tripathy, C. R. Panigrahi, and B. Pati, *AIoT-based water management and IoT-based smart irrigation system: Effective in smart agriculture*, vol. 57. DRIEMS Autonomous, Dept Comp Sci & Engn, Tangi, Odisha, India, 2022.
12. D. Yin, Y. Wang, and Y. Huang, "Predicting soil moisture content of tea plantation using support vector machine optimized by arithmetic optimization algorithm," *J. Algorithms Comput. Technol.*, vol. 17, no. 2, 2023, doi: 10.1177/17483026221151198.
13. B. Kiranmai, S. Venu Vasantha, and S. Rama Krishna, "Techniques for rice leaf disease detection using machine learning algorithms," *Artic. Int. J. Eng. Tech. Res.*, 2021, www.ijert.org.
14. K. M. Hou, X. Diao, H. Shi, H. Ding, H. Zhou, and C. de Vaulx, "Trends and challenges in AIoT/IIoT/IoT implementation," *Sensors*, vol. 23, no. 11, p. 5074, 2023, doi: 10.3390/s23115074.
15. L. B. Chen, G. Z. Huang, X. R. Huang, and W. C. Wang, "A self-supervised learning-based intelligent greenhouse orchid growth inspection system for precision agriculture," *IEEE Sens. J.*, vol. 22, no. 24, pp. 24567–24577, 2022, doi: 10.1109/JSEN.2022.3221960.
16. W. T. Su, L. Y. Jiang, O. Tang-Hsuan, Y. C. Lin, M. H. Hung, and C. C. Chen, "AIoT-cloud-integrated smart livestock surveillance via assembling deep networks with considering robustness and semantics availability," *IEEE Robot. Autom. Lett.*, vol. 6, no. 4, pp. 6140–6147, 2021, doi: 10.1109/LRA.2021.3090453.
17. Y. Yi, M. Lu, L. H. Wu, and Z. G. Chen, "AIoT-based drum transcription robot using convolutional neural networks," *4th International Conference on Informatics Engineering and Information Science (ICIEIS 2021)*, vol. 12161, no. 4, Alibaba Inc, Hangzhou, Zhejiang, Peoples R China, 2022, doi: 10.1117/12.2627208.

18. S. S. Yamaç, "Artificial intelligence methods reliably predict crop evapotranspiration with different combinations of meteorological data for sugar beet in a semiarid area," *Agric. Water Manag.*, vol. 254, p. 106968, 2021, doi: 10.1016/j.agwat.2021.106968.

19. M. Rahmouni, M. Hanifi, C. Savaglio, G. Fortino, and M. Ghogho, "An AIoT framework for precision agriculture," In *2022 IEEE International Conference on Dependable, Autonomic and Secure Computing, International Conference on Pervasive Intelligence and Computing, International Conference on Cloud and Big Data Computing, International Conference on Cyber Science and Technology Congress (DASC/PiCom/CBDCom/CyberSciTech)*, Sep. 2022, pp. 1–6, doi: 10.1109/DASC/PiCom/CBDCom/Cy55231.2022.9927989.

20. S. Sankar, P. Srinivasan, A. K. Luhach, R. Somula, and N. Chilamkurti, "Energy-aware grid-based data aggregation scheme in routing protocol for agricultural internet of things," *Sustain. Comput. Informatics Syst.*, vol. 28, p. 100422, 2020, doi: 10.1016/j.suscom.2020.100422.

21. M. Wazid, A. K. Das, and Y. Park, "Blockchain-envisioned secure authentication approach in AIoT: Applications, challenges, and future research," *Wirel. Commun. Mob. Comput.*, vol. 2021, pp. 1–19, 2021, doi: 10.1155/2021/3866006.

22. E. Kristen, R. Kloibhofer, V. H. Díaz, and P. Castillejo, "Security assessment of agriculture IoT (AIoT) applications," *Appl. Sci.*, vol. 11, no. 13, p. 5841, 2021, doi: 10.3390/app11135841.

23. L. Emmi, M. Gonzalez-de-Soto, G. Pajares, and P. Gonzalez-de-Santos, "New trends in robotics for agriculture: Integration and assessment of a real fleet of robots," *Sci. World J.*, vol. 2014, pp. 1–21, 2014, doi: 10.1155/2014/404059.

24. Z. Boulouard, M. Ouaissa, M. Ouaissa, F. Siddiqui, M. Almutiq, and M. Krichen, "An integrated artificial intelligence of things environment for river flood prevention," *Sensors*, vol. 22, no. 23, p. 9485, 2022, doi: 10.3390/s22239485.

25. Y. Q. Zou and L. Quan, "Resource management and scheduling policy based on grid for AIoT," *Mod. Phys. Lett. B*, vol. 31, no. 19–21, 2017, doi: 10.1142/S0217984917400668.

26. H. K. Adli, et al., "Recent advancements and challenges of AIoT application in smart agriculture: A review," *Sensors*, vol. 23, no. 7, p. 3752, 2023, doi: 10.3390/s23073752.

27. Y. Chen, Y. Ning, Z. Chai, and H. Rangwala, "Federated multi-task learning with hierarchical attention for sensor data analytics," *Proceedings of International Joint Conference on Neural Networks*, 2020, doi: 10.1109/IJCNN48605.2020.9207508.

28. L. B. Chen, X. R. Huang, and W. H. Chen, "Design and implementation of an artificial intelligence of things-based autonomous mobile robot system for pitaya harvesting," *IEEE Sens. J.*, vol. 23, no. 12, pp. 13220–13235, 2023, doi: 10.1109/JSEN.2023.3270844.

29. A. Alzuhair and A. Alghaihab, "The design and optimization of an acoustic and ambient sensing AIoT platform for agricultural applications," *Sensors*, vol. 23, no. 14, 2023, doi: 10.3390/s23146262.

16 Introduction to Deployable AI for Cutting-Edge Technologies
An Overview, Scope, Opportunities, and Challenges

Aayushi Goenka, Shobhit Srivastava, and A. Helen Victoria

16.1 INTRODUCTION

Interpreting chest X-rays is a critical component of medical diagnostics, playing a pivotal role in the timely and accurate identification of various thoracic diseases. However, traditional human interpretation of these images is not without its limitations. It is inherently subjective, often time-consuming, and susceptible to errors stemming from factors like fatigue and variations in expertise. In the pursuit of enhancing this process, our proposed system harnesses the capabilities of CV [1] and NLP to automatically generate meaningful captions for chest X-ray images [2–4]. This innovative approach aims to provide valuable support to radiologists and healthcare professionals in their decision-making processes. The foundation of our system lies in a meticulously trained algorithm, which has been exposed to an extensive dataset of annotated chest X-rays and their corresponding captions. Through this training, the algorithm has acquired the ability to comprehend the intricate details present in these medical images and translate them into coherent, standardized textual descriptions. By doing so, it not only expedites the interpretation process but also elevates the correctness and the generated reports' consistency. The potential impact of our system on healthcare is profound. By reducing the potential for misdiagnosis and enhancing the quality of medical reports, we aim to improve patient outcomes significantly. Additionally, the efficiency brought by automation can lead to cost savings in the healthcare sector, relieving some of the burdens associated with escalating expenditures.

Furthermore, our approach employs an encoder-decoder architecture for captioning of the image, representing a notable advancement in the application of artificial intelligence in healthcare [5]. This technology not only streamlines the interpretation of chest X-rays but also augments the capabilities of healthcare professionals, allowing them to provide more accurate diagnoses and reducing the risk of misdiagnosis.

In conclusion, our innovative system holds the promise to revolutionize the field of radiology by offering healthcare professionals a powerful and efficient tool. It aligns with the broader trend of harnessing AI to enhance medical diagnostics and enhance patient care. By automating and standardizing the interpretation of chest X-rays, our approach seeks to usher in a new era of precision medicine, ultimately benefitting both healthcare providers and the patients they serve.

16.2 LITERATURE SURVEY

The literature survey delves into the realm of automated medical report generation [6], image captioning [7,8], and encoder-decoder architectures, with a particular emphasis on the ChexNet [9] framework. These technologies hold tremendous potential to revolutionize the field of medical imaging diagnosis and patient care. Several research papers are highlighted for their valuable contributions to

DOI: 10.1201/9781003457176-16

this evolving field. One notable study, referenced as [10], introduces a ground-breaking approach that combines deep learning and NLP to generate accurate reports from complex medical images. In reference [11], the "TieNet" framework harnesses both image and textual data to classify and report thorax diseases, thereby improving diagnostic accuracy and consistency. This approach not only benefits healthcare providers but also encourages knowledge sharing among them. Additionally, the same study showcases that deep neural networks are being used to identify hip fractures. in X-ray images, achieving radiologist-level accuracy. This innovation is particularly promising for resource-limited settings, as it accelerates diagnosis and enhances precision in patient care. In another key contribution from reference [12], the FHDO Biomedical Computer Science Group focuses on caption prediction using CNNs and LSTM-RNNs. Their research emphasizes the significance of data pre-processing, hybrid models, and transfer learning techniques, which collectively enhance the generation of meaningful captions. This not only reduces interpretation time but also elevates the quality of medical reports, ultimately streamlining healthcare workflows. Work contributed by reference [13] helps us draw the conclusion that data pre-processing is vital in such a problem statement. References [14,15] also make use of LSTM solidifying its credibility. Reference [16] helps us understand image recognition in a large dataset containing varying sets of images. Additionally, Reference [17] presents an innovative method for automating medical report production from chest X-ray images. Employing a dual-word LSTM, this approach generates more diverse and unbiased paragraphs, leading to improved report quality. Clinicians and patients alike stand to benefit from the resulting clarity and accuracy in medical documentation. The literature review also spotlights the "Show and Tell" approach, which utilizes encoder-decoder architectures for the generation of text reports using chest X-rays. A CNN serves as the encoder to process image data, while an LSTM-RNN acts as the decoder to generate textual descriptions. Furthermore, the integration of the "Show, Attend and Tell" model enhances caption quality through the incorporation of attention mechanisms.

Thus, the study emphasizes auto medical report creation [18], image captions, and ChexNet's encoder-decoder use. In our study, we have explored the various combinations between existing state-of-the-art CV and NLP models [19] and looked at the cross combination of different models to check which has the highest accuracy. We also go one step further by incorporating an extended feature by providing the user with an explanation of the medical terms given as well.

16.3 DATASET

16.3.1 Overview

During our research, we employed a comprehensive dataset comprising 7,470 chest X-ray images, meticulously sourced via the esteemed chest X-ray collection of Indiana University (IU Chest X-ray Dataset). This dataset proved to be an invaluable resource, enriched with a diverse array of annotations that greatly facilitated our investigative work. Among these annotations were the MTI (Medical Text Indexer) encodings, which encompassed a wide spectrum of information, including indications, findings, and impressions, all meticulously documented in textual format. To ensure the accuracy and relevance of the data, we took the step of carefully curating the dataset. This involved the systematic removal of catchphrases that might have been present in the MTI encodings, thereby ensuring that our dataset was as precise as possible. This curated dataset ultimately featured 121 distinct MTI markings, each of which provided an additional layer of contextual information, enhancing the depth of our analysis.

Furthermore, the dataset benefitted from the diligent efforts of its creators, who thoughtfully supplemented it with MEDLINE Clinical Subject Headings (Lattice) comments linked to the individual X-ray images. This additional layer of metadata not only boosted our dataset but also provided valuable insights into the clinical aspects of the chest X-rays, further enhancing the depth and context of our research.

In summation, this publicly accessible dataset represents a treasure trove of medical image data, comprising 3,955 narrative reports, each intricately linked to Lattice labels and capturing chest

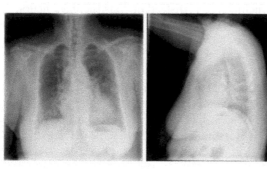

UID: CXR1001
Impression: Diffuse fibrosis. No visible focal acute disease.
Indication: dyspnea, subjective fevers, arthritis, immigrant from Bangladesh
Findings: Interstitial markings are diffusely prominent throughout both lungs. Heart size is normal. Pulmonary XXXX normal.
Problems: Markings; Fibrosis
MeSH: Markings/lung/bilateral/interstitial/diffuse/prominent; Fibrosis/diffuse

FIGURE 16.1 Indiana University chest X-ray dataset example showing an abnormal case alongside findings.

X-ray images from two distinct perspectives—namely, a posteroanterior (Dad) view and a horizontal view. In alignment with established practices in the field, we treated the specialist's report as a composite entity, encapsulating both impressions and findings, thus enabling a comprehensive and nuanced analysis of the chest X-ray images.

In leveraging this meticulously curated and richly annotated dataset, our research endeavors were significantly bolstered, enabling us to explore the field of medical image analysis in greater depth and contribute to the advancement of knowledge and practices in radiology and healthcare (Figure 16.1).

16.3.2 Preparation

In this research project, a dataset is being compiled that consists of XML radiology reports and their corresponding image files. The primary objective is to create a structured and well-organized dataset that seamlessly integrates both textual and image data, which can then be leveraged for subsequent analysis and the development of ML models.

To achieve this, the project utilizes the ElementTree module for parsing and navigating the hierarchical XML structure of the radiology reports [20]. Within these reports, key components such as radiological findings and the radiologist's impression are identified and extracted [21]. These extracted elements are concatenated to form an informative report column that captures the essential textual information.

Furthermore, the cv2 (OpenCV) module is employed to read the image files linked to each report. This allows for the correct association of each image with its respective report, establishing a clear connection between textual and visual data.

In addition to this, NLP techniques are applied to preprocess the textual data. This includes tasks such as tokenization, stemming, and removing stop words to make the text amenable to analysis and modeling. Additionally, all images are resized to ensure a uniform height and width, facilitating their compatibility and ease of use in subsequent stages of the project.

16.3.3 Transfer Learning Model

From [22], we gathered a list of potential methods for transfer learning. The suggested method incorporates the use of a pre-trained CheXNet model, a deep CNN with 121 layers, initially trained on the ChestX-ray14 dataset. This dataset contains over 100,000 X-ray images of the frontal view and is one of the most comprehensive freely available collections of chest X-ray images showcasing 14 distinct chest disorders. The primary objective of employing CheXNet as a pre-trained model is to tap into its learned representations and features, which encapsulate critical patterns and characteristics found in the chest X-ray images, particularly those related to the presence or absence of various diseases.

Transfer learning plays a pivotal role in this methodology. Instead of constructing a neural network from the ground up, which can be computationally expensive and data-intensive, transfer learning leverages the knowledge and features extracted by CheXNet from the ChestX-ray14 dataset. When a fresh X-ray of the chest is input into the CheXNet model, it undergoes a forward pass through the network, resulting in the generation of a numerical representation or feature vector. This feature vector encapsulates essential information about the input image, including key diagnostic indicators associated with the various chest diseases. This approach significantly expedites the development of an accurate disease detection system by improving the pre-trained CheXNet model's ability to diagnose illnesses in the images on a smaller, domain-specific dataset.

16.4   FEATURE EXTRACTION

16.4.1   FOR IMAGES

In this study, image feature extraction is accomplished by using CheXNet, a Transfer Learning model trained on a big dataset of chest X-ray images, to extract meaningful features from preprocessed images. CheXNet is used to generate feature vectors that capture essential visual patterns and attributes from chest X-ray pictures. These separate image feature vectors are then concatenated to form a single concatenated image feature vector, which represents the overall visual qualities of the chest X-rays.

1. The photos and portions of the reports serve as inputs for the model. In order for the model to make use of the information included within each photo, each image must first be converted into a vector with a predetermined size. In order to accomplish this, transfer learning will be utilized.
2. In order to extract characteristics from the photographs, we will utilize a CheXNet model that has been trained. We are not concerned with arranging the photographs; rather, our goal is to just acquire the bottleneck highlights for each one. As a result, the very final layer of the arrangement is not required. The weights that have been pre-trained will be put into our ChexNet model, and then we will start the process of extracting features from each image in our data set.
3. Each image is resized to (224,224,3) and then run through CheXNet to produce a feature vector of 1,024 bytes. Combining both of the feature vectors yields a 2,048 feature vector. As you can see, the final layer is an average pooling layer. There is a particular explanation behind this. Given that we are concatenating both images, the model may pick up on a concatenation order. For instance, image1 is typically placed before image2 or vice versa, but that is not the case in this instance. While concatenating them, we are not maintaining any order. Pooling, which generates location invariance, solves this issue.

The image's features are extracted. For later use, we will store these attributes for each image in a pickle file (Figure 16.2).

16.4.2   FOR TEXT

Caption feature extraction involves converting a textual caption into a numerical representation for machine learning tasks.

1. A tokenizer is used to extract text features from the associated reports by dividing them into smaller pieces known as tokens and turning them into numerical sequences. The tokenizer is trained using the textual reports obtained from the training data in this case, allowing it to interpret the word vocabulary and give appropriate numerical values to each word. After the training phase, the tokenizer is retained for later use, maintaining the lexical knowledge that was learned.

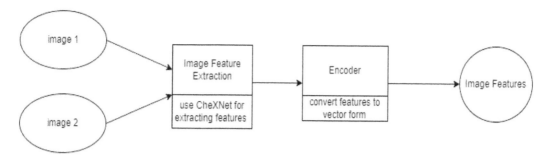

FIGURE 16.2   Diagram explaining image feature extraction.

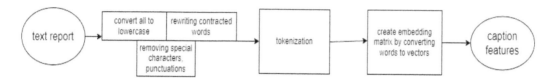

FIGURE 16.3   Caption feature extraction.

2. The use of padding is necessary in order to guarantee a length of continuous sequence, and the size of the tokenizer's vocabulary is determined by counting how many unique words are present in the tokenizer's vocabulary.

3. We then incorporate pre-trained GloVe word embeddings. GloVe word embeddings, short for Global Vectors for Word Representation, are pre-created vectors that encode word semantics. Word meanings and contextual relationships are captured in these embeddings from large text corpora. Each word is a key to a high-dimensional vector representation. GloVe embeddings preserve language semantics' subtleties, making them extraordinary. Words with comparable meanings or contexts have vectors that are geometrically close, while dissimilar words are farther away [23]. The model can understand word contextual relationships, making language translation and sentiment analysis easier. Pre-trained GloVe word embeddings provide our model with a strong understanding of medical report semantics, enabling more accurate and contextually relevant report production.

   These embeddings are simply word vectors that have already been computed, and they capture the common semantic relationships between words. Each word acts as a key to the appropriate vector representation for each embedding, which is kept in an embedding dictionary.

4. An effective approach is to create an embedding matrix, which contains vector representations for words in a vocabulary. Pre-trained words embedding models like Word2Vec, GloVe, or FastText can be used to initialize the embedding matrix. The embedding matrix is created by looking up the vector representation for each word in the pre-trained model and assigning it to the corresponding row in the matrix. This matrix then encodes captions into numerical representations by substituting each word with its corresponding vector. The resulting matrix serves as input into our DL model (Figure 16.3).

16.5   ENCODER-DECODER MODEL

After reviewing the current literature survey of our project, we concluded using an encoder-decoder architecture for our problem statement.

In order to process chest X-ray pictures in a smooth manner and generate relevant captions for them, our model makes use of an encoder-decoder architecture. This brings together two neural network components.

The image encoder, which is driven by a CNN, also performs the function of extracting visual features. It performs a rigorous analysis of the myriad of minute features that are contained within chest X-ray pictures, isolating critical visual traits and patterns that capture important medical discoveries. After that, these characteristics are compressed into a representation of the image that has a fixed-size vector, which efficiently encodes the most important information in the image.

On the other hand, the caption decoder is controlled by an RNN, and it creates captions in a sequential fashion using the encoded picture characteristics as input. It accepts the encoded image features as input. The RNN constructs captions one word at a time, considering both the visual context of the image and the linguistic context of previously generated words. This iterative procedure ultimately results in the development of textual descriptions of the X-ray pictures that are consistent with one another and contextually appropriate. Our model acquires the ability to match the extracted visual characteristics with the provided captions by undergoing training on data that has been manually annotated. This ensures that it is capable of producing medical reports that are both descriptive and instructive.

This combined architecture not only closes the information gap between medical imagery and natural language, but it also gives medical practitioners a strong tool that can increase the accuracy of the diagnosis and treatment quality they provide to their patients.

16.5.1 ENCODER

In the image captioning pipeline, the encoder serves a crucial role in extracting relevant visual information from the input image and transforming it into a condensed, meaningful representation. This process is essential for bridging the gap between the image's visual content and the generation of textual captions. In many instances, a pre-trained CNN model like CheXNet is employed as the encoder due to its effectiveness in learning hierarchical features from images. The encoding process begins with the pre-processed image as input, which has often undergone resizing, normalization, and other transformations to ensure consistency and enhance the model's performance. After that, the image is processed through a succession of layers within the CNN. These layers include convolutional layers, pooling layers, and non-linear activation functions, like ReLU.

As the image progresses through these layers, it undergoes a hierarchical transformation. Initially, the lower layers of the CNN focus on capturing low-level characteristics of the image, such as edges, textures, and simple patterns. These low-level features are essential for understanding the fundamental building blocks of the image. As the image data moves through the network, the spatial dimensions of the features decrease while the number of channels, often referred to as feature maps, increases. This transformation aids in the abstraction of visual data, gradually building more complex and high-level representations of the image. These representations encompass not only shapes and objects but also their spatial relationships within the image. The culmination of the encoding process is the extraction of a fixed-length vector known as the image feature vector or visual embedding. This vector encodes the most salient visual information from the input image. It encapsulates the image's content, its distinctive visual characteristics, and context. The image feature vector, as produced by the encoder, is crucial in the image captioning process. It is used as the model's initial input for the decoder component, acting as a bridge between the visual information extracted from the image and the generation of textual captions. This feature vector carries the rich visual context required for generating coherent and contextually relevant captions. The decoder, often implemented as an RNN or transformer-based model, takes this feature vector and generates a sequence of words that form the textual description of the image.

In essence, the encoder's role is to transform the raw visual data of an image into a compact and representative feature vector, enabling the subsequent decoding process to produce accurate and meaningful textual captions that describe the content of the image in a human-understandable way. This two-stage process of encoding and decoding forms the foundation of image captioning systems, allowing machines to explain images in natural language.

16.5.2 DECODER

The image captioning pipeline is a fascinating application of deep learning that combines CV and NLP techniques to produce image captions that are logical and contextually appropriate [19]. This process relies on a decoder, which often employs RNNs like LSTM or GRU models to achieve its goal.

The first key component of this pipeline is the encoder, which takes an input image and converts it into a feature vector. This vector encapsulates essential visual information about the image, such as objects, shapes, and textures. Importantly, this feature vector acts as the RNN decoder's initial hidden state during the caption generation phase. This initial state acts as the decoder's context or memory, allowing it to access and utilize the visual information from the image. Caption development begins with the words being represented as dense vectors in an uninterrupted space using word embeddings. The semantic and syntactic links between words are captured by these embeddings, allowing the model to comprehend the meaning and context of each word in the vocabulary. During the decoding phase, the RNN model processes these word embeddings and updates its hidden state iteratively. The current word embedding and the previous hidden state are used in combination, effectively blending information from both the visual characteristics and the words created thus far. This iterative process enables the model to dynamically adjust its predictions based on the context it has acquired. The decoder output is processed through a softmax activation function at each time interval, creating a probability distribution for the vocabulary. This distribution depicts the likelihood of each word becoming the following word in the caption. The next word is picked based on its likelihood, and its matching word embedding is given into the decoder for the subsequent time step. This decoding process continues recursively, one word at a time until a predefined end token or a maximum caption length is reached. The produced caption for the supplied image is formed by the resultant sequence of predicted words. This approach effectively marries visual information with linguistic context, ensuring that the generated captions are both accurate and contextually relevant.

In essence, the image captioning pipeline demonstrates the power of deep learning in understanding and bridging the gap between different modalities of data, in this case, images and text. By leveraging encoded image attributes and a sequential word generation process, this model can produce captions that do more than only explain the content of the image but also capture its context and nuances. This technology finds applications in various fields, from assisting the visually impaired to enhancing content accessibility and enriching user experiences in the realm of CV.

The BERT and GPT models are widely recognized transformer-based architectures that have demonstrated use in the domain of picture captioning tasks. Every model has distinct advantages and characteristics. However, they are frequently employed for the computational analysis of natural languages in diverse settings. The primary objective of BERT, an acronym for "Bidirectional Encoder Representations from Transformers," is to facilitate bidirectional context prediction inside textual data. The ability to achieve proficiency in activities including sentiment analysis, answering questions, and text categorization is facilitated by the acquisition of language comprehension through the consideration of preceding and subsequent words. Conversely, the Generative Pre-trained Transformer (GPT) has remarkable proficiency in the domain of autoregressive text generation. During this procedure, the software produces text in a sequential manner by taking into account the context from left to right. As a result of these capabilities, it demonstrates outstanding proficiency in tasks like text and dialogue generation, as well as language translation.

BERT is commonly selected as the preferred method for image captioning due to its customizable nature. While BERT's primary architecture does not encompass picture processing, it can be effectively modified for multimodal tasks by integrating its textual understanding with visual data acquired from pre-trained CNNs. Due to this amalgamation, BERT exhibits the capability to produce captions that consider both the accompanying image and the provided text, so offering a versatile solution for image captioning assignments. Researchers undergo supplementary training on pre-trained BERT models with datasets specifically designed for picture captioning. This facilitates the investigation of the relationships that are present between photos and captions. The process of fine-tuning utilizes BERT's capacity to comprehend the context from both preceding and succeeding directions, leading to the generation of captions for images that are cohesive and contextually suitable.

In practical applications, BERT models that have undergone extensive training have demonstrated comparable or even greater performance in tasks related to picture captioning. This is achieved by using their contextual understanding and ability to process many modes of information. This capability is made available due to the models' ability to consider a diverse range of inputs. BERT is widely regarded as a favorable option for generating accurate and contextually appropriate captions for photographs due to its versatility and capacity to establish a connection between visual imagery and written language. Although GPT remains an exceptional model for many text generation jobs, BERT possesses the capability to establish a connection between images and textual information. Hence, we have not used GPT here in the architecture.

16.6   SEARCH MECHANISM

Beam search is a vital decoding method in NLP, contrasting with greedy search. It operates by maintaining a "beam" of the most promising partial sequences, scored based on likelihood and language models. This strategy explores multiple-word candidates concurrently, enhancing sequence exploration. Periodically, the beam is pruned to retain the top-k candidates, discarding less likely options. This action is repeated until a predetermined stopping condition is reached, like exceeding the maximum allowed length or an end-of-sentence token, is satisfied. Although computationally intensive, beam search generates more diverse, contextually accurate sequences and is valuable in various language generation tasks.

16.7   FINAL PIPELINE OR INTERFACE

The process described in this pipeline is a remarkable fusion of CV and NLP techniques aimed at automating the generation of text reports from chest X-ray images. This sophisticated approach addresses a critical need in the field of medicine and healthcare, where the interpretation of medical imagery is tedious and requires specialized expertise. By combining feature extraction and an Encoder-Decoder model, this pipeline offers a promising solution to streamline the reporting process and make healthcare more accessible (Figure 16.4).

At the heart of this pipeline lies Feature Extraction, a fundamental step in understanding and extracting valuable information from chest X-ray images [24]. The output of this stage is a CheXNet feature vector with a size of 2048, which serves as the visual input to the subsequent Encoder-Decoder model. This vector encapsulates crucial visual features from the X-ray images, forming the foundation for generating textual reports. The Encoder component of the model plays a pivotal role in transforming the visual information into a format suitable for generating text. It starts by taking the CheXNet feature vector and passing it through a dense layer with 256 units. This layer's purpose is to condense the extracted visual information into a context vector that captures the essential features from the X-ray images. This context vector acts as the bridge between the visual data and the text generation process. The model's Decoder portion is in charge of the sequence-to-sequence conversion, turning visual features into coherent textual reports. It begins by accepting a sequence of words, typically of a predefined length of 153, and converts each word into a 300-dimensional vector using an embedding layer. This transformation makes the textual data amenable to neural network processing. Following the embedding layer, two LSTM layers come into play, each with 256 units. LSTMs are particularly well-suited for sequence modeling, enabling the model to grasp the context and dependencies between words in the input sequence. The initial

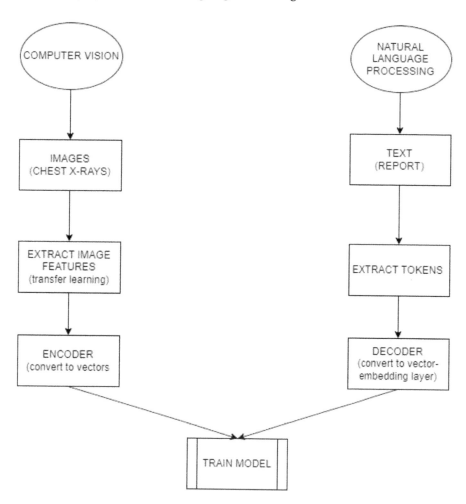

FIGURE 16.4　Architecture of the training model.

LSTM layer creates a vector sequence representing the evolving context, while the second LSTM consolidates these vectors into a single context vector, capturing the overall context of the text.

The Encoder and Decoder contexts works as the context vector from the Encoder's dense layer is combined with the context vector generated by the second LSTM layer through element-wise addition. This merging of visual and textual contexts enhances the model's understanding of the relationship between the image of the X-ray and the generated report. Further refinement occurs as the combined output passes through a 256-unit fully connected layer and a dropout layer with a 0.4 dropout rate. This dropout layer is instrumental in preventing overfitting, ensuring that the model generalizes well to diverse data. Finally, a dense layer with a softmax activation function generates the anticipated word sequence, providing the foundation for the text report. However, generating medically accurate and coherent reports is a nuanced task, and this pipeline takes that into account by incorporating a search mechanism. This mechanism refines the sequence of word vectors into coherent sentences, ensuring that the generated reports are grammatically correct and contextually meaningful. During inference, beam search is employed, showcasing the model's adaptability to new and unseen chest X-ray images. The pipeline's sophistication doesn't end there. After generating the initial report, it undergoes a critical final step: simplification through the OpenAI API. This step is essential for making the report comprehensible to non-medical personnel by converting

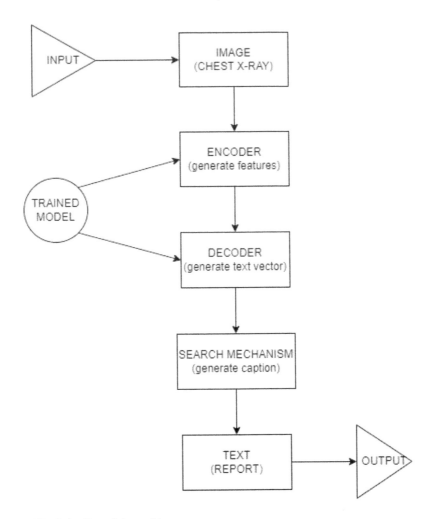

FIGURE 16.5 Final pipeline of the architecture.

complex medical terminology into more accessible language, thereby enhancing healthcare accessibility for a broader audience (Figure 16.5).

In summary, this pipeline represents a harmonious integration of pioneering CV and NLP techniques. Combining Feature Extraction with an Encoder-Decoder model demonstrates the potential to revolutionize the field of medical reporting, aiding healthcare professionals and making healthcare information more accessible to the general public. This amalgamation of technology and medicine stands as a testament to the power of AI in advancing healthcare.

16.8 EVALUATION AND RESULTS

16.8.1 EVALUATION METRIC

BLEU [25,26] is a widely used metric in NLP that evaluates the quality of machine-generated translations or captions by comparing them to human-created references. It operates by assessing n-gram precision, measuring the overlap of n-word sequences between the machine output and the reference. A higher BLEU score indicates a closer resemblance to the reference, with a perfect match yielding a score of 1. BLEU scores facilitate the quantitative evaluation of language generation models, enabling researchers to objectively compare and fine-tune their systems for improved performance. This statistic is critical in assuring the correctness and fluency of machine-generated text in activities like machine translation and image captioning.

16.8.2 RESULTS

Through rigorous testing and evaluation, we meticulously assessed the performance of various neural network architectures in both CV and NLP tasks. Among these architectures, the fusion of InceptionV3 [27] and DenseNet emerged as exceptional in handling complex visual information, while LSTM and GRU stood out for their prowess in NLP. Conclusions drawn from reference [28] were eliminated using EfficientNet.

Significantly, the strategic integration of DenseNet, which is widely recognized for its proficiency in image processing, with LSTM, which is highly regarded for its ability to model sequential sequences, has consistently shown superior performance compared to other configurations. This was seen in consistently achieving the lowest validation loss across multiple experiments. The selection of this synergistic pairing for our project was decisively made due to its perceived ideal configuration. This choice highlights the perfect combination of DenseNet's expertise in analyzing complex image details and LSTM's capability to model elaborate language sequences. The collaborative synergy between different components significantly contributed to enhancing the overall performance of our model. This was particularly evident in the generation of comprehensive and contextually accurate text reports from input medical images. As a result, our work has made significant advancements in the medical image analysis and report creation sector, pushing the boundaries of current knowledge and techniques.

In extensive dataset testing, we obtained detailed results using the BLEU score metric. BLEU evaluates machine translation quality by comparing it to human reference translations. It assigns a score from 0 to 1, indicating the degree of similarity between machine and human translations. A greater BLEU score indicates a better match between machine translation and human reference translations.

As depicted in Figure 16.6, the loss keeps on decreasing epoch by epoch hence proving the accuracy of the prediction (Figure 16.7).

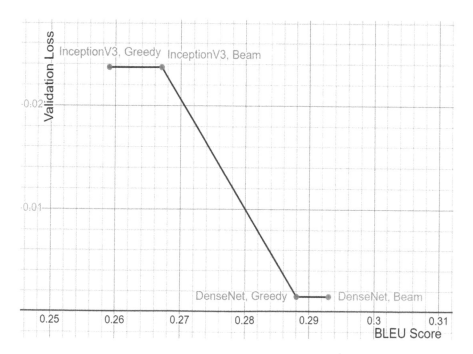

FIGURE 16.6 Experimentation on the entire dataset with BLEU scores.

Loss per epoch

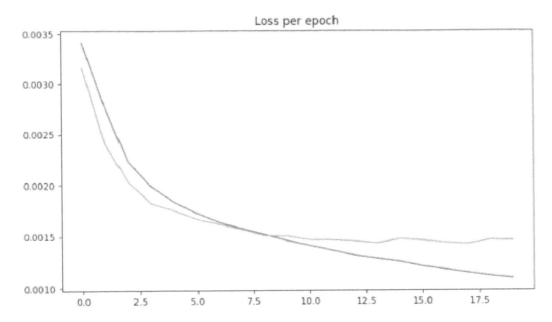

FIGURE 16.7   Loss function.

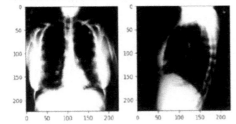

FIGURE 16.8   Predicted report when passed in the images.

16.8.3 Sample Outputs

The results achieved in our study were derived through a complete evaluation procedure.

This process involved processing photos using the final pipeline to generate captions. This methodology provides the flexibility to use either a greedy or a beam search method. Both of these search approaches are essential for improving the quality of generated captions, even though they may produce slightly different results.

Beam search is a notable alternative to greedy search that offers improved efficiency and enhances the clarity and coherence of generated textual descriptions. Through the examination of select illustrative instances, we may gain a deeper understanding of the concrete influence exerted by various search strategies on the precision and coherence of the captions generated by our model. Consequently, this enhances the resilience and efficacy of our picture captioning system.

We have added some examples below (Figure 16.8):

One noteworthy characteristic of our research findings is our dedication to promoting accessibility and comprehension for users who may have limited familiarity with medical terminology.

Predicted Report : no acute cardiopulmonary abnormality . the heart size normal . the mediastinum unremarkable . the lungs are clear . there no pneumothora pleural effusion .
Score is : 0.45926503996307543
WARNING:matplotlib.image:Clipping input data to the valid range for imshow with RGB data ([0..1] for floats or [0..255] for integers).
WARNING:matplotlib.image:Clipping input data to the valid range for imshow with RGB data ([0..1] for floats or [0..255] for integers).

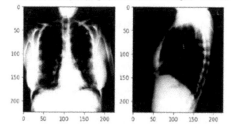

openai.api_key = "sk-KQ4Bk002dtsguXe5wfUT3OlbkFJKFu90N7tdQLYlzi?9ye?"
openai.ChatCompletion.create(model="gpt-3.5-turbo", messages=[["role": "user", "content": Predicted_Report]])

The above paragraph is a summary of the findings of a medical imaging test, such as an X-ray or CT scan. The results show that there are no major abnormalities in the chest area, including the heart, lungs, and surrounding tissues. Specifically, the results indicate that there is no evidence of any acute or sudden problems with the heart or lungs. The heart size and position are normal, and there are no signs of any inflammation or fluid buildup in the chest. Additionally, there are no indications of any air or gas pockets outside of the lungs (pneumothorax) or any buildup of fluid around the lungs (pleural effusion). Overall, the results suggest that there are no major health concerns in the chest area. However, it's important to note that these findings only relate to the specific imaging test performed and do not necessarily rule out any other potential health issues or conditions. It's always best to discuss these results with a qualified healthcare provider to fully understand their implications and determine any necessary follow-up care.

FIGURE 16.9 Report explanation by OpenAI API.

In order to effectively address this pivotal aspect, we have successfully included the OpenAI API into our interface, thereby augmenting the user experience through the provision of explanatory context. In practical application, the process involves providing the created medical report as an input to the OpenAI API, along with a specific inquiry to clarify the information inside the report, with particular emphasis on intricate medical terminology and specialized language. This intelligent technology enables users to not only get medical reports but also acquire full insights and explanations, thereby promoting equal access to crucial healthcare information and facilitating well-informed decision-making in the field of medical diagnostics and patient care (Figure 16.9).

16.9   CONCLUSION

Our efforts resulted in the development of an efficient model for identifying abnormalities on X-rays of the chest. This model integrated DenseNet and LSTM, two robust neural network architectures, in a way that was completely cohesive. The performance of the model was thoroughly examined using the BLEU score, which revealed a significant increase in accuracy with beam search (0.71), in comparison to the baseline greedy search (0.45). Notably, among the many other computer vision and natural language processing (CV-NLP) pairings that were investigated, the DenseNet-LSTM combination emerged as the most powerful. This demonstrated the combination's adaptability to variable-length data, which is an essential quality in medical imaging.

Our objective is to improve the capabilities of the model by including GAN-augmented data [29] and making use of radiologist feedback to further develop our deep learning strategy. In addition, our strategy calls for the investigation of Federated Learning in order to protect users' privacy, which will ultimately lead to the acceleration of the development of X-ray report creation through the application of cutting-edge deep learning approaches.

ACKNOWLEDGMENT

We extend our heartfelt gratitude to SRM University for their indispensable support, and we would like to express our profound appreciation to Indiana University for generously sharing their vital dataset. Their collaborative efforts played an instrumental role in enhancing the quality and success of our research paper.

REFERENCES

1. Onita D, Birlutiu A, Dinu L (2020) Towards mapping images to text using deep-learning architectures. *Mathematics*, vol. 8(9), p. 1606.
2. Sebampitako D (2022). Deep Learning-Aided Image Captioning in Chest X-Rays for TB Screening (Doctoral dissertation, Makerere University).
3. Kumar MA, Ganta S, and Chinni GR (2023). Report generation on chest X-rays using deep learning. In *2023 7th International Conference on Intelligent Computing and Control Systems (ICICCS)*, Madurai, India, pp. 376–381. IEEE.
4. Yang HM, Duan T, Ding D, Bagul A, Langlotz C, and Shpanskaya K (2017). CheXNet: radiologist-level pneumonia detection on chest x-rays with deep learning. arXiv preprint arXiv:1711.05225.
5. Sun L, Wang W, Li J, et al (2019) Study on medical image report generation based on the improved encoding-decoding method. In: *15th International Conference on Intelligent Computing, ICIC 2019*, DongHua University, Shanghai, China, vol. 11643, pp. 686–696.
6. Allaouzi I, Ben Ahmed M, Benamrou B, and Ouardouz M (2018). Automatic caption generation for medical images. In *Proceedings of the 3rd International Conference on Smart City Applications*, Tetouan, Morocco, pp. 1–6.
7. Ayesha H, Iqbal S, Tariq M, et al. (2021) Automatic medical image interpretation: State of the art and future directions. *Pattern Recognition*, vol. 114, p. 107856.
8. Hossain MZ, Sohel F, Shiratuddin MF, and Laga H (2019). A comprehensive survey of deep learning for image captioning. *ACM Computing Surveys (CsUR)*, vol. 51(6), pp. 1–36.
9. Wijerathna V, Raveen H, Abeygunawardhana S, and Ambegoda TD (2022). Chest x-ray caption generation with chexnet. In: *2022 Moratuwa Engineering Research Conference (MERCon)*, Moratuwa, Sri Lanka, pp. 1–6. IEEE.
10. Benzarti S, Ben Abdessalem Karaa W, Hajjami Ben Ghezala H, et al. (2021) Cross-model retrieval via automatic medical image diagnosis generation. In: *19th International Conference on Intelligent Systems Design and Applications, Pretoria, South Africa, ISDA 2019* 1181, pp. 561–571.
11. Wang X, Peng Y, Lu L, Lu Z, and Summers RM (2018). Tienet: Text-image embedding network for common thorax disease classification and reporting in chest x-rays. In: *Proceedings of the IEEE Conference on Computer Vision and Pattern Recognition*, Honolulu, pp. 9049–9058.
12. Pelka O, Friedrich CM, et al. (2017) Keyword generation for biomedical image retrieval with recurrent neural networks. In: *18th Working Notes of CLEF Conference and Labs of the Evaluation Forum, Dortmund, Germany, CLEF 2017*.
13. Tsuneda R, Asakawa T, Aono M (2021) Kdelab at image-clef 2021: medical caption prediction with effective data pre-processing and deep learning. In: *CLEF2021 Working Notes, CEUR Workshop Proceedings*, CEUR-WS.org, Bucharest, Romania.
14. Yao T, Pan Y, Li Y et al. (2017) Boosting image captioning with attributes. In: *Proceedings of the IEEE International Conference on Computer Vision*, Beijing, China, pp. 4894–4902.
15. Wu L, Wan C, Wu Y et al. (2017) Generative caption for diabetic retinopathy images. In: *2017 International Conference on Security, Pattern, and Cybernetics (SPAC)*, Shenzhen, China, pp. 515–519.
16. He K, Zhang X, Ren S and Sun J (2016) Deep residual learning for image recognition. In: *IEEE Conference on Computer Vision and Pattern Recognition*, Las Vegas, NV, USA.
17. Harzig P, Chen Y-Y, Chen F, Lienhar R (2019) Addressing Data Bias Problems for Chest X-ray Image Report Generation.
18. Zeng X, Wen L, Xu Y et al. (2020b) Generating diagnostic report for a medical image by high middle-level visual information incorporation on double deep learning models. *Computer Methods and Programs in Biomedicine*, vol. 197, p. 105700.
19. Hasan S, Farri O (2019) Clinical natural language processing with deep learning. In: *Data Science for Healthcare: Methodologies and Applications*, pp. 147–171. doi: 10.1007/978-3-030-05249-2_5.
20. Alfarghaly O, Khaled R, Elkorany A, Helal M, and Fahmy A (2021). Automated radiology report generation using conditioned transformers. *Informatics in Medicine Unlocked*, vol. 24, p. 100557.
21. Rajpurkar P, Irvin J, Zhu K, Yang B, Mehta H, Duan T, and Ng AY (2017). Chexnet: Radiologist-level pneumonia detection on chest x-rays with deep learning. arXiv preprint arXiv:1711.05225.
22. Ribani R, and Marengoni M (2019). A survey of transfer learning for convolutional neural networks. In: *2019 32nd SIBGRAPI cConference on Graphics, Patterns and Images Tutorials (SIBGRAPI-T)*, Rio de Janeiro, Brazil, pp. 47–57. IEEE.

23. Haritha D, Pranathi MK, and Reethika M (2020). COVID detection from chest X-rays with DeepLearning: CheXNet. In *2020 5th International Conference on Computing, Communication and Security (ICCCS)*, Patna, India, pp. 1–5. IEEE.

24. Shin H, Roberts K, Lu L et al. (2016) Learning to read chest x-rays: Recurrent neural cascade model for automated image annotation. In: *2016 IEEE Conference on Computer Vision and Pattern Recognition (CVPR)*, Las Vegas, NV, USA, pp. 2497–2506.

25. Papineni K, Roukos S, Ward T, and Zhu W-J (2002). BLEU: A method for automatic evaluation of machine translation. In: *Proceedings of the 40th Annual Meeting of the Association for Computational Linguistics (ACL)*, Philadelphia, pp. 311–318.

26. Wu C, Xia F, Deleger L, and Solti I (2011). Statistical machine translation for biomedical text: Are we there yet? *AMIA Annual Symposium Proceedings, 2011*, Washington DC, USA, pp. 1290–1299.

27. Guan Q, Wan X, Lu H, Ping B, Li D, Wang L, Zhu Y, Wang Y, and Xiang J (2019). Deep convolutional neural network Inception-v3 model for differential diagnosing of lymph node in cytological images: A pilot study. *Annals of Translational Medicine*, vol. 7(14), p. 307.

28. Tan M and Le QV (2019) EfficientNet: Rethinking model scaling for convolutional neural networks. In: *International Conference on Machine Learning*, Long Beach, 9–15 June 2019.

29. Aggarwal A, Mittal M, and Battineni G (2021). Generative adversarial network: An overview of theory and applications. *International Journal of Information Management Data Insights*, vol. 1(1), p. 100004.

17 The Role of AIoT in Reshaping the Farming Sector

Leo John and Korhan Cengiz

17.1 INTRODUCTION

In order to completely transform the agricultural sector, a new idea known as Artificial Intelligence of Things (AIoT) in Agriculture 4.0 has been developed. Agriculture 4.0, or the fourth industrial century, utilizes cutting-edge innovations like the Web of Things (WoT), large-scale data analysis, serverless computing, sensors, and machine intelligence to improve farm productivity and sustainability. One of the goals of Agriculture 4.0 is to use modern technologies like machine learning, blockchain, aerial vehicles, and connected devices networks (CDN) to increase agricultural output while decreasing negative effects on the environment and boosting farmers' earnings. Micro and macro crop planning utilizing AI-powered algorithms that connect weather predictions, variable soil data, logistics and warehouse infrastructures, and economic conditions are just a few of the many possible uses of AIOT in Agriculture 4.0. Using artificial intelligence in sensors and automated weather gauge data, smart agricultural solutions may be implemented, such as Internet of Things-enabled irrigation and dynamic soil condition mapping at the farm level. AI-driven pest control, farming input advice platforms, drone-enabled farm mapping, and farming input apps all contribute to better crop health management. Artificial intelligence (AI), spectroscopy (spectroscopy), and blockchain may be utilized to improve quality and traceability and market linkage platforms, while IoT can be used to improve warehousing and logistics. Second, these technology breakthroughs have enormous promise and might speed up digitization across the entire value chain. The Web of Things (WoT) serves as the basis for Artificial Intelligence of Things (AIoT), which is the combination of technological advances in artificial intelligence with the IoT. The objective of the AIoT program is to improve data management and analytics, human-machine interface, and IoT efficiency. Computer systems, especially PC platforms, can mimic human intellect through the use of artificial intelligence [1]. It has several applications, including those in computer vision, detection of speech, and linguistic processing. Networked intelligence (NI) is a network of computers, mechanical and digital devices, and other items that may communicate data with one another using unique identifiers and the internet, without the need for human or machine intervention. Examples of IoT include implanted monitoring devices, vehicles with tire-pressure monitoring systems, and any inanimate item that is capable of sending and receiving data through the web and being assigned an IP address [2].

IoT contributes advantages to AI by providing data acquisition, transmission, and communication capabilities. AI enhances the functionality of IoT using machine learning algorithms and more effective information-generating processes. AIoT is game-changing and simultaneously productive for different categories of devices. AIoT can further develop organizations and administrations by generating more value out of IoT-produced information [3]. Man-made intelligence empowers the IoT device to use the enormous amount of information it has accumulated to be more likely to break down, learn, and settle on choices without a human. The Internet of Things (IoT) facilitates improved performance by incorporating AI. The objective is to have these frameworks perform precise decisions without human mediation. The inclusion of 5G is one of the most significant AIoT innovations. 5G's higher bandwidth and lower latency make IoT

 DOI: 10.1201/9781003457176-17

devices transfer large data files faster. The price of successful human talent development as well as the complexity of supply chains and delivery models are two examples of operational issues that the Internet of Things (IoT) could help resolve [4]. Understand how organizations in factories, customer service, merchandising, and the motor industry are utilizing the Internet of Things (IoT) to provide assistance in prediction and preventive action. The agriculture sector was clearly adversely affected by COVID-19. Large-scale crop diseases were brought on by bacterial infections and pest attacks. Researchers must examine ways to use IR4.0 innovations to address the issues and revolutionize the farming economy. This is because traditional methods must be more effective at resolving them [5]. In the post-pandemic period, savvy farming is a fitting answer to work deficiencies and a constant food production network. To achieve their sustainable development objectives, only a few nations, including the United States and South Korea, have developed comprehensive conceptualizations and strategies for efficient agriculture management. During the COVID-19 pandemic, the paradigms with the greatest influence were machine intelligence (MI) and smart object networks (SON) technologies. This integrated system that serves as the most widely used tool in the 21st time period is capable of data mining, effective real-time remote control monitoring, and intelligent management [6].

Wireless sensor networks (WSNs) are installed at various locations to capture location-based and real-time metrics in a typical IoT network. A grouping of "everything" or elements attached to microcontrollers, incorporating computing power, networking technology, detection characteristics, and operation comprise such a system's global visualization. The Internet Protocol (IP) connects all of these items. AI serves as the underlying support for a large number of gadgets and numerous applications in the industrial IoT. These include ecological observing, food production, computerized grids, townships, residences, habitations, telecommunications, and public health [7]. AI makes IoT technology management, application, and implementation easier. The use of artificial intelligence in IoT conditions supports functional effectiveness, gives better chances of winning, triggers upgraded items/administrations, and expands IoT adaptability. Fujitsu has created an innovation for assessing human body stances utilizing millimeter wave sensors and cloud information. Photo analysis, sensor analysis, data communication, and decision-making are all AI techniques. High-speed stream transmissions, reliable connectivity, quick computation times, and immediate response to the Internet of Things are all necessary for these processes. The system executes in the small data volume of Internet of Things equipment and is based on reinforcement learning models. For pre-processing and preparing massive amounts of IoT records to decrease ambiguity, reduce complexity, and eliminate potential duplications, effective AI methods are required. The majority of reports use AI techniques like fuzzy systems, genetic computation, neural models, pattern recognition, modeling, communication handling, estimation, estimation guidance, and data dissemination. This is for a variety of reasons. Deep learning techniques are extensively incorporated into security surveillance methods because of their learning capabilities [8].

Pests and plant diseases directly affect crop production. Pests appear on plants' leaves at night or in the evening after hiding behind them through the daylight to hide from the temperature. As a result, monitoring insects' activities on food through the hours is difficult. In the event gardeners discover pest problems, the pests are likely to have multiplied and spread out of control [9]. As the harvests approach, a huge amount of chemicals is expected to splash over the harvests to mitigate irritations and reduce harm. However, even after washing, pesticide residues remain after crops are sprayed during the growing season. Pests that cause widespread crop diseases infect crops with bacteria. Burning infected crops to stop bacteria from spreading is necessary to avoid these conditions. However, this method fails to effectively address pest issues and damages agricultural production significantly. Consequently, the objective of the aforementioned studies is to utilize AIoT and deep learning innovations to a natural investigation of yield development and the expectation of bug events. This is to increase harvest efficiency and reduce the size of the rural labor force [9].

17.2 LITERATURE REVIEW

According to reference [10], for the purpose of pest identification, the technologies of AI and image classification are combined with atmospheric monitors and the IoT. Intelligent pest recognition and ecological IoT metrics are used to evaluate current farming conditions and pest monitoring applications for wireless networks. Researcher applied deep learning and the current, mature AIoT technology to smart agriculture. The researcher involved profound awareness YOLOv3 for picture acknowledgment to acquire the area of *Tessaratoma papillosa* and dissect the ecological data from climate conditions places through lengthy transient memory (LSTM) to anticipate the event of bugs. The outcomes of the experiment revealed that the accuracy of pest identification was 90%. Pesticide harm to the soil and the amount of pesticides used can mutually be concentrated with precise positioning. It allows farmers to administer pesticides at the right time based on the correct location and extent of pests. As a result, pest control can be executed quickly and smart agriculture can be achieved. In the envisaged system, farmers are made aware before pests increase in large groups. It contributes to the profitability and value of agriculture by eliminating crop destruction and ecosystem harm incurred by unsustainable chemical use.

In [11], River floods are one of the weather-related emergencies that could have a direct impact on a variety of aspects of life, including the economy, infrastructure, agriculture, and human lives. In order to find more effective methods for preventing them, businesses are making significant investments in research. The Man-made brainpower of Things (AIoT) is a new idea that joins the finest of mutually computerized reasoning and Web of Things and has proactively shown its capacities in various areas of expertise. According to the study, the researcher presents the Smart Internet of Things (SIoT) engineering where waterway flood monitoring device, in every district, can communicate their information by means of the LoRaWAN to their nearest nearby transmission place. The latter will transmit the composed statistics by connecting to a centralized cloud server using 4G or 5G technology, where an effective Artificial Intelligence strategy will be used to assess the data and forecast the state of the rivers nationwide, assisting in the prevention of future deluge or floods. This study has demonstrated its effectiveness at each level. LoRaWAN-based statement between broadcast centers and monitoring devices has, on the one hand, enabled greater range and lower energy consumption. The AI-based data analysis, on the other hand, has made better predictions about river floods.

In today's era of the connected devices network (CDN), an immense number of monitoring devices and equipment accumulate and analyze environmental data. These devices transmit the data to cloud centers and utilize internet connectivity for feedback and perception. However, the transmission of large volumes of diverse data, understanding complex environments based on this data, and making prompt intelligent decisions present significant challenges. Artificial intelligence (AI), particularly advanced machine learning, has emerged as a proven solution in various domains, including computer modeling, communication notification, and computational linguistics. The integration of AI into the IoT introduces the idea of artificial intelligence of things (AIoT). This article aims to provide a comprehensive survey on AIoT, demonstrating how AI can enhance the IoT ecosystem to make it quicker, keener, greener, and harmless [12].

The low work [13] cooperation by youthful grown-ups and a maturing farming populace, Taiwan and the remainder of the earth are confronting work deficiencies in horticulture, which will influence hydroponics creation. The projected structure is expected basically for taking care of the issues looked at by the hydroponics cultivating area in Taiwan through planning a shrewd IoT-driven fish observing and organizing framework furnished using various IoT gadgets to empower ongoing information assortment, so that remote monitoring, adjusting, and evaluation of fishpond water purity parameters and various components information is simple. As part of their research, the authors created a feature learning simulation that combined the numerous features included in the complex agricultural method for estimating the size of the California Bass fish population. To determine the best deep learning model design to offer precise expectations on the given trial informational index, we used Bayesian progress-driven hyper-boundary tuning. The experiments have shown that the DL model can be used in the automated nutrient delivery process to reduce the quantity of supply that is left over. Hence, hydroponics in view of the man-made reasoning of things (AIOT) can help fish ranchers shrewdly maintain and oversee an entirely new fishpond hardware from a distance and help hydroponics administrators in performing proficient hydroponics, bringing down the business' entrance hindrance, and advancing hydroponics.

Reference [14] explained that the accuracy horticulture is a significant level farming creation process that accomplishes great and high effectiveness by joining conventional rural innovation with the web of things (IoT) innovation and man-made reasoning (computer-based intelligence) innovation. High-tech, high-quality, and high-level agricultural production is achieved through this approach. The goal is agricultural goods with added value. By utilizing sophisticated analysis and strategic planning, intelligent greenhouse planting technology makes it easier to control and manage the greenhouse environment. At the same time, it preserves the ancient agricultural practice and understanding and governance, expands the working zone, and reduces the effort and cost of crop maintenance. In this editorial, an orchid development examination framework is proposed for identifying the development position of orchids in nurseries. The greenhouse orchids' growth status, flower names, and environmental factors can all be managed with this system. What's more, an arising self-managed learning strategy is projected for preparing and distinguishing orchid simulations to perceive the development position of orchids. The shape, color, and appearance of numerous orchid species are identical. Orchid management can be hampered by the difficulty of identifying them. Therefore, the orchid greenhouse managers will be able to manage orchid growth more effectively if the orchid's name and stage of growth can be established. A 98.6% accuracy rate was found for orchid identity in the research.

17.2.1 THE CHALLENGES AND OPPORTUNITIES OF AIoT IN SMART AGRICULTURE

Despite being commonly informed for additional applications, there are still only a few review of publications on AIoT in smart agriculture. By providing an overview of AI and IoT, we purposely spotlight on the AIoT impression in this section. Literature review benefits and drawbacks are also discussed. The following is a summary of the study's contributions.

1. Research talks about the AIoT idea, from the use of gadgets in IoT frameworks to the reception of computer-based intelligence methods.
2. Study presents an efficient writing survey to highlight the rising pattern in article distribution regarding AI and IoT in various applications and AI and IoT development.
3. Analysis provides a synopsis of a few capable implementations of AIoT and associated technologies that enable AI or IoT.
4. Study emphasizes AIoT adoption obstacles.

17.3 ARTIFICIAL INTELLIGENCE OF THINGS (AIOT) ON AGRICULTURE

According to [15] studied that agribusiness implements IoT by using robots, machines, sensors, and PC imaging incorporated with scientific equipment to gather knowledge and observe homesteads. On ranch screens, hardware records information, which is then used to get significant pieces of data.

IoT in horticulture is a method that coordinates physical equipment with scientific programming. Analytic dashboards are software that processes equipment data. Therefore, to operate, maintain, and comprehend the insights of this valuable equipment, a solid technical understanding of robotics and automated intelligent systems is essential.

Due to the physical limitations of IoT, farms will need to integrate their own sensors and automated systems. It is only meaningful data that will be gathered by these sensors and bots for that farm. This will be reflected in each farm possessing its own user interface where insights can be acquired. With

IoT, it is inconceivable to scale a single platform for various farms, unlike SaaS technologies such as Cropin, an app that enables worldwide operations using a single system.

It has been a long time since sensors were implemented in agricultural operations. However, the fact that this conventional method of sensor technology did not provide live data was the issue. The sensors stored the information in the appended memory and were then used.

Modern sensors can now be utilized in agriculture thanks to industrial IoT. A cellular/satellite network connects these sensors to the cloud. We are able to make informed decisions and obtain live and real-time data thanks to this system.

Internet of Things (IoT) has helped farmers in numerous endeavors, including tank water level monitoring. Since all of this is done in real time, the irrigation process is more effective. Moreover, another innovation that has been made available with IoT innovation is the emergence of seeding. Ranchers can presently monitor the utilization of an asset and the rate at which it takes for plants to mature into mature plants.

The presentation of IoT in Horticulture resembles a second signal of the Green Upheaval. IoT has given ranchers two advantages. With precise IoT data, they can successfully complete the required number of efforts in a shorter length of duration and maximize production results.

17.3.1 Applications of IoT in Agriculture

According to [16], savvy farming is conceivable because of the Web of Things. Now that smart production has been identified, some may delve into what it is precisely. Using sustainable farming, agriculture can be managed cleanly and economically at high levels of technology and economic investment. Agricultural ICT can also be known as agriculture ICT. Artificial Intelligence of Things (AIoT) is revolutionizing the agriculture industry in the era of Agriculture 4.0. This powerful combination of AI and IoT technologies is enhancing the efficiency and productivity of farming operations like never before. AIoT in agriculture involves the integration of smart sensors, drones, and other IoT devices with AI techniques to gather and examine current data from farms, assisting farmers in making decisions based on data to maximize crop yields, reduce resource wastage, and improve overall sustainability.

One key application of AIoT in agriculture is precision farming. Through the deployment of IoT sensors and drones, farmers can monitor various environmental factors such as soil moisture levels, temperature, and crop health in real time. The data are then processed by machine learning techniques to produce useful insights that assist farmers in making educated decisions regarding fertilization, crop irrigation, and pest management. This degree of accuracy not only increases crop yields but also minimizes the environmental impact by reducing the unnecessary use of water and chemicals.

AIoT in Agriculture 4.0 is not only transforming farming practices but also contributing significantly to resource conservation and sustainability. One of its remarkable applications is in the realm of water management. Through the integration of AI-driven IoT sensors, farmers can closely assess the soil wetness level and weather conditions. These instant-time data enable them to implement precise irrigation strategies, reducing water wastage and ensuring that crops receive just the right amount of hydration. As a result, water resources are conserved, and the environmental impact of agriculture is greatly reduced, aligning perfectly with the global push for more sustainable farming practices.

An IoT-based intelligent cultivating approach that uses sensing devices to screen the productivity of the field is explored within the perspective of IoT-based innovative cultivating. Further, these sensors automate the water system framework and keep track of each fundamental for harvest creation, which includes soil moistness, stickiness, light, heat, etc. From any location, farm owners can observe field occurrences through this framework. Farming dependent on IoT is more efficient than standard farming.

In addition to modernizing old-fashioned production practices, IoT-based modern agricultural production can also improve other agricultural practices like ecological cultivation, communal livestock (with specific cattle and/or cultures, complex or small spaces, retention of specialized or high-quality plants, etc.) and make farming more reliable. IoT-powered smart agribusiness can equally be supportive of climate change issues. It is able to make water use easier, and information and medicines are better available to ranchers.

17.3.1.1 The Challenges of Integrating Agricultural Robots with Other Systems

Several obstacles arise from agricultural robots' connection with other systems, which must be overcome before smart farming technologies can be widely used. Interoperability is a significant obstacle. Because of the wide variety of hardware and software used by agricultural robots, it can be challenging to integrate them with existing infrastructure on a farm. For the sake of efficient communication between robots and other equipment, efforts toward standardization are essential.

Data handling is an additional difficulty. Soil conditions, crop health, and gear efficiency are just some of the many metrics that may be tracked by agricultural robots. Integrating this information with farm management software and decision support systems may be challenging and call for advanced data processing and analytics tools.

Moreover, handling electricity and other forms of energy is crucial. All of the farm's electrical components, including the robots' batteries and other power sources, must be compatible with one another. In order to keep robots functioning, reliable power management systems and charging infrastructure are essential.

The issue of safety is also very important. Safety measures are essential for agricultural robots that interact with humans and other animals. It is crucial that farm robots be designed such that they do not endanger humans or animals.

Another issue is that many farmers may not be able to afford to implement agricultural robots. Robots and the supporting infrastructure needed to run them can be expensive upfront. Farmers who are thinking about using this method should analyze the pros and downsides carefully.

Finally, it's important to think about the learning curve. Training is necessary for farmers and farm workers to efficiently use and maintain agricultural robots. Education and assistance are essential components of successful integration, since they enable users to reap the full benefits of new technology.

Interoperability, management of data, energy and power consumption, security, costs, and user training are just some of the hurdles that must be cleared before agricultural robots may be properly integrated into existing farm systems. The full promise of agricultural automation and smart farming methods cannot be realized without overcoming these obstacles.

Various sensors, automatons, autonomous vehicles, and cameras are needed on agriculture to control and run it. Experienced operational support is required to develop and supervise bots, as well as an understanding of the Internet of Things [17].

1. Equipment is expensive and fragile.
2. Hardware requires regular maintenance. There are large introductory payments.
3. Electronic photography is accomplished using sensor technology and unmanned aircraft with manual controllers.
4. There is no supply chain management.
5. A farm's statistics needs to be monitored by itself.
6. There is no recorded information. It is a challenge to integrate with products that have

17.4 AGRICULTURE 4.0: THE RISE OF THE ROBOTS IN THE FIELD

Food and agricultural system sustainability, poverty, and food security are all affected by global trends.

In conjunction with Oliver Wyman, the World Government Conference released a report called Agriculture 4.0 – The Next Generation of Agribusiness Technology for the 2018 event. The report discusses four primary advancements putting strain on agribusiness to live up to assumptions representing things to come: Food waste, natural resource scarcity, demographics, and climate change [18].

According to the report, even though demand rises, we will need to produce 70% more food by 2050. In the meantime, agribusiness' portion of the worldwide gross domestic product has decreased to about 3%, 33% of its involvement some many a decade before. Around 800 million people are hungry. By 2030, 650 million people, or 8% of the world's populace, will continue to be malnourished in a business-as-usual scenario. In fact, innovation has been scarce lately. However, that doesn't mean hunger and food insecurity won't be a problem in the coming decades.

Governments, investors, and cutting-edge agricultural technologies will need to band with each other to eliminate these limitations. Water, chemicals, and substances will not need to be distributed uniformly across entire areas in Agri 4.0. On the contrary, farm owners will only use what is absolutely necessary and concentrate on very specific regions. In addition, the document emphasizes that lands and agribusiness companies will need to be governed drastically otherwise in the future. This is mostly attributed to developments in information science, sensing devices, and automation. Robots, sensors for monitoring heat and wetness, aerial pictures, and GPS equipment will be prevalent in tomorrow's farms. Agricultural production will become significantly less expensive, productive, reliable, and considerate of the environment thanks to these cutting-edge tools, robotic systems, and precision agriculture practices [19].

Governments can solve the problem of food shortages. Governments can challenge the conventional framework approach and pursue similar policies; governments must embark on a bigger and more visible position than just the existing controlling and supporting activities; Increase productivity and assist the transformation toward an innovation-focused and digital economy by becoming a net exporter of products, intellectual property, and cutting-edge solutions.

With the aim of cultivating more food with smaller amount of resources and lower production costs, precision farming involves accurately managing field variations.

According to [20], There is a wide range of climates from one location to another, including soil, climate, vegetation, and water. Additionally, crop growth and farming success are determined by all

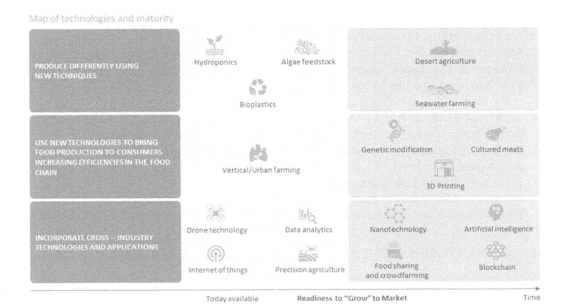

FIGURE 17.1   Technology and Agriculture 4.0 map.

of these factors. Farmers have always known this, but they did not have the equipment to precisely measure, map, or manage these variations. Consequently, Precision Cultivating can affect food production confronting the increasing population and can assist ranchers in:

• More prominent supportability and ecological insurance
• Higher efficiency
• Financial advantages
• Key innovations and ideas

Below is a rundown of the most widely recognized innovations applied to Accuracy Cultivating drills. Then, the following logical things were investigated:

High-accuracy situating frameworks (like GPS and Galileo) are vital innovations to achieve precision while driving in the field. Basic accuracy will be achieved much faster and more consistently with the European global satellite-based navigation system Galileo.

Automatic steering systems allow for the control of specialized drivability functions like steer-by-wire, overhead rotation, adhering to field contours, and row interlocking. These innovations decrease human faults and convince executives [21].

Using satellite navigation systems like GPS, assisted steering systems direct drivers in the field. This permits more precise steering; nonetheless, the rancher has to control the vehicle.

The driver can take their hands off the wheel while driving down the road thanks to automated steering systems. This will also give them the ability to watch the sprayer, planter, or other piece of machinery.

Depending on the shape of the field, intelligent steering techniques can create various maneuvering designs (guidance patterns) and must be utilized in conjunction with the preceding controls. In this way, movement cultivation may be utilized for this multitude of frameworks and limits the % of soil being compacted [22].

Geomapping: used to create layers of maps with information about soil type, nutrients, etc., and to link that information to a specific field location. Remote sensing and sensors: gather information from a distance to assess soil and yield wellbeing (dampness, supplements, compaction, crop infection). Sensor Devices can be installed on moving machines [23]. Seamless electronic communication among system components, such as between a tractor and farm office or dealer, or between a spray can and sprayer, for example. The majority of these systems remain in private ownership.

Variable rate innovation: Ability to alter boundaries on equipment to deliver, for instance, plant food or compost as per the specific plant types in plant propagation, or fertilizer ingredients and type.

17.4.1 Digital Agriculture: What Exactly Does It Imply?

Furthermore, what is the industry's vision for Agriculture 4.0/Digital Farming in Europe?

According to [24], Digital farming is the move away from manual harvesting and toward digital, computerized farm harvesting machinery in agriculture and agricultural engineering. Digital farming employs intelligent communications and records keeping software in addition to Precision Farming technology. Digital farming aims to automate sustainable agricultural processes by utilizing all available information and expertise.

Data is essential if the European farming industry is to grow in productivity, sustainability, and global competitiveness. A vast amount of information is as of now accessible in farming.

According to reference [25], In digital farming, information provided by sources that are not simply present or accessible is transformed into actionable intelligence and added value. "Connectivity," i.e., machine-to-machine, cloud-to-cloud, and cloud-to-cloud, are the primary tools for digital farming. A consistent, simple information stream is key for information suppliers and information specialist organizations to see one another.

So how might the computerized upheaval potentially impact farming? Furthermore, what is the homestead hardware industry's vision for computerized cultivating?

17.4.2 Key Technologies in Smart Farming

Digital information practice in the food and farming industry is not a recent innovation, but the possibility of digitizing the market is, as stated by reference [26]. Consistency in agriculture statistics and the technology used to collect, record, alter, manage, and send these numbers is also crucial. Improvements in both process and output have resulted from advances in wireless technology and robots, respectively. In addition, the availability and decrease in the price of computing power have enabled the development of novel agricultural decision-support instruments. For instance, machine learning algorithms may transform the massive amounts of real-time and historical data collected by big data into actionable insights and useful information. Figure 17.2 shows how information travels across the chosen systems.

Connectivity between Agriculture 4.0's major tenets is seen in the preceding diagram. Data interpretation (including big information and AI-based techniques for data exploration), data interpretation, information support applications (for data exploration, suggestion functions, and interactive interfaces), and the IoT make the five key areas of development that have been identified.

In the field, Internet of Things devices (such as sensors, AI, etc.) collect the relevant information, which is then transmitted through a wired or wireless connection to a cloud-based data storage system for archiving, computation, and analysis. It can be accomplished to fit unstructured records into content with additional assessment using data-intensive approaches and AI-driven solutions. Ultimately, a decision support system (DSS) provides the data that decision-makers need to maximize the benefits of the interconnected system and work together to enhance operations. However, the sequence of operations may vary depending on the IoT architecture and computing methods actually employed. To begin with, while some platforms analyze data in the public cloud, others use edge and fog technologies to pre-process findings before pushing them. Therefore, the following part will provide a brief summary of the aforementioned technologies' responsibilities as they are typically characterized and implemented under Agriculture 4.0.

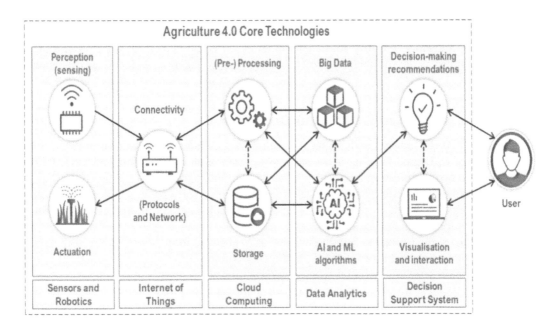

FIGURE 17.2   Core technologies of Agriculture 4.0.

17.4.2.1 Sensors the Key to Smart Farming

One of the main forces behind the Internet of Things is sensors. This is because of technological innovations that have made them smaller, smarter, and less expensive. In the past few eras, wired and remote devices have remained generally used in farming. Information collected about plants, animals, and the countryside is invaluable to agricultural activities. It is an urgent innovation for IoT deployment in horticulture. There are two ways to address spatial and temporal variables that affect agricultural production: the sensor-based strategy and the map-based strategy. Both methods require massive data collection and analysis and involve mobile or permanent sensors. This is done to make better use of farm inputs, which results in better crop yield and environmental sustainability [27].

17.4.2.2 Remote Sensing for Crop and Soil Monitoring

Gathering data about something without physically interacting with it is called "remote sensing." Remote sensing applications make use of a limited range of energy frequencies within the electromagnetic spectrum. These include microwave, thermal infrared, visible, and reflective infrared energy measurements. Satellites, drones, UGVs (unmanned ground vehicles), farm machinery, and portable sensors are just some of the platforms used to take these readings. Proximal sensing refers to readings made with hand-held sensors and tractors. In agricultural remote sensing applications, vegetation indices play a crucial role in assessing the quantity and condition of vegetation. This is accomplished by determining whether the crop is undergoing any stress or homogeneous growth Artificial Intelligence algorithms, electronically detectable data, and vegetation indicators may all be used to estimate future harvests. Other methods focus on soil properties like organic matter, moisture, minerals, pH, and salinity, as well as crop nutrients, weed infestations, insect and plant diseases. Taking the well-known normalized difference vegetation index (NDVI) as an illustration, values that are higher can be taken as a sign of the high density of green leaves. On the contrary, lower values indicate that a crop or region has less chlorophyll (and/or leaves). This has to do with the fact that healthy vegetation is more active in its photosynthesis processes. It will absorb an increased amount of red wavelengths associated with leaf chlorophyll. The leaf area index (LAI), which is linked to ecosystem leaf cover, is another example in this field. It is a non-dimensional quantity that measures the amount of photosynthesis occurring in a given area of land [28].

17.4.2.3 WSN for Transforming Agriculture for Efficiency and Sustainability

WSNs show up as one of the arising patterns, since they have been broadly applied in different Agrarian applications to work on the conventional techniques for cultivating are increasing. There are three fundamental roles that sensor networks play: (1) detecting; (2) correspondence, between the different parts of the organization; and also (3) calculation, by utilizing equipment, programming, and calculations. A telemetric sensor and sensor controller network, on the other hand, is a variation of a WSN that includes an additional mechanism: a controller, the controller is an actual gadget (lights, fans, siphons, valves, water system sprinklers, etc.) liable for interacting with the surrounding environment. These organizations are based on the appropriate plans of a few sensors and actuators as well as hubs interconnected by remote connection. These nodes typically consist of a number of parts, each in charge of a specific role, such as power, supervision, data exchange, and sensing [29].

In Agriculture 4.0, numerous applications that use WSNs and WSANs are currently being utilized to optimize agricultural production. These frameworks have facilitated the checking of a few safety boundaries (such as water boundaries, landscape attributes, and air surroundings) and prepared it simpler to react in the field, as well as timely. In this way, they contribute to increasing effectiveness and efficiency. What's more, they benefit from numerous rural creation frameworks, reducing the data sources (water, agro-compound items, etc.), and reducing waste, while limiting climate adverse consequences.

17.4.2.4 Robotics in Agriculture: A Growing Field with Many Applications

As robots have been implemented [30] to improve some agricultural procedures like crop surveying (plant monitoring and identification), staking and planting, water distribution, crops sprayed, climate research, herbicide and pest eradication, disease surveillance, clipping, milking, and categorizing, this field of robotics has gained interest in previous time periods. While remotely operated aerial platforms and unmanned aerial vehicles were mentioned earlier in relation to remote sensing, it is essential to emphasize that they can also be utilized directly in the fields to carry out specific agricultural tasks. Industrial settings typically use fixed robots. Mobile robots, on the other hand, might be more useful in agriculture. They are seen as having a lot of potential to improve agricultural management because of their ability to shield a large part of arenas, smart farming tasks, and traverse various types of terrain in a variety of landscape conditions that may be difficult to reach by ground transportation.

UAVs are referenced with frequent use, with a few applications in the farming space like yield assessment, crop sickness identification, weed acknowledgment, and planning. By preventing health issues associated with manual agrochemical spraying in crop fields, incorporating drones into the workplace can also be thought of as a protective mechanism for the employees' well-being. The UGV is another type of mobile robot that has been used in the agricultural industry in recent decades. Its main goal is to make agriculture more efficient and cut down on manual labor. This is especially helpful in places where humans can't get in. Field planting, soil assessment, sprinkler management, automated spraying, robot-assisted weeding, and crop gathering are just a few of the agricultural tasks performed by these robots.

17.4.2.5 IoT: The Key to Sustainable Agriculture

Conceptually, the smart objects networks (IoT) allude to the connectivity of digital and physical "things" using standard, interoperable communication protocols. It has infiltrated medical care, smart homes, smart cities, and modern creation. Farming is no exemption for IoT arrangements, since horticultural activities should be constantly monitored and controlled. Weather forecasting, crop, soil, and water management, as well as AFSC transparency, are amid them, which are discussed in additional detail. The blend of various Agriculture 4.0 Inventions with the Internet of Things (IoT) has demonstrated a significant possibility for enhancing smart farming activities' efficiency, each with its own set of requirements. In the agricultural literature on IoT, various communication protocols and technologies have been used to match these [31].

17.4.2.6 The Future of Agriculture: AI and Machine Learning

One of the primary factors behind Agriculture 4.0 is synthetic intelligence, particularly in the form of computational learning, along with IoT and cloud computing. One of the most promising methods being investigated in this area is machine learning (ML), which has applications in monitoring and managing weeds, soil, crops, and animals, as well as monitoring and managing weather and climate change [32]. Because they can recognize intricate trends, variations, and interactions in diverse, interdisciplinary agricultural statistics, ML techniques have been utilized to maximize production yield and reduce operating charges. They also accurately forecast events and give areas of strength for a further developed rural direction and tasks to the executives. According to a recent review, crop management accounted for 61% of ML-based articles published in the agricultural sector, followed by livestock management (19%), soil management (10%), and water management (10%). Random forests, SVMs, ANNs, and a variety of deep learning algorithms, including CNN for machine learning applications, are among the more common ML algorithms utilized in Agriculture 4.0, as shown in Figures 17.1 and 17.2. However, in response to the innovative tasks posed via increased connectivity and the requirement to develop scalable solutions within smart farming, additional techniques, such as preserving confidentiality techniques and integrated education, are emerging from the scientific community in order to address the information security and privacy problems arising in the context of the digital era. These strategies place an emphasis on dispersing the process of training across a number of nodes, which then work together to construct ML formulas avoiding exchanging any private or private data sets, but rather only private settings. This eliminates or reduces the confidentiality and performance issues mentioned earlier, making it a promising research area for AI applied to smart farming

17.4.2.7 Agriculture 4.0 Applications

To answer the research question, "What really are today's Agriculture 4.0 applications domains?". The primary application areas and the importance they have to the overall agri-food supply chain (AFSC) will be identified through a more in-depth analysis of the existing literature on Agriculture 4.0 in this section. FAO's Horticulture 4.0 initiative focuses on cultivating and transforming agri-food frameworks. The process of distributing agricultural products to end users is called the "AFSC" process. Typically, the AFSC is made up of several organizations that are in charge of production, processing, distribution, and marketing.

Horticulture 4.0 brings development potential to open doors in heterogeneous spaces across the whole AFSC. As shown in Figure 17.3, these purpose domains can be divided into four main categorizations: (1) surveillance; (2) control; (3) forecasting; and (4) operations. Despite this diversity, one thing that all of these innovations have in common is that they are the result of current developments in innovative techniques like IoT, sensors innovations, robotics, private and public cloud computing, and artificial intelligence. In addition, despite their apparent segregation, these domains are actually intertwined. For example, a shrewd control framework really requires checking and estimating functionalities to completely use the capability of information-driven emotionally supportive networks [33].

In addition, this section provides responses to RQ3 (How can Agriculture 4.0 support sustainable development?), and it does so by highlighting a few of the advantages provided by these domains. Finally, this section concludes with applications relevant to the entire AFSC's monitoring, control, predictive, and logistic activities.

17.4.2.8 AIOT in Agriculture 4.0 Access for Farmers

The Artificial Intelligence for Agriculture Innovation (AI4AI) program, announced in August 2020 by the Centre for the Fourth Industrial Revolution India of the World Economic Forum [34], aims to revolutionize the farming industry and operate in a way that benefits farmers and

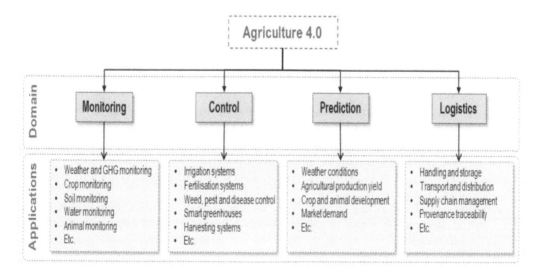

FIGURE 17.3 Agriculture 4.0, applications, and domains.

is sustainable and profitable. Future technologies like artificial intelligence (AI), blockchain, unmanned aerial vehicles (UAVs), and smart object networks (IoT) present both possibilities and difficulties, and this effort aims to improve collaboration across different groups. The chapter delves into the possibilities of cutting-edge technologies that might hasten digitalization across the agriculture value chain.

There are a number of ways that farmers might have access to this kind of technology. For instance, they can use artificial intelligence (AI) in remote sensing and autonomous weather station data to improve irrigation and dynamic soil health mapping on farms. Drones may help with farm mapping and applications that advise on agricultural inputs, while AI-powered pest control helps farmers maintain crop health. Furthermore, companies may employ IoT to improve storage and transportation, artificial intelligence (AI) to improve quality and traceability, and spectroscopic and blockchain to improve market linkage platforms.

"Think big, start small, and scale fast" is the motto of the AI4AI project. Therefore, it is crucial to begin with a pilot program for implementing these technologies. The project is building multi-stakeholder collaborations to harness the opportunities and address the challenges of emerging agricultural technologies, with the goal of reshaping the farming ecosystem in an efficient and long-term manner for farmers.

17.5   OPEN CHALLENGES IN AIOT IN AGRICULTURE

17.5.1   SOCIAL AND ETHICAL CHALLENGES OF AIoT IN AGRICULTURE

The integration of AIoT (Artificial Intelligence of Things) in agriculture offers numerous benefits, including increased efficiency, improved crop management, and sustainable resource use. However, it also raises important ethical and social considerations that need careful attention. Here, we examine three key factors: data privacy, algorithmic bias, and the impact on rural communities.

Data Privacy
   Data Collection and Ownership: AIoT systems collect vast amounts of data from farms, including weather data, crop conditions, and soil information. Concerns arise regarding who owns and controls this data. Farmers must be assured that their data will not be misused or shared without consent.
   Data Security: Safeguarding this sensitive data from cyber threats is crucial. A breach could expose personal information, trade secrets, and potentially disrupt agricultural operations. Robust cybersecurity measures are essential.
   Informed Consent: Farmers should have clear and informed consent mechanisms regarding how their data will be used and shared. Transparency in data practices is essential to maintain trust.
Algorithmic Bias
   Bias in Decision-Making: AI algorithms may inadvertently introduce bias into decision-making processes. This could result in unequal treatment of different farmers or regions. It's vital to continuously assess and mitigate algorithmic biases.
   Fair Access: Ensuring that AIoT technologies are accessible and beneficial to all farmers, regardless of size or location, is essential. This prevents the exacerbation of existing disparities in agriculture.
   Accountability: Establishing accountability for algorithmic decisions is challenging but crucial. Responsible organizations and regulatory bodies should oversee the fairness of AIoT systems.
Impact on Rural Communities
   Labor Displacement: As AIoT systems automate tasks, there may be concerns about job displacement in rural areas. Transitioning the workforce to adapt to new roles and skills is essential.

     Economic Disparities: The adoption of AIoT technologies may favor larger, wealthier farms, potentially marginalizing smaller farms. Policies should aim to support the sustainability of small and family-owned farms.

     Community Dynamics: Changes in agricultural practices due to AIoT can impact the social fabric of rural communities. Balancing technological progress with the preservation of community cohesion is a challenge.

17.5.2 Assess the Environmental Impact of AIoT in Agriculture

The adoption of AIoT (Artificial Intelligence of Things) in agriculture offers significant potential benefits in terms of increased productivity and resource optimization. However, it also presents potential environmental impacts that need to be carefully considered, including energy consumption, waste management, and overall sustainability.

Energy Consumption

     Increased Energy Demand: AIoT systems, especially those involving sensors, data processing, and communication networks, can consume additional energy. The deployment of sensor nodes, data centers, and communication infrastructure may lead to increased electricity usage.

     Renewable Energy Integration: To mitigate this impact, it's crucial to promote the use of renewable energy sources to power AIoT systems. Solar panels, wind turbines, or other clean energy sources can offset the environmental footprint.

     Energy-Efficient Hardware: Developing and deploying energy-efficient hardware and low-power sensors can help reduce the energy demands of AIoT devices.

Waste Management

     Electronic Waste: The rapid turnover of technology can lead to electronic waste (e-waste) concerns as older AIoT equipment is replaced. Proper e-waste disposal and recycling programs must be in place to minimize environmental harm.

     Sustainable Design: Designing AIoT devices with sustainability in mind, including longer lifespans and upgradability, can help reduce e-waste.

Overall Sustainability

     Resource Optimization: AIoT's core purpose is to optimize resource use in agriculture. By fine-tuning irrigation, fertilizer application, and pest control, it can reduce resource waste, enhance efficiency, and support sustainability.

     Data-Driven Precision: Leveraging AIoT data can lead to more precise decision-making, reducing the overuse of water, chemicals, and energy. This precision can enhance the overall sustainability of agricultural practices.

     Life Cycle Assessment: Conducting a life cycle study of AIoT systems can aid in locating potential environmental hotspots and directing design and operational improvements.

Carbon Footprint Reduction

     Telecommuting and Remote Monitoring: AIoT can enable remote monitoring and control of agricultural operations, potentially reducing the need for frequent travel to rural areas, which can contribute to a lower carbon footprint.

     Transportation Efficiency: Optimization of transportation logistics through AIoT can minimize fuel consumption and emissions in supply chain management.

To mitigate the potential environmental impacts of AIoT in agriculture, stakeholders, including farmers, technology developers, and policymakers, should prioritize sustainable practices. This includes implementing energy-efficient technologies, adopting renewable energy sources, promoting circular economies for electronic devices, and using AIoT for resource-efficient farming practices. Ultimately, the responsible adoption of AIoT can contribute to both agricultural productivity and environmental sustainability.

17.5.3 Other Challenges

Data Privacy and Security: The large amounts of data generated by AIoT devices can be a security risk if it is not properly protected. Farmers and agricultural businesses need to be alerted of the threats and initiate steps to protect their data, such as implementing robust encryption and access controls.

Interoperability: AIoT devices and systems from different vendors often do not interoperate with each other. This can make it difficult to integrate AIoT into existing agricultural operations. Farmers and agricultural businesses need to carefully consider the interoperability of different AIoT solutions before making a purchase.

Cost: AIoT can be a costly investment for farmers and agricultural businesses. The cost of AIoT devices, systems, and data analytics can be a barrier to adoption. Farmers and agricultural businesses need to carefully consider the cost-benefit of AIoT before making a decision to invest.

Training and Skills: AIoT requires a new set of skills and knowledge for farmers and agricultural businesses. Farmers and agricultural businesses are essential to capitalize on training and learning to confirm that their organizations have the skills they need to use AIoT effectively.

Regulation: AIoT is a rapidly evolving field, and regulations are still catching up. Farmers and agricultural businesses need to be aware of the latest regulations and how they may affect their use of AIoT.

Despite these challenges, AIoT has the potential to revolutionize agriculture. By addressing these challenges, farmers and agricultural businesses can reap the benefits of AIoT, such as increased productivity, improved yields, and reduced costs.

Here are some additional challenges that are specific to AIoT in agriculture:

Limited Connectivity: Many agricultural areas have limited or no connectivity, which can make it difficult to deploy and use AIoT devices and systems.

Varying Environmental Conditions: Agricultural areas are often subject to harsh environmental conditions, such as extreme temperatures, moisture, and dust. This can make it difficult to deploy and use AIoT devices and systems that are not designed for these conditions.

Scalability: AIoT systems need to be scalable to accommodate the large number of devices and sensors that are used in agriculture.

Data Management: The large amounts of data generated by AIoT devices and systems can be challenging to manage and store.

Interpreting Data: AIoT systems need to be able to interpret the data they generate in a way that is meaningful to farmers and agricultural businesses.

These challenges are being addressed by researchers and developers, and as AIoT technology continues to mature, they are likely to be overcome.

17.6 CONCLUSION

Real-time statistics compilation, automation, and AIoT-enabled devices are significant factors that can boost the smart agriculture sector. This chapter summarizes the existing use of AI/IoT technology and highlights some of the advantages of AIoT. A few benefits of AIoT in horticulture, for example, illness recognizable proof, shrewd ranch observing, and effective farming information examination, were likewise featured. In addition, it should be noted that the adoption of technology in the smart agriculture sector is constrained in part by the fact that the policies and mechanisms necessary to push for this assessment are still in their infancy. Last but not least, the application of

AIoT in smart agriculture faces a number of obstacles, including the complexity of the technology, privacy and security concerns, and inadequate infrastructure. It ought to be noticed that the techniques introduced depend on AI and profound learning calculations, which have seen significant improvement and forward leaps in shrewd farming. The machine learning system's verification and validation, on the other hand, require additional investigation due to the wide range of agricultural data sources. Hardware and software machine learning systems are the subject of rigorous investigation and verification in this field of study. This is also called the formal method. A number of strategies have been proposed to provide validation procedures for machine learning algorithms' high complexity, unpredictability, and lack of certainty.

REFERENCES

1. Mukhopadhyay, C.S., et al., "Artificial intelligence-based sensors for next generation IOT applications: A review," *IEEE Sensors Journal*, vol. 21, no. 22, pp. 24920–24932, 2021.
2. Poolayi, S. and Assadiyan, H.A., "Governance of IOT in order to move ahead of the calendar & live the future today," *Journal of Management and Accounting Studies*, vol. 8, no. 3, pp. 38–42, 2020.
3. Li, Y., et al., "Retrospective thinking based multi-agent system for wireless video transmissions," *ICC 2021- IEEE International Conference on Communications*, Montreal, QC, Canada, 2021.
4. Painuly, S., Kohli, P., Matta, P., and Sharma, S., "Advance applications and future challenges of 5G IOT," *2020 3rd International Conference on Intelligent Sustainable Systems (ICISS)*, Tuticorin, India, 2020.
5. Adli, K.H., et al., "Recent advancements and challenges of AIoT application in smart agriculture: A review," *Sensors*, vol. 23, no. 7, p. 3752, 2023.
6. Ritambhara, Shukla, K.S., and Shukla, S., "Automation, modern tools and technique for sustainable agriculture - an important parameter toward advance plant biotechnology," *Green Technological Innovation for Sustainable Smart Societies*, pp. 281–300, 2021. doi: 10.1007/978-3-030-73295-0_13.
7. Shukla, S., Hassan, M.F., Khan, M.K., Jung, L.T. and Awang, A., "An analytical model to minimize the latency in healthcare internet-of-things in fog computing environment," *PloS One*, vol. 14, no. 11, p. e0224934, 2019.
8. Mahbub, M., Hossain, M.M., and Gazi, S., "IOT-cognizant cloud-assisted energy efficient embedded system for indoor intelligent lighting, air quality monitoring, and ventilation," *Internet of Things*, vol. 11, p. 100266, 2020.
9. Rustia, J.D., et al., "Towards intelligent and integrated pest management through an aiot-based monitoring system," *Pest Management Science*, vol. 78, no. 10, pp. 4288–4302, 2022.
10. Van Bruggen, A.H., Gamliel, A. and Finckh, M.R., "Plant disease management in organic farming systems," *Pest Management Science*, vol. 72, no. 1, pp. 30–44, 2015.
11. Chen, L.-B., Huang, G.-Z., Huang, X.-R., and Wang, W.-C., "A self-supervised learning-based intelligent greenhouse orchid growth inspection system for precision agriculture," *IEEE Sensors Journal*, vol. 22, no. 24, pp. 24567–24577, 2022.
12. Boulouard, Z., Ouaissa, M., Ouaissa, M., Siddiqui, F., Almutiq, M., and Krichen, M., "An integrated artificial intelligence of things environment for river flood prevention," *Sensors*, vol. 22, no. 23, p. 9485, 2022.
13. Zhang, J., and Tao, D., "Empowering things with intelligence: A survey of the progress, challenges, and opportunities in artificial intelligence of things," *IEEE Internet of Things Journal*, vol. 8, no. 10, pp. 7789–7817, 2021.
14. Chiu, C.M., Yan, M.W., Bhat, A.S., and Huang, F.N., "Development of smart aquaculture farm management system using IOT and AI-based surrogate models," *Journal of Agriculture and Food Research*, vol. 9, p. 100357, 2022.
15. Chen, L.B., Huang, G.Z., Huang, X.R., and Wang, W.C., "A self-supervised learning-based Intelligent greenhouse orchid growth inspection system for precision agriculture," *IEEE Sensors Journal*, vol. 22, no. 24, pp. 24567–24577, 2022.
16. Jain, A., Ranjan, N., Kumar, S. and Vishwakarma, S.K., "Internet of things (IOT) in the agriculture sector: Challenges and solutions," *Sustainable Computing*, pp. 69–85, 2023. doi: 10.1007/978-3-031-13577-4_4.
17. Relf-Eckstein, J.E., Ballantyne, A.T., and Phillips, P.W., "Farming reimagined: A case study of autonomous farm equipment and creating an innovation opportunity space for broadacre smart farming," *NJAS-Wageningen Journal of Life Sciences*, vol. 90, p. 100307, 2019.

18. Benos, L., Sørensen, C.G. and Bochtis, D., "Field deployment of robotic systems for agriculture in light of key safety, labor, ethics, and legislation issues," *Current Robotics Reports*, vol. 3, no. 2, pp. 49–56, 2022.

19. De Clercq, M., Vats, A. and Biel, A., "Agriculture 4.0: The future of farming technology," *Proceedings of the World Government Summit*, Dubai, UAE, pp. 1–30, 2018.

20. Harfouche, A., Saba, P., Aoun, G. and Wamba, S.F., "Guest editorial: Cutting-edge technologies for the development of Asian countries," *Journal of Asia Business Studies*, vol. 16, no. 2, pp. 225–229, 2022.

21. Harkness, C., Semenov, M.A., Areal, F., Senapati, N., Trnka, M., Balek, J. and Bishop, J., "Adverse weather conditions for UK wheat production under climate change," *Agricultural and Forest Meteorology*, vol. 282, p. 107862, 2020.

22. Addicott, J.E., *The Precision Farming Revolution*, pp. 1–35, 2019. doi: 10.1007/978-981-13-9686-1.

23. Murali, P.K., Kaboli, M. and Dahiya, R., "Intelligent in-vehicle interaction technologies," *Advanced Intelligent Systems*, vol. 4, no. 2, p. 2100122, 2022.

24. Zhang, Y. and Hartemink, A.E., "Digital mapping of a soil profile," *European Journal of Soil Science*, vol. 70, no. 1, pp. 27–41, 2019.

25. Klerkx, L., Jakku, E. and Labarthe, P., "A review of social science on digital agriculture, smart farming and agriculture 4.0: New contributions and a future research agenda," *NJAS-Wageningen Journal of Life Sciences*, vol. 90, p. 100315, 2019.

26. Hachimi, C.E., Belaqziz, S., Khabba, S., Sebbar, B., Dhiba, D. and Chehbouni, A., "Smart weather data management based on artificial intelligence and big data analytics for precision agriculture," *Agriculture*, vol. 13, no. 1, p. 95, 2022.

27. Araújo, S.O., Peres, R.S., Barata, J., Lidon, F. and Ramalho, J.C., "Characterising the agriculture 4.0 landscape-emerging trends, challenges and opportunities," *Agronomy*, vol. 11, no. 4, p. 667, 2021.

28. Bibri, S.E., "The IoT for smart sustainable cities of the future: An analytical framework for sensor-based big data applications for environmental sustainability," *Sustainable Cities and Society*, vol. 38, pp. 230–253, 2018.

29. Khanal, S., Kc, K., Fulton, J.P., Shearer, S. and Ozkan, E., "Remote sensing in agriculture-accomplishments, limitations, and opportunities," *Remote Sensing*, vol. 12, no. 22, p. 3783, 2020.

30. Landaluce, H., Arjona, L., Perallos, A., Falcone, F., Angulo, I. and Muralter, F., "A review of IoT sensing applications and challenges using RFID and wireless sensor networks," *Sensors*, vol. 20, no. 9, p. 2495, 2020.

31. Javaid, M., Haleem, A., Singh, R.P. and Suman, R., "Enhancing smart farming through the applications of agriculture 4.0 technologies," *International Journal of Intelligent Networks*, vol. 3, pp. 150–164, 2022.

32. Georgios, L., Kerstin, S. and Theofylaktos, A., "Internet of things in the context of industry 4.0: An overview", *IJEK*, vol. 7, no. 1, pp. 4–19, 2019.

33. Ahmad, L. and Nabi, F., *Agriculture 5.0*, 1st ed, vol. 1. Boca Raton, FL: CRC Press, 2021.

34. Sott, M.K., et al., "A bibliometric network analysis of recent publications on digital agriculture to depict strategic themes and evolution structure," *Sensors*, vol. 21, no. 23, p. 7889, 2021.

18 Unleashing the Power of XAI (Explainable Artificial Intelligence)

Empowering Decision-Making and Overcoming Challenges in Smart Healthcare Automation

G. Arun Sampaul Thomas, S. Muthukaruppasamy,
Nandha Gopal J., Sudha G., and Saravanan K.

18.1 INTRODUCTION

Since artificial intelligence (AI) emerged a decade ago, many improvements have been made, and AI continues to be an upcoming technology. AI is best for interpreting the outcomes in a manner that is easy for the user to grasp. AI is being employed in the healthcare industry as a decision-making tool and productivity booster. These models cannot be employed in clinical exercise because doctors have difficulty in understanding them due to their black-box nature. AI systems are not in the situation of commonly recognised for medical decision-making situations, particularly when it comes to the identification of epilepsy and other symptoms. However, AI systems will be far more trustworthy if the rationale is explained in terms a human can comprehend. Logic can be interpreted using a wide variety of methods. Different XAI methods (gradient, integrated gradient, LRP, Deeplift) are utilised to decipher the reasoning [1,2].

Despite the popularity of explainability studies, there is still no consensus on how to precisely define explainable artificial intelligence. "Explainable AI" is defined as a context with an approach to developing AI systems that ensures human users can understand and rely on the outcomes and outputs generated by machine learning algorithms. This concept incorporates many kinds of explanations and audiences, as well as the fact that explainability approaches are added to a system rather than being inherent to it. In what ways does "explainable AI" differ from "regular" AI? To guarantee that every ML decision can be tracked and explained, XAI employs several different tools and strategies. While AI uses an ML algorithm to arrive at a conclusion, the AI architects are not completely comprehending the algorithms' thought process in arriving at that conclusion. Because of this, control, accountability, and auditability are all compromised, making it harder to verify correctness [3].

The advantages of explainability have been studied by experts in academia, business, and government, and algorithms have been developed to deal with a variety of settings. Researchers have identified explainability as a requirement for AI clinical decision support systems in the healthcare domain because it allows collaborative decision-making between doctors and patients. To satisfy regulatory standards and provide analysts with the knowledge to audit high-risk judgements, financial institutions provide explanations of AI systems [4]. Without proper model monitoring and

DOI: 10.1201/9781003457176-18

accountability for AI, businesses put faith in their algorithms and miss important insights. When it comes to explaining AI, humans benefit from explainable AI. This is especially true for ML algorithms, deep learning, and neural networks. Many people have the preconceived notion that ML models are opaque black boxes that cannot be understood. Deep learning employs neural networks that are notoriously difficult for humans to grasp. Training AI models has always included the potential for incorporating bias, gender, age, or geographical kind. Furthermore, since production data is different from training data, AI model performance likely to be drift or deteriorate. It emphasises the need for quantifying the business effect of deploying such algorithms and maintaining a continual monitoring and management cycle for models that increase AI explainability. Trust from users, auditability of models, and effective use of AI are all bolstered by AI that can explain itself. Risks associated with production AI are reduced in areas like compliance, law, security, and reputation.

Responsible AI is an approach for the widespread use of AI technologies in actual organisations that prioritises transparency, fairness, and explainability models. Organisations facilitate responsible AI adoption by designing AI systems based on trust and transparency, which are in turn embedded into AI applications and processes [3].

There are three primary components to an XAI system.

Decision Understanding: caters to human requirements, while prediction precision and traceability cater to technological needs. Future soldiers will need explainable AI, and particularly explainable machine learning, to be able to comprehend, properly trust, and competently handle the next generation of AI peer machines.

Reliability of Predictions: The practical usefulness of AI depends critically on how well it performs in actual situations. The accuracy of predictions is measured by performing simulations and comparing XAI output to findings in the training data set.

Local Interpretable Model-Agnostic Explanations (LIME): It is a widely used method for this purpose; it provides an explanation for the ML algorithm prediction of classifiers.

One further important strategy for achieving XAI is traceability. One method to do this is to restrict the range of possible options and the applicability of Machine Learning rules and features. DeepLIFT (Deep Learning Important Features) is an XAI approach that provides an example of traceability by comparing the activation of each neuron to its reference neuron. Thus, it provides a connection between the active neurons and their dependencies. Although faith in AI is necessary for productive collaboration, many individuals still struggle to do so [3].

18.2 SMART HEALTHCARE BASED HUMAN CENTRED XAI

For many years, the healthcare sector has relied on AI technologies to analyse and diagnose patient data. Smart wearable gadgets are increasing healthcare's reliance on AI, which is good news for the future of personalised treatment. Early diagnosis of illness is directly correlated with their ability to be cured or prevented from advancing to severe stages. Artificial intelligence (AI) combined with smart wearable devices aids in early illness identification by allowing for continuous monitoring of vital signs. However, trusting AI systems is difficult because of the lack of explainability of the AI model-based predictions, necessitating extensive technical and statistical understanding. AI models that can be explained are necessary due to the lack of confidence in the black-box functioning of AI systems and the difficulty in comprehending the outcomes. Since expert systems supported reasoning structures in the 1980s, the concept of explaining sophisticated AI systems is not new. When it comes to patients' lives, doctors in the healthcare business need to know the reasoning behind an AI model's recommendation before they can put their faith in it. Since Explainable AI (XAI) illustrates the machine judgements and predictions produced by AI systems, it has increased user confidence in AI systems. Using XAI techniques, AI systems become more open, and it becomes possible to determine what elements contributed to a certain prediction. To make accurate predictions, artificial intelligence systems learn from data. By using XAI techniques, the system will be able to comprehend the newly acquired rules and rectify any mistakes. As a result, medical personnel are better equipped to enhance the quality of care they provide by making choices that are grounded in evidence. Integration of XAI models has been shown to increase the effectiveness and reliability of healthcare AI systems [5–7].

All forms of life rely critically on the healthcare sector. The healthcare sector makes significant contributions to both a nation's economy and its international standing. Expanding medical technology is essential and Artificial Intelligence (AI) has the potential to revolutionise healthcare by making it more efficient and intelligent. Humans will always have a part in this industry, but we can find ways to have them coexist with machines. There was a time when we had to wait until the doctor had reviewed our body scan data before giving any prescribed medication. A computer powered by artificial intelligence can do this task in minutes today. With the use of Artificial Intelligence (AI) software-based Natural Language Processing (NLP), it is scanning our prescriptions and find out exactly what drugs have been prescribed [8]. Ultimately, the use of AI will lead to beneficial and even necessary progress in the medical field. This article discusses the present state and potential applications of AI and XAI in the healthcare industry, with a focus on the significance of human oversight and control over these innovations via human-centred AI.

18.2.1 Progression of AI in Healthcare

As people learn more about AI, the healthcare industry is progressing. Machines are taking over many formerly human-only jobs in medical and scientific settings. When most of us were children, many healthcare procedures required human labour. Rather than waiting 2 days for our blood test results, we now have access to intelligent equipment that can measure our glucose and oxygen levels instantly. The healthcare industry is making extensive use of intelligent AI applications for a wide variety of purposes, including drug research, patient care, therapy recommendation, early diagnosis, and so on. Machines can quickly analyse a patient's X-rays and provide a diagnosis if any signs of illness are detected. The employment of these intelligent tools for early illness detection has a direct positive impact on patient health. Patients can communicate with hospital and clinic staff using chatbots. These chatbots are intelligent enough to answer simple queries about health and to query hospital databases for an open appointment time [1]. Patients waiting times are drastically decreasing. Radiologists are using test analysis and early identification to interpret CT scans and X-rays. As demonstrated in Figure 18.1, these devices identify diseases early and initiate therapy at an optimal time [9].

Advanced technology is also assisting doctors in their work [10]. Artificial intelligence programmes are assisting medical professionals in monitoring patients' health, identifying possible

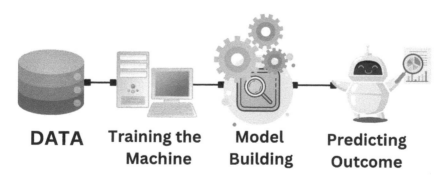

DATA   **Training the Machine**   **Model Building**   **Predicting Outcome**

FIGURE 18.1 AI and data model for healthcare.

risks, and issuing alerts. Officials' workloads are lighter, and patient care and preventative measures are improved as a result. The most effective course of therapy is determined by modern medical device, history of health issues, and current way of life, among other factors. Both the doctor and the patient find them helpful. Everyone can learn it quickly since there is less time spent in waiting, and a machine can provide a second view. Because of their ability to quickly digest vast amounts of data and provide the results of studies, AI machines are also a tremendous aid in research projects pertaining to the study of medical conditions and viruses. Technological advances in healthcare research are very helpful. The accuracy and intelligence of AI-based device is improved over time with regular training using client data. Training for the same objective takes significantly longer. There have been several advancements in both treatment methods and scientific inquiry with the use of AI in the healthcare industry.

However, there is always a chance of harm when new technologies are introduced. There is a danger of poor trust in the data offered by the machine when it is used as a second opinion in healthcare, either for suggesting treatments or for detecting diseases at an early stage. These AI-based models are trained on data from several patients, and these data are likely to include a lot of variation. It narrows the margin of error for the AI-based healthcare machine's findings. This highlights the need for XAI (Explainable Artificial Intelligence) in the medical field [8].

The debate over explainability in healthcare is complex and far-reaching effects. Figure 18.2 illustrates the rising prevalence of AI in health care administration, clinical decision-making, predictive medicine, patient data, and diagnostics. Despite its impressive performance, artificial intelligence is still seen as mysterious. The lack of trust that results from being secretive is a contributing factor. For instance, the doctor should be able to justify the benefits of a certain treatment plan. Adoption of AI is hindered if the AI system lacks explainability. Therefore, explainable AI (XAI) in healthcare refers to tools that shed light on the "why" behind the system's judgements. In other words, it clarifies the reasoning behind the AI system [11].

The success of many black-box models is attributed to the use of ambiguous or misleading inputs. For instance, a physician-guided deep learning network trained on asthma patients mistakenly predicted a low death risk from pneumonia. The location of the scanner was employed as an irrelevant feature in another deep learning model that screened X-rays for pneumonia. At last, hardware-related information was used to predict risk in a model that classified patients into

FIGURE 18.2 AI and robotics use cases in healthcare.

high- and low-risk categories based on X-rays. These cases demonstrate that it is not sufficient to depend just on the precision of the models. More confidence-building frameworks, such as explainable AI, are needed.

In addition to promoting value-based treatment, explainable AI in healthcare has incentivised providers to concentrate on results rather than service quantity. Patient data are analysed by XAI algorithms. It is to determine whether patients are at a greater risk of having a certain disease. Integration with wearables is likely to increase as the use of explainable AI in healthcare becomes more widespread. Wearables collect a wealth of information on their users' health since they track their activity and vitals all day long. Using this information, explainable AI can provide precise diagnoses and recommendations [11].

18.3 BENEFITS OF XAI AND HAI BASED APPROACHES

Artificial intelligence (AI) is being used in the medical and healthcare fields to aid doctors' decision-making, increase productivity, and decrease mortality rates. However, the final consumer is blind to the logic behind these results. These models cannot be used in clinical exercise because they are too complex for clinicians to grasp. Users are more likely to have faith in AI systems when they can understand the reasoning behind the system's decisions, which is achieved through the application of XAI techniques [5,6].

Since the integration of clinical knowledge with AI systems produces more trustworthy outcomes, clinical feedback lends greater credence to the AI system's output. The dependability of an AI system is much improved when an XAI is used to interpret the AI-based findings [7].

18.3.1 BENEFITS OF XAI

- Increased openness: XAI methods promote openness in healthcare by presenting the reasoning behind an AI system's decision. Higher levels of trust are a natural consequence of greater openness and comprehension. Furthermore, XAI approaches explanatory power used to track the influence of individual components on an AI system's prediction accuracy.
- AI forecasting systems make data-driven improvements to the model. There are times when conventional wisdom fails, leading to faulty forecasts. The explanations supplied by XAI methods are useful for assessing the learned rules, which in turn helps identify errors and enhance models.
- XAI improves the precision of medical diagnosis and treatment plans by explaining the reasoning behind an AI system's findings. Medical professionals benefit from XAI since it increases the likelihood of an accurate diagnosis and effective therapy.
- Knowledge transfer: XAI makes it easier for AI systems to share their expertise with medical staff so that better results can be achieved for patients. An AI system identifies a link between symptoms and diseases that doctors had not considered before. The AI technology helps doctors see new connections they apply to future diagnoses by explaining their reasoning.
- By evaluating large amounts of patient data, XAI helps physicians catch potentially fatal infections before they spread. Some people are genetically predisposed to illnesses, and XAI can explain why, how it came to this decision, and what steps can be taken to avoid this [11].

18.3.2 XAI IN HEALTHCARE WITH THE PROCESSING OF THE AI MODEL

The data used for training AI models allows for faster processing, analysis, and outcome prediction. However, it is not always clear to us how the model processed the input data to arrive at the displayed findings. This model is often referred to as a "black box," since even its designers do not fully understand it. In healthcare, this kind of uncertainty has no place. Even though the machine is working very quickly. The healthcare industry has heightened demand for the explainability of AI models so that physicians and other authorities can comprehend the procedure and make informed decisions about whether to implement the advice. Numerous healthcare jobs require the use of XAI. For instance, when the patient needs more clarification before making an educated choice about the diagnosis and treatment options presented to them, AI has come up with a new hypothesis that has to be checked by humans [8,12].

The degree to which a doctor or patient needs explanations from an AI system, which is very context dependent. A doctor would need to know more about the reasoning behind an AI's recommendation. Results improve if explanations are tailored to user roles and needs [12]. Due to high variance data, healthcare AI models are more susceptible to error, creating a higher demand for XAI. While explanations are helpful, humans must always oversee smart healthcare technologies to prevent them from making a mistake. Technology has increased the pace of work, but it will never be able to fully replace human labour.

18.3.3 HAI in Healthcare – The Need of Human Control Over Smart Machines

Scientists are now developing AI with a human focus. If we are already succeeding with AI and XAI in healthcare, why do we need HAI? The obvious solution to this problem is to ensure that humans oversee any intelligent robots serving humanity. In a variety of ways, the healthcare industry is indispensable. Testing an AI machine's accuracy and precision or the quality of its explanations at the expense of a patient's life is unacceptable. To be certain of the beneficial effects of a therapy or newly discovered condition, every choice must be supported by strong confidence and a doctor's monitoring [13]. Intelligent AI systems are predicated on the premise that they can learn from the information they are given about patients' health issues in various contexts and circumstances, ultimately producing the desired outcomes. The computer is learning to generalise the principles, it finds in the data, and it applies them to real-world problems. The main flaw with this setup is that generalisations cannot be made with any degree of certainty, since the dataset used to train the system represents just a tiny fraction of the whole set. This is why the intelligent system needs human input right now. Very accurate machine learning has been accomplished, it can shift the attention to training and monitoring machines. AI is focused on humans is called "human-centred AI," and examples are shown in Figures 18.3 and 18.4.

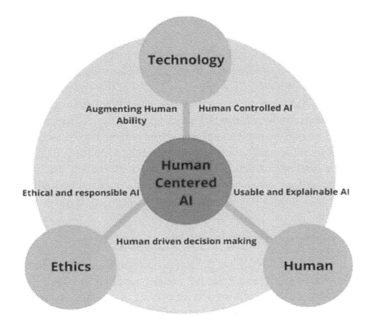

FIGURE 18.3   XAI-based HAI in healthcare.

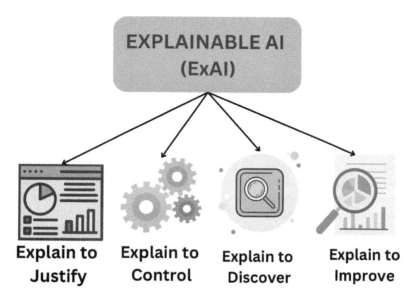

FIGURE 18.4 Human-centred AI in healthcare.

Treatment success rates, surgical outcomes, illness identification, and even life-or-death decisions greatly benefit from HAI in healthcare. Together, human and AI brainpower allow for rapid pattern recognition, machine learning, and intelligent decision-making based on accessible data. This potent mix has allowed for greater precision in medical treatments and studies. Both people and healthcare science need the capabilities of artificial intelligence. The solution to this issue is AI, designed with humans in mind [12,13].

18.4 SMART XAI BASED HEALTHCARE TECHNOLOGIES

Nowadays, technology is developing at a lightning-fast rate. The impact of the industrial revolution on contemporary life is immense, although most of us are oblivious to it. The modern conveniences are made possible by the industrial revolution [14]. This is due to the rise of industrialisation. The Industrial Revolution is to blame for this situation. Undoubtedly, know that our culture has gone through three distinct periods of industrialisation.

From around 1760 to roughly 1830, the first industrial revolution was in full swing. During this period, the steam engine was invented and went on to play a significant role in the development of the first industrialised nations. Water, coal, and steam were the primary forms of energy production at the time. Between the late 19th and early 20th centuries, the second industrial revolution took place, between 1850 and 1914 to be exact. Energy was generated from petroleum and electricity [15,16].

In the year 1950s, marked the beginning of the third industrial revolution. Also called the "digital revolution," this period seeks the development of semiconductors, mainframe computers, personal computers, and the Internet.

18.4.1 INDUSTRIAL REVOLUTION AND HEALTHCARE

There will always be implications from the Industrial Revolution. Many people were impacted. We are on the cusp of the next industrial revolution, which will go down in history as the fourth [17]. Progress in artificial intelligence, nanotechnology, synthetic biology, data science, genetic engineering, and stem cell research are all contributing to the fourth industrial revolution's impact on medicine and healthcare. This is developing at a breakneck pace.

Our lives get altered in ways we have not foreseen before this upheaval. It will have a greater effect on healthcare [18] than all the preceding industrial revolutions put together.

18.4.2 STEM CELL TREATMENT

Regenerative medicine with stem cell treatment is a subset, is an emerging field of medical study. It is very much wondering how regenerative medicine differs from conventional exercise. When compared to conventional medicine, which primarily treats the disease's symptoms, regenerative medicine prioritises restoring health by growing, repairing, or replacing diseased tissues or cells using different cutting-edge technologies. Stem cell treatment, tissue engineering, and even artificial organs are all used. The medical specialty of regenerative medicine has only been around for a short while. This trend emerged only in the 20th century. Regenerative medicine as a word did not appear, presumably in the 1990s. "Any time you have healing after an injury, it's a stem cell-mediated event," said Harry Adelson an orthopaedic stem cell researcher [19,20]. Stem cells are responsible for initiating all tissue healing in the body. However, everyone knows that wounds heal at different rates for different people. This is due to the patient's stem cells not performing at an ideal level or to a lack of sufficient stem cells to mend the injured region. Stem cell or regenerative treatment involves transplanting stem cells into a region where they are needed but are in insufficient supply. These stem cells come from another part of the patient's body or from a donor. Stem cell treatment is now being used to slow down the ageing process and cure conditions associated with ageing. It's also effective in treating a wide range of other medical illnesses, including Multiple Sclerosis (MS), Rheumatoid Arthritis (RA), Osteoarthritis (OA), Spinal Cord Injury (SCI), Ankle Brachial Index (ABI), and a host of others. Since stem cell treatment threatens to undermine the pharmaceutical and medical device industries, no firm in either sector is likely to extol its virtues.

18.4.3 MEDICAL ROBOTIC SURGERY

Already, many surgeons rely on robotic surgery [19]. The term "robotic surgery" now refers mostly to robot-assisted surgical procedures. The surgeon makes all the choices at the console; the robot just executes them. Surgeons do the procedures themselves with the assistance of several robotic arms. In this universe, robots have no ability to act alone or make choices. These robotic surgeries [19] are helpful in procedures requiring a high degree of accuracy, such as those involving organ transplants. It is a huge time saver for the operating room staff. These operations are also safer and less likely to cause infection than standard procedures.

The Soft Tissue Autonomous Robot (STAR) now outperforms human surgeons when it comes to stitching soft tissue. Bionaut Labs [20], an Israeli business, is developing a miniature robot. It travels at a rate of 60 cm/h through tissues. Future applications include illness diagnostics, targeted drug administration, and less invasive surgical procedures.This technique has infinite potential. Researchers are working to create robots that can replace human surgeons in the operating room. There is still a long way to go before robots are completely autonomous, but progress is being made.

18.4.4 GENETIC ENGINEERING-BASED ROBOTICS

Genetic modification, often known as genetic engineering, is the process of altering or manipulating the DNA of an organism. Gene editing (also known as "gene therapy"), exon skipping, and gene therapy are all examples of genetic engineering techniques.Agriculture, industrial biotechnology, and medicine are just a few of the areas that have made use of genetic engineering. There is a very long way to go. Diseases with genetic causes will be treatable using methods like gene therapy. More than 10,000 human disorders are traced back to a mutated gene. The process of altering genes was previously time-consuming and costly. However, a new gene-editing tool called CRISPR (Clustered

Regularly Interspaced Short Palindromic Repeats) has just been developed. Thus, the price has dropped significantly, and the time required has shrunk from years to a few weeks. "Clustered regularly interspaced short palindromic repeats" is the full name for CRISPR. Together, CRISPR and AI are bringing revolutionary changes to the medical industry. Bad or dangerous genes are found with the help of AI. The CRISPR system was first discovered in bacteria. This technique is used to eliminate the genetic material of pathogens like viruses. In 2018, a Chinese researcher named He Jiankui used CRISPR to generate the first gene-edited infant. Heart disease, inherited blindness, cystic fibrosis, and even certain mental health disorders are just some of the diseases that experts believe, using CRISPR to cure soon.

18.4.5 NANOMEDICINE-BASED MEDICAL TECHNOLOGY

Nanotechnology's potential use in medicine holds great promise for improving disease diagnosis. Diseases and genetic predispositions are detected and treated sooner with the help of nano-sized diagnostic devices implanted all over the body. It is possible to diagnose many illnesses using only one bodily fluid sample. Drug delivery systems greatly improved with the use of nanotechnology. Targeted medicine delivery to the damaged location using nanotechnology will reduce unwanted side effects. Nanotechnology has shown promising results in the treatment of cancer. Many of the cancer drugs never make it to the tumour. The use of nanoparticles in this context is proving fruitful. Nanoparticles allow us to concentrate anti-cancer medications in a specific location. Besides cancer, other illnesses benefit from the use of targeted nanoparticles. It will lessen the medication's negative effects.

18.4.6 3D PRINTING-BASED ORGANS TREATMENT

With a digital file or design as a starting point, a real item is made via 3D printing or additive manufacturing by adding layers of material. It is used to make intricate pieces of machinery, vehicles, and aircraft for a fraction of the cost of conventional production processes. In recent years, 3D printing has also shown promise as a potent instrument in the field of tissue engineering. Unlike other techniques of 3D printing, in which materials like metals or plastics are used to make human organs, this technique relies on natural biomaterials. In addition to skin and a thyroid gland, scientists have successfully 3D printed human ears. There will no longer be a scarcity of transplantable organs by means of 3D printing. Prosthetics is made through 3D printing. Many individuals will benefit greatly from 3D-printed prosthesis. The low cost is the key perk. When compared to the thousands of dollars that a conventional hand or limb cost, a 3D-printed one would only cost approximately $50–$60. The quality of 3D-printed materials is currently lower than that of conventionally manufactured ones.

Artificial organs are being made using a variety of methods, not only 3D printing. The use of stem cell technology has allowed, for instance, the development of a "Lung in a dish" by scientists. It is not perfect, but it is a step in the right direction towards a human lung. Bio-artificial kidneys are very near being created by another group of Dutch researchers led by Roos Masereeuw of the University of Utrecht and Dimitrios Stamatialis of the University of Twente [11]. Number of interesting approaches are available to organ development, but 3D printing stands out as the most promising since it has the potential to create an exact copy of the patient's original organ. There is no chance of the patient's body rejecting the organ by using the patient's own biomaterial.

18.5 THE FUTURE OF XAI IN HEALTHCARE

The growth in the artificial intelligence healthcare software market is rapid. Research and Markets predicts that the worldwide market for explainable AI will grow from $3.5 billion in 2020 to $21 billion in 2030 [11,21]. The benefits of AI will become more obvious as the volume of data generation increases.

The XAI framework strikes a balance between data security and potential advantages to be agreed upon by government, industry, and advocacy organisations soon. According to research by the World Economic Forum [18], the year 2030 will be a watershed moment for artificial intelligence in healthcare, with a plethora of new use cases coming together to provide a genuinely proactive, predictive healthcare system [22]. In addition, the future of XAI in healthcare suggests consumers will have more say over their data and how it is used.

By the year 2030, AI will have altered medical treatment in three distinct ways. There used to be a significant backlog of patients waiting to see doctors and nurses at this time of year a decade ago, but now both professionals and patients can move quickly through the system [22].

There are many ways in which data are enhancing medical treatment. Robot nurses provide medical care in the future. Lessons for improving healthcare in developing nations from the Fourth Industrial Revolution AI now be able to identify patterns in large datasets that are too subtle or complicated for human detection. It achieves smart healthcare by bringing together data from many sources, such as internet-connected appliances, medical files, and, increasingly, other types of data that were formerly kept in isolation.

The first major repercussion of this is by the year 2030, healthcare systems will be able to provide completely proactive, predictive treatment.

18.5.1　AI-Powered Predictive Care

The use of artificial intelligence and predictive analytics has allowed us to learn about the numerous factors that affect our health. From where we are born to the food we consume to the quality of the oxygen around us to the stability of our housing and income situations, many factors influence our lives. To a certain extent, these are examples of what the World Health Organisation (WHO) refers to as "the social determinants of health" (SDOH).

By the year 2030, XAI will allow healthcare systems to warn patients when they are at risk for acquiring a chronic condition like diabetes. Because of this progress, SDOH (Social Determinants of Health)-related diseases, including diabetes, heart failure, and COPD (Chronic Obstructive Pulmonary Disease), are on the decline.

18.5.2　Hospital Networks and Electronic Health Records

A further development concerning the physical location of treatment coincides with the advent of predictive medicine., Future hospitals of the future will focus on the most critically ill patients as shown in Figure 18.5, and the most complex procedures while referring less urgent care to smaller facilities like retail clinics, same-day surgery centres, specialist treatment clinics, and even patients' own homes.

Each of these hubs is linked to the same digital network. Command and control hubs assess geographical and clinical data to track supply and demand in real time. This network can not only use AI to predict which patients will see a decline in health but also eliminate bottlenecks in the system and send both patients and medical staff to the locations where they will get the greatest treatment Location is no longer the cement-holding smart healthcare-based network together. The major change in 2030 will be focused on the experiences of the individuals it serves.

18.5.3　Better Patient and Staff Experiences

Studies have demonstrated for quite some time that patients have a significant impact on whether they improve. Since physicians began experiencing high rates of burnout a decade ago, mostly due to the stress of attempting to serve too many patients with few resources, it has become vital to provide them with better work experiences.

FIGURE 18.5　Size of the global healthcare challenge in numbers.

Predictive healthcare networks powered by AI have reduced waiting times, increased staff productivity, and taken on the ever-increasing administrative load. As AI becomes increasingly commonplace in healthcare settings, professionals are more likely to put their faith in the technology to supplement their own expertise during procedures and diagnoses. Artificial Intelligence (AI) produces experiences that adapt to the professional and the patient by learning from every patient, diagnosis, and operation. It not only makes the system more financially stable but also helps alleviate clinician shortages and fatigue while enhancing health outcomes. To promote health and well-being across the course of a person's life, a networked system spans communities and is driven by linked care.

In the year 2020, it is far from realising that smart healthcare everywhere is a dream. Complexity in technology, information technology, and data systems continues to be a bottleneck in therapeutic domains where it is utilised to diagnose, treat, monitor, and (ideally) prevent and cure illnesses.

However, all three of these concepts have the potential to be actualised in the future. Intelligent technologies assist humans in their work as if they were experts themselves. Artificial intelligence (AI) can examine and quantify physician notes, optimise patient flow in emergency rooms, and even identify malignant tumours in images. The use of predictive analytics is already saving lives in critical care units of hospital. Hospitalisations can be avoided or reduced by providing preventative treatment in primary or community settings which are outside of hospitals.

However, this is a lengthy and difficult trip that cannot be accomplished by a single business or organisation. Generally, governments, healthcare systems, and private businesses keep cooperating to make AI systems completely interoperable and transparent, it is to eliminate prejudice and inequity. The requirement for universal safeguards insisted governing how AI processes individual data will grow in importance as the healthcare industry continues to expand internationally.

Perhaps most importantly, I think it is important to remember that AI's greatest potential use is to augment, not to replace human talents. The patients who need care and the carers who work diligently to provide it are at the centre of connected care, not cutting-edge technology. For less-developed nations, the issue is not if the benefits of the fourth industrial revolution will eventually trickle down to their citizens. Just as there are huge differences in the wealth of countries, there are also huge differences in the creation, storage, and access to data. The Big Data Gap was narrowed by LMICs (Low and Middle-Income Countries) due to their vast populations and the decreasing cost of technology. Effective and timely investments in scalable digital systems are necessary to achieve this goal. While statistics on individual and population health are among the most useful, they are scarce in developing nations.

The public health and healthcare of both wealthy and impoverished nations will be revolutionised by the fourth industrial revolution, which represents the biological, social, and digital systems; the only remaining issue is when this will occur. For people living in developing nations, the question of when healthcare reforms brought about by the fourth industrial revolution will be implemented is one of the greatest sources of anxiety.

Big data [23,24] is starting to reach a statistical tipping point where "$n =$ all" in terms of health benefits. The current state of research and planning for population health improvement in LMICs (Low and Middle-Income Countries) requires reliance on sampled populations drawn from the past. The idea is like a full and continuous census, in which all individuals who have any kind of contact with the healthcare system become part of a larger data set and are subject to monitoring. When information on family finances, location, social variables, biology, sickness, and genetics is merged, a surveillance system is created.

Existing healthcare and data infrastructure provide the basis for the entire healthcare system's infrastructure. There are two types of facilities that must be in place: (1) easy, linked smartphone-based applications that connect to facility-based data, including labs; and (2) professional community healthcare professionals who continually engage with a defined, entire population, in health and in disease.

This framework is essential for accelerating the performance improvement of health systems and achieving universal health care. Disease monitoring is enhanced by merging facility-level laboratory data with community-level syndromic data to better detect and respond to epidemics as they unfold. It avoids the devastating health and financial effects of epidemics. Healthcare practitioners respond to patients with chronic diseases by combining the prevalence of these disorders with the efficacy of different therapies. Entire populations are registered and monitored to spot holes in coverage and fill them. The healthcare system has the potential to become more flexible and research based [22,25].

Nonetheless, that framework predates the Fourth Industrial Revolution by a generation. The Fourth Industrial Revolution presents the chance to take advantage of recent breakthroughs in machine learning, genomics, proteomics, and the microbiome and apply them to the development of personalised medicine at the population level. The foundational infrastructure continually counts residents and connects them with community healthcare staff. It allows for seamless integration of various features. LMICs can build most of the public health infrastructure and will be in the best position to adopt these innovations and persuade businesses and other organisations to fund their widespread implementation.

The type of personalised medicine here raises significant privacy, security, and ethical concerns. To adjust, citizens and governments will have to modify existing regulations and safety nets. It is hard to conceive of a deployment of all healthcare systems that respect human rights in the absence of democratic institutions, which is why democratic governance is so crucial in this area. There should be no way for governments to abuse citizens' privacy, expression rights, or other liberties using the public health surveillance data architecture.

Nepal has made a firm commitment as an international pioneer in the development of cutting-edge, low-cost digital technologies for scientific monitoring and research. The established groundwork for this is through a novel Public-Private Partnership that combines the strengths of Nepal's maturing democratic governance heritage with our own organisation, Possible, which has a solid history of providing public healthcare to the underserved. A continuous surveillance system by Community Healthcare Workers, a biometrics application, and an Electronic Medical Record located in a hospital have all been developed thus far as foundational pieces of the platform. Our next steps will be to refine our scalable strategy, discover novel scientific applications, expand our operations in Nepal, and engage in cross-national conversation and knowledge exchange.

There are numerous obstacles that low- and middle-income countries (LMICs) now face, but we believe that they "leapfrog" these obstacles and become active participants in the technological advances that are driving the Fourth Industrial Revolution. To improve healthcare delivery, it is necessary to first establish a solid foundation of reliable, complete, and well-structured data [25].

18.6 CONCLUSION

As a direct consequence of the rapid development of technology and artificial intelligence, businesses are showing a growth in the integration of intelligent technologies into existing workflows. One of the businesses is healthcare, which is currently adopting technologies based on AI and its applications to give consumers enhanced and more customised healthcare services. Another one of the industries is the retail industry. Nevertheless, consider all of them to be black box models. People should have the capacity to manage how artificial intelligence system must analyse the data to achieve solutions. For this reason, more transparent artificial intelligence systems are needed. In addition, it is essential to provide an explanation of why certain results are achieved to direct further stages in the process of enhancing the system's ability to diagnose illnesses or prescribe medications. This is essential for all patients and medical professionals. HAI is the future of intelligent healthcare on our planet, and AI is now making healthcare more intelligent. XAI is making AI in healthcare more visible and understandable to people. Since the beginning of this decade, robotic surgery has been helped by XAI. The XAI has garnered broad acceptance and favourable feedback from the medical professionals who exercise it and the patients who are treated by it. Initially, the use of robotic arms for training purposes and actual operations is restricted to surgeons. In recent years, skilled surgeons and students have been getting training and briefings for each medical case. This has also been occurring more frequently. It is plausible that XAI performs a significant and productive function in the field of medicine.

REFERENCES

1. https://medium.com/@diyaannamathew_85240/explainable-ai-xai-in-healthcare-cb5028392f32.
2. Beddiar, D., Oussalah, M. and Tapio, S., 2022. Explainability for medical image captioning, In: *2022 Eleventh International Conference on Image Processing Theory, Tools and Applications (IPTA)*. IEEE, Salzburg, Austria, pp. 1–6. https://doi.org/10.1109/IPTA54936.2022.9784146.
3. IBM Explainable AI, https://www.ibm.com/topics/explainable-ai.
4. Insight of Explainable AI, https://insights.sei.cmu.edu/blog/what-is-explainable-ai/.
5. Cavaliere, F., Cioppa, A., Marcelli, A., Parziale, A. and Senatore, R., 2020. *Parkinson's Disease Diagnosis: Towards Grammar-based Explainable Artificial Intelligence.* IEEE Symposium on Computers and Communications (ISCC), Rennes, France, pp. 1-6. doi: 10.1109/ISCC50000.2020.9219616.
6. Chen, D., Zhao, H., He, J., Pan, Q. and Zhao, W., 2021. An causal XAI diagnostic model for breast cancer based on mammography reports, In: *2021 IEEE International Conference on Bioinformatics and Biomedicine (BIBM)*. IEEE, Houston, TX, USA, pp. 3341–3349. https://doi.org/10.1109/BIBM 52615.2021.9669648.
7. Davagdorj, K., Jang-Whan, B., Van-Huy, P. and Theera-Umpon, N., 2021. Explainable artificial intelligence based framework for non-communicable diseases prediction. *IEEE Access*, vol. 9, pp. 123672–123688.
8. https://medium.com/@shahooda637/smart-healthcare-and-human-centered-ai-73d3a9d1c8b7.
9. Working of Gene Therapy, https://futurismhub.com/how-does-gene-therapy-work/.
10. Kumar, A. and Joshi, S., 2022. Applications of AI in healthcare sector for enhancement of medical decision making and quality of service, In: *International Conference on Decision Aid Sciences and Applications (DASA)*, Berkas University, Indonesia.
11. The importance of AI in Healthcare, https://www.encora.com/insights/the-importance-of-explainable-ai-in-healthcare.
12. Capestart, How Explainable AI (XAI) for Health Care Helps Build User Trust - Even During Life-and-Death Decisions. https://www.capestart.com/resources/blog/how-explainable-ai-for-health-care-helps-build-user-trust/.

13. Zhang, Y., Chen, Y., Yang, W., Yu, H. and Lv, Z. 2022. Human-centered intelligent healthcare: Explore how to apply AI to assess cognitive health, In: *China Computer Federation (CCF) 2022*, China.

14. Future Healthcare Technology, https://medium.com/@judaspriest2/future-healthcare-technology-5-upcoming-technologies-that-will-change-healthcare-forever-a3a9469240f4.

15. Muthukaruppasamy, S., Abudhahir, A., Gnana Saravanan, A., Gnanavadivel, J. and Duraipandy, P. 2018. Design and implementation of PIC/FLC plus SMC for positive output elementary super lift Luo converter working in discontinuous conduction mode, *Journal of Electrical Engineering & Technology* 13(5): 1886–1900.

16. Nandha Gopal, J., Muthuselvan, N.B. and Muthukaruppasamy, S. 2021. Model predictive controller-based quadratic boost converter for WECS applications, *International Transactions on Electrical Energy Systems*, Wiley, 31(12). doi: 10.1002/2050-7038.13133.

17. Fourth Industry Revolution, https://www.salesforce.com/blog/what-is-the-fourth-industrial-revolution-4ir/.

18. Arun Sampaul Thomas, G. and Harold Robinson, Y. 2020. Real-time health system (RTHS) Centered Internet of Things (IoT) in healthcare industry: benefits, use cases and advancements in 2020, In: Raghavendra Kumar, Rohit sharma and Prasant Kumar (eds.) *Springer's Multimedia Technologies on the Internet of Things Environment (Scopus Indexed)*, 29 September 2020, pp. 83–93. ISSN: 978-981-15-7965-3.

19. Robotics Surgery, https://futurismhub.com/robotic-surgery-its-advantages-disadvantages-and-future/.

20. Bionauts – Robots in our Body, https://www.diamandis.com/blog/bionauts-robots-in-the-body.

21. Markets Ltd., Research and Explainable AI Market by Offering, Deployment, Technology, End-Use Industry, and Application-Global Opportunity Analysis and Industry Forecast, 2021–2030. https://www.researchandmarkets.com/reports/5481228/explainable-ai-market-by-offering-by-deployment/.

22. Here is 3 ways AI will change healthcare by 2030. 2020. World Economic Forum. https://www.weforum.org/agenda/2020/01/future-of-artificial-intelligence-healthcare-delivery/.

23. Arun Sampaul Thomas, G. and Harold Robinson, Y. 2020. IoT, big data, blockchain and machine learning besides its transmutation with modern technological applications, In: Lakshmi C. Jain (ed.) *Internet of Things and Big Data Applications* - Part of the Intelligent Systems Reference Library book series (ISRL, volume 180), 25 February 2020, Springer, pp. 47–63. ISSN: 978-3-030-39118-8.

24. Arun Sampaul Thomas and Muthukaruppasamy, S. 2023. Green IoT use case approaches for blockchain technology taking industry 5.0 to the next level, In: Saravanan, Raghavendra Kumar and Valentina (eds.) *Green Blockchain Technology for Sustainable Smart Cities*, Elsevier, pp. 119–141. ISSN: 978-0-323-95407-5.

25. https://www.weforum.org/agenda/2017/07/n-all-digital-foundations-for-universal-health-coverage-and-beyond.

Index

9 781032 598864